DICTIONARY OF ASIAN PHILOSOPHIES

DICTIONARY
OF
ASIAN PHILOSOPHIES

by

ST. ELMO NAUMAN, JR.

Philosophical Library
New York

Dedicated to
the Memory of
Captain John Y. Whitley, USAF

PREFACE

The DICTIONARY OF ASIAN PHILOSOPHIES by Dr. St. Elmo Nauman, Jr., is no doubt the most timely work for the benefit of western students, teachers, as well as the general reader. Eastern philosophies with which the West came into contact as far back as the 16th and the 17th centuries, which were studied by selected western scholars during the 18th and the 19th centuries, are not only creating interest, but even being adopted as a way of life by thousands of Westerners today.

Our age is the age of transformation, comparable to the Renaissance Period which brought about the advancement of science and technology. The present Neo-Renaissance, which is unveiling Far Eastern culture in the West, is bound to lead to the advancement of humanities and philosophy in the near future. The DICTIONARY not only acquaints the reader with philosophical terms and philosophers, but it also gives a historical background of Asian philosophies. The style is lucid and elegant. In this volume Dr. Nauman has made a scholarly contribution to the better understanding of Asian philosophies in the West, and has also supplied useful material for scholars who are interested in a comparative study of Eastern and Western philosophies.

I recommend this work to all scholars, teachers, students and general readers interested in Asian philosophy.

I. C. Sharma

Visiting Full Professor of Philosophy
Cleveland State University
Cleveland, Ohio

Adjunct Professor of Philosophy
Old Dominion University
Norfolk, Virginia

Formerly Chairman and Professor
of Philosophy
Udaipur University
Udaipur, India

Cleveland, Ohio
11-12-77

INTRODUCTION

From Buddha to Gandhi, Chu Hsi to Hu Shih and Kitabatake Chikafusa, the wisdom of the East, hidden mysteries from India and Tibet, China, Japan, and Persia are opened to the interested reader. The doctrines of *Karma, Maya, Satori* and *Nirvana*, the key teachings of such thinkers as Confucius, Lao Tzu, Mo Ti and Mao Tse-Tung, are presented. Lesser-known Eastern thinkers, Chou Tun-i, Wang Yang-Ming, Ho Yen, Kung-Sun Hung, Wang Pi, and many others are also included. Whether we wish to consult the *I Ching*, with its predictions about the future, learn "The Way" (Tao), or read the Zen "Koan", such as: "He put his sandals on his head and walked out," these pages contain the needed reference information. Every major stream of Eastern thought, whether idealistic or materialistic, is represented.

Why should we spend time studying Asian philosophies? Primarily to avoid the mistake of thinking that "If I don't know it, it must not be important." The study of human thought is incomplete and incoherent without the valuable contributions from the East. Western civilization never was all the civilization there was, even when it so imagined. Cultural imperialism is no proper replacement for military imperialism. The sneer is no better than the gun. To ignore the East is to miss its insights and to lessen the humanity which should be education's gift to us. Mankind shrinks with ignorance, and surrenders the life of man for the life of a brute. Barriers of distance and language may have excused such intellectual poverty in the past, but advances in translation have made Eastern works generally accessible to the generalist. No one knows philosophy if he knows "all philosophy except Eastern." The ignorance of an educated man is no excuse, in the eyes of the universe, and the laziness of an educated individual may lead to the death of civilization through misunderstanding.

A second reason for the study of Asian philosophies is that, despite many notable accomplishments, Western philosophy is still not complete. A general unity, even the unity of sciences, is still missing.

The East may not turn out to have the answer, either, but many Eastern thinkers do attempt to state the conditions of a coherent unity. Whether these formulations succeed will be for the reader to judge.

A third reason for the study of Asian philosophies is for unique insights. Besides a unified world-view, most notable in Indian thought, we may appreciate the importance of meditation, or the phenomenalism characteristic of Japanese thought, the social emphasis of Chinese thought, or the intense interest in spiritual forces in Tibetan teachings. These topics, among others, merit attention.

Contemporary Western thought is deficient in:

(1) value theory, which is inadequately grounded, a kind of poor orphan in the midst of the wealth of Western technology;

(2) the coherent explanation of non-material phenomena;

(3) the explanation of teleology (purpose), which oddly appears to be miraculous on Western scientific principles;

(4) an adequate model for later adult life, which, after the Western rites of initiation (confirmation, bar mitzvah, or sweet sixteen parties), is supposed to stay unchanged until death;

(5) the integration of knowledge, an explanation of how the universe can be the universe. Western philosophy can explain partial coherence *par excellence*, but cannot adequately account for the coherence of parts into a universal whole; and

(6) an explanation of dis-value, evil. While the West succeeded in mapping the dark side of the moon, it cannot cope with the dark side of human behavior. Except for the contributions of Freud and of the Existentialists to this topic, contemporary Western thought has nothing significant to say. Are we expected to think

of value as some kind of "warp" in an otherwise value-free universe? What is the origin of evil? Why is it the case that, in a monistic universe, there should exist a sort of hostile sub-environment?

These are some possible questions not answered well in contemporary Western philosophical works. Thus, deficiencies of Western thought, together with the insights of Eastern thinkers are more than sufficient to justify the time we may spend turning Eastern pages.

The characteristically metaphysical caste of Eastern thought often produces suspicion in Western readers, who prefer a reality they can touch, feel, and make into an experiment. Western empiricism, experimental and pragmatic, has succeeded scientifically. In the process, however, it has presented a world-view so fragmented that it is difficult even for a well-educated individual to make sense out of all its separate parts. Partial coherence replaced an understanding of the whole.

We need to ask, however, whether Eastern philosophies which do not make this mistake are dream-castles or deep visions. In Eastern meditation do we discover truth, or do we simply find an infinite emptiness? Is the universe, after all, a null class?

Recent Western methods of determining truth have been uniformly, almost fanatically, singleminded. The verification principle has been the only way. However, why should we prefer one hypothesis over another? Because of the simplicity of its operation in calculating or forecasting new results? Is it not conceivable that another hypothesis may serve equally well? Perhaps there are parallel ways to truth. Perhaps each perspective provides a special insight which is indispensable to the complete picture.

Some will study Eastern texts for salvation. Others will read them for absurdities. Let us read them for whatever knowledge they prove to contain.

I

CHRONOLOGY OF ASIAN PHILOSOPHERS

This chronological listing is presented as a tool to help orient the reader. Names which appear in capital letters signify major thinkers. Some Western names are included in the right-hand column to indicate which key philosophical or religious figures were contemporaries.

Every one of these dates, without exception, is problematical. The first, for example, Zoroaster, is dated by Diogenes Laertius as "five thousand years before the fall of Troy," a date which we have declined to credit with any great degree of accuracy. It would probably require a book of equal size to sift all the evidence pro and con each date. These dates are presented with no thought other than that it is better to have something rather than nothing at all. Adjustments can be made according to the evidence later produced.

		ASIAN PHILOSOPHER	COUNTRY	WESTERN THINKER
B.C.	660-583	Zoroaster	Persia	
	630-583	Yajnavalkya	India	
	599-527	Mahavira	India	
	580-520	Gautama	India	
	570-517	LAO TZŬ	China	
	563-483	BUDDHA	India	Thales
	551-479	CONFUCIUS	China	
	550-500	Kapila	India	
	483-402	Tsŭ Ssŭ	China	
	479-438	Mo Tzŭ	China	
	450-375	Lieh Tzŭ	China	
	440-380	Badarayana	India	
	430-370	Jaimini	India	
	400-338	Shang Yang	China	
	399-295	CHUANG TZŬ	China	Plato
	372-289	Yang Chu	China	
	371-289	MENCIUS	China	
	320-250	Kung-Sun Lung	China	
	298-238	Hsün Tzŭ	China	
	280-233	Han Fei Tzŭ	China	
	273-232	Ashoka	India	
	250-175	Sirach	Palestine	
	240-180	Patanjali	India	
	180-122	Huai-nan Tzŭ	China	
	179-104	Tung Chung-shu	China	
	90-30	Shammai	Palestine	
	53-A.D. 18	Yang Hsiung	China	
	30-A.D. 10	Hillel I	Palestine	
A.D.	3-60	Gamaliel	Palestine	
	27-97	Wang Ch'ung	China	St. Paul
	50-132	Akiba	Palestine	
	80-150	Meir	Palestine	
	100-165	Nagarjuna	India	
	135-220	Judah Ha-Nasi	Palestine	
	160-247	Rab	Babylonia	
	189-249	Ho Yen	China	
	223-262	Hsi K'ang	China	
	226-249	Wang Pi	China	
	268-334	Ko Hung	China	
	250-312	Kuo Hsiang	China	
	320-365	Hillel II	Palestine	
	334-416	Hui-Yüan	China	St. Augustine

xiv

384-414	Seng-chao	China
470-543	BODHIDHARMA	China
476-542	T'an-luan	China
596-664	Hsüan-tsang	China
613-681	Shan-t'ao (Zendō)	China
617-649	Song-tsen Gampo	Tibet
638-713	Hui-Neng	China
643-712	Fa-tsang	China
670-762	Shen-hui	China
690-750	Kumarila	India
700-767	Abu Hanifa	Persia
750-810	Hui Hai	China
767-822	Saichō	Japan
768-824	Han Yü	China
774-835	Kūkai	Japan
785-867	Rinzai (Lin-Ch'i)	China
788-820	SHANKARA	India
800-850	Huang Po	China
800-855	Ibn-Hanbal	Arabia
809-873	Hunein Ibn Ishak	Syria
810-873	Al-Kindi	Arabia
870-950	Al-Farabi	Arabia
880-937	Al-Mukammas	Babylonia
892-942	Saadia	Babylonia
920-990	Udayana	India
942-1017	Genshin (Eshin Sōzu)	Japan
958-1055	Rinchen Sangpo	Tibet
960-1030	Ibn Maskawaih	Arabia
973-1048	Beruni	Arabia
980-1037	Avicenna	Arabia
1011-1077	Shao Yung	China
1012-1096	Marpa	Tibet
1016-1100	Nāropa	India/Tibet
1017-1073	Chou Tun-i	China
1020-1077	Chang Tsai	China
1032-1085	Ch'eng Hao	China
1033-1108	Ch'eng I	China
1040-1123	Mila Rêpa	Tibet
1040-1137	Ramanuja	India
1059-1111	Al-Ghazzali	Persia
1063-1135	Yüan-Wu Ko-Chin	China
1079-1153	Gampo-pa	Tibet
1110-1170	Phagmotru	Tibet
1130-1200	Chu Hsi	China

1133-1212	Hōnen	Japan	
1139-1193	Lu Hsiang-shan	China	
1199-1260	Madhva	India	
1141-1215	Eisai	Japan	
1155-1225	Jien (Jichin)	Japan	
1173-1262	Shinran	Japan	
1182-1251	Sakya Panchen	Tibet	St. Francis of Assisi
1200-1253	Dōgen	Japan	
1222-1282	NICHIREN	Japan	
1268-1369	Veṅkaṭanātha	India	
1293-1354	Kitabatake	Japan	St. Thomas Aquinas
1357-1419	Tsongkha-pa	Tibet	
1379-1449	Jamyang Choje	Tibet	
1385-1464	Thangton Gyelpo	Tibet	
1389-1449	Jamchen Choje	Tibet	
1391-1474	Gedün-truppa	Tibet	
1469-1538	BABA NANAK	India	Martin Luther
1472-1529	Wang Yang-Ming	China	
1475-1542	Gedün Gyatso	Tibet	
1534-1572	Isaac Luria	Palestine	
1543-1588	Sönam Gyatso	Tibet	
1543-1620	Chaim Vital	Palestine	
1579-1655	Shōsan Suzuki	Japan	
1583-1657	Hayashi Razan (Dōshun)	Japan	
1608-1648	Nakae Tōjyū	Japan	
1610-1695	Huang Tsung-Hsi	China	
1613-1682	Ku Yen-Wu	China	
1617-1682	Ngawang Lopsang Gyatso	Tibet	
1619-1691	Banzan Kumazawa	Japan	
1619-1693	Wang Fu-Chih	China	
1622-1685	Yamaga Sokō	Japan	
1627-1705	Itō Jinsai	Japan	
1635-1704	Yen Yüan	China	
1657-1725	Arai Hakuseki	Japan	
1659-1735	Li Kung	China	
1666-1728	Ogyū Sorai	Japan	
1669-1736	Kada Azumamaro	Japan	
1683-1706	Tshangyang Gyatso	Tibet	
1685-1768	Hakuin	Japan	
1688-1734	Muro Kyūsō	Japan	
1708-1757	Kesang Gyatso	Tibet	
1715-1746	Tominaga Nakamoto	Japan	
1723-1777	Tai Chen	China	
1723-1789	Miura Baien	Japan	

1730-1801	Motoori Norinaga	Japan	
1755-1817	Kaiho Seiryō	Japan	
1758-1804	Jampal Gyatso	Tibet	
1834-1886	Ramakrishna	India	Kierkegaard
1856-1875	Trinley Gyatso	Tibet	
1858-1927	K' ang Yu-Wei	China	
1861-1941	Rabindranath Tagore	India	
1863-1902	Vivekananda	India	
1865-1898	Tan Ssu-T'ung	China	
1866-1925	Sun Yat-sen	China	
1869-1948	GANDHI	India	
1872-1950	Sri Aurobindo	India	
1876-1933	Thubten Gyatso	Tibet	
1879-1942	Ch'en Tu-Hsiu	China	Einstein
1883-1931	Kahlil Gibran	Lebanon	
1888-1975	Sarvepalli Radhakrishnan	India	
1889-1960	Watsuji Tetsurō	Japan	
1891-1962	Ho Shih	China	
1893-1976	MAO TSE-TUNG	China	
1895-1976	Lin Yutang	China	
1895-	Fung Yu-Lan	China	
1935-	Tenzin Gyatso	Tibet	

II

THE TEN GREATEST ASIAN PHILOSOPHERS

In the preceding chronological listing, many names may seem outstanding, according to one's point of view. Of these, the ten most influential Asian philosophers may be said to be:

1. Zoroaster   (660-583 B.C.)
2. Lao Tzǔ   (570-517 B.C.)
3. Buddha   (563-483 B.C.)
4. Confucius   (551-479 B.C.)
5. Chuang Tzǔ   (399-295 B.C.)
6. Mencius   (371-289 B.C.)
7. Shankara   (788-820)
8. Nichiren   (1222-1282)
9. Gandhi   (1869-1948)
10. Mao Tse-Tung (1893-1976)

Of these, one is Persian, three are Indian, five Chinese, and one Japanese. None of them, in contrast with the West, or at least, with common Western opinion on the subject, had any significant tie with an institution of higher learning. Four of them founded religions (Zoroaster, Zoroastrianism; Lao Tzǔ, Taoism; Buddha, Buddhism; Confucius, Confucianism). Four significantly developed religious systems (Chuang Tzǔ, Mencius, Shankara, Nichiren). The last two on the list (Gandhi, Mao Tse-Tung) were political figures and revolutionaries, one non-violent, the other armed.

ASIAN PHILOSOPHY: As the greatest philosophical work in the West may be said to be Plato's *Republic*, the greatest work in India may be said to be the *Brihadāraṇyaka-upanishad*. The following quotation from this *Upanishad* expresses well the spirit of much of the philosophy of Asia:

From the unreal lead me to the real.
From darkness lead me to light.
From death lead me to immortality.

However, Eastern thought cannot be forced into one single, unified theme. Its five major cultures, Indian, Chinese, Tibetan, Persian, and Japanese, and its long time-span, covering three thousand years, lead us naturally to expect major divergences.

India may be characterized generally as the source of great universal formulations. To be an individual, on the Indian view, is to be less than complete. To be all is to be all in all. Only the universal is the real. All particular beings perceived by the senses are merely illusions.

This lofty attitude is more than a view from Mount Olympus. It is a view from Mount Everest, looking down on Olympus. Olympus is like a foot-hill to the heights of the Himalayas. In the words of Bhartrhari:

Now, as it was testified in the sacred book, these two things, true and non-true, are present within every thing; and the true thing is the species, the individual is non-true.

Even the individual gods, on the Greek style, would be less than ideal. Thus, in India, biographies of authors or leaders who have witnessed to the truth are secondary, and, more importantly, the dating of texts is so problematical because of the lack of historical references, as to be without parallel.

China is the source of most of the great classics on social theory. The Indian thinkers had defined hell as "the state of bondage to others," but the Chinese considered that state to be the mandate of heaven. China taught the art of successful society. Opinions may have differed on whether utopia was possible, or, more precisely, about whether utopia could be attained by more or less institutionalization, but society was definitely the focus of her philosophers, both ancient and modern.

Tibet is the source of mystic meditation. The huge Tibetan monasteries were practically universities of the occult. They taught initiates how to run faster than a horse, walk through walls, keep warm in sub-zero temperatures, and materialize companions to keep them company on a long, lonely trip. The mysterious, occult, magical powers were the reward for long years of study with and submission to a lama.

Japan is the source of phenomenological philosophy, and of the extraordinary application of meditation to the ordinary tasks of daily life. Truth was beauty, and beauty was simplicity. Zen, as applied to Japanese culture, produced a simple, direct, and natural view of life, one which enhances swordsmanship, archery, and motorcycle maintenance, among other things. The ideal was tea and simplicity. Meditation was on the flow of life.

Eastern thought as a whole may be said to be strong on synthesis and life. The price it has paid for this strength is that it has been weak on the kind of analytic thought characteristic of the scientific frame of mind. Eastern generalizations have been strong, even powerful. The reasons needed to support those generalizations have often been underdeveloped.

Currently, Eastern philosophy is in as much of a crisis as Western. Desperate for Western technology, military, industrial, medical, and agricultural, Eastern countries needed the mechanistic and scientific philosophy to support it. In China, attacked by imperialists and militarists, one thing was certain, that Confucianism would not survive. Neither indigenous leadership, Nationalist or Communist, could tolerate it. The old ways of thinking could not accommodate technology; therefore, a new way must be embraced, whether Christianity or Marxism. In fact, throughout the breadth of Asia, the ancient regimes all fell, in the latter part of the nineteenth century, under the onslaught of the successes of Western powers. Now that such a process has been slowed, there is time for a new synthesis to be developed of East and West.

A

ABHIDHARMA: The Sanskrit term designating that division of the Buddhist canon dealing with metaphysics and philosophy.

ABU HANIFA (700-767): A Persian scholar who developed Moslem law into the liberal Hanifite school. He applied the code of behavior found in the *Koran* to contemporary cases by means of analogy, deduction, or *ra'y* ("considered opinion," or "recognized justice"). He paid little attention, in this process, to the *Tradition* (*Hadith*). To illustrate how this kind of reasoning might work, the *Koran* states punishment for theft as chopping off the hand. That punishment may be regarded as applicable only to the semi-nomad society of the times, which did not have the ability to keep track of thieves, so that the best possible warning for those sitting around a campfire would be a stranger who joined them with only one hand. People would be warned to watch their possessions, and the one-handed man could not carry off much. However, in the more cosmopolitan parts of Persia, such an extreme punishment is not necessary. Different circumstances call for different punishments. By analogical deduction from other parts of the *Koran*, we may conclude that an appropriate punishment for theft in more modern times and civilized situations is imprisonment.

Hanifite rulings are generally followed in Iran, Iraq, Pakistan, and central Asia.

ĀDI GRANTH: The Sacred Book of the Sikhs, more highly venerated than the scripture of any other religion, including the *Bible, Koran*, or *Torah*. Verses from the *Ādi Granth* are chanted at the Golden Temple in Amritsar, and considered the perpetual *guru* (spiritual guide). Initially compiled in 1604 by Arjan, the fifth *guru*, it was edited into final form in 1705 by Gobindh Singh (1666-1708), the tenth *guru*. Singh said that there would be no more *gurus* after him, that the *Ādi Granth* should henceforth be regarded as the living voice of all the prophets. Containing writings by religious leaders of Hinduism and Islam, among others, the *Ādi Granth* is noted for its intense emotional mysticism.

ADVAITA: (pronounced ud-VEE-tuh) "Not two," or "non-dualism," term used to describe *Vedānta* philosophy (one of the six systems of orthodox Indian thought), especially Shankara's version. It indicates that the world, the self, and God are not absolutely one, yet in reality are not two, not essentially different. God (*Brahman*) is, on this theory, totally beyond human experience. Further, the empirical world is phenomenal, neither existent nor non-existent. Thus, it can never be fully explained. We may say that the world "rests on" God as its basis, but God is not directly involved in the world in a cause-and-effect way. The world developed through illusion (*maya*), and is "transient, impure, unsubstantial, like a flowing river or a burning lamp, lacking in fiber like a banana, comparable to foam in appearance, a mirage, a dream." The development of the world was by means of the creative, personal manifestation (*Ishvara*) of the unmanifest God (*Brahman*).

Non-dualism thus differs from both monism and pantheism. A negative term, it nevertheless expresses a process of subtle reasoning which otherwise would be obscured by a positive summary statement, such as "pantheism."

AHURA MAZDA (or ORMAZD): "Wise Lord," or "Lord of Light," the name of the supreme deity in the teaching of Zoroastrianism. The light in the (heavenly) presence of *Ahura Mazda* was so brilliant that Zoroaster could not see his own shadow on the floor. Perfect in wisdom and goodness, this highly ethical conception of God as Truth is opposed by "the Lie," the "Evil Spirit," named *Angra Mainyu*. The *Gathas* (or Hymns of Zoroaster, part of the *Avesta*, Zorastrianism's sacred book) describe *Ahura Mazda* as "clothed with the massy heavens as with a garment."

AKIBA (50-132): One of the greatest Palestinian teachers of the Law, Rabbi Akiba ben Joseph was an illiterate shepherd, forty years old, when his wife urged him to get some education. After twelve years of study, he was recognized as a master, and became the leading light of his generation. He is often called the "father of rabbinic Judaism." Akiba deduced laws not only from the clear text of the Bible, but also from its arrangement and superfluous words.

When a revolt was led by the Zealot, Bar Kochba, Akiba proclaimed him the long-awaited Messiah. Within three years, the Romans crushed the revolt and the country. Rabbi Akiba was put to death with pincers and fire, but died with the name of God on his lips.

AL-FARABI (870-950): The son of a Persian general, Abu Nasr ibn Mohammed ibn Tarkhan ibn Uzlag al-Farabi was born in Turkish Transoxiana. Educated in Bagdad, he became interested in philosophy and music. He wrote a treatise entitled *On the Agreement of the Philosophy of Plato and Aristotle*, and was called "the Second Teacher," that is, "the Second Aristotle." As a physician, the medication he prescribed was entirely spiritual.

He opposed the Dialecticians for accepting the testimony of sense-experiences without testing them, and he opposed the Natural Philosophers for being too bound to this earth and failing to appreciate what was transcendent.

Logic, in his view, is divided into two parts: *tasawwur* (ideas, definitions) and *tasdiq* (judgments, inferences, proofs).

He provided commentaries on the works of Aristotle and anticipated the controversy over universals which dominated Western thought beginning with the twelfth century.

AL-GHAZZALI (1059-1111): The brilliant Persian philosopher Abu Hamid Mohammed ibn Ghazzali was born at Tos in Khorasan and educated, after his father's death, in the home of a Sufi friend. Studying law, theology, and philosophy, he was appointed professor of law at the Nizamiya Academy in Bagdad, where he taught for four years (1091-1095).

In his book, *The Destruction of the Philosophers* (*Tahafut al-Filasifa*), he argues that reason leads to doubt, skepticism, moral deterioration, and social collapse. Arguing against cause, as Hume would later, and observing, as would Kant, that philosophy cannot prove the existence of God or the immortality of the soul, he concluded that only direct intuition can assure belief, and thus guarantee the survival of moral order and civilization. Although reason was higher than sense experience, he taught, intuition was higher than reason.

He abandoned his teaching career, ostensibly to go on the pilgrimmage to Mecca, but actually to go into seclusion, seeking peace through meditation. For ten years he lived the life of a wanderer.

His principal contribution to theology and ethics is entitled *Revival of the Science of Religion* (*Ihya Ulum al-Din*), urging the revival of belief in the horrors of hell as necessary to popular morality. Religion is more than the law and doctrine; it is the experience of inner being, the soul.

AL-KINDI (810-873): Arabian philosopher, astrologer, physician, and budget director at the court of Al-Mamoon, Caliph of Bagdad, Abu Yaqub ibn Ishaq al-Kindi wrote *The Theology of Aristotle*, which was a translation of parts of Plotinus' *Enneads*. It was not this confusion, which harmed Arabic philosophy for centuries, but his lack of orthodoxy that led to his downfall and the confiscation of his library. In 870, he forecast the future of The Bagdad Caliphate on the basis of the stars, predicting it would last about 450 more years. He was right within 62 years (1258 A.D., or 656 A.H.). He was the first to apply mathematics to medicine, calculating the effect of drugs by the proportions of the mixtures. In any single existing thing, he taught, we hold a mirror, so that if we know it thoroughly, we may behold the entire scheme of things. Al-Kindi was the first Islamic philosopher to develop the doctrine of the Spirit, or Mind, *'aql*. He developed a

4

fourfold division of Spirit; Cause (God), Reasoning Capacity, the Habit or actual possession of the soul (as in the gift of writing), and Activity (Man himself).

AL-MUKAMMAS (880-937): Born in Babylonia, David ibn Merwan Al-Mukammas was the author of a commentary on the *Book of Formation* (*Sefer Yetzirah*). Influential in the development of the Cabala, he wrote that the three ascending categories of science were (1) practical philosophy, (2) theoretical philosophy, and (3) knowledge of the Torah. His manuscripts lay forgotten for centuries, one being discovered as recently as 1898 in the Czarist Library.

AMIDA (or *AMITA*): (Japanese or Korean term; *O-mi-t'o* is the Chinese term) One of the five principle aspects (*Jinas*) of the Buddha-wisdom; "Boundless Light." Eons ago, many existences ago, he was a monk who took the vow to become a *Bodhisattva* (Buddha-of-the-future). Succeeding, he now presides over the Western Paradise, the "Pure Land" (named *Sukhavati*, the Land of Bliss), to which he will freely admit all who ask entrance in faith. He is thus one of the most popular Buddhist fig-ures.

ANALECTS: (from the Latin *analecta*, "select," or "collect") The book of the collected sayings of Confucius, written by his disciples after his death. The *Analects* (in Chinese *Lun Yü*, which may also be translated "Conversations," "Discussions," or "Dialogues") is one of what are termed the "Four Books," the others being the *Great Learning* (*Ta Hsio*), the *Doctrine of the Mean* (*Chung Yung*), and the *Book of Mencius* (*Meng-tze*). The Four Books, together with the Five Classics, the *Book of Filial Piety*, and the *Book of Hsün Tzŭ* were studied intensively in later generations. From this common core of shared experience the fundamental values of Chinese civilization were to emerge.

The *Analects* barely survived a fanatical attempt at extermination by the government censors. The reigning emperor, Duke Chen of Ch'in, who built the Great Wall and wrote on silk, instead of bamboo, attempted to improve life even more by ordering all books burned, except "how to" manuals on farming, medicine,

5

and foretelling the future. He believed his citizens were being corrupted by books of poetry and history and ordered everyone to turn in their copies under pain of being branded with a hot iron and compelled to work at hard labor for four years on the Great Wall. He did not want to be either restricted or out-classed by tradition. This project was carried on between 213 and 211 B.C. Some four hundred and sixty scholars were buried alive for the "treason" of refusing to obey this order. Some American scholars, evidently overcome with admiration for the wall, have attempted to excuse Chen for this action, evidently feeling that it is all right to burn the books a little, or that the scholars buried alive have not complained much lately.

One copy of the *Analects* was hidden somewhere in the house of Confucius and thus escaped. Duke Chen died after three years. Sixty years later, the copy of the manuscript was rediscovered, and the book was saved.

The *Analects* is one of three main sources of information about the life of Confucius, the others being Ssu-ma Ch'ien's biography of Confucius and the *Doctrine of the Mean* by Tzŭ Ssŭ, Confucius' grandson. The *Analects* portrays him as a philosopher, rather than as a man of action (as does Ssŭ-ma Ch'ien) or saint and sage (as does Tzŭ Ssŭ).

The most important translations of the *Analects* include the following:

Legge, *Confucian Analects*, in *The Chinese Classics*, 1;
Ezra Pound, *Confucian Analects*;
Soothill, *The Analects of Confucius*;
Waley, *The Analects of Confucius*; and
Ware, *The Sayings of Confucius*.

Among the many notable quotations from the *Analects* are the following:

The Master said: "A man who is blind to doom can be no gentleman. Without a knowledge of courtesy, we have no place to stand. Without a knowledge of words, there is no understanding men." (Book XX, Section 3.)

The Master said: "The superior man thinks of virtue; the small man thinks of comfort." (Book IV.)

ANGRA MAINYU: "The Bad Spirit," the evil deity of Zoroastrianism. He created 99,999 diseases, was the author of death, and made demons to help him, such as Aka Manah, "Bad Thought," and Druj, "the Lie."

ARAHAT: In Buddhist usage, a saint, or enlightened Buddhist monk.

AŚOKA: (pronounced aw-SHOW-kuh) The great Indian Emperor (reigned c. 269-232 B.C.) who converted to Buddhism and was influential in its spread. Aśoka's grandfather had established the Mauryan Empire, indirectly helped by the disruptive effects of Alexander the Great, whose invasion of the Indus Valley had destroyed local defense alliances. Aśoka extended the empire which he inherited by adding central and southern India, with the exception of the extreme southern tip.

After his conversion to the faith, he built shrines to house Buddha's ashes and publicized his laws by means of the "pillar edicts." For a while, primarily through his efforts, it seemed as if Buddhism would become the sole religion of India.

After Aśoka's death, his empire split into various warring factions, and new invaders, displaced by pressures on the steppes caused by clashes between a newly-united China and the Turkish-speaking peoples of Mongolia, poured through the passes.

ASTIKA: (from the Sanskrit asti, "it is") The term applied to those systems of Indian philosophy which affirm the authority of the Vedas, although this does not necessarily mean that they also affirm the existence of God. Opposed to Nastika systems, which deny the authority of the Vedas.

ĀTMAN: (pronounced AWT-mun) Sanskrit term for the soul or self, derived from ān, found in the Rig Veda as tmān, originally meaning "breath." The word gradually acquired the meaning of "the individual soul," the unseen inner essence of an individual which is distinct from the body, mind, or senses. It is the transcendental self. It is also the ultimate, as discovered introspectively.

7

An important distinction is to be drawn between forms of this word which seem almost identical. The word "*Ātman*" refers to the ultimate principle, and is generally translated "Self," with a capital "S." On the other hand, the word "*ātman*" refers to the individual principle in a human being, and is generally translated "self," with a lower-case "s."

Many of the Upanishads assert the Vedānta doctrine of Advaita (non-dualism), that there is a unity between *ātman* and *Brahman*, so that every *ātman*, whether in man, beast, fish, insect, or flower, is one with the infinite. If *Brahman-Ātman* alone exists, the objective and the subjective may be said to be one. As the *Khāndogya Upanishad* states:

> This self of mine within the heart is smaller than a grain of rice, smaller than a mustard-seed, smaller than a grain of millet, or the kernel of a grain of millet. This self of mine within the heart is greater than the earth, greater than the sky, greater than the galaxy, greater than the universe. ... This self of mine within the heart, this is *Brahman*.
>
> (—III, 14, 3 & 4)

It may be of interest to observe that Martin Luther, in one of his sermons, used an image almost exactly like this to describe God.

On the Hindu view, truth lies within. Self-realization is the supreme good. One reaches ultimate reality by an inward journey. This inward ascent is marked by discipline and persistence, by becoming "calm, controlled, quiet, patiently enduring, and contented."

AUROBINDO, SRI (1872-1950): The great mystic-philosopher of modern India, Sri Aurobindo (Arabinda Ghose) wrote that the Absolute was manifest in and developed through a series of grades of reality, progressing from physical matter up to the plane of absolute spirit. His works include *Essays on the Gītā* (1926-1944, 1950), *The Renaissance in India* (1946), *The Riddle of the World* (1946), *The Life Divine* (1947), *The Synthesis of Yoga* (1948), *More Lights on Yoga* (1948), *The Human Cycle* (1949), *The Ideal of Human Unity* (1950), *Savitri-a Legend and a Symbol* (1951), *The*

8

Problem of Rebirth (1952), *The Supramental Manifestation upon Earth* (1952), and *The Mind of Light* (1953).

He intended his philosophy to be faithful to the original Vedānta position, and took issue with Shankara's Advaita Vedānta on several points.

According to Sri Aurobindo, Shankara could not successfully explain, on his negativistic principles, why it was that the Absolute should descend into the finite. Sri Aurobindo accounted for that descent on the grounds that it was the inevitable expression of the essential power of *Brahman*.

With regard to humanity, he wrote that the mental level is not the highest possible level. The individual must prepare for a leap beyond the mind, into the limit of one's fundamental nature. The preparation for this leap is called "integral yoga", and is an elaborate discipline capable of transforming one's state of mind and one's life.

Sri Aurobindo believed it important to reconcile matter and spirit, man and God, the finite world and absolute reality, the many and the one.

AVALOKITESVARA: (pronounced aw-vuh-LOW-kee-TASH-vuh-ruh) One of the most prominent Bodhisattvas (Buddhas-to-be), Lord Avalokita, in Mahayana Buddhism, is "he who looks down upon the world with compassion." Compassion and Wisdom are the two major aspects of the Buddha-nature. As Avalokitesvara represents Compassion, Mañjuśri represents Wisdom. The latter is less popular than the former.

Avalokitesvara is said to have miraculous powers to protect men from storms and disasters and to grant fertility to childless women. These miracles work by *mantras* and spells. Avalokitesvara became important for the "Buddhism of Faith," in contrast with the earlier Buddhist emphasis upon self-reliance.

Tibet made the most prominent use of Avalokitesvara by making him its patron saint. Songtsen Gampo (617-649), the famous king who introduced Buddhism to the country, was believed to be his reincarnation. The Dalai Lama is also said to be the reincarnation of Avalokitesvara (in Tibetan, *Chen esigs*).

In China, he was changed into a she, *Kwan-Yin*, the goddess of

9

mercy (in Korea, *Koan-Eum*, and in Japan, *Kwannon*). Gracious and beautiful, she is often portrayed as a madonna.

Avalokitesvara is believed to have come to earth to help people with their problems over three hundred times in human form and once as a horse.

AVESTA: Sacred scripture of the Zoroastrian faith. Preserved for centuries by word of mouth, but not finally written down until the third or fourth century A.D., it is our source of information on the life and teachings of Zoroaster (Zarathustra). The *Avesta* is also noted for containing many spells against demons.

AVĪCCI: "No Interval," the eighth and lowest of the eight Buddhist hells. Although none of the Buddhist hells are eternal, they do last for a very long time, and are said to be extremely unpleasant.

This hell lasts for two thousand years. Those sentenced to it have committed one of the five traditional sins:

(1) premeditated murder of one's natural mother;

(2) premeditated murder of one's natural father;

(3) premeditated intention to harm The Enlightened One and rejoicing at such an action;

(4) premeditated intention to destroy the Buddhist Community; or

(5) premeditated murder of *Arhats* (saints).

AVICENNA (980-1037): Known as "the Bagdad Aristotle," Abu Ali al-Hosain ibn Abdallah ibn Sina (Avicenna) was noted for his work in natural philosophy, metaphysics, and medicine. Born in Bokhara, he memorized the *Koran* by the age of ten, studied philosophy and medicine, and when seventeen, cured a prince. As his reward, he was given free access to the prince's library. At twenty-four, he travelled to "lone Khiva in the waste" and then to "the lone Chorasmian shore," pursuing his fortunes in the services of the smaller states, in a manner similar to Confucius. Avicenna became vizir at the court of Shems Addaula in Hamadan, until the prince died, and Avicenna was thrown into prison by the son. Upon his release, he went to Ispahan where he taught philosophy and medicine, returning to Hamadan when Ala Ad-daula, the ruler of Ispahan, conquered it. There he died at the age of fifty-seven, and his grave is pointed out to this day.

He wrote the *Canon of Medicine* and the *Encyclopaedia of Philosophy*. He frequently commented on the defectiveness of the intellectual constitution in man, saying that it is in urgent need of some logical rule.

Avicenna's formula on universals became St. Thomas Aquinas' position, via Averroes and Albertus Magnus, that genera are *before* things in God's understanding, *in* things in natural objects, and *after* things in human thought.

AVIDYĀ: (pronounced uh-VEED-yuh) The Sanskrit term for ignorance (in Pali: *Avijja*). It is the failure to see the true nature of things, the object-side of illusion by which the intellect mistakenly thinks that it knows the real. According to Buddhism, ignorance is one of the links in the cycle of rebirth, a link which may be interrupted if one faithfully follows the Buddhist path.

B

BABA NANAK (1469-1539): The first (human) *guru*, or spiritual guide, and founder of Sikhism (literally, "Disciple-ism"). Born in the village of Talwandi, which is located some thirty miles from Lahore, capital of the Punjab, his father was a village accountant and farmer. Too much of a daydreamer for anything but a government job, he worked in Sultanpur, married, and had two children. Evenings he spent singing hymns while his friend, Mardana, accompanied him on a small stringed rebeck. One day, after taking a bath in the river, Nanak was given a cup of nectar by God, and three days later returned home. After a day of silence, he said these words: "There is no Hindu and no Moslem." Soon he left again, with his friend, this time to be gone for years, wandering to all the places of pilgrimmage visited by Hindu and Moslem, Hardwar, Delhi, Benares, the temple of Jaganatha, and Mecca. In Mecca, he went to sleep with his feet toward the sacred Kaaba. Kicked awake by an irate Moslem, who shouted at him: "Who is this sleeping infidel? Why, O sinner, hast thou turned thy feet towards God?" He replied: "Turn my feet in any direction in which God is not." The angry Arab, not thinking what he was doing, then seized the *guru's* feet and dragged them around in the opposite direction.

In the process of singing and preaching to the pilgrims along the way, Nanak wrote most of the hymns now found in the *Ādi Granth*, including:

I was a minstrel out of work;
The Lord gave me employment.
The Mighty One instructed me:
"Night and day, sing my praise!"
        Again:
There is but one God whose name is True,
The Creator, devoid of fear and enmity,
Immortal, unborn, self-existent,
Great and bountiful.
        Again:
The age is a knife;
Kings are butchers;
They dispense justice when their palms are filled;
Decency and laws have vanished;
Falsehood stalks abroad.

It was back in the Punjab that Nanak had the most success, a prophet honored primarily in his own country. There his efforts to unite the two great faiths attracted followers. At sixty-nine, he decided to appoint a successor, but passed over his own two sons, because they did not show any spiritual qualities. He appointed one of his disciples, Angad.

When Nanak lay dying, the Hindus and Moslems began arguing about who would be in charge of taking his body, Hindus wanting to cremate it, Moslems wanting to bury it. He told them to place flowers beside him, Hindus on the right, Moslems on the left, and whichever were fresh in the morning may have the disposal of the body. Then he pulled the sheet over his head and lay still. When the morning came, the flowers on both sides were in bloom, and when the sheet was removed, nothing was found beneath it.

Probably, as the historian Toynbee has observed, Nanak would disclaim being the "founder" of the religion, preferring rather to say that he merely brought to light the religious truths expressed by others before him.

Self-denial, he taught, was the correct approach to God, whose true name is True Name.

BĀDARĀYAṆA (440-380 B.C.): Founder of Vedānta and teacher of Jaimini, who founded Mīmāṁsā, Bādarāyaṇa wrote the first text of the school, the *Vedānta Sūtra*, also called the *Brahma Sūtra* or *Sārīraka Sūtra*.

BARDO: Tibetan for the disembodied state of an individual after death and prior to rebirth, an intermediate and indeterminate state of existence. To Tibetans, the Art of Dying was at least as important as the Art of Living. Dying is the art of going out of the physical body, transferring consciousness from the earth-plane to the after-death plane.

Evans-Wentz, the noted Tibetan scholar, in his preface to *The Tibetan Book of the Dead* (*Bardo Thodöl*, or, literally translated: "Liberation by Hearing on the After-Death Plane"), remarks that the West is ignorant of the Art of Dying. Medical science, materialistically inclined, unwittingly interferes with the natural process of death. The dying person is not allowed to die in familiar surroundings or in an undisturbed state of mind. The result is an undesirable death, fully as bad as that of a shell-shocked soldier on a battlefield.

The Tibetan Book of the Dead is read on the occasion of death, as a guide for the dying, or even, surprisingly, for one who is already dead. Sometimes it is recited for the entire forty-nine days, which is the length of the *Bardo*.

BEING: (*Be* is an irregular verb with parts from three unrelated stems: (1) Indo-European base *es-*, as in Sanskrit *ásmi, asti*; (2) Indo-European base *wes-*, stay remain, as in Sanskrit *vasati*, lingers, stays; (3) Indo-European base *bheu-*, grow, become, as in Sanskrit *bhávati*, occurs, is there, Latin *fieri* (*fis, fit, fimus*), be, become, occur.)

Reality, in the Eastern view, ranges from knowledge of self (Indian) to social relationships (Chinese) to phenomenal relationships (Japanese) or spiritual-magical-sexual activities (Tibetan).

1. *Indian*. P. T. Raju quotes the *Brahmasūtra* to summarize the Vedāntic theory of reality, that ultimate reality is known and realized within us as the Self (*Ātman*).

The Vedic tradition refers to several other theories, listed in

14

the Śvetāśvatara-upanishad: that reality was explained in terms of time (kāla), the nature of things (sva-bhāva), fate (niyati), chance (yadrcchā), elements (bhūtāni), womb (yoni), or person (purusa). While not all Indian schools do accept the view that self is the only reality, this seems to be the best general summary of Indian thought in general. Our own self exists everywhere, dividing itself into subject and object, matter and form. Categories of material and social existence are ultimately inward and immediate. The realm of thought with which Indian philosophy deals is the inward spirit.

2. *Chinese.* Wing-Tsit Chan observes that Chinese metaphysics is simple, unsystematic, and sometimes superficial. Both ancient and modern Chinese philosophers have been primarily interested in ethical, social, and political questions. Theoretical foundations are seldom addressed in Chinese thought.

One of the metaphysical topics that is dealt with is the problem of being and non-being. Buddhism, whose introduction into China presented a strong challenge to Confucianism, denied both being and non-being. To *be*, something has to be produced. To be produced, something either has to come from something else or from itself. To *be* means to have self-nature. But everything is composite, and has no "nature." Thus, being is an illusion. As also is non-being.

Taoism, instead of denying being and non-being, reduced everything to non-being.

Neo-Confucianism did not deny being or non-being, but affirmed them both as essential to change. The system was stated in these terms:

In the system of change there is the Great Ultimate (*T'ai-chi*). It generates the Two Modes (*yin* and *yang*). The two Modes generate the Four Forms (major and minor *yin* and *yang*). The Four Forms generate the Eight Trigrams. The Eight Trigrams determine good and evil fortunes. All good and evil fortunes produce the great business (of life). (—*I Ching*, Appendix I.)

3. *Japanese.*

Hajime Nakamura remarks that the Japanese are willing to accept the phenomenal world as Absolute because they emphasize intuitive sensible concrete events, rather than universals.

The image is on the fluid character of events, rather than solid masses. The phenomenal is the real.

On the Asian continent, "enlightenment" meant the ultimate comprehension of what is beyond the phenomenal world. In Japan, "enlightenment" meant the understanding of things within the phenomenal world.

Nichiren Buddhism, for example, rejected "Action according to principles" in favor of "Action according to things." It lay emphasis upon an empirical turn of thought.

Zen Buddhism, in Dogen, held that the truth for which people search is nothing but the world of daily experience:

The real aspect is all things.

The ever-changing flux of time is identified with ultimate being itself.

Again, Dogen said:

There are many thousands of worlds comparable to the sacred scriptures within a single spade of dust. Within a single dust there are innumerable Buddhas. A single stalk of grass and a single tree are both the mind and body (of us and the Buddhas).

Ogyū Sorai rejected and denounced the static character of Chu Hsi's School of Principle, holding that the fundamental mode of existence is phenomena.

Ryōkan wrote:

For a momento of my existence
What shall I leave? (I need not leave anything.)
Flowers in the spring, cuckoos in the summer,
and maple leaves in the autumn.

This emphasis on phenomenalism has helped Japanese scientists do exceptionally well forming hypotheses to explain the behavior of sub-atomic particles in high-energy physics.

4. *Tibetan.*

Noted for miraculous events, Tibetans do not attribute them to supernatural agents. When a companion is materialized to provide company on a long, lonely trip, that phenomenon is considered the reasonable result of traditional learning. So-called won-

16

ders are as natural as common everyday events. According to Alexandra David-Neel, the "secret lore" which can produce magical results is not necessarily esoteric Buddhist doctrine (although the traditional Buddhist idea that the world can be altered by altering states of consciousness would seem to be compatible with Tibetan theories), but rather traditional (Tibetan) knowledge of methods for realizing aims not necessarily spiritual. Thus, Tibetans do not consider magical phenomena to be supernatural events. Rather, they are the result of the clever handling of little-known laws or forces of nature.

BERUNI (973-1048): An Arabian thinker who was a contemporary of Avicenna, Beruni remarked:
> India, not to mention Arabia,
> has produced no Socrates:
> there no logical method
> has expelled phantasy from science.

His philosophy was that only sense-perceptions united by logical intelligence can yield sure knowledge:
> It is enough for us to know that
> which is lighted up by the sun's rays.
> Whatever lies beyond, though it
> should be of immeasurable extent,
> we cannot make use of. For
> what the sunbeam does not reach,
> the senses do not perceive, and
> what the senses do not perceive,
> we cannot know.

BHAGAVAD-GĪTĀ: (pronounced bawg-uh-vawd GEE-tah.) Probably the most widely-known book from India, the Bhagavad-Gītā (which means Song of the Blessed Lord) is one part of the lengthy epic, the Mahabharata. The Bhagavad-Gītā dates from perhaps the third century A.D., although its date of specific origin is under dispute. It has influenced many Western thinkers, from Hegel and Schopenhauer to Emerson and Thoreau.
Thoreau once remarked:

17

In the morning I bathe my intellect in the stupendous and cosmogonal philosophy of the *Bhagavad-Gītā* in comparison with which our modern world and its literature seem puny and trivial.

Of the "Three Ways," the Way of Knowledge, the Way of Works, and the Way of Devotion, the *Bhagavad-Gītā* recommends the third, Devotion, or *bhakti*. In a typically tolerant manner, the book grants that Knowledge and Works may both lead to unconditional release. But, as the hero-god Krishna explains while he acts as the great warrior Arjuna's charioteer, the Way of Devotion is best of all.

A notable quotation from the *Bhagavad-Gītā* reads:

The Blessed Lord said:

Many births have been left behind by me and by thee, Arjuna.

I remember them all, but thou knowest not thine.

One of the most visually attractive English editions of this work is the Bhaktivedanta Book Trust's version, *Bhagavad-Gītā: As It Is*.

Although it is the most popular and best-loved book of devotion from India, it is not generally considered *shriti*, that is, the literally inspired word of God, as are the *Vedas*.

BODHIDHARMA (470-543): According to tradition, Bodhidharma, the founder of Zen (Ch'an) Buddhism, journeyed from India to China in 520 A.D. He crossed the Yangtze River "on a reed," and rapidly displayed outstanding abilities in other ways.

Emperor Wu Ti of the Southern Liang Dynasty sent for him to ask how much spiritual merit he had earned by the imperial subsidies of the translation of sacred Buddhist books into Chinese. Bodhidharma answered: "No merit at all!" Furthermore, Bodhidharma added, the knowledge gained from reading books is worthless. All good works are worthless. The only thing of any value at all is meditation upon the Great Emptiness of the Buddha-reality. Only the Buddha in one's heart is of any real worth.

The Emperor was infuriated by this reply. He expelled him. Bodhidharma went to Mount Su in north China and sat with his face to the wall, meditating for nine years. Whether Emperor Wu had anything to do with this posture is not clear.

Basing his teachings on the *Lankāvatāra Sūtra*, Bodhidharma proclaimed that:

(1) A special transmission (from master to disciple) is possible outside the Scriptures;

(2) We should not be dependent upon words or letters as authorities;

(3) We should point directly to the soul of man; and

(4) We should see into our own nature and thus attain Buddhahood.

This latter point has its similarities to Jesus' saying, "The kingdom of God is within you," which was so admired by Tolstoy, as well as to Meister Eckhart's doctrine that within each of us there is a "castle of the soul." (See also: Zen.)

BODHISATTVA: (pronounced bode-he-SUT-vuh) Sanskrit for "being of enlightenment," in other words, one who has passed through the ten stages and is thus qualified to enter Nirvana immediately and to become a full Buddha. However, wishing to work for the salvation of mankind, he remains on this side of eternity to help others. Entirely freed from self, he is qualified to free others who are in bondage to their illusions. He undergoes great suffering and toil in working for the salvation of others.

The ten vows the Bodhisattva takes are:

1) to abstain from violating the discipline;

2) to refrain from acting superior;

3) to refrain from anger;

4) to avoid envy;

5) to avoid jealousy;

6) to refrain from being attached to material things;

7) to practice the four "acceptances:" charity, loving words, helpful deeds (working together to help others), and detachment;

8) to free all beings from suffering;

9) to protest all violations of discipline; and

10) to keep the true law.

19

One popular *Bodhisattva* is Avalokitesvara (of Tibet). In China and Japan, the term *Bodhisattva* was applied to include many non-Buddhist deities brought into Mahayana Buddhism.

BONPO: The Bon Religion, which was predominant in Tibet (and also Nepal, Sikkim, and parts of Southwest China) prior to the introduction of Buddhism. A shamanistic religion, Bon depended for its expression upon mediums possessed by spirits who uttered prophecies. Animistic, Bon taught that the world is filled with spirits which caused good or evil to people. The medium could then perform a miracle with the help of a spirit, cure illness and turn misfortune into blessing.

Many features of Bon were incorporated into the form of Tantric Buddhism which developed in Tibet, particularly with regard to magic and super-normal abilities.

Alexandra David-Neel, who wrote *Parmi les Mystiques et les Magiciens du Tibet* in 1929 (translated as *Magic and Mystery in Tibet*) describes such rites as *rolang*, "the corpse who stands up," in which the celebrant shuts himself up alone in a dark room with a corpse. He lies on the body, mouth to mouth. Holding it in his arms, he mentally repeats the magic formula. After a while, the corpse moves feebly, arises and, unless conquered, will kill the one who has disturbed it.

BRAHMĀ: (pronounced bruh-MA) To be distinguished from *Brahman* (q.v.), *Brahmā* is the first of the gods in the Hindu trinity: *Brahmā* (the creator), *Vishnu* (the sustainer of the world) and *Shiva* (the destroyer).

The key distinction between the two is that *Brahmā* has attributes, whereas *Brahman* has no attributes.

Brahmā began the creation by meditation and thought, thus producing the Golden Egg, the first stage in the world process.

Brahmā, the creator, is not worshipped in India, surprisingly. The only temple to *Brahmā* is located at Bhuvaneshwara, and no worship is conducted there.

BRAHMAN: (pronounced BRA-mun) God, the ultimate, understood to be without attributes. According to Vedānta, God

(*Brahman*) is not in the image of man, nor can it be described by any human words or categories of thought. *Brahman* is: not divided among beings, but standing in them as though divided, maintaining all beings, . . . seated in the hearts of all. *Brahman* is the being of all existence. *Brahman* is also the being of all non-being.

The word *Brahman* is neuter, when used to mean the supreme all-inclusive Being. *Brahmā* (q.v.), in the masculine gender, refers to the first member of the Hindu trinity. *Brahma* (with no lengthening of the final vowel) is the nominative form of *Brahman*.

BRAHMAN-ĀTMAN: The doctrine, in the Upanishads, of the connection between the universe and humanity, the ultimate and the individual, God and man: "Truly, He is the Inner Self (*Ātman*) of all."

BUDDHA (563-483 B.C.): "Don't just *do* something,"
Buddha said: "*stand* there!"
—Daniel Berrigan

One of the most remarkable geniuses in the history of the world, the Buddha was the only atheist ever to have founded a religion successfully. Bertrand Russell tried later, expressing regret for not having died in China so they could have built a religious shrine to an agnostic. Where Bertrand failed, the Buddha succeeded.

Buddha (which means "the Enlightened One," from the Sanskrit *budh*, to know, to wake up) was born Siddhartha Gautama (Siddhartha of the clan of Gautama) in northern India, at the foot of the Himalayan mountains, about a hundred miles from Benares.

This was a time period in which many of the great figures in world cultures arose: Confucius and Lao Tzŭ in China; Thales, Xenophanes, Pythagoras, Heraclitus in (greater) Greece; Zarathustra in Persia; Jeremiah and "Second" Isaiah in Israel.

Siddhartha's father, Shuddhodhana, was the ruler of the Gautama clan of the Sakya tribe. He was a member of the Kshatriya caste, trained in military science. As Siddhartha's mother had

21

died in childbirth, his father evidently tried to protect him from the harshness of life by surrounding him with luxuries: garments of silk and forty thousand dancing girls and three palaces. When he came of age, five hundred ladies were sent to him that he might choose one for his wife.

That he did choose, shows strength of character. He married Yasodhara and became the proud father of a son, Rahula. When he was twenty-nine, Siddhartha saw the "Four Passing Sights:" the first an aged man, wrinkled and feeble, broken-toothed, gray-haired, crooked and bent over, trembling, leaning on a staff. The next day, he saw a man sick with disease. The third, he saw the cold and rigid corpse of a dead man. The fourth, he saw a monk who had renounced the world. He became obsessed by the thought: "One must die!"

Later, he described his feelings:

"Then, O monks, did I, endowed with such majesty and excessive delicacy, think thus: 'An ignorant, ordinary person, who is himself subject to old age, not beyond the sphere of old age, on seeing an old man, is troubled, ashamed and disgusted, extending the thought to himself. I, too, am subject to old age, not beyond the sphere of old age; and should I, who am subject to old age, . . . on seeing an old man, be troubled, ashamed and disgusted?' This seemed to me not fitting. As thus I reflected, all the elation in youth suddenly disappeared. . . . Thus, O monks, before my enlightenment, being myself subject to birth, I sought out the nature of old age, of sickness, of sorrow, of impurity. Then I thought: 'What if I, being myself subject to birth, were to seek out the nature of birth, . . . and having seen the wretchedness of the nature of birth, were to seek out the unborn, the supreme peace of Nirvana? . . . Life is subject to age and death. Where is the realm of life in which there is neither age nor death?' "

He then described the next step:

"A lamp of scented oil was burning. On the bed strewn with heaps of jessamine and other flowers, the mother of Rahula was sleeping, with her hand on her son's head. The Bodhisattwa, standing with his foot on the threshold, looked, and thought, 'If I move aside the Queen's hand and take my son, the Queen will awake, and this will be an obstacle to my going. When I have become Buddha I will come back and see him.' And he descended from the palace."

Siddhartha became a wanderer, an ascetic, trying for the next six years to attain spiritual peace and enlightenment through the renunciation of pleasure.

He first tried the path of the Yogis. He lived on seeds and grass and gradually reduced his food to one grain of rice a day. In one experiment, he ate only dung.

He next tried the way of the ascetics. He wore hair cloth, lay upon thorns, let dust and dirt accumulate upon himself until he resembled an old tree.

He slept in a yard where rotting human corpses were laid out to be eaten by vultures and scavengers. Describing his frame of mind at the time, he said:

"I thought, what if now I set my teeth, press my tongue to my palate, and restrain, crush and burn out my mind with my mind? I did so. And sweat flowed from my armpits. . . . Then I thought, what if now I practice trance without breathing? So I restrained breathing in and out from mouth and nose. And as I did so there was a violent sound of winds issuing from my ears. . . . Just as if a strong man were to crush one's head with the point of a sword, even so did violent winds disturb my head. . . . Then I thought, what if I were to take foods in small amounts, as much as my hollowed palm would hold, juices of beans, vetches, chick-peas, or pulse . . . My body became extremely lean. The mark of my seat was like a camel's footprint through the little food. The bones of my spine, when bent and straightened, were like a row of spindles through the little food. And as, in a deep well, the deep, low-lying sparkling of the waters is seen, so in my eye-sockets was seen the deep, low-lying sparkling of my eyes through the little food. And as a bitter gourd, cut off raw, is cracked and withered through rain and sun, so was the skin of my head withered through the little food. When I thought I would touch the skin of my stomach I actually took hold of my spine. . . . When I thought I would ease myself I thereupon fell prone through the little food. To relieve my body I stroked my limbs with my hand, and as I did so the decayed hairs fell from my body through the little food."

He fell into a faint, and if his companions had not fed him some warm gruel, he might have died.

But no matter how little he ate, he did not understand life any better. Unable to reach truth by this self-denying means, Siddhartha abandoned this way to seek another. He began eating, to the great disgust of his five companions, who abandoned him.

Siddhartha went to sit under a shade-giving fig tree, the Bo-tree (Bodhi—"Enlightenment-"tree, still shown to tourists at Bodh-gaya, near the current town of Patna), and resolved not to move from that spot until he understood. It was May, the night of the full moon. The literature describes in vivid terms the assaults of the Evil One, Mara, to tempt him to move from his place, to distract him from his goal.

Mara sent three dancing goddesses to parade before him the temptations of Desire. When this failed to move Siddhartha, the Evil One sent storms, lightning, torrential rains, and showers of flaming rocks, splashing steam and boiling mud, to frighten him away by the prospect of sudden and violent Death. But these burning missles were transformed into blossom petals when they entered Siddhartha's field of concentration. Finally the Evil One marched his full army of fiends and demons to challenge his right to be there. When he saw them, Siddhartha touched the earth with his right finger, and the earth thundered its support for him, replying to his touch: "I bear witness!"

Siddhartha then saw a vision of the infinite succession of deaths and births in the ever-flowing stream of life. Every death he saw frustrated by a new birth, every peace and joy balanced by new desire and discontent, disappointment, grief and pain, and he said:

"Thus, with mind concentrated, purified, cleansed, . . . I directed my mind to the passing away and rebirth of beings.

24

With divine, purified, superhuman vision I saw beings passing away and being reborn, low and high, of good and bad color, in happy or miserable existences, according to their *karma* (in other words, according to that universal law by which every act of good or evil will be rewarded or punished either in this life, or in some later incarnation)."

The Evil One and his army, seeing that he could not be moved, and being basically cowardly, hastily advanced to the rear and vanished. All night long Siddhartha meditated, until, as the morning star shone, he at last reached his goal, Enlightenment. He thus became the Buddha, and sat in rapture.

Mara then came back, with one final temptation: "Why stay on earth?" he whispered. "No one will appreciate you, or even listen. Go at once into Nirvana. Leave the whole hot world to the Evil One." The argument had so much truth that it almost worked. But Buddha answered: "There will be some who will understand." Whereupon Mara vanished.

Buddha could have entered Nirvana immediately, had he so desired, separating himself from the world of pain and illusion. He chose instead to share his way of salvation with others, spending the remaining forty-five years as a wandering teacher among nearby tribes. He was called the Sage of the Sakyas (Sakyamuni).

The Buddha's insight was that the cause of suffering is desire, craving, due to ignorance. The path to its removal is right living and mental discipline. He summarized this in his address in the Holy City of Benares, the deer-park at Sarnath, in an address called "Turning the Wheel of Doctrine," containing The Four Noble Truths and The Noble Eightfold Path. The Four Noble Truths recommend "the middle path," a path between self-denial and self-indulgence.

The Four Noble Truths are:

1) the Noble Truth of Pain;
2) the Noble Truth of the Cause of Pain;
3) the Noble Truth of the Cessation of Pain; and
4) the Noble Eightfold Path (which leads to the cessation of pain).

The Noble Eightfold Path is:

1) Right beliefs,
2) Right thought,
3) Right speech,
4) Right conduct,
5) Right vocation,
6) Right effort,
7) Right attention (meditation), and
8) Right concentration.

Addressed to "him who has given up the world," convinced that worldly life cannot give true happiness, Buddha condemns as unsatisfactory two ways of life: (1) profitless indulgence in sensual pleasure and (2) equally profitless self-mortification. By avoiding these two extremes, one can gain "the enlightenment of the middle path which produces insight, produces knowledge, and conduces to tranquility, to higher knowledge, to enlightenment, to Nirvana." This is something like the sermon on the mount, only Buddhists believe theirs more literally.

Enlightenment is summarized by the Four Noble Truths:

1) The Noble Truth of Pain (or suffering, sorrow) is this: birth is pain, old age is pain, sickness is pain, and death is pain. Union with the unpleasant is pain, separation from the pleasant is pain, not getting what one wants is pain. The five groups of clinging to existence are pain.
2) The Noble Truth of the Cause of Pain is: the craving that leads to rebirth, accompanied by delight and passion, the rejoicing at finding delight here and there, the craving for lust, for existence, or for non-existence. Any craving is a cause of pain. The cause of sorrow is desire, want, likes and dislikes.
3) The Noble Truth of the Cessation of Pain is: the complete cessation of craving, its forsaking, relinquishment, which brings release and detachment from pain. Sorrow can be eliminated.

4) The Noble Truth of the Path which leads to the Cessation of Pain is the Noble Eightfold Path, namely:

1) Right beliefs, the right views, freedom from superstition, represented by understanding the Four Noble Truths;
2) Right thought, right resolution or aspiration; in other words, encouraging thoughts free from lust, ill will, cruelty, or untruthfulness;
3) Right speech, abstaining from gossipping, lying, tattling, talebearing, harsh language, vain talk, or revelling; or positively, speech that is kindly, open, and truthful;
4) Right conduct, or right action, means, negatively, abstaining from killing, stealing, and sexual misconduct; or, positively, action that is peaceful, honest, and pure;
5) Right vocation, or right livelihood, means earning a living in a way which is not harmful to any living thing: no butchers, no exterminators;
6) Right effort means self-training and self-control, self-discipline, so as to avoid evil thoughts and overcome them, to arouse good thoughts and maintain them;
7) Right meditation, attention, or right mindfulness, means to pay attention to every thought in an active, watchful, vigilant way, and to examine every state of feeling in body or mind;
8) Right concentration, also called right relation or absorption, rapture, means to concentrate on one single object so as to induce a special state of consciousness in deep meditation. This can be a trance-like state.

By following this Path, the disciple aims at complete purity of thought and life, hoping to become an *arahat*, one freed from the necessity of rebirth, ready for the peace of Nirvana.

We desire not to desire, and eventually that desire, as well, passes away. The state of Nirvana is Nothingness, oblivion, lack of suffering.

The key to this system of thought is the consideration that suffering is so awful we should re-structure our way of living, thinking, and reacting, so as to escape suffering and pain. Nothing is bliss. Bliss is nothing. When we attain everything, we attain nothing.

Buddhism's view of the six key concepts of Vedic thought was that:

(1) *Brahman*, the transcendent source of reality, was rejected;
(2) the soul was also rejected: Buddhism taught a doctrine of "no soul" (*Anatta*); the question arises, how can something be reborn if there is no soul; the answer given is that it is not the soul that is reborn, but karmic matter;
(3) *Moksha*, release or liberation from all the pains of existence, was kept;
(4) *Samsāra*, the time process, was also kept;
(5) *Karma* was retained and reinterpreted; and
(6) *Dharma*, righteousness, moral law, merit, or virtue, was reinterpreted.

Buddha died after eating some poisoned mushrooms at the home of Cunda the Smith. By mistake they had gotten into his dish. He forgave Cunda for this accident, saying it was the second best meal he had ever eaten. The best was the meal before his Enlightenment. This second was the one before he entered Nirvana.

BUDDHA: Either the historical founder of Buddhism (see previous article) or any fully Enlightened being or principle of Enlightenment.

BUDDHISM: From the Hindu point of view, Buddhism is a heresy. It reinterprets many of Hinduism's major concepts.

Buddhism is devoted to the elimination of pain and human suffering through the middle path between extremes of self-indulgence and self-denial. Founded by Siddhartha Gautama (Pali: Gotama) Buddha (*q.v.*) in the sixth century B.C., Buddhism virtually died out in its homeland, but spread through the rest of south and east Asia, exercising a profound influence upon the life and culture of such countries as Ceylon, Burma, Thailand, Cambodia, Viet Nam, China, Tibet, Korea, and Japan.

Buddhism is primarily suited for monastic expression. Only monks can live the complete Buddhist life. Ordinary laymen will find no help for the crises of life or the rites of marriage, puberty, and death. Further, where monasteries are challenged or attacked, as happened most dramatically in Tibet, there seems little chance for the survival of the system of belief.

(See also Hinayana Buddhism, Mahayana Buddhism.)

BUDDHISM IN CHINA: Such scholars as Fung Yu-lan make a distinction between Buddhism in China and Chinese Buddhism, using the first expression to refer to those forms of Buddhism which, though technically in China, were not congenial to the Chinese mind and consequently not lasting. The second expression is used to refer to those forms of Buddhism which changed sufficiently to fit Chinese culture more closely.

This article covers both forms.

According to certain second-century Chinese circles, Buddha was actually a disciple of Lao Tzŭ. When Lao Tzŭ, late in life, had gone west, he disappeared, and no one knew exactly where he had gone. India was his destination, according to this theory, where he taught Buddha and twenty-nine other disciples. The Buddhist *sūtras* (sacred texts) thus were simply versions of the *Tao Te Ching*. This theory, unlikely as it may seem, helped prepare the way for a cooperative spirit of acceptance between Taoism and Buddhism, the two philosophies of the Way (Tao) and the Way (Middle Path).

Buddhism was first brought to China in 2 B.C., when a Chinese official took lessons from a foreign diplomat on the Buddhist scriptures. Buddhism initially was considered to be an occult science, desired for its magical powers.

29

Another Chinese tradition relates how the Emperor Ming Ti (reigned 58-75 A.D.) dreamed he saw a golden image of the Buddha flying into the room, its head glowing like the sun. Upon waking, he ordered twelve envoys sent to India to bring back more accurate information on The Blessed One. They returned with two monks and a horse full of books. Unloading this four-legged library, they entered a monastery which the emperor had built for them, and began to translate the books into Chinese.

The Chinese did not accept Buddhism in its purely Indian form. They declined to translate the sexual passages of the holy books into Chinese. They also changed the abstract language of the Indian texts into more personal images.

Chinese Buddhism had seven divisions: first, the Seven Schools; secondly, *Seng-chao*; thirdly, the Three Treatise School; fourthly, the Conciousness-Only School; fifthly, the *T'ien-T'ai* School; sixthly, the *Hua-yen* School; and seventhly, the *Ch'an (Zen)* School. As the scholar Liebenthal observed: "The Chinese asked all the questions and Indian Buddhist revelation supplied the answers."

The main controversy concerned the concepts of being or non-being. Some schools held that matter is empty, without denying its conditional existence. Others maintained that matter is empty and does not have any sort of existence whatsoever, not even conditionally. All the phenomena of the universe, or, to be more exact, of the universe of an individual sentient being, are manifestations of one's mind.

Let us now consider the schools of Chinese Buddhism.

(1) THE SEVEN SCHOOLS

(i) The School of Original Non-Being (or Pure Being) was founded by the monk Tao-an (312-385), an orphan who joined the Buddhist order at twelve. Non-Being, he argued, existed before the things were evolved. Emptiness, the Void, was the beginning of all things with shapes.

The obstructions of man's mind are derived entities. If we

could get back to simplicities, we would then understand the universe and its true nature:

I, Monk Tao-an, cut a desert path to open up a way, and signal to the world the doctrine of the emptiness of the nature of things as a profound concept.

Later, the school of *Seng-chao* would teach a doctrine similar to Tao-an's.

(ii) The Variant School of Original Non-Being was founded by Fa-shen (286-374), a Teacher of the Law. "Original" non-being, he said, meant non-being before there was any form of matter (or color or thing or appearance). In the beginning was Non-Being. Out of Non-Being came Being.

Seng-chao (see section 2, following) criticized this theory sharply on the grounds that if Non-Being came before Being, the Buddha and the Bodhisattvas had to come into existence, which involved suffering, and this would therefore mean that they had sinned.

(iii) The School of Matter As We Find It (*Chi-Se*) was the school of matter as-it-is, actual things. Matter as-it-is is empty, because matter has no self-nature. It is not self-existent, but exists because of various causes.

This theory is imputed not to a person, but to a place, Kuan-nei (modern Shensi). Seng-chao (the person, not the place) criticized this theory on the grounds that it holds that: "matter has no self-nature but does not understand that matter is really not matter at all."

Another variation of the Matter As We Find It School is that of Chih Tao-lin (314-366). Chih Tao-lin was a nobleman turned monk, who wrote extensively. All his works are lost except for one introduction, which proves that prefaces are more important than people realize. His immortal masterpiece was entitled *Roaming in the Supremely Profound State Inherent in Matter As It Is*, and he explains in it that matter "as it is" is empty, because it depends on certain conditions for its existence.

We can see that this is virtually the same as Tao-an's theory of the emptiness of original nature.

31

(iv) The School of Non-Being of the Mind was noted for Fa-wen's (344-404) theory that one should not have any fixed opinions of the physical universe, no state of mind which clings to or is in any way affected by external things. The physical universe, however, is not non-existent. Whenever scriptures spoke of physical things as empty, they really meant not that they are actually empty, but that we should not allow ourselves to become attached to them.

This theory is criticized by Seng-chao on the grounds that: "The theory is right about the tranquility of the spirit but wrong in not realizing the vacuity of things."

(v) The School of Consciousness Contained in the Spirit was founded by Yü Fa-k'ai (334-394), a famous medical doctor. He drew a distinction between spirit and consciousness, holding that consciousness is a function of the spirit. What is "awakened" in enlightenment is the spirit.

The Three Worlds (of desire, matter, and pure spirit) are the abodes of one long night of worldly existence. The mind is the basis of a great dream. We dream the world, our lives, and our sufferings. When we awaken from the great dream, the long night will turn into dawn, the consciousness which produced such illusions will be extinguished, the Three Worlds will be seen to be empty, we will be awakened, and we shall attain enlightenment.

(vi) The School of Tao-i (370-431) taught that all the *dharmas* of worldly truth are illusory (however, the spirit is not illusory). There is no wisdom, and the scripture has always correctly said so.

(vii) The School of Chance, by Yü Tao-sui. Yü and Yü (fa-k'ai) both studied under the same teacher (whose entire class seems to have consisted of Yü's, or at least of Yü Yü's). Yü (Tao-sui) accompanied his teacher on a trip to India, which was a mistake, because, reaching Annam, he fell sick and died, aged thirty-one, and never did that again.

Dharmas, Yü wrote, are causal unions. They are the results of combinations of causes. This is all that can be said about worldly wisdom. As causes dissipate, the *dharmas* will cease to exist. This is absolute truth, or highest wisdom. Wisdom is more than science fiction: science *is* fiction.

(2) SENG-CHAO AND REALITY

Seng-chao (384-414) was born a poor boy, who learned to earn his living by repairing and copying books. He took to reading them as well as fixing them. Eventually, he wrote his own. The obsession of all the previous schools with Being and Non-Being, he believed, was suicidal. He taught that substance and function are identical, tranquility and activity the same. In the *Chao lun (Seng-chao's Treatises)*, he remarks:

People seek the past in the present. . . . I seek the present in the past. I know that it does not go anywhere. If the present passes on to the past, then there should be the present in the past. If the past reaches to the present, then there should be the past in the present. Since there is no past in the present, we know that it does not come (into the present). And since there is no present in the past, we know that it does not go (into the future). As neither does the past reach to the present nor does the present reach to the past, everything, according to its nature, remains for only one period of time.

According to Seng-chao, time is impossible. Hence, motion, which depends upon time, is illusory. This theory appears similar to Parmenides and Zeno, in Western philosophy, who argued that the concept of motion was self-contradictory and that nothing moved.

Seng-chao produced a kind of philosophical realism, completely empty of all substance. Another of Seng-chao's concepts may be compared to medieval nominalism:

If we look for a thing through a name, we shall find that there is no actuality in that thing which would correspond to the name. If we look for the name through a thing, we shall find that the name is not capable of helping us to discover a thing. A thing that has no actuality corresponding to a name is not a thing, and a name that is not capable of discovering a thing is not a name. Consequently, a name does not correspond to an actuality and an actuality does not correspond to a name. As

33

name and actuality do not correspond to each other, where do the myriad things exist?

(—in Wing-tsit Chan, *A Source Book in Chinese Philosophy*, Princeton, 1963, p. 356.)

All things can be said to resemble a man produced by magic. The man is not non-existent, but he is a man produced by magic and not a real man.

(3) THE THREE TREATISE SCHOOL

The philosophy of emptiness was developed to its fullest extent by Chi-Tsang (549-623), native of Nanking, who drew all emptiness together into one great system of nothingness.

All *dharmas*, elements of existence (in Chinese, *Fa*, "that which is held to," all things with or without form, real or imaginary), are unreal. Their causes are unreal. The Three Treatise School (named for the three treatises of Nāgārjuna (*Treatise on the Middle Doctrine* and the *Twelve Gates Treatise*) and his disciple Āryadeva (*One Hundred Verses Treatise*) may also be called the School of Non-Being, to be contrasted with the School of Being (or the Consciousness-Only School).

Emptiness is its central tenet. All things and causes are devoid of reality. Any differentiation, whether of being, non-being, cause, or effect, are only temporary names, empty in nature. Reality is Emptiness. The Absolute is the Void.

The nominalism of the Three Treatise School had social implications as it reinforced opposition to the whole Confucian theory that names, ranks, stations and classes are based on natural differences.

The Three Treatise School taught that there are Two Levels of Truth, one (worldly truth, or opinion) holding that all things exist provisionally as dependent beings, temporary names, and the other (absolute truth, or knowledge) holding that all things are really empty.

Existence and non-existence are both denied. Both are the results of causation, and, as such, are empty. If we were to combine being and non-being, we would form a synthesis. But that

34

synthesis itself is a new extreme with its own antithesis. This Hegelian-like doctrine reaches its final synthesis in Emptiness, the True Middle, as ultimate truth.

This Middle Doctrine employed a logical method of refutation and negation. Refutation of errors is just as beneficial as the explanation of right views. However, even a right view in itself becomes one-sided and is soon in need of refutation. This process will lead to the ultimate, Emptiness, which is "inexplicable in speech and unrealizable in thought."

This negative approach to knowledge and reality is nihilistic and destructive. It gave rebellious Chinese philosophers, including Neo-Taoists, a sense of freedom, but it offered nothing new except disproofs of existing ideas.

The Absolute as Emptiness, perfect and pure, devoid of specific content and separated from everyday reality was too abstract for the Chinese mind to accept. It did not lead to any new approach to life or reality. Later, *Ch'an (Zen)* would be able to rise to this challenge with conspicuous success.

(4) THE CONSCIOUSNESS-ONLY SCHOOL

Hsüan-tsang, the key figure in the Consciousness-Only School, went to India in 629, and returned in 645 with 657 Buddhist texts. Although the emperor had forbade him to go, he was so glad to have him back that he subsidized the translation of 75 of these texts into Chinese, before the emperor ran out of funds and Hušan-tsang ran out of time (d. 664).

Hsüan-tsang was not all translator, however, taking time to write the most difficult book in Chinese philosophy, the *Treatise on the Establishment of the Doctrine of Consciousness-Only (Ch'eng-wei-shih lun)*. His assistant, K'uei-chi (632-682) wrote a sixty-chapter explanation of the work, which he entitled *Notes On the Treatise on the Establishment of the Doctrine of Consciousness-Only (Ch'eng-wei-shih lun shu-chi)*, which won a prize for the most original title of the year. These works are notable for the same kind of hair-splitting analysis usually characteristic of medieval scholasticism or contemporary linguistic analysis.

"Consciousness-Only" refers to the detailed analysis of the mind conducted by the school. The mind consists of eight consciousnesses:

(1) sight,
(2) touch,
(3) smell,
(4) sound,
(5) taste,
(6) the sixth consciousness, the sense-center which forms ideas,
(7) the thought-center which reasons and wills on a self-centered basis, and
(8) the "storehouse" consciousness, a kind of memory.

These consciousnesses are involved in three transformations, the first of which is the storehouse consciousness, so called because it stores the effects of good and evil deeds (called "seeds") which have existed since the beginning of time. These seeds become the energy to produce manifestations.

The storehouse consciousness is constantly changing, being influenced (called "perfumed") by incoming perceptions and ideas from the external manifestations, which in turn are produced by the seeds, and so on:

A seed produces a manifestation;

A manifestation perfumes a seed;

The three elements (seed, manifestation, perfuming) turn on and on;

Cause and effect occur simultaneously.

The second transformation makes up the seventh consciousness, the thought-center. Unlike the first six consciousnesses, the second transformation does not have the external world as its object, but rather its object is the storehouse consciousness. Its intellectual deliberation considers the storehouse consciousness to be the self. The flaw in this kind of analysis is its strengthening of self-interest.

The third transformation involves a combination of the first five consciousnesses (the five senses) with the sixth, sense-center consciousness. The first five has as their objects the particular objects of sense. The sixth has as its object the external world as a whole. Thus this third transformation is not self-centered, as was the second transformation. However, it suffers from superficiality and the lack of continuity which characterize the consideration of the external world.

These three transformations all occur at the same time, and, further, each one influences all the others. This is how all things are caused.

(5) *T'IEN-T'AI*, THE PHILOSOPHY OF PERFECT HARMONY

Rather than take sides with any of the preceding schools of Chinese Buddhism, *T'ien-T'ai* taught the synthesis, the essential harmony between opposites, phenomena and noumena, transcendence and immanence, so that "every color or fragrance is none other than the Middle Path."

Threes seem to be predominant in *T'ien-T'ai*'s central doctrines:

(1) the True nature of all elements of existence;

(2) the perfect harmony of the Three levels of Truth; and

(3) the Three Thousand worlds immanent in an instance of thought.

The truth about existence is that all things are empty. The Three Levels of Truth are:

(1) the Truth of Emptiness,

(2) Temporary Truth, and

(3) the Truth of the Mean.

If all things are empty, that is the first truth. They are empty because they depend upon external causes for their being, but at the same time they *are* produced, and thus possess existence, even if only a temporary and dependent existence. This is Temporary Truth. The Truth of the Mean is that both emptiness and temporary existence involve each other. The Mean embraces both emptiness and relative reality.

T'ien-t'ai was the name for the Heavenly Terrace (Mountain) in Chekiang, where the school's monastery was located. Chih-i (538-597) lived there, lectured, and became so noted that he was invited to lecture at the palace in Nanking. He had thirty-two disciples who spread his word far and wide.

37

In contrast with the Consciousness-Only School, which had taught that some people are devoid of Buddha-nature, and thus are unable to attain Buddhahood, *T'ien-T'ai* taught universal salvation, since everything involves everything else.

Mind, unlike the teaching of Consciousness-Only, does not change. It involves all. The world is a manifestation of the mind, not consciousness itself. Calmness of mind is brought about by the cessation of erroneous thoughts, such as the false thought that the elements of existence come into or go out of existence.

T'ien-T'ai, when taken to Japan, became very influential, and was named *Tendai*.

(6) *HUA-YEN*, THE FLOWERY SPLENDOR SCHOOL

Fa-tsang (643-712) impressed Wu, the Empress, with his sixty books and his lecture on the *Flowery Splendor Scripture*, speaking with words so moving that "even the earth shook." Although the Empress was an Empress, she was not quick-witted. To make his point, Fa-tsang pointed at the statue of a lion in the palace, and used it as a visual aid. This was the origin of the *Treatise on the Golden Lion*.

Hua-yen may be characterized as *T'ien T'ai*, plus. That is to say, it is Perfect Harmony raised to the nth degree. Not only is it true, as *T'ien T'ai* had stated, that everything *involves* everything else, but it is also true that everything *implies* everything else. Particularity implies generality. Generality implies particularity. *Hua-yen* used the metaphor of the ocean and its many waves, each said to imply the other. The one is all, and the all is one. The universe is a complete concord of pre-established harmony:

the tendency of harmonious combination becomes unrestricted because it has no nature.

(7) *CH'AN (ZEN)*

The long history of the six Chinese Buddhist schools illustrates how none of them was able to complete its project of thought successfully. The advent of the school of *Ch'an* with riddling

38

answers to serious questions may seem to make more sense in that historical context than it would taken in isolation. The Chinese Buddhists had attempted to deal with various kinds of emptiness as recommended by various Buddhist schools. As the discussions became more and more acrimonious, the hoped-for result, enlightenment, receded into the futile future. The Chinese philosophers must have felt frustration. When the perfect harmony schools appeared, with the theory that all things (even Buddhist theories bitterly opposed to each other) work together, it was too late. So many abstractions and distinctions within abstractions had been developed that the weary intellect was ready to accept question-and-answer sessions like:

"What is the Buddha?"

"Three pounds of flax."

Or, again:

"Whenever I ask questions, I get so confused. What is wrong?"

"Kill! Kill!"

Ch'an Buddhism was not attempting to say that there is no serious truth, but rather that one was never to tell the truth too plainly, because a student needs to discover the truth for himself. Education must be indirect. *Ch'an* has proven to be one of the most interesting reformations in human thought. Part of its appeal may be in the celebrated Chinese tendency to express abstract ideas in concrete images.

The mind rather than ultimate reality was the focus of *Ch'an*. The Buddha-mind is everywhere. Anything at any moment may be taken as the occasion for enlightenment.

Bodhidharma (*q.v.*) brought Meditation (*Ch'an*) to China. Hung-jen (601-674) clarified it and made *Ch'an* the radical philosophy it is, based on the *Diamond Scripture* (*Chin-kang ching*), which became probably the most popular Buddhist text in China.

With Hung-jen's two disciples, Shen-hsiu (605-706) in the north, and Hui-neng (638-713) in the south, Zen developed two divergent tendencies, gradual enlightenment, and sudden enlightenment.

The methods devised by *Ch'an* for helping one achieve understanding include the *koan* (in Chinese, *Kung-an*), paradoxical or irrational answers to philosophical questions, the shout ("Ho!"), and corporeal persuasion (beating the questioner). Each method is designed to jar a student from the usual way of thinking. The point is that regular conceptual thinking cannot reach the truth. We must look to our own minds for a ray of light. Look at yourself! Look at the world! Then, we shall understand.

It is worth emphasizing again that such a method of looking at the world is characteristically Chinese. It offers a pronounced opposition to withdrawing from the world, the characteristically Indian response to problems.

The Chinese Confucian scholars, who dislike Buddhism in general for what they take to be its filial irresponsibility, are particularly unhappy with *Ch'an*, because it has no place for principle. The rectification of names has no place if it is recommended that we get away from words altogether. It is irony, charge the Confucians, that the Ch'anists use words to attack the adequacy of words.

After 845, Buddhism ran into systematic persecution. The emperor confiscated much of the land of the monasteries. In the end, the Confucians succeeded in suppressing Buddhism, except for remote provinces beyond effective government control and among those who would like whatever their social superiors opposed.

BUDDHISM IN JAPAN: Strong and original thinkers, men such as Hōnen and Dōgen, adapted Buddhist teaching to the cultural requirements of Japanese life.

The Mahayana (*q.v.*) form of Buddhism was almost the exclusive form of the religion in Japan. It was first introduced into Japan in the mid-sixth century (552 A.D.). The Emperor Kimmei received, in the tribute from Korea, a gold-plated image of a Buddha, together with several writings saying that these excellent and difficult doctrines could bring to the land either good fortune and true wisdom, or painful retribution. It was also noted that Buddhist doctrines had been reverently accepted from India to China.

A policy struggle within Japan ensued, with court families dividing into two bitterly opposed groups. One was composed of Shinto ritualists and imperial guards, who were threatened by the new philosophy. The other was led by the noted Soga family, which welcomed the change. When the emperor gave the golden image to the Soga, to see whether the old gods (the *kami*) would object, pestilence broke out. Obviously, said the conservatives, the *kami* objected. The golden image was then thrown into the canal.

Some time later, the experiment was repeated, and pestilence again broke out. This time, however, the pestilence continued to rage even after the statue had been disposed of. The Soga then argued that the disease had been caused not by the *kami*, but by the Buddha, unhappy at his cold reception.

The Soga were then permitted by the emperor to practice Buddhism as a family cult. Soga Buddhism was primarily the worship of relics for the sake of the magical qualities and material goods to be gained.

A dispute broke out over the question of succession to the throne. The Soga went to war against the other side. The Soga won. However, the next Emperor, Sujun, expressed his dislike for the Soga family. They promptly had him assassinated and enthroned one of their nieces as the Empress Suiko. Her nephew was the famous Prince Shōtoku (574-622). Born in a stable (nicknamed *umayado*, "stable door"), he became regent when his aunt, the Empress, became a Buddhist nun.

Greatly idealized by history, Prince Shōtoku vigorously supported the full-scale introduction of Buddhism into Japan. He sent delegations of scholars to study in China, adopted various Confucian ideas for organizing the ethics of court life and vigorously promoted social change. Once Japanese scholars had learned how to pronounce Chinese ideographs, it was possible for them to read them off without any further need for translation.

However, Prince Shōtoku had no intention of allowing Japan to become a vassal state of China. In one communication he sent to the Chinese Emperor (Sui court, 607), he wrote:

"From the sovereign of the land of the rising sun to the sovereign of the land of the setting sun."

The Chinese Emperor refused to reply to such an insulting note.

Some temples built by Shōtoku still survive, most notably the

41

Horyuji (607), which is the oldest wooden building still standing in the world.

(1) THE NARA PERIOD (710-784)

Once established, Buddhism became a powerful influence in Japan. During the period when the capital was located at Nara, the Buddhist monasteries became progressively more influential until, at the end, the civil government had to move from the city to escape their influence. Bound by loyalties to their beautiful temples in Nara, the priests did not follow the government in its flight.

Of the six schools of Buddhism during this period, two were Hinayana (*q.v.*), and four Mahayana (*q.v.*).

The two Hinayana schools were *Kusha* and *Jō Jitsu*. According to the *Kusha*, the self was unreal but the world real. The *Jō Jitsu* (which means "Completion of the Truth") taught that both self and world were unreal, that there is no substance, no duration, no bliss, but only *Nirvana*.

The four Mahayana schools were *Sanron, Kegon, Hossō*, and *Ritsu*. The *Sanron* (which means "Three Treatises") school was the first concentrated attempt by the Japanese to understand and assimilate Buddhist philosophical systems in depth. The three treatises referred to are the *Treatise on the Middle Path (Chūron)*, the *Treatise on the Twleve Gates (Jūnimonron)*, and the *One Hundred Verse Treatise (Hyakuron)*. A fourth text, sometimes added to these, is the *Great Treatise on Knowledge (Daichidoron)*. According to these treatises, all phenomena are unreal and relative. Any question can be answered in one of four ways: (1) yes, (2) no, (3) either yes or no, depending upon the circumstances, or (4) neither yes nor no, depending upon the circumstances. Thus all opposites, extremes, or polarities, can be suppressed. There is no absolute positive or negative, left or right, up or down. The correct teaching is the Middle path, which begins when verbal teaching ends, and which has no name.

The *Kegon* ("Flower Ornament") school used the image of "Indra's Net" to illustrate its teaching. Indra's Net was a large net with reflecting jewels sewn into each intersection. Each jewel

42

reflects its neighbor's image. The entire net represents the universe. The reflections in the jewels represent cause. Thus, no single being exists independently. The only truly independent state is *Nirvana*.

The *Hossō* ("Characteristics of the Dharmas") school taught that things exist only when we are conscious of them. It is the projection of their image on our minds that make them exist for us. Fact and principle are different. The thing in itself is different from the thing for us.

The *Ritsu* ("Discipline") school taught that the most important element in establishing correct doctrine was correct transmission. Proper ordination was necessary to prove the orthodoxy of a teacher or of a temple. Ordination of priests took place on a special platform built just for that ceremony. The vows taken at ordination were an active moral force affecting the mind and the actions. The *Ritsu* texts were intended to organize monastic life.

The high point in Nara Buddhism was reached in the year 752. A cleric from India arrived in Japan for the "eye-opening" ceremony of the *daibutsu*, the "great Buddha," a bronze statue fifty-three feet high. He had come to paint in the pupils of its eyes, thus giving it symbolic life. Ten thousand Buddhist priests were in attendance. Just before the ceremony began, the former emperor, Shomo, appeared and dramatically declared himself a servant to the three Buddhist treasures, the Buddha, law, and priesthood.

(2) THE HEIAN PERIOD (794-1185)

Heian ("peace and tranquility"), or, more familiarly, Kyoto, was a city approximately twenty-eight miles north of Nara. The imperial court moved there to escape the constant interference by Buddhist priests in the business of state. The kind of Buddhism they encouraged was whatever would devote itself to spiritual rather than political matters. The main such types were called *Tendai* and *Shingon*.

Tendai is named for the mountain in Southern China where the original monastery of the school was located. It is also called *Hokke-shū* ("Lotus sect") because it is based primarily upon the

43

Lotus Sutra. Tendai is an eclectic philosophy, incorporating into its system all the theories of truth in the older Buddhist schools. No particular doctrine is unique to Tendai.

One noted Tendai slogan is: "One heart, three meditations," expressing the conviction that one truth is found in three inseparable aspects, the "Triple Truth" of (1) the Void, (2) the Temporary, and (3) the Middle Path. Cause and effect produce the elements of the world, although in reality they are non-existent, the Void. Everything that we see is Temporary, mere appearance. Further, the Void is also the Middle Path, and the way to enlightenment and salvation. Tendai uses the illustration of a mirror to explain this doctrine. The reflections we see in the mirror are only temporary, only present as long as the objects it reflects are present. The mirror itself, that is, its brightness when no objects are in it, is really non-existent. The physical mirror itself is understood as the Middle Path, and symbolizes the true state of all things.

The court favored Tendai because it was conciliatory. In addition, the monastery on Hiei was located beyond the city limits to the northeast, at a "demon entrance" to the capitol (a dangerous direction, according to Chinese geomancy). Political leaders were happy to have a monastery protecting their flank.

The *Lotus Sutra* admonished its readers to "choose the straight way and cast aside expediencies. . . . We should now practice Budda's wisdom alone."

Shingon (the Japanese pronounciation for Chen-yen, the Chinese name of the school), the second main form of Buddhism in the Heian period, is the esoteric worship of the sun-god, Vairochana. "Shingon" is compounded of *shin* (true) and *gon* (word), meaning mantra, correct formula. Brought back to Japan by the monk Kūkai, Shingon is a branch of the so-called "right-handed tantrism," devoted to the masculine divinities (as "left-handed tantrism" worshipped female deities, the Tārās, savioresses). Kūkai himself was called "the universally illuminating thunderbolt." Shingon's monastery was built on Mount Koya, removed from "the world" of politics.

Shingon, like Tendai, is an eclectic philosophy, embracing in addition to Buddhism elements of Hinduism, Confucianism, and

Taoism. One of the outstanding features of Shingon is its advocacy of "Twofold Shinto," a blend of Buddhism with the ancient religion of Japan. According to Shingon, the whole universe is the body of the Great Sun Buddha, Vairochana or Mahavairochana. It provides a comprehensive worldview, answering cosmological, physical and psychological questions.

Shingon differs from Tendai in teaching that the Buddha had a secret or private doctrine which was superior to his public teachings.

In the late Heian Period several significant changes took place. For one thing, Tendai developed a very militant clergy. A factional dispute between the Enchin and Ennin lines of Tendai led to violence, the one sacking the monastery of the other, leaving it in ashes (1081). Warrior monks developed, large monk armies retained by all the great Tendai monasteries. Mercenaries were sometimes recruited for protection. Then the "bad monks" arose. The monk armies attacked rival monasteries and also, in a worse development, began to attack civil authorities. Several thousand such troops at a time (this was between 981 and 1185) would storm into the capital, at first to demonstrate peacefully, then to attack violently and, finally to loot. The attacking monks would often bring along the sacred carriage in which the god was transported. Government troops would not dare attack this carriage, for fear of sacrilege. This put government troops at a definite disadvantage. When the monks retreated back to their monasteries, leaving the sacred carriage behind and unguarded, the god inside was supposedly angered at having been abandoned. The civil authorities then had to beg and bribe the monks to return and take the angry deity back home.

The enthusiasm of the earlier Heian period was replaced by disillusionment. Genshin (942-1017), a Tendai priest, founded the Amida cult, urging the worship of Amida (Sanskrit: *Amitābha*), the Buddha of long life. The end of an era seemed to be approaching, with crime and civil disorder, weak rulers, greedy clergy, and generally disintegrating moral values. In such a situation, the teaching of the older Hinayanist sects, stressing one's own powers to save oneself, seemed useless. Monks like Genshin and Kūya, with evangelistic zeal, promised help from an outside source, Amida Buddha. Believers will be saved by being born again into the Western Paradise, which is open to all who call upon the name of Amida.

Another feature of Amidism was *mappō*, "the end of the Law." *Mappō* was the name for the third and last period in the cosmic cycle. History was divided into three periods of a thousand years. The first, called "the period of the *perfect* law," began with the Buddha's death. The second, "the period of *copied* law," was one in which the true faith declined but piety was preserved by being copied and studied. The third, in which we are currently, is "the period of the *end* of the law," states that religion and government are united by the Dharma (Buddhist Law). This divine law is higher than any human law. A king who obeys it will be rewarded by Buddha:

the people shall flourish, the earth shall be fertile, the climate temperate, and the seasons shall follow in the proper order. . . . All treasures shall be abundant. No meanness shall be found in human hearts.

The implication of the Sutra was that the right to rule was not based on heredity nor on the will of heaven but upon merit earned in previous existence, which presumably could be recognized as the ruler performed his duties properly. The king who disobeyed the Dharma would be punished.

In this period of *mappō*, Buddha's teaching will decline, the world will be overwhelmed by vice and strife, and we can be saved only by the mercy and compassion of Amida Buddha.

(3) KAMAKURA PERIOD (1185-1333)

The rule of the Shoguns (generalissimos), Minamoto and Jojo, was headquartered at Kamakura, a small village east of Kyoto which became the former capital. During this period, the Mongol attempt to invade Japan was repelled.

The philosophy of the Kamakura period emphasized faith and experience rather than the intellectual or moral topics characteristic of earlier forms of Buddhism. Amidism, Zen, and Nichiren were predominant.

Amidism, as we have seen, taught that calling on Amida's name was all that was necessary to attain paradise. Amida (or some other deity in the Mahayana pantheon of gods) was not used merely as an aid to meditation.

The founder of Amidism as an independent sect, called Jōdo-shin, or Pure Land (Amida's Western Paradise), was Hōnen (Gen-kū, 1133-1212). Honen sought and taught religious peace of mind. He read through the entire Buddhist *Tripitaka* five times, but still he felt dissatisfied. It was not until he abandoned all dependence upon his own strength (*jiriki*) and accepted the outside strength of another (*tariki*) that was he able at last to attain inner peace. According to Hōnen, anyone, even sinners, may receive salvation simply by "recitation with faith," that is, by calling on the name of Amida (1) with a sincere heart, (2) with a deeply believing heart, and (3) with a longing heart, longing for birth in the Pure Land.

Another form of Amidism, besides the Pure Land sect, was the True Pure Land sect (Jōdo Shinshū). Founded by Shinran, a disciple of Hōnen, he allowed a married priesthood and (since one thing leads to another) the eating of meat.

Zen ("Meditation"), while not the largest Buddhist group in Japan, is one of the most influential. Rinzai Zen has about six thousand temples, but Shingon, Jodo, and Shin are larger. Zen taught that study, of the kind carried on by earlier Buddhist sects, is unnecessary. Inner enlightenment, without which the ultimate cannot be comprehended, is all that is needed. Words, which are completely incapable of expressing essence, are futile. Understanding is a kind of imaginative insight.

Rinzai Zen, the type of Zen most familiar to the West, due to the efforts of D. T. Suzuki, emphasizes the virtue of sudden enlight-enment. This is the Zen of the *kōan*, absurd exchanges, riddling answers to devout questions.

Sōtō Zen emphasizes the virtue of gradual enlightenment, "si-lent enlightenment." Sōtō recommends the practice of sitting in meditation (*zazen*), the importance of daily living, and the partici-pation of the whole personality in the experience of illumination.

Zen has profoundly influenced Japanese culture from the tea ceremony to the art of archery. The best form of art is simplicity and understatement. Nature and everyday life are highly valued.

Another Zen art is called "the art of protecting life," swordsmanship.

The Zen master Eisai introduced tea to the country in 1191. Another master, Dōgen, improved the teacup. When the two got together, the result was irresistable. Eisai wrote (1214) a famous book entitled *Drink Tea to Improve Health and Prolong Life* (*Kissa yojo-ji*), taking a Madison Avenue approach to the topic before Madison Avenue. Tea was important to the monks engaged in long hours of silent meditation because it kept them awake.

The famous and formalized "tea ceremony," often performed in a tea hut, derived from Zen's interest in perceiving the divine in the commonplace.

Nichiren was the third school of Buddhism to arise in this period. Named for its founder, Nichiren (Risshō daishi, 1222-1282), it is a singularly polemical sect. Nichiren (which is a name he took for himself, meaning "sun-lotus," *nichi* meaning sun, the sunlight of the true faith, and also for Japan; *ren* meaning lotus, also referring to the *Lotus Sūtra*) had practiced the Amidist *nembutsu*, calling on the name of Amida for assistance, but after a while began to doubt whether it would work. Spending ten years in the monastery at Mount Hiei, he decided that Tendai doctrine was better than Amidist. The Tendai, he believed, however, was not the current doctrine, but rather the old-fashioned Tendai of Saicho. Nichiren's attempts to purify Tendai simply got him expelled.

According to Nichiren, a better *nembutsu*, better than calling on the name of one single Buddha alone, would be to call upon the entire *Lotus Sūtra*, which taught the essential oneness of the three bodies of the Buddha (transformation, bliss, and law). The devout believer was counseled to say: "reverence to the wonderful Law of the *Lotus*" (*namu myōhō renge-kyō*). This became the slogan of the Nichiren movement.

Nichiren was compelled to spend three years (1271-1274) on the island of Sado, under sentence of death for having been such a troublemaker. During this time he became convinced that he was the manifestation of the Bodhisattva Jōgyō, the chief of the hosts of Bodhisattvas in the *Lotus*. Writing *The Eye Opener* (1272), he vowed three things: that he would be (1) the pillar of Japan, (2) the eyes of Japan, and (3) the great vessel of Japan. Released following a miraculous stay of execution (1274), he witnessed the Mongol invasion, which he had prophesied formerly. The national crisis which ensued made people more receptive to the kind of radical conservatism he presented with such singular zeal.

Buddhist history, he taught, divides into (1) *shōbō*, the True Law, Hinayana, lasting a thousand years from the time of Buddha's death, which he reckoned on the Chinese fashion to be 947 B.C.; (2) *zōbō*, the Image Law, Mahayana; and (3) *mappō*, the End of the Law, beginning around 1050 A.D.

Nichiren's fiercest teaching was that killing heretics was not murder, but rather one of the duties which government is dutybound to perform. In particular, Nichiren said, Hōnen, the founder of Japanese Amidism, was the chief heretic. However, since he had died before Nichiren's life-time, he was unsuccessful in having him put to death.

The most outstanding Buddhist group today is Sōka Gakkai ("Value Creating Study Group"). It claims more than ten million members in Japan alone, making it the largest single religious organization in the land. Sōka Gakkai is based on the Nichiren True Sect branch.

(4) THE POST-NICHIREN PERIOD (1334-1600)

The Ashikaga Shoguns replaced the Kamakura, and two centuries of peace ended. There was constant political strife. The third Shogun, Yoshimitsu (1358-1408) was a member of Zen. Zen monks who learned Chinese were used as government clerks. Zen monks managed the commercial trading fleets.

By the time of the Tokugawa Shoguns, most of the Buddhist orders had again taken political sides. Mount Hiei, which made the fatal mistake of joining the enemies of Nobunaga, was destroyed. The monks had allowed rebels to hide in the monastery. Nobunaga sent two envoys to warn them to give up his enemies or see their sanctuaries destroyed.

All buildings without exception, including the central cathedral and the Shrine of the Mountain King, would be burned ... and all the inhabitants—religious or otherwise—would be beheaded.

Since they refused to yield, the army surrounded the mountain under cover of darkness, leaving no room for escape, and burned all three thousand buildings, libraries, sacred scriptures, and records of the imperial capital. Twenty thousand inhabitants were killed:

> Great scholars, men of rare talents, aged priests and young boys, still with their innocent, delicate features, were either beheaded or taken captive. Some pleaded innocence, claiming that they held no enmity, but they were told merely to cease their pretense and their connivance. Some begged to be spared while others remained steadfast in their faith, saying ... "Let us concentrate our attention on the Moon of Perfect Enlightenment, and chastise our hearts in the water that flows from the hillside of Shimei (Mount Hiei). Scalding water and charcoal fire are no worse than the cooling breeze." So saying, they threw themselves into the raging flames ... The roar of the huge burning monastery, magnified by the cries of countless numbers of the old and the young, sounded and resounded to the ends of heaven and earth.

Although Ieyasu later rebuilt it, it was never quite the same. Shingon resisted Hideyoshi and was smashed. Nichiren fortified a temple at Kanazawa and a castle at Osaka. Although never beaten, in the end the Nichiren had to surrender their fortresses, and the temporal power of Buddhism was broken.

(5) THE TOKUGAWA PERIOD (1600-1868)

During the period of stability brought to Japan by the Tokugawa family, only one new Buddhist sect was introduced into the country, a Zen sect called Ōbaku. Both the koan and zazen were considered the best ways to *satori* (enlightenment), but the nembutsu, invocation of the name of Amida, was also recommended. The Pure Land was said not to be an actual place, but rather within one's heart. "The unity of scriptures and Zen" was the slogan of Ōbaku Zen. Respected for its Chinese style, the architecture and customs favored by the Tokugawa, Ōbaku was said to represent a kind of Chinese enclave in Japan.

(6) THE MEIJI PERIOD (1868-1911)

When the American naval officer, Commodore Perry, opened Japan to trade with the West, a crisis was precipitated. In 1867 the Shogunate collapsed. In 1868 Buddhism was disestablished, and violent attacks were led against Buddhist temples and statues, with the slogan: "Exterminate the Buddhas and abandon the scriptures." The statues lost.

Shintō was proclaimed the national religion in 1870, and called the "Great Doctrine" (*Daikyō*).

(7) TAISHŌ AND SHŌWA PERIODS (1912-Present)

The main ideological challenge for Japanese thought during the current period has been from Christian missionaries and Western technological ideas. Western scientific concepts may sometimes operate with a great degree of compatibility in Japan. The Mahayana deities, unlike the Christian concept of a providential God, do not interfere with the chain of cause and effect. The resulting phenomenalism of Japanese thought may enable concentration on present phenomena rather than upon essences or substances. This Japanese acceptance of phenomenalism is accompanied by a reduced emphasis upon universals. The emphasis is upon intuitive, sensible, concrete events. The phenomenal is the real. According to Tendai, for example, the real aspect is all things. Dōgen, in agreement, maintains that:

> The real aspect is all things. All things are this aspect, this character, this body, this mind, this world, this wind, and this rain, this sequence of daily going, living, sitting and lying down, this series of melancholy, joy, action, and inaction, this

51

stick and wand, this Buddha's smile, this transmisssion and reception of the doctrine, this study and practice, this evergreen pine and ever unbreakable bamboo.

(—*Shōbōgenzō*, section on "The True Nature of the Law.")

BUDDHISM IN TIBET: In Tibet, Buddhism took a distinctive turn toward the occult. By the seventh century A.D., Buddhism in India had developed similarities to tantric Hinduism, magic and animism playing the key part in both. Female deities had been developed as counterparts to the male, and sexual elements entered the system. It was during this period that Buddhism spread to Tibet.

The first division of Tibetan history is the ancient era, from prehistory to 600 A.D., characterized by the absence of royal authority. The people were said by Tibetan sources to be "stupid" barbarians, and the country was called gloomy and "dark."

The second period (600-846) is the "Earlier Spread" (*sngadar*) of Buddhism. The famous King, Songtsen Gampo (r. 634-650) tamed the country, introduced Buddhism, and established the monarchy at Lhasa. He was considered an incarnation of Tibet's patron saint, Avalokiteśvara. He married a Chinese princess (and also, not wanting to play favorites, a Nepalese one). The two powers on Tibet's borders contended in more ways than providing brides for the king. For example, in 730, the Chinese classics, the *I Ching, Tso Chuan*, and *Wên hsüan*, were sent to Tibet. In 791 Buddhism was declared to be the official religion. During the following two years, 792-4, a debate was held at Samyê between a Chinese monk, Mahayana, advocating the "sudden path," and an Indian, Kamalasila, advocating the "gradual path." The Chinese lost the debate and were expelled from the country.

Other religious influences in the land at that time included (Christian) Nestorianism, from Iran, Manichaeanism, from the Turks, and Islam, from the Arabs.

This period ends with persecutions initiated by Lang Darma (r. 844-846), called "the wicked king." He was soon assassinated by a monk, Pelgyi Dorje of Lhalung.

The third period (846-1641) is called the "later spread" (*phyi-*

dar) of Buddhism. During this period Rinchen Sangpo (958-1055) was active, the translator of texts and founder of temples (Toling in Guge, Tabo and Nako in Spiti).

Phagmotru (1110-1170), (the name of the region where this noble family's founder settled), also called the "precious protector of beings," or "the great man of Kham," founded the great monastery of Thil (Thel). He won the kingdom of Tsharong in a chess game, as a civilized way to conduct war. The office of abbot of these monasteries was often handed down from uncle to nephew.

Other notable figures were Marpa (1012-1106), who brought from India the art of transferring the conscious principle into another body or into paradise; Mila Rêpa (1040-1123), the poet hermit who sang the mystic songs of the tantric poets of Bengal, and who is noted for the doctrine of "the Great Seal;" Gampo-pa (1079-1153), the physician (or the medium) of Dakpo; Sakya Panchen (1182-1251), the "great scholar," famed for having worsted "the heretics" in theological debates in India. He was invited to do the same in Mongolia. Later he gave religion lessons to Godan (the grandson of Genghiz Khan), which may be compared to Aristotle's tutoring Alexander the Great. Thangton Gyelpo (1385-1464) was the great yogin-type saint, celebrated for building iron suspension bridges. Tsongkha-pa (1357-1419) wrote the *Lam-rim* and the *sNgags-rim*, and was the founder of the Geluk-pa order ("those who follow virtuous works"), commonly known as the Yellow Hat Sect. Insisting upon the need for monastic discipline and the gradual path (morality, etc.), he wrote (in two volumes) the *Lam-rim* and the *sNgags-rim* in 1403. Invited to China, he said he was too busy to go, and instead sent his disciple.

Jamchen Choje Shakya Yeshe, "the king of religion," was the founder (in 1419) of the great monastery of Sera.

Another disciple of Tsongkha-pa's, Jamyang Choje Trashi Pelden, founded (in 1416) the monastery, Drêpung, in the neighborhood of Lhasa. These monasteries were like university cities, containing a variety of faculties, some of which specialized in knowledge of the Tantras.

Gedün-trup (1391-1474) was the founder (in 1447) of the

53

monastery of Trashil-hünpo, retrospectively called the First Dalai Lama. He was believed to be the incarnation of Avalokiteśvara, patron saint of Tibet, who earlier had been incarnated in their monkey ancestor and also in the first Buddhist king, Songtsen Gampo.

Gedûn Gyatso (1475-1542) was abbot of Drêpung (1517), Trashil-hünpo (1520) and Sera (1526). Retrospectively, he was called the Second Dalai Lama.

Sönam Gyatso (1475-1538) of the house of Phagmotru, was the first to be called (by the Mongols) "Dalai Lama" (*Dalai* meaning "ocean" in Mongolian, a translation of *gyatso*), and was reckoned the Third Dalai Lama. He had approached various foreign patrons, including the Altan Khan (related to Kublai Khan) to secure an edict abolishing the Mongols' practice of blood-sacrifice. He travelled widely throughout Kham, Koko Nor, and Inner Mongolia. His authority to reign over all Tibet came from the Gushi Khan, under the oversight of a governor nominated by the Mongols.

The Fourth Dalai Lama was Yönten Gyatso.

The fourth period in Tibetan culture is the modern era, from 1641 to the present. Ngawang Lopsang Gyatso (1617-1682), the Fifth Dalai Lama, instituted the high office of Panchen Lama (of Trashil-hünpo). He also built (or started) the Potala palace (1645-1694) in Lhasa. His famous regent was Sanggye Gyatso (r. 1679-1705).

Tshangyang Gyatso (1683-1705), the Sixth Dalai Lama, liked women and love-poems. He was once attacked by a Qosot. He died while being kidnapped and taken to China.

Lhapsang Khan tried to force a false Dalai Lama on Tibet, which caused great disturbances. Shortly thereafter, Kesang Gyatso (1708-1747), the true Seventh Dalai Lama, was enthroned at the Potala.

The eighth to the twelfth Dalai Lamas (1758-1875) were either unimportant or died young, or both. Many of the Panchen Lamas, on the other hand, earned distinction. Lopsang Pelden Yeshe (1738-1780), for example, the Sixth Panchen Lama was a great friend of China's.

The Thirteenth Dalai Lama was Thupten Gyatso (1875-1933).

During his reign, China was at bay. Russia was occupied by war with Japan. Britain had set up a protectorate over Sikkim. In 1904, the British marched on Lhasa and occupied the city temporarily. The Dalai Lama fled, after firing the court magician for having predicted the British would never attack Lhasa.

In 1910, a Chinese army advanced on Lhasa, and again the Dalai Lama fled, this time to India. Revolution within China forced her to withdraw from the attack. Not until 1949 did China begin to effectively control Tibet. In 1959, revolt broke out, started by the Khampas. Once broken by the Chinese, the Dalai Lama fled to India.

The great monasteries have been closed, and many of the spiritual leaders of Tibet have fled to India, Indiana, Switzerland, Scotland, Colorado, New Mexico, and other high places around the world. The teachings of the lamas, once secret, are being published and old manuscripts, when they become available, are translated and studied with great interest.

BURMA, PHILOSOPHY IN: The Burmese were the original Pagans, the Kingdom of Pagan lasting from 1044 to 1287, centered at the city of Pagan on the left bank of the Irrawaddy river. There is a Pagan river in Virginia, but Virginia was settled after Burma. Pagan is a city of temples, considered by art historians to be one of the landmarks of Asia, the Ananda temple is one of the most beautiful. Some five thousand temples were built in the city. In the summer of 1975, a severe earthquake damaged more than half of the five hundred most important surviving temples. High spires fell, pinnacles lost many of their bells, and one entire pagoda, the Buphaya, even tumbled into the river.

Buddhism first came to Burma in the fifth century A.D., in the Theravada (or Hinayana) form. Many vividly illustrated books on Buddhism are available, depicting the transitory character of life. Some show the progression in appearance of a beautiful young woman, a "Miss Burma," from youth to old age, and on to a small pile of bleached bones.

In the nineteenth century, Christian missions were introduced into the country coincidentally with the entrance of the British Empire. Rangoon hosted the construction of Judson Church

(Baptist), a newcomer compared with the gold-covered Shwe-Dagon Pagoda. Western religious efforts made little headway in the cities, and efforts were directed at the more primitive tribes in the hill country.

Today the hill tribes in Burma are either head-hunters or Christians, or both.

Western-style education was also introduced into the country, and produced the benefit of a larger number of university graduates than the country can employ. Many who have earned college degrees are working at low-class jobs.

Burma has currently withdrawn into a self-imposed isolationism.

BUSHIDŌ: Japanese term for "the way of the warrior," or "the way of the Samurai." Ruth Benedict objects, in her study of Japanese culture entitled *The Chrysanthemum and the Sword*, that *bushidō* is a misleading term, a modern official word which does not have any deep folk-feeling behind it. *Bushidō* is best understood as part of a more general ethical principle, that of *giri* to one's name, which means the duty of keeping one's reputation unspotted. Whatever the social class, this obligation is the same, the only difference being that it is more important the higher the class.

C

CAMBODIAN PHILOSOPHY: The early cultural influences on Cambodia were from India. The *Mahābhārata* was known in Cambodia as early as the sixth century A.D. Temples to Shiva and Ganeśa (Ganeśa was the elephant headed god) may be found in the country, dating, for example, from the tenth century. The chief masterpiece of Khmer architecture was Angkor Wat, built in the early twelfth century. It is a galleried temple complex adorned with scenes from the Hindu epics.

The political use of Hindu philosophy was to establish a god-king on the throne, ruling in an authoritarian manner over the land. An irrigation system composed of a vast number of canals supported extensive agricultural enterprises. However, weak rulers, together with the introduction of Buddhist ideas, which sharply criticized the traditional Hindu culture and royal household, opened the empire to invasion by Thais and Mongols during the thirteenth and fourteenth centuries. The invaders occupied Angkor Wat and destroyed the canal system. The devastation was too great to be dealt with, and Cambodia became a pawn in struggles between her neighbors, a role which has persisted for centuries, recently aggravated by French Colonialists and American presidents. In 1962, the population of the country was about six million, including as sizeable minorities 350,000 Vietnamese ("Annamites") and 230,000 Chinese immigrants. The Indian settlers had long since intermarried freely with the Mongolians they found in Cambodia. Most Cambodians practiced Theravada Buddhism.

CĀRVĀKA: Materialistic philosophy, one of the three heretical schools of Indian thought (together with Jainism and Buddhism). Cārvāka ("*Charv*" means "eat!") is named after its founder, Cārvāka. Scholars doubt that Cārvāka (the founder) actually existed, but they do not generally doubt the existence of Cārvāka (the philosophy), although, given time, they may. Regardless of the outcome of this serious scholarly controversy, let us leave Cārvāka to the historians and instead discuss the influence of Cārvāka.

Not only did the founder die (if he existed), but the chief source book, the *Bṛhaspati Sūtra*, was lost as well, and is only available in the form of quotations in books written by orthodox authors for the purpose of refuting it. The main source is the *Lion Assaulting All Philosophical Principles* (*Tattvopaplavasiṃha*), dating from the seventh century A.D.

The main doctrines of Cārvāka evidently were that only this world is actually real, that our knowledge about it comes from sense perception. Inference, reasoning from analogy, and testimony from authorities are all defective, and not to be trusted.

Matter, which is the only reality, is composed of air, earth, fire, and water (this formulation is similar to medieval European alchemists and also to the pre-Socratic philosopher, Empedocles).

This world, according to Cārvāka, is all there is. There is no other:

> Heaven is found in eating delicious food, keeping company with young women, wearing fine clothes, perfumes, garlands. . . . Hell is found in the troubles caused by enemies, weapons, diseases. . . . Liberation (*moksha*) is death.

We may see how this kind of skepticism could provide the setting for the answer to the question of life developed by Buddhism. Buddhism accepted the last of Cārvāka's doctrines, that liberation is death, and merely added the power of a positive image to that form.

Consciousness, according to Cārvāka, is not independently real, but only a function of matter. The "soul" is only a word for the body or the senses or breath or thought (opinions within the school differed). There is no life after death. The soul dies when the body dies:

> While life is yours, live joyously;
> None can escape Death's searching eye:
> When once this frame of ours they burn,
> How shall it e'er again return?

The world was not created by any divine power. The world made itself. God is a myth, and history does not bear witness to any sort of divine providence. Nature is indifferent to good and evil. Virtue and vice are only conventions. The only good is the pursuit of pleasure.

Chastity and other such ordinances are laid down by clever weaklings.

Hedonism is its ethical theory.

Cārvāka refused to draw any inspiration from the Veda, and refused to justify doctrines by any reference whatever to orthodox texts. The *Vedas* were written by "clowns, fools, and devils."

Cārvāka argues (in the *Tattvopaplavasiṁha*) against the notion of cause and effect. The argument for cause, that "There is a cause, for there is an effect," is criticized as no better than the argument that "The crow has a soul, for it is black."

The force of *karma* (*q.v.*), merit and demerit as determining the lot of the individual, is also denied. Materialism, the philosopher Radakrishnan has observed, may be interpreted as "the first answer to the question of how far our unassisted reason helps us in the difficulties of philosophy."

Materialism died out in India, at least officially, until it was reintroduced by the merchants of the British East India Company.

CASTE: The Indian practice of dividing society into exclusive classes, called *varna* (Sanskrit, "color") or more correctly, *jati* ("sub-caste").

There are four classes (*varna*) and more than three thousand sub-castes (*jati*), according to the 1961 census. The four classes are: (1) priests, (2) warriors, (3) merchants and craftsmen, and (4) menials. The caste system is a stratified system of social classes given religious sanction. It was said to be a divinely ordained feature of the universe.

The religious sanction comes from a hymn in the *Rig Veda* which describes the ancient sacrifice from which the world was made. The priests, the *Brahman* class, came from the head of the primeval man; the warriors, the *Ksatriya* class, came from the arms; the merchants and craftsmen, the *Vaishya* class, came from his thighs; the menials, the laborers and peasants, the *Sudra* class, came from his feet. Below these are the out-castes, the "untouchables," called *Harijans* ("children of God") by Gandhi. *Harijans*, traditionally employed as executioners, undertakers, or garbage collectors, were not allowed to enter temples, use the roads, or go to school. They were required to have a separate water supply.

Untouchability was outlawed in 1955, and Prime Minister Nehru carried on a campaign for a casteless society. However, fourteen years later a government commission reported that many police and even higher officials were unaware of the law in that regard.

The caste regulations govern such features of life as marriage, eating, occupation and travel. Marriage is required to be between members of the same caste. Eating should be only with a member of the same caste. To be a vegetarian is higher than being a meat-eater. To eat only fish or pork is higher than eating beef. To drink tea is higher than drinking alcohol. Occupation is generally, although not exclusively, prescribed by caste. For example, the Ahirs are traditionally herdsmen; the Chamars are leather workers; the Chuhras are scavengers; the Goalas are milkmen; the Kayasths are writers; the Humhars are potters. The Brahmans are the priests or professionals.

Travel outside India was forbidden. Whenever young Hindus sought their education abroad, the stricter families would hold a ceremony of purification upon their return from a foreign country, to wash away those features of travel and associations abroad which were considered tainting.

Many social changes have taken place in modern India, with

upper- and lower-caste individuals travelling side by side in trains, working side by side in factories, and eating side by side in restaurants. This is a change from the days when a Brahman would be defiled if even the shadow from an untouchable touched him. The attitude of many toward the changes was expressed by a clerk who said: "When I go to the office, I put on my shirt and take off my caste; when I come home, I take off my shirt and put on my caste."

No specific hierarchy of castes exists for the whole country. Instead, the place of the caste is decided on a village by village basis. The *Sudra* castes, for example, are dominant in some regions, while in others they are so low as to be regarded as almost untouchables.

Some caste mobility is possible, an interesting illustration provided by the Nadars (formerly Shanans) of Tamilnadu. In the nineteenth century, they were traditionally brewers, and barely above untouchability. Improving their activities, they finally claimed Kshatriya status before the census commissioner in 1901. Their attempt at upward mobility was successful, and their new position approved.

CHANG TSAI (1020-1077): The "Master of Heng-ch'u" (or Chang Heng-ch'u), from the province now called Shensi, Chang Tsai was a neo-Confucianist noted for his theory of cosmology. His main work was the *Correct Discipline for Beginners* (*Cheng Meng*).

He based his theory on "Appendix III" of the *I Ching*, which states: "In the *Yi* there is the Supreme Ultimate which produces the Two Forms (*Yin* and *Yang*)."

According to his interpretation, the "Supreme Ultimate" is the concept of *Ch'i* ("gas" or "ether"). The Master's "gas" was understood to mean the physical matter which constitutes all existing individual things. The *Ch'i*, also described as "wandering air," is called, in its unity, the Great Harmony. *Yang* rises. *Yin* falls. When influenced by *Yang*, the *Ch'i* rises. When influenced by the *Yin*, the *Ch'i* sinks and falls.

This process of alternating attraction and repulsion, mixing and separating, seems to bear some similarities to the pre-Socratic philosopher Empodocles, who held that love and strife were the moving forces in the universe.

Chang Tsai denies Non-being (*Wu*), by saying: "If one knows that nothing is the Real (*Ch'i*), one knows that there is no Non-being (*Wu*)."

The most famous passage from the *Cheng Meng* is the "Western Inscription," so called because it was inscribed on the western wall of Chang Tsai's study. According to the words of the Western Inscription, all things in the universe have the same reality (*Ch'i*). We are therefore all a part of one great body. We should serve Heaven and Earth as if they were our own parents. All men are brothers. Every normal moral action serves the universal parents well. The passage ends with the moving words:

"In life I follow and serve, and when death comes, I rest."

CH'ENG HAO (1032-1085): (pronounced jung how) One of the two brothers who divided Chinese Neo-Confucianism in the Sung Dynasty into two divergent schools. The two are known as the Ch'eng Masters. Ch'eng Hao, also called Master Ming-tao, was the elder brother, and his branch was called "The School of Mind" (*Hsin hsüeh*). The younger brother, Ch'eng Yi, founded "The School of Laws (or Principles)" (*Li hsüeh*).

The main difference between the two schools is over whether the laws of nature are actually found in nature, or whether they are supplied by the mind. In a somewhat Kantian manner, Ch'eng Hao maintained that the laws of nature are supplied by the mind. Wang Yang-ming would later champion this point of view.

Some well-known quotations from Ch'eng Hao are:
There is no spirit outside of material force, and there is no material force outside of spirit. . . . Nature and man are basically not two. There is no need to speak of combining them.

CH'ENG YI (1033-1107): (pronounced jung yee) The younger of the two brothers who divided Chinese Neo-Confucianism in the Sung Dynasty into two divergent schools. Ch'eng Yi, also called Cheng Yi-Ch'uan, or Cheng-shu, or Ch'eng I, founded the

"School of Laws (or Principles)" (*Li hsüeh*). If something exists, it must exist according to some principle (*Li*). Somewhat like Plato's theory of forms, *li* was contrasted with material substance, or *ch'i*. One of the most celebrated philosophical slogans in China was Ch'eng Yi's: "Principle is one, but its manifestations are many." Chu Hsi would later champion this point of view.

Ch'eng Yi lived a long and influential life. A brilliant man, his uncomprising attitude and critical opinions of the dullards who, as usual, were in positions of power, created bitter enemies. While he was supervisor of the Directorate of Education (1092), his enemies constantly petitioned for his impeachment. In disgust, he resigned. His teachings were prohibited in 1097. His land was confiscated, and he was exiled.

Pardoned, he served again for a few years. In 1103, his enemies succeeded in securing an edict to have his books burned. His highly moralistic teachings were prohibited.

He was again pardoned, a year before his death, but when he died, official antagonism was so intense that only four people were sufficiently courageous to attend his funeral.

In one of his writings, he criticized the Buddha for "deserting his father and leaving his family. . . . Such a person should not be allowed in any community." He also criticized the followers of Buddha, because their "feelings are basically love of life and fear of death. This is selfishness."

One of Ch'eng Yi's positive statements is often quoted: "Empty and tranquil, and without any sign, and yet all things are luxuriously present."

A man of principle, dedicated to a good society, he died persecuted by society, which was happy with its evils. High principles brought him down, but his fall brought them up.

CH'EN TU-HSUI (1879-1942): A Chinese communist philosopher, the first interpreter of Marxism in the country. He was the editor of *La Jeunesse Nouvelle*, the most influential review of the period (1915-1920). He firmly supported Hu Shih's campaign for literary reform. Confucianism was denounced as being conservative and backward, the enemy of progress. One of Ch'en's slogans was:

Republican government in politics and science in the domain of ideas; these seem to me the two treasures of modern civilization.

Ch'en's democratic ideas were acquired from France. He did not want to abolish all morals, he said, only Confucian morals. Ethics is relative, not absolute.

By 1920, he was emphasizing the importance of economic goals to social improvement:

The republic cannot give happiness to the masses

and:

Evolution goes from feudalism to republicanism and from republicanism to communism.

In 1921, he founded the Communist Party, directing it until 1927. He was called "the Chinese Lenin." Later he was expelled from the party, tried to organize an opposition, called "Trotskyist," and was imprisoned by the Nanking government.

Freed by the Japanese war in 1937, he died in 1942, unnoticed.

CH'I: (1) Concrete thing; ch'i opposed to Tao (which is unrestricted and spiritual, rather than physical). In popular use, ch'i means an instrument, implement, or vessel, but the philosophical use of the term is more technical, and should not be misinterpreted in the popular sense. Nor should ch'i be misunderstood to mean matter or substance. Ch'i in the technical sense does also include systems and institutions, any thing which has a concrete and limited form.

(2) Material force; ch'i (matter-energy) opposed to li (principle). Sometimes, prior to the development of thought in Neo-Confucianism, ch'i was translated "vital force," or (as with Mencius) "strong, moving power."

CHINESE PHILOSOPHY: The Chinese have always been masters of society, and the Chinese approach to philosophy is primarily concerned with the theory of society rather than metaphysics or epistemology. The non-human portion of the universe may be all right in its place, but it is the source of too many floods, famines and earthquakes to be entirely trustworthy. God may be all right in His place (Confucius was not much more religious than Chairman Mao), but He is less a source of happiness than a woman, and an emperor is more to be feared than God.

For a time, China was corrupted by Buddhism, according to Confucian scholars, but her polite revenge was achieved when Buddhism was changed to fit the Chinese image. The sacred scriptures were translated with fewer sexual images than in their Indian form. Further, in the translations, the Chinese displayed their tendency to express abstract ideas in concrete images. The exegesis of Chinese classics has produced an immense variety of interpretations, many directly opposite to each other. This is because the Chinese language is grammatically ambiguous, allowing, for example, one character (*jen*) to denote "a man," "men," "some men," or "mankind."

Immanual Kant attacked whatever interest in metaphysics Chinese thinkers displayed, presumably Taoism's interest in mysteries, by observing:

> Thence arises Lao-kiun's monstrosity of the highest good which is supposed to consist in nihility (*im Nichts*), that is, in the consciousness of feeling oneself swallowed up in the abyss of the Godhead through fusion with it, and therefore, through the destruction of one's personality. To have the presentiment of this condition, Chinese philosophers strive in their dark rooms with their eyes closed to experience and contemplate their nihility. . . . This is really a concept in company with which their understanding disintegrates and all thinking itself comes to an end. (—Kant, *On History*)

Despite this opinion, thinking did not come to an end in China, nor did understanding disintegrate. The major forms of philosophy in China were Confucianism, Taoism, Moism, Legalism, and Buddhism. The impact of the West upon China brought the philosophies of Pragmatism and Marxism. We shall look at each of these in turn.

One striking feature about Eastern thought in general and Chinese thought in particular was the pronounced lack of a rapid influx of new ideas. When Buddhism was imported into China, for example, the next thousand years were spent assimilating it.

Only one Marco Polo made the long trip east, and he learned more than he taught. When western powers appeared off the coast in warships, convulsions in Chinese society were caused whose effects are still being assimilated today.

The West, on the other hand, was used to dealing with new ideas more rapidly. The West accepted and sought change. The East remained stable, unable to absorb new ideas quite as effectively as the West. The first priority to the East was social stability, and this worked against intellectual change. The strength of this approach, perhaps, is that the East is able to offer more human stability even in the most unstable of times.

(1) CONFUCIANISM

Confucianism is a philosophy which strongly emphasizes the individual's place in society, and is interested only minimally in metaphysical questions. Confucius (*q.v.*) was interested in reforming social life, to rid government of its repressive tendencies. Metaphysical questions were viewed as distractions. Talk of gods and demons, heavens and hells, leaves society as unredeemed as before. Therefore, they should not claim the attention of intelligent human beings.

Later developments in Confucianism attempted to broaden somewhat the scope of this system of philosophy, but the prime interest still remained political and social. Bad social institutions, it was held, are the main corrupters of mankind, and his main salvation will be better institutions.

Confucius followed a middle course between Taoism on the one hand, and Mo Tzŭ, the vigorous defender of the ancient faith, on the other, with a leaning toward the latter. Confucius taught the importance of moral perfection (*chin shan*) for the individual, and of social order (*li*) for the group. The way to attain these virtues is not by reliance upon some miraculous power from heaven or the spirits, but by entirely natural means:

(1) being true to one's nature (*chung*), and

(2) applying those principles in relationships with others (*shu*).

Chung and *shu* may be said to form a continuous thread through all Confucian teaching. The objective is Central Harmony or the Golden Mean, *chung yung*, the central basis of moral

66

being, harmony with the universe. According to Confucius, the most important features of social life were those in which respect was paid to superiors, and protection was supplied by them to their inferiors.

Confucius supplied Chinese philosophy with its humanistic foundation. However, because of his reluctance to discuss metaphysical questions, he left the door open to Taoism in later centuries, to complete the concerns of the people. The subsequent development of Confucianism began with attempts to answer the question how attainment of moral perfection is possible. According to Mencius (q.v.), human nature is originally good, so of necessity we must develop our good nature, exercising our minds to the fullest. According to Hsün Tzǔ (q.v.), human nature is originally evil, so we must discipline our tendencies to do evil, by means of moral discipline, education, and the rules of social conduct.

Chu Hsi (q.v.), called by Wing-tsit Chan "the greatest of the Neo-Confucianists," emphasized the continuity between humanity and the universe by saying: "The great Ultimate is nothing but the Reason of ultimate goodness." If we try to understand hard enough, we will realize our nature and fulfill our destiny. We will then know that: "all humans are brothers and sisters, and all things are my companions."

Wang Yang-ming (q.v.) argued that desire is an impediment to the mind. Only the disinterested can truly understand anything. Only the bored can appreciate the truth. Opposed to this theory that we must yawn our way to knowledge was Tai Tung-yuan (q.v.), who maintained that desire has a rightful place in human life, since it is part of our human nature.

Confucianism was the basis of the old educational system in China. The Confucian Classics were required texts.

All government officials were selected through passing examinations on the Classics. Since the advent of the Intellectual Renaissance in 1917, Confucianism has been condemned as the chief cause of China's weaknesses in the face of hostile international pressures. The slogan was: "Destroy the old curiosity shop of Confucius." Communism has developed and extended this theme. However, such Confucian sayings as: "The world is a great commonwealth," which have been quoted favorably by Sun Yat-sen, do not necessarily seem antithetical to Marxism.

(2) TAOISM

Taoism is a philosophy which strongly emphasizes man's place in nature. Unlike Confucianism, it is not concerned with society, except as something to escape from. While not dealing with metaphysical questions directly, at least not in a manner familiar to Western thinkers (the *Tao Te Ching* rarely refers to heaven, and only once, in passing, to God), Taoism does leave the subject open, with the result that many supernatural theories have been developed as time went on.

Taoism has occupied several diverse positions in Chinese culture. Initially, it commanded the respect of the powerful, until Confucianism replaced it as the guardian of official values. It then appealed to those interested in religious themes, who wanted to deepen their spiritual life, until Buddhism displaced it from this position. Finally, it functioned as a system of magic, with incantations for healing disease, avoiding death, and warding off vengeful spirits from the other world.

Lao Tzǔ (*q.v.*) taught that the Tao (the Way) is most fully revealed, not through righteous living, nor through action, but through tranquility. Virtue is not achieved by a lifetime of strenuous effort, but by quiet submission to the power of the Tao. The image is used of water coursing over a stone. By going around obstructions, the water finds its own way, and, in the end, wears down the boulders. What is the Tao? The Tao cannot be defined. As the first lines from the *Tao Te Ching* say: "The way (Tao) that can be walked is not the true and unchanging way. The name that can be named is not the true and unchanging name."

Chuang Tzǔ (*q.v.*) emphasized in a memorable manner the superiority of conforming to the Tao and of avoiding all strife.

In later years, Taoist priests specialized in various occult practices, locating lucky sites for graves, telling fortunes, and purifying houses where demons were said to lurk. The so-called "Taoist Pope," chosen by the family and descendants of Chang Tao-ling, led a small Taoist sect located in a stronghold in the Szechuan-

Shensi area. Almost every aspect of Taoism makes its appeal to the contemporary reader.

(3) MOISM, THE SCHOOL OF NAMES, LEGALISM, AND THE SCHOOL OF YIN-YANG

When the Feudal society of the latter years of the Chou period disintegrated, many individuals lost their hereditary positions in the various states, and were forced by circumstances to become itinerant teachers, free-lance military experts, or political consultants, offering their skills to anyone who would support them. This led to much freer thinking than before, and to the spread of education, which previously had been confined to a privileged few.

(i) Mo Tzŭ (q.v.) was the founder of Moism, the school of universal love. Those most attracted to Moism were disillusioned veterans who, having seen enough of senseless wars, were willing to do no more than defend their cities from attacking armies. Political leaders were not impressed. Loving land more than men, they rejected a philosophy which would encourage soldiers to defend their own families rather than extend the boundaries of an emperor's empire.

The five marks of Moist philosophy are:

(1) universal love,

(2) agreement with the Superior,

(3) belief in spirits,

(4) simplicity in living, and

(5) opposition to ceremonials and music (which, of course, were greatly loved by Confucianists).

Later Moists developed an interest in mathematics and physics, an extension of the art of protecting cities from siege. Still later, Chinese secret societies preserved some of the beliefs of Moism, although its influence disappeared from society at large.

(ii) The School of Names may be characterized as the philosophy of lawyers who used sophistic tricks on behalf of their clients to make wrong seem right, and right seem wrong.

Difficult to study because all the works of the school except parts of the *Kung-sun Lung-tzŭ* have been lost, the doctrines of

69

Hui Shih, Teng Hsi, Kung-Sun Lung and others in the school are known chiefly through hostile quotations in the *Chuang-tzŭ* (12, 33), where they are called "Dialecticians." Ssŭ-ma T'an says of them that they:

> made minute examinations of trifling points in complicated and elaborate statements, which make it impossible for others to refute their ideas. They specialized in the definition of names, but lost sight of human feelings.

Hui Shih is known for ten "paradoxes:"
(1) The greatest has nothing beyond itself, and is called the Great Unit (*ta i*, Universal Class). The smallest has nothing within itself, and is called the Little Unit (*hsiao i*, Null Class). The infinitely small has no form, and the infinitely great is beyond all measurement;
(2) That which has no thickness cannot be increased in thickness, yet in extent it may cover a thousand miles;
(3) The sky is as low as the earth; mountains are on the same level as the marshes;
(4) The sun at noon is the sun setting; the creature born is the creature dying;
(5) In one way, all things are similar, in another way, all different;
(6) The South has no boundary and has a boundary;
(7) I go to the state of Yüeh today and arrived there yesterday. Suppose I go to Yüeh today and arrive there tomorrow. Tomorrow, today will be yesterday;
(8) Connected rings can be separated. Separation is the same as construction, and construction is the same as destruction;
(9) I know where the center of the world is: it is north of north and south of south;
(10) Love all things equally, because the universe is one.

Hui Shih argued that because the greatest has nothing beyond itself, all things are limited and relative. "The universe was created when I was born, and with me all things are one."
Chuang Tzŭ dismisses Hui Shih by saying:

70

Weak in virtue, strong in dealing with things, his way was dark and narrow.

Yet, on Fung Yu-lan's interpretation, Chuang Tzŭ's philosophy is Hui Shih's advanced one step further, skepticism made into mysticism, intellectual paradox transformed into life experience.

(iii) Legalism was a school of thought dedicated to the development of a strong, centralized, totalitarian state. There were three schools of Legalist thought, each emphasizing what it considered the most important feature of politics, first, *shih*, second, *shu*, and third, *fa*. *Shih* (power, or authority) was the choice of Shen Tao, a contemporary of Mencius. *Shu* (managerial ability) was stressed by Shen Pu-hai. *Fa* (law, or regulations) was promoted by Shang Yang.

Han Fei Tzŭ, the greatest of the Legalists, unified these theories by arguing that all three are indispensable to the well-functioning state. Han Fei Tzŭ, like his teacher, Hsün Tzŭ, contended that human nature is originally evil. Han Fei Tzŭ went even further, holding that since humanity is evil, no time need be wasted attempting to improve human behavior. Totalitarian government is exactly what man deserves, and is unquestionably the most practical form of state organization:

> The intelligent ruler . . . handles men as if he were God. Being like Heaven, he commits no wrong. Being like a divine being, he falls into no difficulties. His power enforces his strict orders, and nothing he encounters resists him. . . . Only when this is so can his laws be carried out.
>
> (—*Han-fei-tzŭ*, 48.)

(iv) The Yin-yang school was initially a school of wizards (*fang shih*) specializing in astrology, divination, and almanacs. The milfoil plant, tortoise shells, or shoulder bones from oxen were used as main methods for divination. First a hole was bored in the shell or bone. Then it was heated. The cracks which radiated from the hole were then read to answer the question asked of the bone.

As time went by, reliance upon supernatural influences began to decline, and a more naturalistic explanation of phenomena began to predominate in the Yin-yang school. The stage was thus set for the school to combine with Confucianism.

(4) CHINESE BUDDHISM

Introduced into China initially as an occult science, Buddhism then became a refuge for refugees in the Period of Disunity (221-589 A.D.) during which many short-lived dynasties were competing for power. During the Sui (590-617) and T'ang (618-906) dynasties, Chinese Buddhism reached its highest point. Striving to become intellectually respectable, the Buddhist schools (Seven Schools, Seng-chao, Three Treatise, Consciousness-only, *T'ien-t'ai*, and *Hua-yen*) did so well at splitting hairs and debating subtle points that the calculated nonsense of *Ch'an (Zen)* seemed to be the only reasonable development for those who still cared about the great questions. As written in the *Recorded Conversations of Zen Master I-HSÜAN*: "After all, there is not much in Huang-po's Buddhism," to which was added, in another version of the story: "There is not much in Buddhism itself!" *Ch'an* was a way of teaching someone to get out of the way of understanding himself, as if he were blocking the view of himself in a mirror.

(5) WESTERN PHILOSOPHIES IN CHINA

The impact of Western philosophies on China was felt in three ways: religious, technological, and the modern philosophies of science (chiefly through the influence of John Dewey and Bertrand Russell). China could have resisted these all but for the intense military pressures generated by European nations interested in empire. Calling their intrusions "carving up the melon," Western imperialists exposed the military weakness of China and her incapacity to defend herself. Between 1842 and 1940, a bitter series of foreign policy reverses shook successive Chinese governments. Great Britain seized Hong Kong, Russia seized eastern Siberia, France seized Indo-China, and Japan seized Taiwan, Korea, and Manchuria. The demonstration of governmental im-

	1 Confucianism	2 Taoism	3 Mohism	4 Warring States Strategy	5 Legalism	6 Buddhism
570-517 B.C.		Lao Tzŭ				
551-479	Confucius					
479-438			Mo Tzŭ			
400-338					Shang Yang	
399-295		Chuang Tzŭ				
398-337					Shen Pu-hai	
397-336					Shen Tao	
372-289		Yang Chu				
371-289	Mencius					
335-288				Sun Tzŭ		
298-238	Hsün Tzŭ					
280-233					Han Fei Tzŭ	
180-122		Huai-nan Tzŭ				
179-104	Tung Chung-shu (New Text School)					
53 B.C.-A.D. 18	Yang Hsiung (Old Text School)					

Confucianism

334-416

384-414

Buddhism

Seven Schools
(4th-5th Century)

Hui-yüan

Seng-chao

Three-Treatise School
(4th-7th Centuries)

Consciousness-Only
School
(6th-9th Centuries)

T'ien-t'ai School
(6th Century)

Hua-yen School
(7th Century)

Ch'an (Zen) School
(7th-9th Centuries)

potence at coping with these challenges was taken as proof that the Confucian system, the basic education of government officials, was not adequate for the times. Confidence was shaken, and people were ready for new ideas.

Dr. Sun Yat-Sen overthrew the Manchu, in 1911, and moved the capital from Peking, the ancient Manchu city, to Nanking. Mao Tse-tung, about this time, joined the army of the new Republic of China.

Yen Fu translated a series of Western books into Chinese of the classical style: Huxley, Spencer, Adam Smith, Spencer, John Stuart Mill, and Jevons' *Lessons in Logic*. Then, in 1919 and 1920, John Dewey and Bertrand Russell were invited to lecture at the University of Peking. Well received, they were little understood, for the history of Western philosophy was not well-enough known for proper appreciation of their theories. During the next several decades, many interpreters of western philosophy, science, and logic, produced explanatory works.

After Sun Yat-Sen's death in 1925 of cancer, General Chiang Kai-Shek took power, backed by several warlords, the bankers and merchants of the port cities, and foreign interests. Mao Tse-Tung opposed him, and was left with nothing but the support of the masses. In Szechuan, Chiang proceeded to endear himself to the people by ordering the collection of all taxes for sixty years in advance. Many could not afford to pay. Few appreciated the benefits of this policy. Chiang improved agriculture by unleashing the warlords to run across the best crop lands in pursuit of their enemies. Chiang restricted his excellent air force and good roads to military operations and neglected to help the common people suffering the worst floods and famines in a hundred years. Over thirty million refugees were estimated in one part of China alone.

(6) CHINESE COMMUNISM

In 1919, Ch'en Tu-hsiu and Li Ta-chao first published essays explaining Marxism to Chinese readers of the magazine entitled *La Jeunesse*. In 1927, Li was seized by the Peking authorities and executed for his social agitation.

Sung Neo-Confucianism

1011-1077 Shao Yung
1017-1073 Chou Tun-i
(Chou Lien-hsi)
1020-1077 Chang Tsai
(Chang Heng-ch'u)
1032-1085 Ch'eng Hao
(Ch'eng Ming-tao)
1033-1108 Ch'eng I
(Ch'eng I-ch'uan)
1130-1200 Chu Hsi

Ming Neo-confucianism

1139-1193 Lu Hsiang-shan
(Lu Chiu-yüan)
1472-1529 Wang Yang-ming
(Wang Shou-jen)
Ch'ing (Manchu)
Confucianism
1619-1693 Wang Fu-Chih
1650-1725 Li Kung

In 1940, Mao Tse-tung (*q.v.*) published his famous article, "The Government and Culture of the New Democracy," in *Chinese Culture*. This became the charter for Marxist intellectuals in China. Li Ta and Li Chi were among the notable Marxist writers, although the latter was later expelled from the party for Trotskyite tendencies. Ai Ssu-ch'i's *Philosophy of the Masses* was so popular that it went through thirty-two editions in only twelve years. In it he wrote:

The mission of progressive philosophy . . . (is to) help us to penetrate problems more quickly and more exactly, to destroy all mystery, to discover the origin of all things, to combat all oppression.

The victory of Marxist leaders in China inaugurated a period of comparative stability, and gave China the ability to manage her own internal and external affairs, free from any uninvited foreign influences.

CHORTEN: The Tibetan term for a sacred tower.

CHOU LIEN-HSI: see Chou Tun-I.

CHOU MAO-SHU: See Chou Tun-I.

CHUANG TZŬ (369-286 B.C.): The "hermit of Meng," Chuang Tzŭ (pronounced jwawng dzuh) or Chuang Chou, was one of the greatest of the early Taoists. The suggestion (by Eichhorn, among others) that parts (chapters 1-7) of Chuang Tzŭ's *The Identity of Contraries* antedate the *Tao Te Ching* would make him a sort of co-founder of Taoism with Lao Tzŭ.

One of the great scholarly controversies about early Taoism is whether Chuang Tzŭ (the man) wrote *Chuang tzŭ* (the book), or whether Kuo Hsiang (the man) wrote *Chuang tzŭ* (the book). If, of course, Kuo Hsiang wrote *Chuang tzŭ*, we might ask why he did not call it the *Kuo Hsiang*? No one has yet suggested that Chuang Tzŭ wrote *Kuo Hsiang*, perhaps because no such book by that name exists, although such a detail has not stopped scholars before.

A contemporary of Mencius, he was an official in the Lacquer

Garden of Meng, in Honan Province. He was offered more eminent positions in government, including the prime minister-ship of Ch'u. Chuang laughed at the messengers who brought the offer and refused their gifts, saying:

Go away. Do not defile me. I prefer to enjoy my own free will!

Confucians were critical of Taoism in general and Chuang Tzŭ in particular, objecting to his rejection of government on the grounds that such thought was thereby "useless to the rulers of men," which was, however, precisely what he intended. Chuang Tzŭ, for his part, ridiculed efforts by philosophers to improve the governing of states. A state, he said, is like a strong-box into which a careful man places his money. He puts strong iron bands around it: rituals, the law, and civic morality. He fastens it with locks: the police and the military. However, when a strong thief comes along, he will not try to break into the money-box. He will simply pick it up and carry it off with him. If anything, he wants the iron bands and locks all to hold securely until he gets the box to his destination. Thus, all those Confucian sages who have labored so hard to make the state more efficient have simply improved it for the day when the entire apparatus is stolen by some political super-thief, who will then use the improved system for his own purpose.

This analogy infuriated his critics. Chu Hsi, one of those later critics, wrote:

Lao Tzŭ still wanted to do something. But Chuang Tzŭ does not want to do anything at all. He even says that he knows what to do but he just does not want to do it.

Chuang Tzŭ's reply would most likely be that the more human effort is expended, the more misguided the result. What we need is to get back to Nature. Not education, but things themselves will transform the world. We cannot, as Confucian scholars think, participate in the creative work of nature. We must simply return to our destiny. Writing of far-off lands, Chuang Tzŭ held "con-versations" with shadows, skeletons, and the north wind. This mystical approach to thought also irritated the practical, struc-tured, down-to-earth Confucians. Hsün Tzŭ complained: "Pre-judiced in favor of nature, (he) does not know man." Chuang Tzŭ would reply that he knows man only too well, and he prefers to talk to the north wind!

Chuang Tzŭ's ideas have not been followed by any leading thinker since the fifth century, but he has had some influence. In particular, Zen Buddhism, Chinese landscape artistry, and poe-try have been influenced by him. The transformation of ancient Confucian thought into Neo-Confucianism was stimulated by his concepts.

Chuang Tzŭ strongly opposed traditional, conventional stan-dards. Man is not understood through the study of institutions, but through human *nature*. Whatever is natural is best. Whatever is artificial is worst. The entire world should be "doin' what comes naturally:"

> What is of nature is internal. What is of man is external.
> . . . That oxen and horses have four feet is what is of nature.
> That a halter is put on a horse's head, or a rope through an ox's nose, is what is of man. Following nature will bring happiness. Following what man does is the source of all pain and evil. . . . The duck's legs are short, but if we try to lengthen them, the duck will feel pain. The crane's legs are long, but if we try to shorten them, the crane will feel grief. Therefore we should not amputate what is by nature long, nor lengthen what is by nature short.
>
> (—*Chuang Tzŭ*, 8.)

He taught that all laws and institutions, all customs and morals, and all forms of government are negative and destructive in their result. All these things are unnatural. Each is an attempt to establish uniformity, to suppress differences. Regardless of the good intentions of the founders or leaders, the result is always disastrous:

> Once, in the capital city of the Kingdom of Lu, a seagull alighted. The Lord Mayor went out to welcome such a rare bird. He served it wine in the temple, had the special Chiu-

shao music played to amuse it, and even had a bullock butchered to feed it. But the seagull was too dazed and timid to eat or drink a thing. In three days it died. This was doing unto the bird as one would do unto oneself, not treating the bird as a bird. . . . Water is life to fish but death to man. Being different by nature, their likes and dislikes must necessarily differ. Therefore the early sages did not make all men equal in abilities and occupations.

(—*Ibid*., 18.)

The best government, he argued, is the least government. Chuang Tzŭ and Lao Tzŭ differed in degree, but not in kind, on this point. Lao Tzŭ said that the more effort is expended in governing, the less desirable the result achieved:

Reversing is the movement of the *Tao*.

According to Chuang, that the rule of the *Tao* is in leaving mankind alone and letting everyone develop his own natural abilities freely. The more man prevails in "taming" nature, the more misery and unhappiness there will be.

Distinguishing between relative and absolute happiness, he says that relative happiness depends upon something else, whereas absolute happiness is the identification of man with universe:

There was once a man who could ride even on the wind. Among those who have attained happiness, such a man is rare. Yet although he was able to dispense with walking, he still had to depend upon something (the wind). But suppose there is one who chariots on the normality of the universe, rides on the transformation of the six elements, and thus makes excursions into the infinite. What has he to depend upon? Therefore, it is said that the perfect man has no self, the spiritual man has no achievement, and the true sage has no name.

The *Tao* is nameless. Hence the sage who is one with the *Tao* also has no name. Ultimately, Chuang Tzŭ argues, the goal is to have no knowledge. This is not in the sense of being ignorant, but in the sense of being child-like, understanding that our understanding is incomplete. It is an achievement of the spirit, an attainment of what Taoists call the "knowledge that is not knowledge." For example, in a passage using the name of Confucius to make the same point:

"Yen Hui said: 'I have made some progress.'

'What do you mean?' asked Confucius.

'I have forgotten human-heartedness and righteousness,' replied Yen Hui.

'Very well, but that is not enough,' said Confucius.

Another day Yen Hui again saw Confucius and said:

"I have made some progress.'

'What do you mean?' asked Confucius.

'I have forgotten rituals and music,' replied Yen Hui.

'Very well, but that is not enough,' said Confucius.

Another day Yen Hui again saw Confucius and said:

'I sit in forgetfulness,' replied Yen Hui.

At this Confucius changed countenance and asked: 'What do you mean by sitting in forgetfulness?'

To which Yen Hui replied: 'My limbs are nerveless and my intelligence is dimmed. I have abandoned my body and discarded my knowledge. Thus I become one with the Infinite. That is what I mean by sitting in forgetfulness.'

Then Confucius said: 'If you have become one with the Infinite, you have no personal likes and dislikes. If you have become one with the Great Evolution [of the universe], you are one who merely follows its changes. If you have really achieved this, I should like to follow your steps.'"

(—*Ibid.*, 6.)

We should not search for "useful" knowledge. The more useful we are to others, the less we can be our natural selves. A great oak tree whose wood is useless will be allowed to live. Otherwise, it will be cut down and used to make houses, ships, firewood, and coffins.

A very attractive contemporary edition of part of Chuang Tzu's major work is entitled: *Chuang Tsu: Inner Chapters*, by Gia-Fu Feng and Jane English.

81

CHU HSI (1130-1200): Ranked with Confucius, Mencius, Lao Tzŭ, and Chuang Tzŭ for his influence on Chinese thought, Chu Hsi (or Chu Yüan-Hui or Chu Wen-kung) synthesized all the previous kinds of Confucianism. Chu Hsi's achievement was to combine all these in the "Great Synthesis," setting the form of Neo-Confucianism.

The Great Synthesis combined the following theories into one:

(1) Chou Tun-I's cosmogony, from the *Diagram of the Supreme Ultimate Explained*;
(2) Shao Yung's numerology;
(3) Chang Tsai's theory of material force (*ch'i*); and
(4) The two Ch'engs' distinctions between what is above shapes and what is within shapes, principle (*li*) and material force (*ch'i*), the way (*Tao*) and instruments (*ch'i*—a different character from the foregoing).

Chu Hsi's father was a government official who left the capital in protest against humiliating peace terms imposed by northern invaders and accepted by the political leaders. Chu Hsi, born at Yu Hsi in central Fukien, persisted in making the same error as his father, namely blaming incompetent officials for their incompetence. Believing that this habit would not endear him to employers, he refused offers of government posts, preferring instead to live a life of poverty and peace. Severely blamed for this obviously unpatriotic attitude, he was finally persuaded to accept various jobs for some nine years in the departments of education, agriculture, and defense. When thus employed, he began to criticize shirkers for shirking. Shocked, his superiors first transferred and then fired him. He held one job—as prefect of Hunan—for only one month. He was not considered a perfect prefect. Thus proving his unsuitability for the life of a good little bureaucrat, he took a job more suitable to his tastes, as guardian of some temple or the other, and used his time and solitude to study, write, and talk with prominent scholars. He lectured at the White Deer Grotto (in Kiangsi province).

By 1196, his various enemies succeeded in having his teachings prohibited. A censor accused him of ten crimes, including spreading false learning and "refusing to serve." He accused the censor of incurable stupidity. Someone petitioned for Chu Hsi's execution, but Chu Hsi declined to serve in this capacity, as well.

Not everyone disliked him, however. When he died, in 1200, of dysentery, almost a thousand people attended his funeral, and a wonderful time was had by all. Posthumously, he was ennobled as a duke. In 1241, his tablet was placed in the Confucian temple.

Chu Hsi's philosophy was called the "School of Principle," which may be one reason why it did not appeal to politicians. His synthesis of previous Confucian theories was based on the idea that the Great Ultimate involves both matter and form (principle). It is the principle of things to be actualized, rather than to remain purely potential. That actualization requires both principle as its substance and material force as its actuality:

"The mind of Heaven and Earth is to produce things" [Chu Hsi is probably quoting Ch'eng Hao]. In the production of man and things, they receive the mind of Heaven and Earth as their mind.

Chu Hsi had studied Buddhism and Taoism, but decided against them in favor of Confucianism when he was about thirty. Buddhism held nature to be empty, whereas Confucianism held it to contain principle.

Chu Hsi criticized non-Confucianists for what he perceived to be their anti-social tendencies:

The Buddhists and Taoists, for example, even though they would destroy the social relationships (by becoming monks), are nevertheless quite unable to escape from them. Thus, lacking the relationship of father and son, they pay respect to their teachers as if they were fathers, and treat their acolytes as if they were sons. . . . They are thereby clinging to something false, whereas the Confucian sages and worthies have preserved the reality.

Chu Hsi formed a rationalistic version of Neo-Confucianism. Chu Hsi quotes the opening sentence from Chou Tun-I's *Diagram of the Supreme Ultimate Explained*, and then comments upon it in an important way:

"The Ultimateless! And yet also the Supreme Ultimate!" These words do not mean that it is a physical something glittering somewhere in a glorious manner. They only mean that in the beginning when no single physical object yet existed, there was nothing but Principle (*li*). . . . The Supreme Ultimate . . . lacks shape but contains Principle.

(—Conversations, 94.)

Chu Hsi recommended the method of the "examination of individual things." Study everything. Everything should be investigated to the utmost. Nothing is unworthy of attention. Pay no attention to names. Investigate into the reason things are as they are. One cannot succeed if one wants to hurry.

One should be discriminating, and not allow the mind of the body to mingle with the mind of the spirit. The mind of the body is unstable. The mind of the spirit is small. Be discriminating, be undivided, that you may sincerely hold fast to the middle way.

Chu Hsi's thought had an almost mystical dimension to it:

When one has worked at this for a long time, a day will dawn when suddenly everything will become clear, . . . and the mind and its operations will be completely enlightened.

According to Chu Hsi:

If one could but realize that it is human desire that thus obscures his true nature, he would be enlightened.

There must be a Principle for every individual thing. This includes the state. If the ruler governs in accordance with the proper Principle, good government will result. If not, bad government will result. When asked when was the last time good government was observed, Chu Hsi's answer would delight a conservative's conservative—not for the past fifteen hundred years. The Way (*Tao*) for governing a state properly had been obscured by leaders who followed human desire instead of correct reason.

The so called 'heroes' of later ages never exerted [the proper] effort, but only bobbed their heads up and down in the realm of profit and desire.

Chu Hsi described *jen* ("humanity," sometimes translated "benevolence," "love," "altruism;" it means properly both the particular virtue of benevolence and also general virtue, the basis of all goodness) in a famous epigram:

The character of man's mind and the principle of love.

CHOU TUN-I (1017-1073): Lover of lotus flowers and pioneer (if not the actual founder) of Neo-Confucianism, Chou was forced to change his given name, which had been Tun-shih, because an emperor took it (the emperor Ying tsung's personal name had been Tsung *shih*, and this name was declared tabu upon his assuming the emperorship). Chou Tun-i then preferred to call himself "Stream of Waterfalls," (Chou) Lien-hsi, after a stream by that name where he had once lived. Nature, kinder than politi-cians, did not deprive him of his name. Perhaps in gratitude, he refused to let the grass in front of his window be cut. He was also styled, honorifically, Chou Mao-shu.

Through the influence of his uncle, who was a Scholar (the highest rank) of the Dragon Chart Pavilion, Chou Tun-I worked at a succession of government jobs, such as district keeper of records, magistrate, prefectural staff supervisor, professor of the directorate of education, and assistant prefect (of Fen-ning, now Hsiu-shui hsien in northern Kiangsi). He became ill and resigned a year before he died, some fifty-six years old.

His philosophical significance was described by Huang Po-chin (fl. 1695) in these terms:

Since the time of Confucius and Mencius, Han Confucianists merely had textual studies of the classics. The subtle doctrines of the way and the nature of man and things have disappeared for a long time. Master Chou rose like a giant. . . . Although other Neo-Confucianists had opened the way, it was Master Chou who brought light to the exposition of the subtlety and refinement of the mind, the nature, and moral principles.

His major works were the *Diagram of the Supreme Ultimate* (*T'ai-chi T'u*), and the *Explanatory Text* (*T'ung-shu*, originally known as the *Yi T'ung, Explanation of the Changes*). It has sometimes been argued that the *Diagram Explained* was not written by Chou Tun-I, but by someone else with the same name.

Inspired by the *Book of Changes* (*I Ching*), Appendix III, Chou Tun-I writes:

Great is the *Changes*. Herein has been expressed its fullest meaning.

The superior man, according to Chou Tun-I, by cultivating the virtues of the wise, enjoys good fortune. The petty man, by violating them, incurs bad fortune. The virtues of the wise are moderation, correctness, love, righteousness, and peaceful contentment.

Having no desire, he is therefore in a state of peaceful contentment.

The diagram of the ultimate has at the top the Ultimateless, yet also the Supreme Ultimate, the nothing which is everything. Perhaps after hearing this, Ch'eng I, one of his students, called him the "poor Zen fellow."

Through movement, the Supreme Ultimate produces the *yang*, whose opposite is the *yin* (quiescence). By transformations of the *yang*, and the union therewith of the *yin*, the five elements (*ch'i*) are produced: fire, water, earth, wood, and metal. The four seasons are produced in their course.

Someone has accused Chou of stealing the diagram from the Taoists, who had a diagram carved on the face of a cliff on the sacred mountain of Hua Shan in Shensi. On the bottom was a circle labeled "Doorway of the Mysterious Woman;" above it, "Changing the Essence into Vital Force," and "Changing Vital Force into Spirit;" above it, the five elements, etc. However, even granting the existence of this carving, which is in doubt, there seem to be significant differences, not the least of which is that, while this diagram goes from the particular to the general, Chou's goes from the general (the universe) to the particular (mankind).

The five elements are the one *yin* and *yang*. The *yin* and *yang* are the one Supreme Ultimate. The Supreme Ultimate is fundamentally the Ultimateless. When all these unite, the true substance of the Ultimateless, the essences of the Two (*yin-yang*) and the Five (fire, water, earth, wood, and metal), and consolidate mysteriously, the male element (from the *ch'ien* principle) is formed, and the female (from the *k'un* principle). These, by their interaction, are the cause of the production and evolution of all things. Mankind receives all these qualities in their highest excellence. When people react to external phenomena, the distinction between good and evil emerges, and the many kinds of conduct appear.

Yin and *Yang* are established as the way of heaven, the weak and the strong as the way of earth, and love (*jen*) and righteousness (*yi*) as the way of mankind. In other words, the universe is characterized by positive and negative, the earth by the survival of the fittest, and humanity by love and justice.

"Wisdom," said Chou Tun-I, "is nothing but sincerity," perhaps anticipating the statement by Noam Chomsky of M.I.T. that "the first duty of intellectuals is to tell the truth." Chou goes on to say: "Sincerity lies in the state of non-activity (*wu wei*); with the stirrings of activity come good and evil."

Again, Chou writes: If one person does good, and two do evil, learn from the one and exhort the two.

With regard to principle, human nature, and destiny, he writes:

Only the intelligent can understand what is obvious and what is concealed. Strength may be good or it may be evil. The same is true of weakness. The ideal is moderation. . . . Purify the heart, that is all.

CLASSICS: In Chinese Confucian philosophy the *Book of History*, the *Book of Poetry*, the *Book of Changes* (*I Ching*), and the *Book of Rites*, edited by Confucius, were held to be the basic books necessary for a good education.

CONFUCIUS (551-479 B.C.): K'ung Fu Tzŭ (K'ung the Grand Master), called Ch'iu ("hill," because of a bump noticed on his head at birth) or Chungni, was undoubtedly one of the greatest figures in the history of human thought. He shaped the pattern of Chinese civilization for much of twenty-five centuries. "If the ruler is virtuous, the people will also be virtuous," he said. Stern laws are not necessary for good government. Advisors to government officials should always express their criticism of bad policies fearlessly and persistently. Mankind is essentially good. Character is the root of all civilization.

We know more about Confucius' life than we know about any other ancient Chinese philosopher, due largely to the excellent biography by Ssŭ-ma Ch'ien and contained in the *Shiki*. Ssŭ-ma Ch'ien was not a partisan for Confucianism. He was the father of Chinese historians, notably objective. He wrote about three centuries after Confucius.

The personal life of Confucius was difficult. Born at Ch'ufu, in the small kingdom of Lu (now in the province of Shantung), which is across the Yellow Sea from Korea, he was, in his own words, born "without rank and in humble circumstances." Born illegitimate (of a "wild union"), which would tend to diminish one's rank, he had to go to work early to help support his mother, because his father died (he had been seventy when K'ung was born). His mother, a girl of the Yen family, concealed the truth from him about the place of his father's tomb.

He became an excellent student because he had such an excellent teacher (he was largely self-taught). He read historical records in the state archives of Lu, Sung, and Ch'i.

Married at nineteen, divorced at twenty-three, he began using his home for a schoolhouse. Poor, as teachers often have been, he charged whatever students could afford to pay. Because students could usually not afford to pay much, he worked at such other tasks as bookkeeper for grain stores (he was known for the fairness of his measures), and caretaker of a ranch (the cattle and sheep multiplied).

The basic components of education, he taught, were:
(1) history,
(2) poetry, and
(3) rules of propriety (*li*).
"A man's character," he observed, "is formed by Poetry, de-

veloped by Liturgy (by the rules of ceremony and courtesy), and perfected by Music." He left Lu to do some travelling, was given the bum's rush from Ch'i, Sung, and Wei, threatened with bodily harm in the suburbs between Ch'en and Ts'ai, and so returned from his wanderings.

His friend, Nankung Chingshu, borrowed a carriage, two horses, and a page from the ruler of Lu, and they set out for the capital, Chou, to study ancient rites and ceremonies. While there, he saw Lao Tzŭ, who left him with these words:

I have heard that rich people present people with money, and kind persons present people with advice, and I am going to present you with a piece of advice: A man who is brilliant and thoughtful is often in danger of his life because he likes to criticize people. A man who is learned and well read and clever at arguments often endangers himself because he likes to reveal people's foibles. Do not consider yourself only as a son or as a minister at court.

When Confucius returned, he continued teaching and advising on government policy, with mixed success. His own outline of his life's stages is interesting:

At fifteen, I began to be seriously interested in study; at thirty, I had formed my character; at forty, doubts ceased; at fifty, I understood the laws of Heaven; at sixty, nothing that I heard disturbed me (literally: "ears accord"); at seventy, I could do as my heart lusted without breaking the moral law.

His counsel to the Duke of Ch'i was well received, for a time. Asked what made good government, Confucius replied:

The king should be like a king, the ministers like ministers, the fathers like fathers, and sons like sons.

Again:
Good government consists in limiting state expenditures.

His good advice aroused the hostility of the Duke's other ministers, who made their living by giving the Duke bad advice. With a few well-chosen slanders, they were able to destroy the Duke's faith in Confucius, who then left.

Back in Lu, while he was identifying dinosaur bones from some excavation, the government was going to pot. Barons seized power from the Duke, and Confucius decided not to pursue the life of a government employee. Instead, he thought, it would be a good time to study poetry and music.

Duke Ting, having gained power, appointed Confucius magistrate of Chungtu, then Secretary of Public Works (or Labor), and Secretary of Justice. As chief law enforcement officer of the land, he protected Ting not only from physical attack, but also from false ceremonies, such as performances by sword dancers, actors, and dwarfs. He also instituted a policy of attacking the private armies and levelling the fortress cities of various Barons, so no private armies could threaten the ruler's power.

Promoted to Chief Minister, Confucius had Shaochengmao, a minister who had plunged the government into disorder, executed. Within three months there was such an improvement in public order that mutton and pork butchers did not adulterate their meats, things lost on the street were not stolen but returned to their owners, and foreigners were safe visiting the land.

Such success was perceived, in neighboring Ch'i, as a threat: "If Confucius remains in power, Lu is certain to dominate the other states, beginning with us." The secret weapon dispatched to try to discredit Confucius was a hundred and twenty fine horses together with eighty pretty girls who could dance the *k'ang*. Sent as a diversion, they danced outside the South High Gate of Lu. One of the Barons told the Duke to dress in plain clothes and sneak out to see the dance. Everyone who has seen the *k'ang* knows how seductive it is. Baron and Duke hung around for whole days, neglecting their duties. Finally, they spent three days thinking of nothing but the dance. Confucius quit his job in disgust.

Stopping off in Tun, he was asked why he was leaving. Replying, "May I sing a song?" He then sang:

Beware of a woman's tongue,

For sooner or later, you'll get stung.

Beware of a woman's visit,
For sooner or later, you will get it.
Hi, ho! Hi, ho!
I'm going to run away.

His hearer reported back to the court, the Baron heaved a sigh, and said:

The Master is displeased with me on account of those wenches.

For the next thirteen years, Confucius lived the life of a wanderer. He was in his mid-fifties at the beginning. He worked for the Duke of Wei (west of Lu) for ten months, until he was fired by the Duke, who simply sent a man in full military uniform walking through Confucius' room.

In Ch'en (further west), Confucius was confused with Yang Hu, who had been cruel to the natives, and was arrested. He was almost put to death because of mistaken identity. He said:

Since King Wen died, is not his tradition (the ideal system of government, according to Confucius) in my keeping? If it be Heaven's will that this moral tradition should be lost, posterity shall never share this knowledge. But if it be Heaven's will that this tradition should *not* be lost, what can the people of K'uang do to me?

Confucius was only released when he asked Baron Wu Ning, one of his followers, to work for Wei.

In Sung, he had to flee from a homicidal military officer who was going to kill him with an uprooted tree.

In Cheng, as he stood at the gate of the city, he was "crestfallen, like a homeless, wandering dog."

Confucius spent much of his time, during these years, teaching his disciples. Close to employment in Lu several times, things never quite seemed to work out for him.

The group was criticized. On one occasion, someone said: Oh, the world is full of these people wandering about, but who is ever going to change the present state of affairs? Rather than follow one who avoids certain types of people, why not follow one who avoids society altogether?

Confucius replied:

Birds and beasts, or those who try to imitate them, are not the right company for us.

One time, Confucius' whole group was surrounded by hostile soldiers with orders to keep them from giving advice to the enemy. They ran short of food, and tempers grew short, particularly when Confucius kept singing and accompanying himself on a string instrument. One asked sharply:
Doesn't a gentleman also sometimes find himself in adversity?

Confucius answered:
Yes, a gentleman also sometimes finds himself in adversity. But when a common man finds himself in adversity, he forgets himself and does all sorts of foolish things.

He ought to lower his high standards, they said: "come down a little from your heights." He replied:

"Ah, a good farmer plants the field but cannot guarantee the harvest. A good artisan can do a skillful job, but he cannot guarantee to please his customers. Now you are not interested in cultivating yourselves, but are only interested in being accepted by the people. I am afraid you are not setting the highest standard for yourself."

When he returned to Lu permanently, all possibility of political employment was gone. Some potential employers had been undesirable (Confucius declined one job he was being pressured to accept, saying: "A bird can choose a tree for its habitation, but a tree cannot choose the bird").
The last few years of his life were spent in an intensification of teaching and writing. He emphasized the "rectification of names:"

"How odd and impractical you are," objected one of his companions. "What do you want to establish a correct terminology for?"

"Ah, Yu, you are simple-minded indeed," replied Confucius. "If the terminology is not correct, then the whole style of one's speech falls out of form. If one's speech is not in form, then orders cannot be carried out. If orders are not carried out, then the proper forms of worship and social interaction (ritual and music) cannot be restored. If the proper forms of worship and social interaction are not restored, then legal justice in the country will fail. When legal justice fails, then the people are at a loss to know what to do or not to do. When a gentleman institutes something, he is sure what it should be called, and when he gives an order, he knows that the order can be carried out without question. A gentleman never uses words indiscriminately."

The correct use of language, precise definitions, and clarity of expression were goals Confucius believed important to the correct functioning of a good society.

He edited the ancient texts now known as the *Book of Odes*, the *Book of History*, the *Book of Change* (*I Ching*), the *Book of Rites* and the *Spring and Autumn Annals*. He used them as teaching materials, having attempted to collect and summarize in those texts all that was best in ancient learning.

He taught the "six arts": (1) ceremonies, (2) music, (3) archery, (4) carriage-driving, (5) reading, and (6) mathematics. His manner of teaching meant they included the topics of ethics, politics, literature, music, and the techniques of hunt and war. One should be one's true self, honest in social relationships. He denounced four things: arbitrariness of opinions, dogmatism, egotism, and narrow-mindedness. He said:

I never take a walk in the company of three persons without finding that one of them has something to teach me.

He did not talk about how to make a profit, or about heaven's will, destiny, or fate. In his old age, he became interested in the *I Ching*, turning its pages so often that the binding was worn out three times.

93

He died in 479 B.C., vainly waiting for the appearance of the philosopher-king, saying:
The Mountain is crumbling!
The pillar is falling!
The philosopher is passing away.
Duke Ai sent a prayer to Confucius' funeral, with what almost amounted to the offer of a job:

Alas! Heaven has no mercy on me, and has not spared the Grand Old Man. He has left me, the poor self, helpless and alone at the head of the state, and I am a sick person now. Alas! Father Ni (Confucius)! Great is my sorrow! Do not forget me!

By this foolish display of misplaced sorrow, the political leader demonstrated his need of sound counsel. One Confucian scholar, Tsekung, acidly remarked:

When the Master was living, he could not use him, and waited till he was dead to send a prayer to his funeral. This is improper. In calling himself "a poor self," he also uses wrong terminology.

Buried in Lu, on the River Sze, Confucius' tomb can still be seen. His disciples mourned for three years.

Since his death, Confucius has led a chequered career. Awarded the title of "Duke" five centuries after his death, he lost it again a thousand years afterwards, only to be worshipped equally with Heaven four centuries later. After another century, he is being harshly criticized. No one knows what the future holds with regard to his reputation. True to his reputation for equanimity, he has not complained much about these reversals of fortune.

The current criticism of Confucius can be viewed in one sense as a continuation of criticisms advanced since the 1920's. Because Mandarin China could not protect herself from Western attack, and because all civil servants received their positions through passing an exam on the Confucian classics, the Confucian mode of thought was held responsible for the country's inability to cope with Western military technology. Criticisms of Confucianism in contemporary China may be viewed as scientific, based on a detailed view of the economics of feudal society. In addition, an appreciation of the Legalists, ancient rivals of the Confucianists, is encouraged.

CONSCIOUSNESS: In Buddhism, consciousness (Sanskrit, *vijñana*; Pali, *viññāna*) is that pure state which lies behind all other mental states and illuminates them. Consciousness, in Buddhist thought, is not any sort of transcendent entity like the self or soul. Mahayana Buddhism holds that there is no consciousness in the void. Thus the mind is unobstructed, in its pathway to Nirvana, and there is neither wisdom nor the attainment of wisdom, for there is nothing to be attained. Abandoning all fantasies, the believer penetrates to Nirvana.

According to Shankara, as well, the Highest Self does not have Ego-Consciousness which an individual self has. The Highest Self surpasses all limiting elements, in "absolute knowing." Ordinary people cannot conceive such a state, but the Yogic ascetic knows it through self-nullifying concentration. We must throw away the self to gain reality.

CONSCIOUSNESS-ONLY SCHOOL (*Wei-shih* in China, *Yuishiki* in Japan): One of the most philosophical of Buddhist schools in China, Consciousness-Only, originally called the Way of Yoga, dominated the Chinese intellectual scene from the fifth to the seventh century, rivalled only by the Three-Treatise School. The main figure in Consciousness-Only was Hsüan-tsang (596-664), who had studied in India for sixteen years.

The doctrine of the school could be called "solid-state Buddhism," because of its saying:

A seed produces a manifestation;

A manifestation perfumes (influences) a seed;

The three elements (seed, manifestation, perfuming) turn on and on;

The cause and effect occur at the same time.

No other philosophy analyzes the mind into so many parts, eight in total. There are five sense-consciousnesses, the sense-center consciousness which forms conceptions, the thought-center consciousness which wills and reasons, and the storehouse consciousness which remembers.

The persecution of Buddhism in 845 severely injured this and other Buddhist schools. Soon afterward, the Hua-yen School said that Consciousness-Only was merely elementary doctrine within Buddhism. Overshadowed by the popularity of *Zen*, the various texts of the school were lost or forgotten. Ironically, it was reimported into China from Japan in the 1880's. It enjoyed a brief revival in the nineteenth and twentieth centuries, before interest in all old systems of knowledge was destroyed by the Intellectual Renaissance and the impact of western patterns of thought.

CRAVING: Literally "burning thirst" (Sanskrit, *tṛṣṇa*; Pali, *tanhā*), or the craving for satisfaction, it is, according to Buddhism, the primary factor in rebirth. It is opposed to the peace of mind which can be attained by the true believer.

D

DAIBUTSU: (pronounced die-boo-tsoo) Japanese for the Great Buddha.

DAZAI SHUNDAI (1680-1747): A Japanese Confucian scholar during the Tokugawa Shogunate, and disciple of Ogyū Sorai, Dazai believed there had never been any sign of ethical awareness in the country until Confucianism had been introduced. He developed his philosophy from a naturalistic point of view. The orthodox Chinese interpretation of the love poems in the Book of Poetry had been to change them into moral and political lessons. Dazai opposed this interpretation, and, to drive his point home, declared: "I would rather be an acrobat than a moralist." Shintoism, he believed, was primitive paganism.

DEATH: (Indo-European base *dheu-*, to become senseless)
   In the west, technologies are currently the most conspicuous feature accompanying death. Kidney machines, pancreas machines, blood transfusions and monitoring devices of various kinds populate the hospitals. Their value in prolonging life is firmly established. Yet, while they are part of the process, they should not be allowed to become the whole. Death, the death of the individual, is natural, not artificial. So, in eastern modes of thinking, these artificial means of life-support should be kept in proper perspective, as servant, not master. The medical technician should not think he has cheated death, merely because he has

97

postponed it for a while. When death does arrive, for the individual, even for the one who has been kept alive for a while longer, the fact of death must be faced honestly. Dying can be done well or badly. Death can be allowed to be natural, or it can be made into a violent confrontation. Dying well ought not to be made impossible by the mechanical rush to prolong life. One important feature of life is its quality. Death should be a quality, too, a good rather than evil one.

If it is true, as Gurdieff and Ouspensky hold, that a man's level of being attracts his life, then it may also be true that his life attracts his death. As it should be our aim to live well, so it should be our aim to die well. There is no light without darkness, and there is no darkness without the light.

According to the *Brihadāraṇyaka Upanishad*:

As a man's desire is, so is his destiny. For as his desire is, so is his will; and as his will is, so is his deed; and as his deed is, so is his reward, whether good or bad.

'A man acteth according to the desires to which he clingeth. After death he goeth to the next world bearing in his mind the subtle impressions of his deeds; and, after reaping there the harvest of his deeds, he returneth again to this world of action. Thus he who hath desire continueth subject to rebirth.'

The *Kaṭha Upanishad* says:

'He who lacketh discrimination, whose mind is unsteady and whose heart is impure, never reacheth the goal, but is born again and again. But he who hath discrimination, whose mind is steady and whose heart is pure, reacheth the goal, and having reached it is born no more.'

1. INDIAN:
The proper goal for an individual is to be reabsorbed into the deity. "I do not want to be born again," Gandhi said. The chief fear is that the individual *would* be born again, forced by the

Wheel of Rebirth to suffer again and again and again. The law of Karma demands that all the sins of a past life be repaid by another existence, until the individual is pure enough to deserve reabsorption into the universe.

2. CHINESE:

Much more practical and less metaphysical than Indian views, the Chinese view of death may be exemplified by the following incident:

> Tze Lai fell ill and lay gasping at the point of death, while his wife and children stood around him weeping. Li went to ask for him, and said to them: "Hush! Get out of the way! Do not disturb him in his process of transformation." . . . Then, leaning against the door, he spoke to (the dying man). Tze Lai said: "A man's relations with the *Yin* and the *Yang* is more than that to his parents. If they are hastening my death, and I do not obey, I shall be considered unruly. There is the Great Mass (of Nature), that makes me carry this body, labor with this life, relax in old age, and rest in death. Therefore that which has taken care of my birth is that which will take care of my death. Here is a great founder casting his metal. If the metal, dancing up and down, should say, 'I must be made into a Mo Yeh' (a famous old sword), the great founder would surely consider this metal an evil one. So, if, merely because one has once assumed the human form, one insists on being a man, and a man only, the author of transformation will be sure to consider this one an evil being. Let us now regard heaven and earth as a great melting-pot, and the author of transformation as a great founder; and wherever we go, shall we not be at home? Quiet is our sleep, and calm is our awakening."

3. JAPANESE:

From the *Tale of Genji*:
The priest began to tell stories about the uncertainty of this life and the retributions of the life to come. Genji was ap-

palled to think how heavy his own sins had already been. It was bad enough to think that he would have them on his conscience for the rest of his present life. But then there was also the life to come. What terrible punishments he had to look forward to! And all the while the priest was speaking Genji thought of his own wickedness. What a good idea it would be to turn hermit, and live in some such place! . . . But immediately his thoughts strayed to the lovely face which he had seen that afternoon; and longing to know more of her he asked, "Who lives with you here?"

4. TIBETAN: The most unusual and instructive approach to the phenomenon of death is found in the various Tibetan manuscripts. The great lamas have developed and preserved the idea that an individual should be helped through the transition from life to death by proper knowledge and attendants. The *Tibetan Book of the Dead* is designed as a handbook to use at the side of one who is dying. The proper line of succession for correct doctrine is listed from Tilopa to Nāropa to Mar-pa to Mi-la-ras-pa to Sakyaśrī to one's Guru to oneself.

Death means to exist as fulfillment. The technique of "transference" is for the purpose of avoiding unfavorable situations for rebirth.

A dying person should think about the future life and want to go there. He should also think about the shortcomings of all the pleasures of this life and discard his desires for them.

Following this, the individual should "close the gate to the path of the world" by a mystic view of the nature of body-mind. Commenting on this part of Nāropa's teaching, Padma dkar-po makes it much more definite and less abstract.

According to him, the openings from the body which are more spiritual and less physical should be used for exit at death. Thus, the navel, between the eyebrows, and the top of the head are the best gates from which to leave this life and enter the next. By the same token, the nose, ears, and eyes are of medium quality as gates from which to leave. Finally, the mouth, the anus, and the urinary passage are the worst possible gates from which to leave.

The procedure is to "fill the charge" (using the syllable "*hūṃ*"), gather up all one's mental resources, concentrating on the process of leaving, clearing out the hindrances of any unfavorable conditions (by repeating the mantra "*kṣa*"), outlining the path of favorable conditions (by closing off unfavorable exits with certain mantric syllables), and shooting off the mental capacity like an arrow.

Right dying, thus, is initiation. It is an effort to consciously control the process of death and regeneration. This process, transferring the consciousness from the earth-plane to the after-death plane, is called the art of *Pho-wa*. The state intervening between death and rebirth is called the *Bardo*.

The psychic happenings at the moment of death (*Chikkai Bardo*) are the first part of this kind of knowledge. Then a dream-state full of *karmic* illusions sets in, immediately after death (*Chönyid Bardo*). Finally the birth-instinct and various pre-natal events begin (*Sidpa Bardo*). The lights grow more and more faint, and the visions more and more terrifying. The descent threatens to split the consciousness from liberating truth as it approaches rebirth. The function of the lama is to recite the text in the presence of the dead person, in order to fix his attention on the possibility of liberation, and to explain the nature of the visions.

In the *Chönyid Bardo*, the fantasies which appear in this state are the all-destroying God of Death, the epitome of all terrors; the twenty-eight power-holding, sinister goddesses; and the fifty-eight blood-drinking goddesses. The colors of the Four Great Ones are seen:

(1) White, for mirror-like wisdom;
(2) Yellow, for the wisdom of equality;
(3) Red, for discriminative wisdom (Amitabha); and
(4) Green, for all-performing wisdom.

The supreme vision does not come at the end of the *Bardo*, but at the beginning. What happens after the moment of death is an ever-deepening descent into illusion, until the final degradation, physical rebirth. The degeneration in the *Bardo* state is also indicated by the spiritualistic literature of the West, which tells of the trivial nature of communications from "the other side."

The goal of human existence, Tibetan theory held, was to

101

become able to abide in the perpetual light of the Void without clinging to any object, resting on the hub of the wheel of rebirth, free at last from all the illusions of genesis and decay.

DEWEY, JOHN, IN CHINA: With the break-up of the ancient regime in China, interest grew in western forms of philosophy. Among the philosophers invited to lecture was John Dewey. The Chinese officials who extended the invitation could hardly have chosen better. John Dewey was undoubtedly the most significant driving force in American philosophy at the time. With the possible exception of Santayana, who was in Europe and would probably not have gone, in any case, none of the other Contemporary American philosophers, such as Mead, Woodbridge, Rogers, Boodin, McDougall, Flewelling, or Marvin ever attained the stature of Dewey. From 1919-21, he taught his brand of pragmatism to Chinese students.

Joseph Wu quotes Alfred North Whitehead:

If you want to understand Confucius, read John Dewey. And if you want to understand John Dewey, read Confucius.

Of course, it may be added, it is quite possible to read both and to understand neither. Perhaps it was this apparent compatibility with ancient forms of Chinese thought that led to Dewey's invitation to lecture, and also, to his lack of profound influence on a rapidly changing society.

John Dewey's Impressions of Soviet Russia and the Revolutionary World: Mexico—China—Turkey, with introduction and notes by William Brickman (New York: Teachers College, Columbia University, 1964), records his extensive observations, revealing how he perceived the country and its philosophical status. Like a typical American Puritan, he observes:

As one moves about near the clubhouses and gilded house boats one hears everywhere the click of the gambling dominoes. There is money for dissipation and opium, but little for new industrial developments.

Following along, in economic terms, he asks:

Is the industrial development of China to repeat the history of Great Britain, the United States and Japan until the evils of total laissez faire bring about a labor movement and a class struggle?

Then, as if tiring of economic analysis:

One has considerable difficulty in placing the farmers in the bourgeoisie-proletariat terminology (one is tempted to say patter).

Dewey correctly notes the predominance of village society, crediting it with importance, as Mao Tse-tung did, but Chiang Kai-shek did not. A village near Shanghai is described, in which the villagers were exhorted to join the "patriotic boycott" of Japan, against the policies of the Peking regime "dominated by 'traitors' ":

Then they said, in effect:

This is very well for you. You are Chinese. But we are Jonesvillians. These things are not our business.

Dewey's reference to a village in China as "Jonesville," of all things, is instructive. He brought his western views, perhaps of necessity, to China. Where he seems close to a profound insight, as he sometimes did, his vision seems obscured by his set of presuppositions. Some of those presuppositions, surprisingly, considering his own philosophical development, were almost Hegelian:

Is China a nation? No, not as we estimate nations. But is China *becoming* a nation, and how long will it take? . . . The mind at once recalls that improvement of internal communication and transportation has been a chief factor in developing countries into political units, while oppression from without has been the other great factor.

This mode of thought tended to obscure truly useful insights. Dewey grasped the interesting point that:

It is still conceivable that the future historian will say that the resistance of China to the introduction of the agencies of modern production and distribution, the resistance which was long cited as the classic instance of stupid conservatism, was in truth the manifestation of a mighty social instinct which led China to wait until the world had reached a point where it was possible for society to control the industrial revolution instead of being its slave.

Dewey also correctly grasped the feeling at the time of the villagers toward government:

The professions of soldier and bandit are interchangeable, and upon the whole the peasants prefer the latter. One hears the story of the traveler who met a whole village in flight with their household goods on mules and in wheelbarrows, because the soldiers were coming to protect them from bandits.

Again:

The military governor (of Anhwei) recently closed all schools in the province for a year in order to spend the money on his army.

But in his summary statement, Dewey curiously misses the mark. He says:

The accumulated effect of thousands of petty changes due to contact with western methods and ideas, has been to create a new mind in the educated class. This fact is at present more important than any single big external change or external failure to change that can be singled out. It will take a long time for this new mind to work itself out in definite achievement or even to trace definitely perceptible lines of progress.

Dewey's overestimation of the time factor involved for change, and underestimation of the importance of outside factors badly mars his analysis. Dewey seemed to assume that once Western philosophy was presented to Chinese students, it would remain like a jewel until it was properly appreciated for its greatness, but it would not be allowed to change. Pragmatism claimed that the truth of a theory was proved by its utility. If the proposition were: "It's true if it works," it would not take long for Chinese thinkers to add "for China." And, if pragmatism did not work for the Chinese educational or social scene, it would be abandoned for another theory that would. It was the failure of Western thought in general as much as the successes of Marxism in particular that turned Chinese intellectuals to Marxism.

Not that Dewey did not have followers. They included Hu Shih, Hsü Ch'ung-Ch'ing, Liu Po-ming (Dewey's interpreter during his lecture tour), Chang Tai-nien, Chu Ching-nung, Chou En-jün, and Ch'iu Chin-chang. A number of reforms of education were instituted, including the opening of experimental schools (like Dewey's lab school in Chicago), the founding of schools of education, and the revision of curricula to correspond more closely with the needs and interests of students. Student-centered education was tried.

With some enthusiasm, Dewey's contribution to education in China was called "original, decisive," and "lasting." However, the curriculum of the schools was soon returned to a more subject-oriented approach.

In 1951, the Communists launched a campaign of denunciation against Hu Shih. They also attacked Ch'en Ho-Ch'in, professor of education at Nanking, for his "reactionary educational theories."

John Dewey died in 1952.

DHARMA: Dharma is a word which comes from a root from which many related meanings can be drawn. Some of these are:

1) The universal law which governs all existence.
2) As Buddhism reinterpreted the concept, it is the doctrine of the Buddha, his teaching, the religion founded by him, the way all human beings should follow in order to carry out their moral and social responsibilities and fulfill their true nature.

DHARMAS: The plural term *dharmas* (as opposed to *Dharma*) refers to the brief impulses of energy of which the universe as perceived is said to consist. The *dharmas* are the innumerable things, beings, or entities which compose the universe.

DŌGEN (1200-1253): (pronounced doe-gen) *Zen* master of the *Sōtō Zen* school of Japanese Buddhism during the Kamakura period, Dōgen studied in China. In common with the other religious reformers of the era (such as Hōnen, Shinran, and Nichiren), Dōgen advocated a religion of practical simplicity, absolute faith, and individual spiritual awakening.

Although of aristocratic birth, Dōgen avoided the imperial court, practicing meditation deep in the remote hills of Eihei.

Attaining enlightenment, he taught, is not the function of the mind, but of the body:

"Do away with mental deliberation and cognition, and simply go on sitting. . . . That is why I put exclusive emphasis upon sitting."

Dōgen said:

To study Buddhism is to study oneself. To study oneself is to forget oneself. To forget oneself is to realize oneself as all things (in the world). To realize oneself as all things is to strip off both one's own mind and body and the mind and body of others.

Dōgen's thought is recorded in the *Repository of True Buddhist Teachings* (*Shōbōgenzo*). Dōgen said that he wished to cultivate only one disciple or even only half a disciple during his lifetime, to devote proper care to his instruction.

One of Japan's greatest philosophers, Dōgen wrote, paradoxically, that:

"Life and death matter little, because the Buddha exists therein. And one is not perplexed by life and death, because the Buddha does not exist therein."

Again:

"The mind is neither one nor two. It is neither in the Three Worlds nor beyond the Three Worlds. It is infallible. It is an enlightenment through contemplation, and it is an enlightenment without contemplation. It is walls and pebbles; it is mountains, rivers, and the earth. The mind is but the skin, flesh, bones, and marrow; the mind is but the communication of enlightenment through the Buddha's smile. There is a mind, and there is no mind. There is a mind with a body; there is a mind without a body. There is a mind before a body; there is a mind after a body. A body is generated from the womb, the egg, moisture, or fermentation. Blue, yellow, red, and white are nothing but the mind. Long, short, square, and round are nothing but the mind. Life and death are nothing but the mind. Years, months, days, and hours are nothing but the mind. Dreams, illusions and mirages are nothing but the mind. The bubbles of water and the flames of fire are nothing but the mind. The flowers of the spring and the moon of the autumn are nothing but the mind. Confusions and dangers are nothing but the mind."

DRÊPUNG: (precise transliteration, 'Bras-spung, pronounced dreh-bung) One of the three great monasteries in the neighborhood of Lhasa, Tibet, Drêpung was founded in 1416, by Jamyang Chöje Trashi Pelden, a disciple of Tsongkha-pa, founder of the Geluk-pa order ("those who follow virtuous works"). The order emphasized the need for more discipline, and the gradual path, including moral behaviour. Patterned after the *Tantric* monasteries of India, Drêpung was virtually a religious university which contained a variety of faculties, some specializing in knowledge of the *Tantras*.

Historically important, the monks of Drêpung attacked the Karma-pa military camps in 1546, because of a conspiracy by their enemies to suppress them and their best patrons. A new Mongol invasion ended these local rivalries.

The third Dalai Lama, Sönam Gyatso (1543-1588), was abbot of Drêpung and also, at the time, leader of all Geluk-pas. Political intrigue and religious leadership went hand in hand. Foreign intervention in Tibetan affairs was so much taken for granted that it was actively sought, and what might pass for treason was simply considered prudent statesmanship. Internal rivalries (such as the antagonism between Tsang and U [dBus], the two greatest provinces in Tibet) were perceived as much more intense than external threats.

107

E

EISAI (1141-1215): (pronounced yo-saw-ee) Generally regarded as the first to introduce *Zen* into Japan (in 1191), Eisai studied in China, as did Dōgen. Eisai is connected with the *Rinzai* school of *Zen*, which advocates sudden enlightenment (as contrasted with the *Sōtō* school of *Zen*, which advocates gradual enlightenment). Tea was also introduced into Japan by Eisai. He brought the tea seeds from China, cultivated them, prepared them, and even wrote a book on tea, believing it to be the cure for a variety of diseases.

Monasteries were established at Kyoto and Kamakura. At Kyoto, the older schools of Buddhism, the *Tendai* and *Shingon*, strongly opposed *Zen*, and Eisai had to compromise somewhat by being conciliatory. At Kamakura was the headquarters of the Hōjō government.

Eisai wrote *The Spread of Zen for the Protection of the Land*. Encouraged by the Shogun, a very close relationship was established between *Zen* and the military caste. *Zen* was found to be useful for the developing concentration in such martial arts as archery and swordsmanship.

EPISTEMOLOGY: According to Indian philosophies, new knowledge may be acquired in six ways. Using the Sanskrit term *pramana*, from the root *ma*, "to measure" (the correctness of knowledge), Indian philosophical schools differ on the question of which bases of knowledge are reliable. The following chart summarizes their views on the subject:

108

	Perception	Inference	Testimony	Analogy	Implication	Negative Perception
Chārvāka (materialism)	X					
Buddhism	X	X				
Yoga	X	X	X			
Nyāya (logic)	X	X	X	X		
Mīmāṁsā (exegesis)	X	X	X	X	X	X
Advaita (non-dualism)	X	X	X	X	X	X

F

FA-TSANG (643-712 A.D.): A Chinese Buddhist philosopher, Fa-tsang (styled Hsien-shou) was noted for a famous lecture he gave at the imperial court in 704, called the *Essay on the Gold Lion* (*Chin Shih-tzŭ Chang*). He was speaking to the Emperor (really Empress Wu [ruled 684-705], but she insisted upon the title of "emperor"), trying to explain the "Wreath" (or "Flower Garland," *Hua-yen*) school of Buddhism to her. When young, Fa-tsang had assisted Hsüan-tsang of the Mere Idea theory (whose slogan was: "This man, being a product of magic, is not a real man") in his work of translation, until "differences in viewpoint caused him to leave the translation hall." Explaining he did not agree with Hsüan-tsang that the outside world is simply created by our own minds, Fa-tsang spoke of the ten mysteries of Indra's net, the *samādh*; of the ocean symbol, the harmonizing of the six qualities, and other doctrines. The Emperor became thoroughly bewildered. So Tsang pointed to a golden lion guarding the palace hall, and used it to illustrate his "ten theories":

1) arising-through-causation, because the gold metal of the lion lacks any inherent nature of its own, and the shape of the lion is caused by the technical skill of the artisan;
2) discriminating the emptiness of matter, that the outward aspect of the lion is void, and only the gold substance is real;

110

3) Summarizing the three characters,

(i) that from the viewpoint of the senses, the lion exists (this is called "sole imagination");

(ii) that from a higher viewpoint, the lion seems to exist, being dependent upon others; and

(iii) that from the viewpoint of ultimate reality, the gold of which the lion is made is immutable in its nature;

4) revelation of the qualityless, that the gold completely includes the lion, and apart from the gold, the lion itself has no qualities that may be seized;

5) explaining non-generation, that whereas the lion undergoes generation and destruction, the gold itself incurs neither increase nor decrease;

6) discussing the five teachings,

(i) that there is really no quality to the lion that may be grasped;

(ii) that all things, being the product of causation, lack any nature of their own, and in the final analysis there is only emptiness;

(iii) the final teaching of Mahayana is that although, in the final analysis, there is only emptiness, this does not conflict with the illusory appearance of being;

(iv) being and emptiness are mutually annulled and abolished, so that neither retains any influence, and the mind can rest in non-attachment;

(v) all things of the senses, when revealed in their true essence, become merged into one great mass, so that great functions arise, every one of which represents the Absolute. The all is the one, and the one is the all. All things have equally the nature of non-being. This is called *Yi Ch'eng*, the perfect teaching of the One Vehicle.

7) Mastering the Ten Mysteries:

(i) the gold and the lion are simultaneously complete;

(ii) the pure and mixed attributes of various "storehouses," for example, of taking the eyes of the lion as including the whole of the lion, or the ears the whole, etc.;

(iii) the mutual compatibility between the dissimilarities of the one and the many, since the gold and the lion are mutually compatible;

(iv) mutual freedom among all things, that the ears are part of the lion, and thus part of the lion's nose, and so on, but this interdependence does not result in any one part impeding another part's being what it is;

(v) hidden-and-displayed correlation, that if we look at the lion as a lion, the gold fades into obscurity; and if we look on the gold as gold, the lion fades into the background;

(vi) the peaceful compatability of the very small and the abstruse, that leader and subordinate may interchange their radiance; the one is the other, yet they stand peacefully without interfering with one another;

(vii) the realm of Indra's net, that the gold lion is present in the lion's eyes, ears, and in every separate hair, so that in each hair there could be an infinity of lions, each with many hairs containing in turn an infinity of lions, and so forth;

(viii) relying on phenomenal things in order to elucidate truth, pointing out that we may talk about the lion in order to explain the nature of ignorance and genuine substance;

(ix) the variable formation of the ten ages in sections, that the lion is in the present, and the past, and the future, with the present present, the past present, the future present, the present past, the past past, etc; yet all these nine ages are bound together to form a single moment in time, or, in total, ten ages, all in harmony; and

(x) the excellent achievement according to the evolutions of mind only, that the gold lion lacks a nature of its own, being derived only according to the operations of the human mind.

8) embracing the Six Qualities,
  (i) unity (the lion as a whole),
  (ii) particularity (the parts of the lion),

(iii) similarity (the lion and its parts arise from a single cause),

(iv) diversity (the parts of the lion do not overlap in their functions),

(v) integration (the various parts of the lion taken collectively), and

(vi) disintegration (the various parts of the lion taken individually);

9) the achievement of *Bodhi* (Perfect Wisdom), that looking at the lion, we can see that all things have been from the beginning in a state of "calm extinction"; avoiding both attachment and renunciation, we can appreciate the true Way (*Tao*); like waking from a dream, we realize that illusions have no reality, in emptiness there is nothing, and we come to enlightenment (*Chüeh*); embodying all these wisdoms is called the achievement of Perfect Wisdom (*Bodhi*):

10) entry into *Nirvana*, that in looking at the lion and its gold, and realizing that its qualities are completely extinguished, passions are no longer produced in us; the mind is as tranquil as the sea, beauty and ugliness are simply temporary manifestations; abandoning the source of suffering, casting off our bonds, emerging from our barriers, we enter the state of *Nirvana*.

THE FOUR BOOKS: In Chinese Confucian theory, the *Analects* (*Lunyu*), *Great Learning* (*Tahsueh*), *Doctrine of the Mean* (*Chung-yung*), and the *Works of Mencius* were required of all children in elementary grades. The second and third works listed above are different selections from the *Book of Rites* (*Liki*), the chapters on "Ethics and Politics" and "Central Harmony." The Sung scholar Chu Hsi made this selection. The four Books are to be distinguished from the Five Classics (*q.v.*), but both together were part of the Thirteen Classics.

FUNG YU-LAN (1895-   ): One of the most important philosophers in contemporary China, Fung Yu-lan's influence was first felt with his publication, in 1931, of the *History of Chinese*

Philosophy (translated by Derk Bodde and published in English by the Princeton University Press, 1952-3). This work far outclassed any other study of the subject. It has been criticized, however, for tending to make ancient Chinese philosophers into positivists.

Fung's education and scholarly life span the major changes in modern China, its attempt to suddenly become an effective nation, capable of competing with western technology. When he was an undergraduate student in Shanghai, Fung took a course in elementary logic. The school had a great deal of trouble finding a teacher qualified in the subject. Finally one was found who had them buy and read Jevons' *Lessons in Logic*. The instructor's primary interest was in making sure they could spell the English word "judgment" correctly, without inserting an "e." When a different instructor took over the course, he was unable to do the logic exercises in the book, and vanished from the classroom, never to return.

Fung transferred to the University of Peking, which was said to have three complete departments of philosophy: Chinese, Indian, and Western. However, when Fung arrived for classes, it had only the first, Chinese. A teacher who had been engaged (1915) to teach western philosophy because he had studied in Germany, died before he could begin classes. By 1918, Fung graduated from the University. Receiving a Boxer Indemnity grant to study in the United States, he was admitted to Columbia in February of 1920. There he was influenced by F. J. E. Woodbridge (see St. Elmo Nauman, *Dictionary of American Philosophy*, p. 270, for more information on Woodbridge) and John Dewey. He returned to China in 1923, finishing his Ph.D. degree by 1925.

His significant works (besides the two-volume *History* mentioned above) include:

A *Comparative Study of Life Ideals*, 1927 (his dissertation);
Chuang Tzŭ, A New Selected Translation with an Exposition of the Philosophy of Kuo Hsiang, 1933 (trans.);
Hsin Li-Hsüeh (New Norm or Dogma of the Ideal Pattern, his personal metaphysical system, a modernization of the Neo-Confucianism of Chu Hsi), 1939;

Hsin Shih-lun (*China's Road to Freedom*, or *New Realities*), 1940;
Counsels for the New Age, 1940;
Hsin Yüan-jen (*New Treatise on the Nature of Man*), 1943;
New Treatise on the Nature of Tao, 1945, described as a supplement to the two-volume *History*;
Hsin Chih Yen (*New Understanding of Words*, or *New Treatise on the Methodology of Metaphysics*), 1946, which compares Neo-Confucian methodology with Plato, Spinoza, Kant, and others;
The Spirit of Chinese Philosophy, 1947;
A Short History of Chinese Philosophy, 1948, which is not a condensation of his *History*, but an altogether new work;
"Chinese Philosophy and a Future World Philosophy," *Philosophical Review*, 57(1948), 539-549; which, according to Wing-Tsit Chan, exaggerates the similarities between the Platonic and Confucian traditions as representing an "ontological" approach to metaphysics while the Kantian and Taoist traditions represent the "epistemological" approach;
"I Discovered Marxism-Leninism," *People's China*, 1, no. 6 (1950), 10-11, 21;
"Philosophy in New China according to Fung Yu-lan," *East and West*, (July, 1952), 105-107;
"Problems in the Study of Confucius," *People's China*, no. 1(1957), 21-22, 27-31.

Fung has taught at the Chung-Chow University in Kaifeng, at Chung-shan (Sun Yat-sen) University in Canton, at Yenching University in Peking, at Tsing Hua University in Peking (beginning in 1928), serving as chairman of the Department of Philosophy and (1933) Dean of the College of Arts. Tsing Hua had been known for the use of logical analysis for the study of philosophical problems (which Fung interprets as Platonic, in Western terms, Ch'eng-Chu, in Eastern), in contrast with the University of Peking, which emphasized historical studies and idealistic philosophy (Kantian and Hegelian, in Western terms, Lu-Wang, in Eastern).

After the war broke out, in the summer of 1937, the faculties and student bodies of the schools in Peking fled to the southwest, forming the Southwest Associated University, with the Philosophy Department located at Hengshan, the "South Holy Mountain." After four months, they had to flee again, this time to Kunming. The emotional character of the flight, together with the geographical associations (where Chu Hsi had once lived, and where Huai-jang, the Ch'an master, tried to grind a brick into pieces and make a mirror out of them, saying: "If grinding bricks cannot make a mirror, how can meditation make a Buddha?") made a deep impression upon Fung.

In 1946 he came to the University of Pennsylvania as a visiting professor. There, with the assistance of Dr. Derk Bodde, he wrote his *Short History of Chinese Philosophy*.

His philosophical position begins with the consideration that metaphysical reasoning starts with the experience that something exists. This "something" may be a sensation, emotion, or anything. From this statement, Fung then deduces all the metaphysical concepts of the various schools of Chinese philosophy:

> If we think about the world in its static aspect, we will say with the Taoists that before anything comes into being there must first be the being of Being. And if we think about the world in its dynamic aspect, we will say with the Confucianists that before anything comes to exist, there must first be Movement.

Thus, the idea of Movement is not treated as a cosmological idea for the actual beginning of the world, but rather as a metaphysical idea implied in the idea of existence itself. To exist is an activity, a movement.

The realization of *Li* (principle, form) requires a material basis. In *China's Road to Freedom*, Fung applies this theory to Chinese history and society. The various types of society are the expressions of the various principles of social structure. The material basis required for the realization of each social principle is the economic foundation of a given type of society.

In "I Discovered Marxism-Leninism" (1950), Fung states that his New Rational Philosophy was but the twilight of the old

116

Chinese philosophy. It may be compared to medieval medicine, while Marxism-Leninism is comparable to modern medicine.

In "Philosophy in New China according to Fung Yu-lan" (1952), he maintains that the dialectic, though rudimentary, may be found in Confucianism and Taoism. We should select what is desirable and reject the undesirable in traditional Chinese philosophy.

In "Problems in the Study of Confucius" (1957), he states that in his opinion Confucius was an Idealist and not a Materialist, a progressive and not a reactionary. The contemporary conflicting views on Confucius are, in any case, conjectural.

In 1952, Tsing Hua University merged with Peking University, and Fung Yu-lan has been associated with that institution since that time.

G

GAMALIEL (3-60): Prominent and respected teacher of the Law, Gamaliel the Elder, a grandson of Hillel, was leader of the Sanhedrin, the highest court in Jerusalem. One of his students was St. Paul the Apostle. Gamaliel was one of the principals in the Pharisee (which means "the Separated Ones") party. According to Acts 5:34, he favored leniency toward the Christians, arguing that if things were allowed to take their course, and persecution not imposed, they would soon find out if the work were "of God" or "of men."

Involved in a dispute with the patriarch, he left Palestine and later died in Asia Minor.

GAMPO-PA (1079-1153): (Precise transliteration: Gam-po-pa) Founder of the Dakpo branch of Tibetan Buddhism, "the physician (or medium) of Dakpo" (Dakpo Lharje), as he was called (Gampo-pa means "from Gampo"), founded a school with doctrinal ties to the Kadam-pa. Dakpo was one of the two main branches (the other at Shang in Tsang, founded by Khyungpo the Yogin) of the Kagyu-pa monastic order, whose lineage can be traced to the hermit poet Mila Rêpa (1040-1123). The eleventh century in Tibet was a time of incredible religious and philosophical ferment.

The frequently factious nature of competing doctrinal divisions within Tibet translated into political disagreements between the major monasteries. The resulting national paralysis prepared the country for her only possible future fate, submission to foreign power.

GANDHI, MOHANDAS K. (KARAMCHAND) (1869-1948):

God is never powerless. But His laws are immutable. We do not know them. Nor do we know His will at a given moment. Therefore we adopt, within bounds, such remedies as may commend themselves to us.
(—*The Wisdom of Gandhi*, ed. by Thomas Kiernan, New York: Philosophical Library, 1967, p. 94.)

Of all the modern figures from India, Gandhi has the greatest influence by far. Combining Tolstoy's ideas with traditional Hinduism, he led a non-violent resistance movement which not only gained independence for India, but also inspired such other leaders as Dr. Martin Luther King, Jr., in America.

In *The Story of My Experiments With Truth*, his autobiography, Gandhi wrote:

Tolstoy's *The Kingdom of God is Within You* overwhelmed me. It left an abiding impression on me. Before the independent thinking, profound morality, and the truthfulness of this book, all the books given me by Mr. Coates (a Christian friend in South Africa) seemed to pale into insignificance. ... I made too an intensive study of Tolstoy's books. *The Gospels in Brief, What to Do?* and other books made a deep impression on me. I began to realize more and more the infinite possibilities of universal love.

He founded and lived on "Tolstoy Farm" for some time, simplifying life, diet, and education for the children on the farm.

His world-wide influence is indicated by *Stride Toward Freedom* (1958), in which Martin Luther King, Jr., wrote the story of the Montgomery bus boycott:

As the days unfolded ... the inspiration of Mahatma Gandhi began to exert its influence. I had come to see early that the

119

Christian doctrine of love operating through the Gandhian method of nonviolence was one of the most potent weapons available to the Negro in his struggle for freedom. . . . Nonviolent resistance had emerged as the technique of the movement, while love stood as the regulating ideal. In other words, Christ furnished the spirit and motivation, while Gandhi furnished the method. . . . I came to feel that this was the only morally and practically sound method open to oppressed people in their struggle for freedom. . . . My study of Gandhi convinced me that true pacifism is not nonresistance to evil, but nonviolent resistance to evil. . . . Unearned suffering is redemptive. Suffering, the nonviolent resister realizes, has tremendous educational and transforming possibilities. . . . We will match your capacity to inflict suffering with our capacity to endure suffering.

In 1915, Gandhi was greeted, upon his return to India, by the poet Rabindranath Tagore with the name "Mahatma" (Great Soul), and he was called by this title from then on.

I. LIFE

Gandhi was born on October 2, 1869, at Porbandar (Sudamapuri), the youngest of seven children. Married at thirteen, according to custom, he always felt shame at the free reign he gave to carnal desires with his child-bride. Three years later, his father died in the brief interval of five or ten minutes when Gandhi had left the room to visit his wife. The guilt he felt over that lapse in duty was crushing.

When nineteen, he went to England to study law. Although the family supported his venture, provided he take a vow not to touch "wine, women, or meat," and although his wife, Kasturbai, sold her jewels to raise money for the trip, the caste elders sternly disapproved. He felt the caste should not interfere, but they felt otherwise. He was solemnly declared an outcaste with the dread words: "Whoever helps him or goes to see him off at the dock shall be punishable with a fine of one rupee four annas." The ban against him was later ignored, but never formally rescinded.

In England, his studies were not difficult, the exams were notoriously easy and the percentage of those who passed was very high. Other things, however, were difficult. A diet of boiled cabbage and other vegetarian delights helped Gandhi through.

He was a very shy person. Once, attempting humor in making a speech, began by saying:

When Addison began his maiden speech in the House of Commons, he repeated 'I conceive' three times, and when he could proceed no further, a wag stood up and said, 'The gentleman conceived thrice but brought forth nothing.'

At this point in his talk, he was suddenly overcome with embarrassment, and added abruptly:

I thank you, gentlemen, for having kindly responded to my invitation!

and sat down.

Gandi believed that this natural shyness was an ally in the search for truth:

Silence is part of the spiritual discipline of a votary of truth. Proneness to exaggerate, to suppress or modify the truth, wittingly or unwittingly, is a natural weakness of man, and silence is necessary in order to surmount it. A man of few words will rarely be thoughtless in his speech; he will measure every word.

At twenty-one, he returned to India to practice law in Bombay and Rajkot. To his great sorrow, he found that his mother had died, and that to spare his feelings in a foreign land, his brother had kept the news from him.

It was difficult to earn a living at the private practice of law, so he accepted a job in South Africa as legal advisor to a commercial firm. For the next twenty years he made South Africa his base of operations.

The humiliations of Gandhi encountered in that country were

severe. A bigoted judge ordered him to remove his turban while in his court. An Englishman entered history anonymously by loudly objecting to having a "colored" man (Gandhi) in the first class railway compartment. He complained to officials, demanding that they "remove the coolie!" He was ejected and stranded at a lonely, small-town railway station. He protested against such unjust treatment, refusing to accept prejudice and cruelty as normal behavior. Because of such bitter experiences, Gandhi began to develop the concept and technique of active non-violence.

During the Boer War, while young Winston Churchill was in the country serving as a correspondent seeking adventure and fame, Gandhi was faced with a crisis of conscience. He was a loyal British subject, yet he sympathized with the South African desire for independence. He thought both sides wrong in using force to get their way. He decided to serve with an Indian ambulance corps attached to the British forces. Severely criticized for helping the war effort in any way, he answered:

It is not always given to one to be clear about one's duty. A votary of truth is often obliged to grope in the darkness.

Gandhi, in 1909, wrote a *Confession of Faith*, stating that Germany and England were living in a "Hall of Death." The materialism and militarism of Western Civilization, with its railways, telegraph, telephones, and so on, was negative:

East and West can only really meet when the West has thrown overboard modern civilization almost in its entirety. . . . India's salvation consists in unlearning what she has learnt during the past fifty years. The railways, telegraphs, hospitals, lawyers, doctors, and such like all have to go, and the so-called upper classes have to learn to live consciously, religiously, and deliberately the simple peasant life, knowing it to be a life giving true happiness.

Even medical technology, according to Gandhi, is negative:

122

Hospitals are the instruments that the Devil has been using for his own purpose, in order to keep his hold on his kingdom. They perpetuate vice, misery, degradation, and real slavery. I was entirely off the track when I considered that I should receive a medical training. It would be sinful for me in any way whatsoever to take part in the abominations that go on in the hospitals.

It is possible to find contradictions between what Gandhi wrote at different times. In such a case, he advises, we should take the later statement as more mature. However, we may also ask, in fairness, whether the earlier formulation may not contain some insight which an older man would have missed.

In 1915, he returned to India, in his mid-forties, and began working for his country's independence.

He adopted a simple life of voluntary poverty, and quickly became a popular leader. He announced as aims:

(1) the elimination of the ban against untouchables,

(2) the spread of universal education in the mother tongue, and

(3) the freedom of India from exploitation by foreign industry.

He was leader of the Indian National Congress several times. During the Non-Cooperation Movement, when brought up for trial before the judge, he affirmed that his occupation was "a farmer and a weaver," regarding the peasant's life as the most wholesome occupation for mankind.

He took up the cause of peasant farmers who were required by law to grow indigo at an unprofitable rate for export to Europe. Arrested as an agitator, the court was astounded by his plea of "guilty," and his announcement that he was prepared for any punishment the court may impose upon him. Anxious to avoid mass demonstrations, they released him to serve on a committee to settle the farmers' grievances.

In 1922, he organized the mass campaign against paying taxes. Charged with sedition, he again entered a "guilty" plea and asked for the maximum sentence. He was imprisoned, but released early because of ill health.

123

He then organized the salt march, a march to the sea to distill salt in defiance of the government's salt monopoly. This time, the authorities tried to break the movement by making mass arrests, but only succeeded in clogging the jails, overloading the system, and having to back down.

On another issue, Gandhi won his point from his jail cell, by sending word out that he would fast unto death unless the government amended its voting regulations which discriminated against untouchables. The government changed its policy.

Gandhi was the moving force in conferences which ultimately led to India's independence on August 15, 1947.

It has become fashionable in some circles to disparage Gandhi, saying that India would have gained independence in any event. It may be true that independence for India was inevitable, sooner or later. It would not have come about in that particular way but for Gandhi. He exalted the virtues of non-violence, love and simplicity. To say that a person, if he had not been shot, would have eventually died in some other way, is not to say that it made no difference that he was shot. Gandhi's influence made a great difference to modern India.

Gandhi was deeply disappointed by the partition of the subcontinent into India and Pakistan. Religious bitterness erupted between Hindus and Moslems, and millions fled from one country to the other. Many lost their lives in the religious disputes that broke out. Gandhi called for a return to non-violence, and for fasts to help restore peace. But he was not to be able to continue these efforts for long.

On January 30, 1948, he was assassinated by a Hindu youth who blamed him for the country's partition. Crying out: "*He Rāma*" ("Oh, God"), he slumped to the ground and, within a half hour, was dead. He made the Hindu sign of forgiveness for the assassin.

Karl Marx said that it is not the business of philosophy to merely understand the world, but to change it. By this definition, Gandhi's philosophical contributions are incontestable, for he has profoundly changed the world. But he did so in a special way, true to the spiritual heritage of India's past. This can be illustrated by his approach to the problem of the redistribution of wealth. He wrote:

> Exploitation of the poor can be extinguished not by effecting the destruction of a few millionaires, but by removing the ignorance of the poor and teaching them to non-cooperate with their exploiters. That will convert the exploiters also.

Two of Gandhi's key ideas are explained in the following sections.

II. *SATYAGRAHA*

The "force born of truth, love, and non-violence," *satyagraha*, "Soul-force," was Gandhi's concept of the power exerted by active non-violence.

> The word '*Satya*' (Truth) is derived from '*Sat*' which means being. And nothing is or exists in reality except Truth. That is why '*Sat*' or Truth is perhaps the most important name of God. In fact it is more correct to say that Truth is God, than to say that God is Truth. But as we cannot do without a ruler or a general, names of God such as King of Kings or the Almighty are and will remain more usually current. On deeper thinking, however, it will be realized that '*Sat*' or '*Satya*' is the only correct and fully significant name of God.
>
> (—Gandhi, *From Yeravda Mandir*, 1932)

> Devotion to this Truth is the sole reason for our existence. All our activities should be centred in Truth. Truth should be the very breath of our life. When once this stage in the pilgrim's progress is reached, all other rules of correct living will come without effort, and obedience to them will be instinctive. But without Truth it would be impossible to observe any principles or rules in life.
>
> (—*Ibid.*)

A *satyagrahi* (a person who practices *satyagraha*) sometimes

125

appears momentarily to disobey laws and the constituted authority only to prove in the end his regard for both.
(—Gandhi, *Speeches and Writings*)

The beauty of *Satyagraha* (is that) it comes up to us; we have not to go out in search for it. There is a virtue inherent in the principle itself. A war of righteousness in which there are no secrets to be guarded, no scope for cunning, and no place for untruth, comes unsought; and a man of religion is ever ready for it. A struggle which has to be previously planned is not a righteous struggle.
(—Gandhi, quoted by C. F. Andrews, *Mahatma Gandhi's Ideas*, 226.)

III. *AHIMSA*

Literally: "not hurting" or "non-violence," *ahimsa* was Gandhi's other guiding principle:

If we turn our eyes to the time of which history has any record down to our own time, we shall find that man has been steadily progressing towards *ahimsa*. Our remote ancestors were cannibals. Then came a time when they were fed up with cannibalism and they began to live on chase. Next came a stage when man was ashamed of leading the life of a wandering hunter. He therefore took to agriculture and depended principally on mother earth for his food. Thus from being a nomad he settled down to civilized stable life, founded villages and towns, and from member of a family he became member of a community and a nation. All these are signs of progressive *ahimsa* and diminishing *himsa*. Had it been otherwise, the human species should have been extinct by now, even as many of the lower species have disappeared.

Prophets and *avatars* have also taught the lesson of *ahimsa* more or less. Not one of them has professed to teach *himsa*. And how should it be otherwise? *Himsa* does not need to be taught. Man as animal is violent, but as spirit is non-violent.

The moment he awakes to the spirit within he cannot remain violent. Either he progresses towards *ahimsa* or rushes to his doom. That is why the prophets and *avatars* have taught the lessons of truth, harmony, brotherhood, justice, etc.—all attributes of *ahimsa*.

(—Gandhi, *Harijan*, 1940)

Our motto must ever be conversion by gentle persuasion and a constant appeal to the head and the heart. We must therefore be ever courteous and patient with those who do not see eye to eye with us. We must resolutely refuse to consider our opponents as enemies of the country.

(—Gandhi, *Young India*.)

The end of non-violent 'war' is always an agreement, never dictation, much less humiliation of the opponent.

(—*Harijan*.)

Our business therefore is to show them that they are in the wrong and we should do so by our suffering. I have found that mere appeal to reason does not answer where prejudices are agelong and based on supposed religious authority. Reason has to be strengthened by suffering and suffering opens the eyes of understanding. Therefore there must be no trace of compulsion in our acts. We must not be impatient, and we must have an undying faith in the means we are adopting.

(—*Young India*.)

I have nothing new to teach the world. Truth and Non-violence are as old as the hills. All I have done is to try experiments in both on as vast a scale as I could. In doing so I have sometimes erred and learnt by my errors. Life and its problems have thus become to me so many experiments in the practice of truth and non-violence. As a Jain *muni* once rightly said, I was not so much a votary of *ahimsa* as I was of truth, and I put the latter in the first place and the former in the second. For, as he put it, I was capable of sacrificing non-

127

violence for the sake of Truth. In fact it was in the course of my pursuit of truth that I discovered non-violence.

(—*Harijan*.)

Ahimsa and Truth are so intertwined that it is practically impossible to disentangle and separate them. They are like the two sides of a coin, or rather a smooth unstamped metallic disc. Who can say, which is the obverse, and which the reverse? Nevertheless, *ahimsa* is the means; Truth is the end.

(—*From Yeravda Mandir*.)

Means and end are convertible terms in my philosophy of life.

(—*Young India*.)

GAUTAMA (580-520 B.C.): Author of the *Nyāya-Sūtra*, Gautama (Gotama) is not to be confused with the Buddha, although they were evidently contemporaries. Also called Akṣapāda ("Eye-footed") and Dīrghatapas ("Long-penance"), complimentary titles, he codified logical and epistemological techniques to verify the truth of the Vedas.

Nyāya, also called *Tarkavidyā*, the science of reasoning, or *Vādavidyā*, the science of discussion, takes its rise from doubt (*samśaya*), which Gautama regards as the chief incentive to philosophical thought. To find the truth, we should seek the help of all valid sources of knowledge, harmonize our theory with those previously established (*siddhānta*), use examples which anyone can accept (*dṛṣṭānta*), employ the five-step method of discovery and proof (*pañcāvayava-nyāya*), strengthen the conclusion by indirect hypotheticals or postulates (*tarka*), avoid the five kinds of material fallacies (*hetvābhāsa*), three kinds of quibbles (*chala*), twenty-four kinds of false analogies (*jāti*), and twenty-two kinds of self-defeating steps which would lead to poor debating.

GEDÜN GYATSO (1475-1542): Abbot of the monasteries of Drêpung (1517), Trashil-hünpo (1520) and Sera (1526), Gedün Gyatso (precise transliteration *dGe-'dun rgya-mtsho*) was a great Tibetan leader later believed to be one of the incarnations of

Avalokiteśvara and thus the Second Dalai Lama. The monasteries of Drêpung and Sera are within a few miles of Lhasa, the capital. Trashil-hünpo is located about a hundred and fifty miles to the west, near Shigatse, and it would later become the place where the Panchen Lama held office.

GEDÜN-TRUP (1391-1474): Founder of the monastery of Trashil-hünpo, Gedün-trup (precise transliteration *dGe-'dun-grub*) was so highly regarded that he was retrospectively called the First Dalai Lama. As such, he was said to be the 51st reincarnation of Avalokiteśvara, Tibet's patron bodhisattva, whose statue stands in the capital. The Tibetan texts explain that a given Dalai Lama was always the reincarnation of his historical predecessor, and hence indirectly, not directly, Avalokiteśvara's incarnation.

GELUGPA: The fourth and most recent school of Tibetan Buddhism, Gelugpa puts less emphasis than the others on Tantric practice. Founded early in the fifteenth century by Lobsang Tragpa (Tsong Khapa), both the Dalai and Panchen Lamas belong to this group.

GENSHIN (942-1017): The Japanese philosopher who urged the practice of the *nembutsu* (the phrase: "pay homage to Amitābha Buddha," *namu Amida Butsu*), Genshin (Eshin Sōzu) declared on his deathbed that the world needs only to know that one phrase. He then ordered all his books to be destroyed by fire, on the grounds that they were superfluous.

Genshin vividly described the attractions of the Pure Land, entrance to which could be gained by repeating the *nembutsu*:

> After the believer is born into this land and when he experiences the pleasures of the first opening of the lotus, his joy becomes a hundred times greater than before. It is like a blind man gaining sight for the first time, or entering a royal palace directly after leaving some rural region. Looking at his own body, it becomes purplish gold in color. He is gowned naturally in jeweled garments. Rings, bracelets, a

crown of jewels, and other ornaments in countless profusion adorn his body. And when he looks upon the light radiating from the Buddha, he obtains pure vision, and because of his experiences in former lives, he hears the sounds of all things. And no matter what color he may see or what sound he may hear, it is a thing of marvel. Such is the ornamentation of space above that the eye becomes lost in the traces of clouds. The melody of the wheel of the wonderful Law as it turns, flows throughout this land of jeweled sound. Palaces, halls, forests, and ponds shine and glitter everywhere. Flocks of wild ducks, geese, and mandarin ducks fly about in the distance and near at hand. One may see multitudes from all the worlds being born into this land like sudden showers of rain.

Genshin was a Tendai priest, and in the *Essentials of Salvation* (*Ōjō Yōshū*), he stresses that anyone who wants can obtain help from an outside source (*tariki*), from Amida himself. This salvation meant rebirth in the Western Paradise, available to all who call on the name of Amida. It was a doctrine which greatly appealed to people in troubled times, weary of trying to improve.

GESHE: Tibetan term for the highest degree in religious studies, equivalent to a Th.D. (Doctor of Theology). Conferred by the Gelug and Sakya Orders, it would commonly require twenty years to earn.

In the course of study, *geshes* would develop extraordinary powers of extra-sensory perception, and the ability to read the minds of students.

GIBRAN, KAHLIL (1883-1931): Artist and mystic, the poetry and parables of Kahlil Gibran are drawn from the experiences of Lebanon. Born in the village of Bsherri, near the Cedars of Lebanon, his father was a shepherd dedicated to smoking the water-pipe and playing trick-trak. His mother, the last child of a Maronite priest, read him *The Arabian Nights* when he was young, and encouraged his artistic talents. When he was eleven, he went with his half-brother, mother, and all the family except the father, to seek his fortune in the new world, America. He went

130

to school in Boston while the family lived and worked in Boston's Chinatown. After two years, he returned to Lebanon to study at the School of Wisdom. Following graduation, he went to Paris to study painting. He wrote *Spirits Rebellious* (1903), criticizing high society, hypocritical priests and marriage based on family arrangements, not love. For his honesty, he was excommunicated by the church, exiled by the State, and the book burned in the marketplace of Beirut.

He received a letter in 1903 from his half-brother in Boston, telling him to come at once, that his sister Sultana had just died from tuberculosis and that his mother was sick with the disease. Within a few months, his mother and half-brother were both dead.

In the next years, he moved between Boston, New York, and Paris, writing "prose poems" and drawing. When the Young Turks overthrew the Sultan in 1908, the new government pardoned all exiles, and he could look forward to returning home.

He wrote *The Broken Wings* (1912), *A Tear and a Smile* (1914), *The Procession* (1918), *The Madman*, influenced by Nietzsche (1918), *The Forerunner* (1920), *The Prophet*, first written when he was fifteen and revised twice since (1923), *Sand and Foam* (1926), *Jesus the Son of Man* (1928), and *The Earth Gods* (1931).

Although he had admirers in life, he was not famous until after his death. The posthumous publications include: *The Wanderer* (1932), *The Garden of the Prophet* (1933), *Secrets of the Heart* (1947), *The Nymphs of the Valley* (1948), *The Voice of the Master* (1959), *A Self-Portrait* (1959), *Thoughts and Meditations* (1961), *Spiritual Sayings* (1962), and *Beloved Prophet* (1972).

Kahlil Gibran died April 10, 1931, in St. Vincent's Hospital, New York. He was buried, according to his wish, in the old deserted monastery of Mar-Sarkis in Wadi Kadisha.

"Art," he wrote, "is a step from nature toward the Infinite. . . . Art is a step in the known toward the unknown."

H

HAIKU: The Japanese term for a seventeen-syllable poetic form, *haiku* may be illustrated by the famous poem by Bashō (1643-1694):

Furu ike ka!	The old pond, ah!
Kawazu tobikomu,	A frog jumps in:
Mizu no oto.	The water's sound!

From Buson (1716-1783) comes this example:

Tsuri-gane ni	On the temple bell,
Tomarite nemuru	Perching, sleeps
Kochō kana.	The butterfly, oh!

Bashō's poem is often quoted, written upon meeting two prostitutes on their way to worship at the Ise Shrine, and having heard them tell about their wretched lives which they abhorred:

Hitotsu ya ni	Under one roof,
Yūjo mo netari,	Prostitutes also were sleeping;
Hagi to tsuki.	Clover flowers and moon.

Haiku is an art-form greatly appreciated, especially by Zen masters.

132

HAKUIN (1685-1768): Zen master of the Rinzai school of Japanese Buddhism, Hakuin (Ekaku) was active during the Tokugawa Shogunate, (the Edo period). Known as the second founder of Rinzai Zen, he was born in Hara (Suruga), the youngest of five children. Brought up in the Nichiren sect, he was impressed by the magical formulas and the *Lotus* sūtra, but soon noticed that the magic did not seem to work all the time. At fifteen, he studied at the Zen temple in his village, and then wandered for years before settling in the Myoshinji. His teacher was Dokyo Yetan, better known as Shōjū Rōnin (Shōjū the Outlaw, "rōnin" meaning a samurai without a leader). When Hakuin first met him, Shōjū asked:

Tell me, what is Joshu's "Mu"?

Master Joshu (778-897) was a Chinese Zen master noted for the incident in which he was asked the question, "Has a dog the Buddha-nature or not?" and his reply was: "Mu!"

Hakuin knew the story and had given it some thought, so he proudly replied:

It pervades the whole universe! There is not any particular spot whatever to take hold of.

Shōjū then reached out and caught Hakuin's nose and gave it a sharp twist, laughing and saying:

It is easy to take hold of it!

Then Shōjū let go and shouted at Hakuin:

You dead monk in a cave! Are you satisfied with such a "Mu"?

Hakuin was startled and surprised. But he stayed on, to learn from Shōjū Rōnin. Some of the Zen technique seems to be calculated at finding out whether a student is serious or not. Hakuin was serious. He was not satisfied with the level of knowledge he already had.

Hakuin reorganized the Koan of Zen. He was an artist and poet. One of his poems is:

You, young fellow,
If you don't want to die,
Die now!
Once dead, you don't have to die twice.

Particularly interested in the mystical aspect of Zen, he wrote of the bodhisattva Kwannon (Goddess of Mercy):

With her eyes she hears the song of spring;
With her ears she sees the colorings of the mountain.

The literal nonsense of many Zen formulations may disturb some Western minds, who fail to penetrate beneath the surface. There are some intelligent people who are too dumb to understand Zen. Hakuin once said:

"Mind is Buddha" is like a dragon without horns.
"No mind, no Buddha" is like a snake with horns.

Hakuin's contributions to the "barrier" that Zen deliberately sets up in the way of the student was to say:

Listen to the sound of one hand clapping!

His teaching may be summarized by the statement:

All beings are originally Buddhas. It is like ice and water. Without water there will be no ice. This very earth is the lotus-land, and this body is the Buddha.

HAN FEI TZǓ (280-233 B.C.): The name of Han Fei Tzǔ should command instant recognition, because he was the greatest of the Legalists in ancient China, and Legalism is enjoying a revival in contemporary China as an alternative to the standard ancient philosophies, such as Confucianism or Taoism. The Legalists (*fa chia*: *fa* may mean law, punishment, custom, duty, discipline, method, techniques, or model) advocated strong centralized government, with no regard for individual rights. Man is evil, the Legalists maintained, and it makes no sense whatever to appeal to his higher instincts, whether by education, as Confucius had recommended, or mysticism, as Lao Tzǔ had advised. The only thing man understands and responds to is a system of rewards and punishments.

As for the ruler, it is not his superior virtue that persuades others to do his will, but his position and the power of coercion that goes with it. Legalism was a kind of combination of Machiavelli, Skinner, and Kissinger. It recommended the extension of political power, psychological conditioning, and secrecy.

Legalism emphasized an approach to politics based on contemporary ideas (and a revolt against antiquity), government by law, the correct understanding of terms ("rectification of names"), the evil nature of man, and *wu-wei* (taking no unnatural action) as the best way to govern.

The three tendencies within the Legalist school had been to emphasize power, statecraft, or law. Han Fei Tzǔ's contribution to Legalist theory was to synthesize these three into one coherent system.

Han Fei Tzǔ stuttered, and thus was prevented from effectively engaging in discussions or debates. Therefore, he became most skillful in writing, producing the *Ku Fen, Wu Tu, Nei Wai Chu Shuo, Shuo Lin,* and *Shuo Nan* (these are all parts of the present Han-fei-tzǔ, Chapters 11, 49, 30-35, 22-23, and 12, respectively).

Han Fei Tzǔ sharply criticized the King of Han for choosing "vermin" as state officials, and permitting "itinerant witches and priests" to make and interpret official policy.

Sent to the state of Ch'in as an envoy, he soon ran afoul of the Prime Minister, Li Ssu, a former classmate of his under Hsün Tzǔ. Jealousy proving thicker than old school ties, Li Ssu had him thrown into prison. Han Fei Tzǔ then was handed poison and ordered to commit suicide. The conscience of the King made him rescind the sentence and order him released. The pardon arrived too late. Han Fei Tzǔ's release from jail was not the King's action but the poison's.

Virtue, according to Han Fei Tzǔ, is not rewarded, and he compiled a long and depressing chronicle of the harm done to good and intelligent men:

The honorable Yi was broiled, the honorable Chiu's corpse was dried, Pi Kan had his heart cut open, his excellency Mei's corpse was pickled.

Furthermore, I-wu was bound with chains. Ta'ao Ch'i fled to Ch'ên. Pai-li Tzu was reduced to begging on his way to the capital of Ch'in. Fu Yüeh was sold into slavery from place to place. Sun Tzu had his feet cut off in Wei. Wu Ch'i wiped off his tears at the Dike Gate, lamented over the impending cession of the Western River Districts to Ch'in, and was dismembered in Ch'u. . . . Kuan Lung-p'êng was executed. Ch'ang Hung had his intestines chopped into pieces. Yin Tzǔ was thrown into a trap in the brambles. The Minister of War, Tzu-Ch'i, was killed and his corpse was floated on the Yangtze River. T'ien Ming was stoned to death. Mi Tzǔ-Chien and Hsi-mên Pao quarrelled with nobody but were killed anyway. Tung An-yü was killed and his corpse exposed in the market-place.... Fan Chü had his ribs broken in Wei.

These tens of men were all benevolent, worthy, loyal, and upright persons in the world and followers of the right way and the true path of life. Unfortunately they met such unreasonable, violent, stupid, and crooked masters that they lost their lives in the long run.

Could these worthies and sages have escaped death penalties and evaded disgrace? It was because of the difficulty in persuading fools. Hence every educated man must remain distrustful about speaking. Even the best speech displeases the ear and upsets the heart, and can be appreciated only by worthy and wise rulers.

Han Fei Tzǔ had been a student of the great Confucian scholar, Hsün Tzǔ, but disagreed strenuously with many Confucian principles. In particular, he disliked their appeal to tradition and custom. No one should be blamed for transgressing a tradition, but only for breaking a written law. Laws should be enforced strictly.

The past should not be used as a pattern for the present: The wise man does not seek to follow the ways of the ancients, nor to establish any fixed standard for all time, but examines his own age and prepares to deal with its problems.

To emphasize his point, he told this story:

A farmer in Sung plowed a field in the middle of which stood a tree trunk. One day a rabbit rushed across the field, into the trunk, broke its neck, and died. The farmer threw down his plow, and stood waiting by that tree in the hope that he could catch another rabbit in the same way. He never did, and was ridiculed by the people of Sung.

If someone wished to govern the people today with the policies of the early kings, he would be doing the same thing as the farmer who waited by his tree trunk.

(—*Han-fei-tzu*, ch. 49)

A major point of disagreement with Confucianism was over the theory that the ruler's power comes from his virtuous conduct. This was nonsense, according to the Legalists. A ruler's power really comes from his office. A good man has no influence if he is not in high office. A bad man has tremendous influence if he is highly placed in the state. Virtue does not produce influence, position does. The term used by the Legalists to describe this situation was *Shih*, authority (or circumstances, conditions, trends, power, influence).

The most effective way to govern, Han Fei Tzŭ believed, was the one which controlled people and officials most stringently. Recommending Watergate behavior, Han Fei Tzŭ wrote:

Keep spies watching the officials and know all about their private lives. Send detectives out to learn about their public conduct. Trust your common sense and ask questions about obscure matters. Give your officials false encouragement and thus reduce their attempts to infringe upon the ruler's rights. Change your words and thereby test the suspects. Use contradictory arguments to find out invisible culprits. Establish a system of espionage and trap the liars. Make appointments and dismissals and observe the reactions of wicked officials. Speak plainly and thereby persuade people to avoid mistakes. Humbly follow the advice of others and thereby discriminate between honest advisors and flatterers. Get information from everyone. Know things you have not seen yet. Create quarrels among your followers and thereby keep them from cooperating with each other. Investigate the depths of the corruption of one accused official, thereby warning many to behave themselves. Give out false ideas, and thereby make subordinates think things through. ... Place every subordinate under surveillance by his immediate superior.... Such is called "the systematic thorough way."

If words are divulged and affairs leak out, no statecraft will function at all.

HAN YÜ (768-824 A.D.): Banished to the wild region of northeastern Kwangtung province (to Ch'ao-chou, a city near Shantow, up the coast from Hong Kong, toward Formosa) because he complained about the honors the emperor was planning to bestow upon one of Buddha's bones, about to be received, Han Yü (styled T'ui-chih) vigorously rejected "the two schools" (Buddhism and Taoism) in favor of Confucianism which, at the time, was hanging "as by a thread." He "grievingly quoted the sages," saying that:

What the ancients thus called the rectification of the mind and the search for sincerity in thought, was used by them in their actual conduct. Today, however, persons who wish to set their minds in order, thereby put themselves beyond the pale of the world and the country.

When not in exile, Han Yü established a sort of apostolic succession for Confucianism, saying that the correct philosophy was transmitted from Yao to Shun to Yü to T'ang to (Kings) Wen and Wu and the Duke of Chou, and then to Confucius, who transmitted it to Mencius. When Mencius died, it was no longer transmitted. Hsün Tzŭ and Yang Hsiung selected certain portions from it, but without reaching its essence. "They discussed it, but without sufficient clarity." Because of Han's advocacy, Mencius was (finally) considered superior to Hsün Tzŭ, his rival. The mystical tendencies in Mencius, his method of self-cultivation through "nourishing the mind" and "making fewer the desires" were more suitable answers to the Buddhist debates of the times.

Han objected to the Buddhists for "destroying the natural constant" of family relationships and respect. Theirs is an alien faith, and they "elevate the rules of the barbarians above the teachings of the early kings, thus becoming almost the same as barbarians, themselves."

In his essay, *Yüan Tao* (*On the Origin of the Truth*), Han writes:

138

A love for everyone is called perfect virtue (*jen*). Conduct which proceeds in conformity with this is called righteousness (*yi*). What follows this course to its destination is called the Way (*Tao*). Sufficiency unto oneself without depending on externals is called the Power (*Te*). Perfect virtue and righteousness are fixed terms, whereas the Way and the Power hold indefinite positions. Therefore, there is a Way for the superior man or for the petty man, and there is a power that may be ineffective or effective.

In *Yüan Hsing* (*On the Origin of the Nature*), Han develops a further position:

There are three grades of the nature: superior, medium, and inferior. The superior is completely good. The medium may be led to be either superior or inferior. The inferior is completely evil. . . . The nature comes into being coincident with birth. The feelings come into being as the consequence of contact with (external) objects. . . . (The superior grade) holds to the mean in its operation. The medium grade either goes too far or is deficient in some of these seven (kinds of emotion: joy, anger, pity, fear, love, hate, and desire); nevertheless, it attempts to hold to the mean among them. But the inferior grade is without exception either deficient or too extreme in its operation throughout all the emotions.

Because of his contribution in setting the direction of Confucianism, Han Yü is called "the Great Dipper," and the first real protagonist of later Neo-Confucianism in the T'ang dynasty.

HARE KṚṢṆA (pronounced haw-ray krish-na): An aggressive and highly visible missionary movement, the International Society for Krishna Consciousness has colorfully-robed followers dancing and chanting in most major cities in the West. Dedicated to fulfilling the prediction that "the holy name of Krishna would one day be sung in every town and village in the world," the Bhaktivedanta Book Trust produces an attractive array of publications. Some 489 years ago, born in a village in Bengal, India,

139

Lord Caitanya (pronounced chaw-we-tan-ya), also called "Lord of the universe" and "most munificent incarnation of Godhead," recommended chanting Krishna's holy names. Today representatives of the organization hand out cards which read:

Please try chanting,
"Hare Krishna, Hare Krishna,
Krishna, Krishna, Hare, Hare;
Hare Rama, Hare Rama,
Rama Rama, Hare, Hare"
and be happy!

In the past, there had been many debates and arguments between atheists and believers. Now, such conflicts can be settled simply by chanting the sacred formula. Congregational chanting seems to be best, but one can obtain the benefits by chanting the formula at home, or anywhere. The organization's magazine, *Back to Godhead* (Vol. 10, No. 3, p. 6), contains such advice as: "Anyone who asks anything from a tree never goes away disappointed."

HATANO SEIICHI (1877-1950): Considered to be one of the leading Japanese thinkers during the first half of the twentieth century, Hatano wrote *A Study of Spinoza* (1904) and *Time and Eternity* (trans. Suzuki Ichirō, Tokyo, 1963). Analyzing how knowledge of the self was possible, he concluded that the individual (subject) knows itself in the same way that it recognizes the objective world. The subject expresses itself through objects or in objects. Those objects then become symbols to the subject. Thus, when the subject gets acquainted with itself, when the hidden self (the center of the knowing act) and the disclosed self are separated and at the same time realize their identity, then the subject knows itself.

HAYASHI RANZAN (1583-1657): The most important Japanese Confucian scholar during the early Tokugawa period, Hayashi Ranzan served as advisor to four shoguns. A noted lawyer and historian, he established as the orthodox creed the Chu Hsi theory of Neo-Confucianism. He reinterpreted *Li* to mean Japanese Shintoism, on the grounds that the Way of the Gods is nothing but Reason (*Li*). Nothing exists outside of Reason.

Reason is the truth of nature. Reason is identical with the Spirit.

The Hayashi family became hereditary headmasters of the Confucian academy in Edo (Tokyo). Yamaga Sokō was one of Hayashi Ranzan's students and, later, chief intellectual opponent.

HELL (BUDDHIST CONCEPTION OF): Eight hells await sinners after death and prior to re-birth, according to Buddhism:

1) Hell of Repetition (*Saṃjiva*), for those who kill, lasting 500 years;
2) Black Rope Hell (*Kāla-Sūtra*), for those who steal, lasting 1000 years;
3) Crowded Hell (*Samghāta*), for those who abuse sex, lasting 2000 years;
4) Screaming Hell (*Raurava*), for drunks, lasting 4000 years;
5) Great Screaming Hell (*Mahā-raurava*), for those who lie, lasting 8000 years;
6) Hell of Burning Heat (*Tapana*), for those who hold false views (such as not believing in *Tapana*), lasting 16,000 years;
7) Hell of Great Burning Heat (*Pra-tapana*), for those guilty of sexual defilement of religious people, lasting half a medium *kalpa* (a *kalpa*, according to one account, is the length of time it would take an angel who polished a cube-shaped rock measuring eighty leagues just once in every hundred years to completely wear out the rock); and
8) Hell of No Interval (*Avici*), for murderers, lasting a medium *kalpa*.

Daigan and Alicia Matsunaga, in *The Buddhist Concept of Hell* (New York: Philosophical Library, 1972), have explained all these concepts in great and excellent detail.

HILLEL I (30 B.C.E. - 10 C.E.): Born in Babylonia, Hillel the Elder became the most prominent Jewish teacher of the first

141

century. He travelled to Palestine to study Biblical interpretation under Shemaiah and Abtalion. Despite poverty and great hardship, he pursued his studies and eventually became the recognized authority on the Law. He formulated the seven rules for the systematic exposition of the Bible, which became the basis of all later rabbinic reasoning. His interpretations of the Law were generally more liberal in character than others, especially Shammai, who was a stern stickler for the letter of the law. Asked for a concise statement of the essence of Judaism, Hillel replied:

What is hateful to thee,
do not unto thy fellowman;
this is the whole Law;
the rest is mere commentary.
(—Shab. 31a)

HILLEL II (320-365): Palestinian scholar and patriarch, Hillel established the permanent Jewish calendar in 344, thus resigning the right of the Palestinian Jewish community to determine for all Jews the dates of the festivals. Persecution had become so severe and communication so difficult that a calendar which made possible the independent computation of these dates seemed the most beneficial course. In 361, work on rebuilding the Temple was started in Jerusalem under the blessing of Emperor Julian. However, the work was abandoned due to flames which burst from the ground, burning several workmen to death (according to Ammianus Marcellinus' *Works*, xxiii, I), the death of Julian, and the withdrawal of state funds from the project.

HĪNAYĀNA BUDDHISM: "Lesser Vehicle" Buddhism, a term applied by Mahayana ("Greater Vehicle") theologians to Theravada ("Teaching of the Elders") Buddhism. Predominant in Ceylon, Burma, Canbodia, Laos, and Viet Nam, Hinayana sticks closer than Mahayana to the actual historical teachings of Buddha, to the exclusion of belief in supernatural deities or transcendent manifestations of Buddha.

HINDUISM: (from a medieval Persian term, *Hindu*, derived from Sanskrit for the Sindhu or Indus river; *India* is from the same derivation.) Both a religious and social system of tremendous complexity, Hinduism is not easily characterized. It is both polytheistic and monotheistic. It both commands and forbids animal sacrifice. It is both tolerant and fanatic. It is both geographically limited (to Southeast Asia) and expansionist (see *Hare Krishna*). This paradoxical character of the religion makes generalization risky. Hinduism is an attempt to combine the popular worship of old nature gods with higher spiritual monotheism, but the nature of this combination is difficult to grasp.

Alone among the major religions of the world, Hinduism had no historical founder. There is no figure comparable to Zoroaster, Buddha, Mahavira, Jesus, Confucius, Mohammed, or Nanak. Thus the later Hindu writers could have extraordinary latitude in their interpretations, and could, without getting into trouble, afford to be much more tolerant than interpreters of other traditions.

Hindus call their religion *Santana Dharma*, the Eternal Religion, because it is based on eternal, rather than historical, principles; or *Vaidika Dharma*, because it is founded upon the teachings of the Vedas. This lack of interest in history pervades the writings and thought of most Hindus. Specific dates are often lacking from critical places in the best of books on or about Hinduism. Even Gandhi's autobiography, *The Story of My Experiments with Truth*, has key dates curiously missing. He meant to emphasize his encounter with truth rather than his experiments as a historical process.

The earliest portions of the Vedas are relatively obscure, written in a forgotten language (Sanskrit must be learned, like Latin or classical Greek), and lacking in historical reference. They need interpretation and explanation before they can have meaning to the reader. The Vedas, according to Hindu tradition, contain certain spiritual laws describing the nature of Ultimate Reality, the Soul and its destiny, and the relationship between God, man, and society.

Hinduism is the fourth largest religion in the world, currently. The government census figures include the scheduled castes as well (some fifty million people), and may be affected by the fact that political representation is connected with the census figures.

143

The scheduled castes within India are converting to Buddhism as part of an unusual phenomenon, the revival of a religion in a country after its complete disappearance for centuries.

The distinguishing doctrines of Hinduism may be said to be: (1) reincarnation, (2) monotheism combined with polytheism, and (3) the caste system.

(1) Reincarnation (Sanskrit: *punarjanma*, "again-birth"):
The *Katha Upanishad* says:

The soul is not born, nor does it die. It has not come from anywhere, nor has it produced anything. It is unborn, eternal, everlasting, ancient; it is not slain though the body is slain. If the slayer thinks of slaying the soul, and if the slain person thinks that the soul is dead, both have missed the truth. The soul slays not nor is slain. The soul, smaller than the small and greater than the great, is hidden in the hearts of all living creatures. A man who is free from desires and free from grief sees its majesty through tranquil senses and mind. Though sitting still it travels far; though lying down it goes everywhere. Wise men, having realized the incorporeal, great, and all-pervading soul dwelling in perishable bodies, do not grieve.

The goal of life is to be virtuous enough to be reborn into a higher state, until at last the individual becomes a holy man and escapes from the wheel of rebirth to be reunited with God (*Moksha*).

One corollary of this doctrine teaches that all living beings are the same in essence. Killing animals is forbidden because all life is sacred. One ancient scripture declares: "All that kill cows rot in hell for as many years as there are hairs on the body of the cow they killed."

Indian businessmen support old cows' homes sometimes more readily than old people's homes. Prime Minister Nehru, appealing for more money for rest homes for old cows, said: "The West does not worship the cow but takes care of it. We worship it but do not take care of it."

According to Sri Aurobindo, rebirth accounts for the

phenomenon of genius, inborn faculty, and other psychological mysteries. He writes:

> The true foundation of the theory of rebirth is the evolution of the soul, or rather its efflorescence out of the veil of matter and its gradual self-finding. . . . The soul needs no proof of its rebirth any more than it needs proof of its immortality. For there comes a time when it is consciously immortal, aware of itself in its eternal and immutable essence.

(2) Polytheism combined with monotheism. Compared with the intolerant attitude of revealed religions (Judaism, Christianity, and Islam), Hinduism appears tolerant indeed. Whereas Exodus 20:3 reads: "Thou shalt have no other Gods before me," the incarnate god, Krishna, in the *Bhagavad Gītā*, says: "Whatever god a man worships, it is I who answer the prayer."

The polytheistic aspect of Hinduism is evident from the devotion villagers pay to many different gods at many different temples. India still is very much a country of villages. If asked how many gods there are, the reply is "thirty-three crores," or, in other words, 330,000,000. If one wants to have obstacles removed, a prayer to Ganesha, the elephant-headed god (son of Shiva), would be appropriate. For more muscle-power, the proper god is Hanuman, the monkey-god. Other gods can give relief to one whose father is dying, who wants a safe trip, immunity from cholera or smallpox, health for his cattle, or more children.

On a more sophisticated level, the supreme reality which upholds the universe is called *Brahman* (*q.v.*), not to be confused with *Brahmā* (*q.v.*), masculine, the first member of the Hindu trinity (with *Vishnu* and *Shiva*).

The second member of the Hindu trinity is *Vishnu*, the preserver. Living on Meru, he is generally pictured with a lotus, conch shell, and mace. His wife is Lakshmi, the goddess of fertility. Vishnu rides through the heavens on the man-bird Garuda, and periodically incarnates himself on earth in the form of a fish, or tortoise, boar, man-lion, dwarf, Rama, or Krishna. Vishnu is sometimes seen lying on the multi-headed serpent Ananta, with

the god Brahma issuing from his navel, symbolizing the interdependence of the gods.

The third member of the Hindu trinity is Shiva, the Destroyer.
Living on Mount Kailas, he is sometimes pictured riding a bull,
dancing on the back of a dwarf, or sitting, meditating, with the
sacred Ganges river spouting out of his head. Shiva's wife has
several names, and several aspects. As Parvati or Uma, she is
graceful and beautiful. As Durga, she is fierce. As Kali, she is
bloodthirsty, and is pictured holding a decapitated head, wearing
a garland of skulls. Shiva's sons are Karttikeya, the warlike leader
of the armies of the gods, and Ganesha, the gentle son who
removes obstacles, pictured with a rat for a helper.

Brahman, as the supreme reality, is identified with Atman (the
soul or self). In the Upanishads, Brahman is described as "that
whence all beings come into existence, wherein they reside, and
whereunto they return at the end."

Brahman is conceived in two different ways by different
schools of Hindu thought. On one hand, Brahman is conceived as
identical with the personal God, Brahma, as the all-inclusive
sustaining spirit of the universe. This is the cosmic view (saprapan-
ca) of Ramanuja Vedānta (11th century), and holds that
Brahman is endowed with attributes.

On the other hand, we find the conception of Brahman as the
impersonal Absolute, the reality of which the universe is only the
surface appearance. This is the acosmic view (nishprapanca) of
Shankara Vedānta (9th century), and holds that Brahman is
unconditioned and attributeless (nirguna). According to this
view, Brahman can be indicated only negatively as: "not this, not
this." However, this does not mean that Brahman is "nothing."
Rather, Brahman is the fullness of being (sat), consciousness
(chit), and bliss (ananda).

Both schools of thought appeal to the texts of the Rigveda, with
justification, to support their views.

(3) Caste (q.v.), said to be the only universally recognized feature in Hinduism, because a person can worship or not, as he
pleases, believe what he pleases, not belong to any organization,
and still be counted a Hindu. But an individual must conform to
the usages of his caste. It has been argued that the caste system is

not an accidental outgrowth of Hinduism, but an essential expression of the idea that men are on different levels:

The fact is that under Caste system there can be no equality between man and man. And since the Hindus do not believe in human equality, individual liberty cannot be enjoyed under Hindu dispensation.

(—quoted in Ahmad Abdullah al Masdoosi, *Living Religions of the World, a Socio-Political Study*, Karachi: Begum Aish Bawany Wakf, 1962, p. 249.)

On the other hand, Gandhi consistently objected to the undesirable features of the caste system.

Swami Nikhilananda wrote:

Hinduism is noted for its catholic and universal outlook. Its toleration and respect for other faiths mainly result from the fact that it regards the Godhead, or Ultimate Reality, as unconditioned by time and space. Religion itself is not the Godhead but the means to Its realization. According to the Vedas Truth is one, though the sages call it by various names. The *Bhagavad Gītā* declares that all religions are strung on the Lord like pearls on a necklace. In whatever way people offer their worship to the Lord, He accepts it. All religions lead to the same Truth.

See also: Indian Philosophy.

HIRATA, ATSUTANE (1760-1843): The Japanese Shinto leader during the Tokugawa Shogunate (Edo), Hirata Atsutane (pronounced hee-rah-ta awt-soo-tawn-eh), an ardent nationalist and physician, deeply venerated the work of Motoori Norinaga and claimed to be his true successor. Hirata knew Dutch Studies (*Rangaku*) and Western medicine.

Hirata was the most influential member of the National Learning movement, a Neo-Shintoist group in the early nineteenth century. Hirata reviled alien teachings and glorified the superiority of native Japanese learning. Japanese society, he wrote, had been inherently virtuous, and hence had no need to preach virtue or develop a "Way" as Confucianism did in China. Japan had originally been pure and free from disease until outside contact infected the land and obliged her to seek outside medical remedies. His most surprising innovation was to suggest the doctrine of life after death for a religion (Shinto) notably lacking such ideas.

The Japanese people, according to Hirata, because of their divine connections, are superior to other peoples, and are destined to extend the scope of their rule over all the world. These doctrines contributed to the downfall of the Shogunate and the "restoration of imperial Sovereignty." Along with this, a Department of Shinto was established in the new government, and *saisei itchi* (union of religion and government) became the slogan.

Hirata's works include *Shutsujō shōgo* (*Ridiculing the Teachings of the Buddha*), Tokyo: Kōbundō, 1936, *Kodō-taii* (*Outline of the Ancient Way*) and *Nyūgaku mondō* (*Elements of Study*), in *Hirata Atsutane zenshū* (*Collected Works of Hirata Atsutane*), 1918.

HŌNEN (GENKŪ, 1133-1212): A simple, gentle man, Hōnen (pronounced HO-nen) was the real founder of the Amidist sect of Japanese Buddhism known as Pure Land (*Jōdo*). Amida Buddha would come down to welcome those who called on his name, and would take them up to enjoy the bliss of the Pure Land, the Western Paradise.

Hōnen's father had been a government official, and on his deathbed urged his son with great emotion to become a monk. At Mount Hiei, the Tendai center, Hōnen studied the ancient books, and is said to have read the entire Tripitaka through five times. Still, he felt dissatisfied with traditional ideas.

The stormy civil wars of the time led him to yearn for religious peace, a peace not dependent upon one's own efforts (*jiriki*), but rather upon the strength of another (*tariki*). The divine intervention of the saving Amida was needed in the corrupt age of *mappō*.

In 1175, at the age of forty-three, Hōnen began teaching, and this is the date taken for the founding of *Jōdo*.

In 1198, Hōnen wrote the *Senchaku Shū* (*Collection of Passages*). These were Amida Sūtras (sermons) with commentaries by Zendō and Hōnen's commentaries on Zendō's commentaries. This style of intellectual development was also employed in medieval Europe.

Hōnen was dissatisfied with the current practice of doing good deeds to earn merit. As Hōnen interpreted matters, it was a case of piling up good deeds, one at a time, until the individual saved up enough to cash in for salvation. One had to earn the way to truth. This could well produce a mean-spirited, narrow-minded, selfish saint who entered Nirvana on the strength of his own private hoard of good deeds.

Hōnen decided that the way to truth needed to be rethought. Hōnen criticized Kūkai's arrangement of an "order of merit" within Buddhism, on the grounds that it is false to imply that the truth itself may be more or less complete. Truth is truth, and is indivisible.

There are, he proposed, two paths to Nirvana: (1) the Holy Path (*Shōdō*), which many Buddhas taught, and (2) the Pure Land Path (*Jōdo*), the way taught only by Amida Buddha. It is not necessary to renounce the first path and its Buddhas, but the second path is better. Amida had become a Buddha by taking forty-eight vows. Of these, the eighteenth is the most important. It states: anyone calling on the name of Amida will by virtue of that act be reborn into the Western Paradise, the Pure Land. There everyone will have wonderful powers of body and mind. Meditation, according to Hōnen, is superfluous. Long training in the secret rites is not necessary. The divinity is always immediately available for everyone. We should call on the name of Amida with faith, and be saved. Amida is all-merciful. Sinners will be pardoned. Every sin will be forgiven.

Opponents of Hōnen objected that this would encourage immorality. Hōnen said, to correct that impression, that if faith is not right, Amida cannot save. Good conduct is related in some way to correct faith.

Still, the great Tendai monasteries opposed these new ideas.

149

His old school at Mount Hiei joined in condemning him and his theories.

Hōnen published an open letter attempting conciliation. However, various intrigues continued. Two women from the imperial court became nuns. Gossip said that they did so because they were in love with some of the priests. The priests replied with some heat and sarcasm, saying that unbelievers are always jealous of those who act on purely religious principles (they were quoting from the commentaries of Zendō). Such a reply was too sharp. The priests lost their heads, literally, with the aid of the court executioner. Since Hōnen had also commented on Zendō's commentaries, he was obviously to blame for corrupting his fellow priests. He was exiled from the court (1207). The exile lasted, formally, only ten months, but he was not allowed to return to the capital for another four years. He might have done better to stay away permanently, because as soon as he returned, he fell ill and died, on the 25th of January, 1212. With his death, he evidently ceased criticizing the customs of the court, and was then allowed to remain, the kind of subject most rulers want.

A three-day ceremony is held each year from April 13-15 at the Zojoji Temple in Shiba Park, Minato-ku, Tokyo, in memory of his death, led by a large group of firemen chanting *kiyari*, their professional song. When Tokugawa Ieyasu had come to Edo (Tokyo) to make it the capital, he also made the Zojoji temple his family temple, an honor celebrated to this day.

HOSSŌ (pronounced hoe-SO): One of the six schools of Buddhism which emerged in Japan after Prince Shōtoku extended protection to the religion. Dōshō (628-700) introduced Hossō into the country. A complicated philosophical system, Hossō means "characteristics of the dharmas." Things only exist when we are conscious of them. The world is our world, and only exists for us.

Annual examinations were held to determine who would be an officially authorized monk, and promotion through the ranks depended upon knowledge of the system of thought.

Today there are approximately forty Hossō temples in Japan.

HO YEN (189-249): An outstanding Neo-Taoist, together with Wang Pi, Ho Yen was brilliant as a young man, and despite that fact was a government official. Neo-Taoism, during the Wei and Chin times (220-419) arose as a way to escape from political chaos. The Taoist Metaphysical (*Hsüan*) Schools which flourished then argued against the supremacy of the Confucian Classics, and reacted against the textual and philological studies which served the Classics. Ho Yen and Wang Pi initiated this process by developing a Taoist interpretation of Confucianism. For instance, Confucius once said of his favorite disciple, Yen Hui:

As for Hui, he was near (perfection), yet frequently was empty (poor).

According to Ho Yen, "empty" (*k'ung*) means "in a state of vacuity" (*hsü chung*). In other words, Hui was not poor, but rather a constant practitioner of the Taoist technique of meditation (emptiness).

Ho wrote that *pen-wu* (originally undifferentiated) was nameless, beyond all words and forms. Non-being (*wu*) was interpreted as Pure Being. The universe is one. The sage is a man of social and political achievement, and the supreme sage was Confucius.

HSI K'ANG (223-262): One of the "Seven Worthies of the Bamboo Grove," Neo-Taoist philosophers who met in bamboo groves to drink, write poems, and express disdain for traditional values, Hsi K'ang said we should "transcend morals and institutions and follow nature." These were the "light conversationalists," who avoided the seriousness of the Confucianists, and limited conversation to sex and poetry. Modern readers might wonder how worthy were the Worthies as they interpreted "following nature" not as lessening desires, as in chapter nineteen of the *Lao-tzu*, but rather as satisfying desires. Jüan Chi (*q.v.*) went further than Hsi, so the reader might like to read more about him.

Hsi wrote an essay arguing that in music there is neither sorrow nor pleasure (See *Hsi Chung-shan Chi, Collected Writings of Hsi K'ang*). Holzman has written an important study entitled *La vie et la pensée de Hi K'ang* (Leiden: Brill, 1957).

151

HSÜAN-TSANG (596-664): One of the greatest figures in the history of Chinese Buddhism, Hsüan-Tsang completed the "doctrine of mere ideation," or "consciousness-only" (originally called, in India, the Way of Yoga, Yogācāra, founded by Asanga (410-500)). At the age of thirteen, he entered Buddhist orders (a Pure Land monastery). At the age of thirty-three, burning with the desire to see the sacred places of Buddhism in India, he set off, against orders from the emperor, across the deserts and mountains of central Asia in a famous pilgrimmage which several times nearly cost him his life (his account of this adventurous journey has been translated by Thomas Watters, *On Yuan Chwang's Travels in India, 629-645 A.D.*, London, 2 vols., 1904-05). There he spent sixteen years studying and debating with the great Indian scholars. He returned in 645 with 657 Buddhist books. He received a government grant and a large group of assistants to translate them into Chinese. By his death he had completed seventy-five translations. The essential work was the *Treatise in Thirty Verses on Consciousness-Only* (by Vasubandhu, in Sanskrit: *Vijñatimātratātrimśika*, in Chinese: *Wei-shih san-shih lun*). Hsüan-tsang's summary and systematization of all these works is the famous *Treatise on the Establishment of the Doctrine of Consciousness-Only* (*Ch'eng-wei-shih lun*).

For more see: Consciousness-Only, Buddhism in China (#4, The Consciousness-Only School).

HSÜN TZǓ (298-238 B.C.): The major rival of Mencius, Hsün Tzǔ was the key figure in the naturalistic wing of Confucianian philosophy. He revered Confucius for his learning rather than, as Mencius did, for his virtue. "Every corner of (his) room and each mat on (his) floor was filled with the culture of the kings and the customs of the perfect society." He also argued that the nature of man is evil. Good is the result of education and institutional pressures. Man is born bad and trained to be good.

Hsün Tzǔ (Hsün K'uang, or Hsün Ch'ing) was born in Chao (a state in the south of present Hopei and Shansi, approximately two hundred miles southwest of Peking). He was next heard from at the age of fifty, when he went to the academy of Chi-hsia at Ch'i (in Shantung province, east of Chao), which was *the* place for scholars to congregate at the time. He argued that they were living in a generation of "low scholars" who had no learning. The few who could think, such as Chuang Tzŭ (*q.v.*), appeared good at first glance, but upon more thought are seen to throw the customs into disorder. Rulers then abandoned the Way (*Tao*) and put their trust in magic and prayers and omens and luck. Hsün Tzŭ therefore lectured on the prosperity to come from putting Confucian ideas into practice, and the decay from Mo-ist ideas. He was soon recognized as the best scholar there. His eminence was guaranteed by the indescribable honor of being chosen the officer in charge of the offering of sacrificial wine. This happened not just once, but three times, which is even more than Harvard professors can say for themselves. However, there were those who coveted this honor, and soon they slandered Hsün Tzŭ. He left, and went to Ch'u. There he was appreciated. The Prince appointed him magistrate in Lan-ling (in Southern Shantung). When the Prince died (in 238), Hsün Tzŭ lost his job, remained there, died, and was buried in Lan-ling.

His students included Li Ssŭ, later the Prime Minister of Ch'in, whose advice enabled Ch'in Shih-huang to unify China into one empire (by 221 B.C.). Li Ssŭ was also directly responsible for the Burning of the Books (213). But, after all, if man is evil, as Hsün Tzŭ taught, students are evil too, and prime ministers as well. Han Fei Tzŭ (*q.v.*) was another one of his noted students. Hsün Tzŭ sharply attacked Mencius and his followers:

There were some who, in a general way, followed the early kings but did not know the fundamentals. . . . Their views were peculiar, contradictory, and without standards, dark and without illustrations, confined and without explanations. . . . The ignorant scholars of the world welcomed it, not knowing that it was false.

Mencius believed that human nature is originally good. Hsün Tzŭ said such a theory was mistaken. Rather, human nature is originally evil. Mankind must be trained to be good. As Hsün Tzŭ says in his book, the *Hsün Tzŭ*:

153

Without a teacher or precepts, then if a man is intelligent, he will certainly become a thief; if he is brave, he will certainly become a killer; if he has organizational ability, he will certainly cause disorder; if he has scientific ability, he will certainly become eccentric; if he has logical ability, he will certainly go far from the truth.

But with a teacher and precepts, if a man is intelligent, he will quickly become learned; if he is brave, he will quickly become awe-inspiring; if he has organizational ability he will quickly become perfect; if he has scientific ability, he will quickly arrive at all truth; if he has logical ability, he will quickly be able to determine the truth or falsity of all matters.

Therefore, the possession of a teacher and precepts is the greatest treasure a man can have. The lack of a teacher and of precepts is the greatest calamity a man can have.

"The nature of man is evil; his goodness is acquired training" (*Hsün-Tzŭ*, Ch. 23). Mencius, in a debate with Kao Tzu on human nature, had said that the fact that men are teachable shows that their original nature is good. Hsün Tzŭ says this is not true:

By nature man's eye can see and his ear can hear. But the clarity of vision is not outside his eye and the distinctness of hearing is not outside his ear. It is clear that clear vision and distinct hearing cannot be learned. . . . Now (following Mencius' line of reasoning), considering the nature of man, as soon as he is born, he would already have . . . lost and destroyed (his original nature, because he must be taught to be good, as Mencius admits). Thus, it is evident that the original nature of man is evil and his goodness is acquired. . . .

The sage-kings of antiquity, knowing that man's nature is evil, that it is partisan, corrupt, violent, disorderly, undisciplined, and rebellious, established the authority of rulers to govern the people, set forth clearly the rules of proper con-

154

duct and justice to reform them, instituted laws and government to rule them, and made punishment severe to warn them. Thus they caused the whole country to come to a state of good government and prosperity, and to harmonize with the good.

(—*Ibid.*, 23.)

The problem arises, for Hsün Tzŭ's system: if every man is born evil, what is the origin of good? He answers by arguing that man must have some kind of social organization:

Man is not as strong as an ox. He cannot run as fast as a horse. Yet the ox and horse are used by him. How is this? Because . . . when united, men have greater strength; having greater strength, they become powerful; being powerful, they can overcome other creatures.

(—*Ibid*, 10.)

It is society that distinguishes man from the beasts. It is the bounds of propriety that produce good, well-ordered society. The fact that beasts are male or female and have offspring is a fact of nature. The relationship between husband and wife, father and son, is a product, on the other hand, of culture. It is culture, not nature, that makes a man good.

Hsün Tzŭ also writes of the necessity for punishing crime: The origin of all punishment is the restraint of violence, the hatred of evil, and the warning against its future occurrence. That a murder should not die, or a man who injures another should not be punished, is favoring violence and being liberal to robbers, rather than hatred of evil.

(—*Ibid.*, 18.)

The argument had been raised against harsh punishments by some of Hsün Tzŭ's contemporaries:

The ancient benevolent rulers had no corporal punishment, but instead punished criminals by changing the clothing. Instead of kneeling on a line, there was wearing an inky turban; instead of cutting off the nose, there was wearing

155

straw fringes; instead of castration, there was cutting off the leather knee-pads; instead of cutting off the feet, there was wearing hemp sandals; instead of execution, there was wearing ochre-colored clothes without any hems—the ancient benevolent government was like this.

Hsün Tzŭ argues against this by saying:

Do you think such a government was benevolent? Men certainly did commit crimes! . . . There is no greater confusion than thinking that if a man has committed a crime, his punishments should be directly lightened, so that a murderer should not die, a man who has assaulted another should not be punished, so that for an extremely great crime the punishment should be extremely light—the ordinary man does not know that there is anything to dislike in such punishment! . . . Punishments by changing the clothing are dangerous; they are not born of the ancient benevolent government, but come from the confused and evil present.

(—*Ibid.*, 18.)

Hsün Tzŭ's advice for good government was:

Pay no attention to seniority, but advance the worthy and able. Dismiss the incompetent and incapable without delay. Put incorrigible ringleaders to death without waiting to compel them by laws. . . . Lewd people, gossips, crooks, people of perverted abilities, shirkers, and unreliable people, should be trained, given employment, and time to reform. Stimulate them by rewards. Warn them by punishments. If they are satisfied with employment, keep them. If they do not want to work, then deport them. Hire the handicapped. If they have ability, they should be given positions. . . . Those who are incorrigible should be put to death without mercy.

(—*Ibid.*, 9.)

Hsün Tzŭ wrote further:

It is said: "If you do not know a person, look at his friends. If you do not know a ruler, look at those to the right and left of him." Follow that, and it will be sufficient!

(—*Ibid.*, 22.)

If a person's will is cultivated, then he can be prouder than the rich and the honorable; if he has emphasized the right Way (*Tao*) and justicy (*Yi*), then he can despise kings and dukes; he can contemplate that which is within him and despise outer things. It is said: the superior man employs things; the small-minded man is the servant of things.

(—*Ibid.*, quoted in Wade Baskin (ed.), *Classics in Chinese Philosophy* (New York: Philosophical Library, 1972, p. 214.))

HUAI-NAN TZŬ (172-122 B.C.): Liu An, or Huai-nan Tzŭ (Prince of Huai-nan), the author (possibly) of the eclectic book of philosophy from the Han dynasty known by the name *Huai-nan Tzŭ*, was the fourth Taoist philosopher, following Lao Tzŭ, Yang Chu and Chuang Tzŭ. Huai-nan is a place in Kiangsu province, between Peking and Shanghai.

With thousands of scholars under his patronage, feeling the power of their loyalty, this grandson of the founder of the Han dynasty plotted rebellion. Scholars, however, do not generally stick together. The revolution failed. Finding himself in an embarrassing position, he abdicated by taking his own life, since he could not take the throne.

It was probably prior to dying that he wrote the *Huai-nan Tzŭ*, although scholars still dispute this. The book contains twenty-one chapters on metaphysics, astronomy, government, and military strategy. We may hope that his metaphysics is better than his military tactics. The approach taken to metaphysics and cosmogony is entirely rational.

While the book does not contain notably original thought, it did serve the purpose of maintaining Taoism in the face of the all-pervasive and triumphant Confucianism of the time. The book says:

The *Tao* covers Heaven and supports Earth. . . . There is no limit to its height, and its depth is unfathomable. It encloses Heaven and Earth and endows things [with their nature] before they have been formed. . . . Because of it, animals run and birds fly. Sun and moon shine and the planets revolve by it. Through it the unicorn emerges and the phoenix soars.

Those who are devoted to the unicorn and the phoenix will also be devoted to this book.

HUANG-LAO: A popular religious movement in ancient China (prior to the first century A.D.) named for Huang-ti, the legendary Yellow Emperor, and Lao Tzǔ. Combining Yin/Yang philosophy, with astrology, and divination, it completed the transformation of the philosophy of the time into occultism.

HUANG PO (800-850 A.D.): Below Vulture Peak, on Mount Huang Po in the modern province of Kiangsi (an inland area of South China located at the intersection of a line drawn south from Peking and northwest from Formosa), lived the great Zen Master, Hsi Yün (or T'uan Chi or, in Japanese, Ōbaku). He is variously said to have died in 848, 849, 850, and 855. His posthumous name, Huang Po, was taken from the mountain. Some Confucian scholars have nervously objected to his appropriation of the name of a mountain, but the mountain has not been heard to object, and, since it was done posthumously, no amount of complaint seems likely to rectify the matter. Emperor Hsüan Tsung bestowed on him the posthumous name of "Zen Master Who Destroys All Limitations." The mountain's name endured.

Zen (in China, Ch'an) Buddhism had split into two branches, the Northern, which taught that the process of Enlightenment is gradual, and the Southern, which taught that it was sudden. Huang Po, of the Southern school, was in the tradition of Hui Nêng (Wei Lang), the Sixth Partriarch. The Wordless Doctrine was passed through him to his successors, and Huang Po, having received it, transmitted it to I Hsüan, founder of the great Lin Chi (Rinzai) sect, which flourishes in Japan.

Well known for his paradoxical statements, designed to motivate students to recognize the truth, the *Huang Po Ch'uan Hsin Fa Yao*, a ninth-century Chinese Buddhist text translated by John Blofeld under the title of *The Zen Teachings of Huang Po on the Transmission of Mind* (1957), contains such passages and anecdotes as the following:

> Ordinary people indulge in conceptual thought based on what they see, hence they feel desire and hatred. To eliminate environmental phenomena, just put an end to your conceptual thinking. When this ceases, environmental phenomena are void; and when these are void, thought ceases. But if you try to eliminate environment without first putting a stop to conceptual thought, you will not succeed, but merely increase its power to disturb you. Thus all things are naught but Mind—intangible Mind; so what can you hope to attain? . . . Therefore the Buddha said: 'I truly obtained nothing from Enlightenment.' There is just a mysterious tacit understanding and no more.

The anti-intellectual quality of this approach is indicated by the following:

> The fruit of attaining the śramana (monk) stage is gained by putting an end to all anxiety; it does not come from book-learning.

One of the most puzzling passages in this work, according to Chinese scholars, is the one which follows. Keep in mind the fact that the same word can mean either doctrine or dharma:

> The fundamental doctrine of the dharma is that there are no dharmas, yet that this doctrine of no-dharma is itself a dharma; and now that the no-dharma doctrine has been transmitted, how can the doctrine of the dharma be a dharma?

This version is a famous pun, made possible by Mr. I. T. Pun, a noted Buddhist scholar in residence at Hong Kong some years ago.

Q: Assuming all this is so, what particular state is connoted by the word Bodhi (Enlightenment, or Supreme Wisdom)?

A: Bodhi is no state. The Buddha did not attain to it. Sentient beings do not lack it. It cannot be reached with the body nor sought with the mind. All sentient beings ARE ALREADY of one form with Bodhi.

Another interesting conversation is recorded:

Q: If the Buddha really dwells in matchless tranquility beyond the multiplicity of forms, how is it that his body yielded eighty-four pecks of relics?

A: If you really think like that, you are confusing the transitory relics with the real. . . .

Q: Then, why is it written: 'The Buddha-relics are ethereal and subtle; the golden ones are indestructible?' What does Your Reverence say to that?

A: If you harbour such beliefs, why call youreslf a student of Zen? Can you imagine bones in the Void? The minds of all the Buddhas are one with the Great Void. What bones do you expect to find there?

Q: But if I had actually seen some of these relics, what then?

A: You would have seen the products of your own wrong thinking.

At another time, a questioner asked him:

Q: What is the Buddha?

A: Your Mind is the Buddha. The Buddha is Mind. Mind and Buddha are indivisible. Therefore it is written: 'That which is Mind is the Buddha; if it is other than Mind, it is certainly other than Buddha.'

Then, with matchless humor, not understood by the serious Confucian scholars, Huang Po arranges (by beating him up) for one of his students to ask another monk (Ta-yü) the meaning of what had happened to him:

As soon as the Master heard this, he understood and said:

'After all, there is not much in Huang Po's Buddhism.'

Experiences like these, common in the Zen school, were the inspiration for the eight-century Buddhist layman P'ang Yün, who wrote in a hymn:

In carrying water and chopping wood,
Therein lies the wonderful *Tao*.

Huang Po believed that Buddha had taught three Vehicles of Truth:

1) the elementary teachings for the masses (this was the Hinayana);
2) the more mystical teachings for the middle group (this was the Mahayana); but
3) the strict Zen, for those who could take it!

HUANG TSUNG-HSI (1610-1695): A seventeenth-century Chinese philosopher who expressed ideas so liberal that two centuries later he was hailed as an early revolutionary, Huang Tsung-Hsi (T'ai-ch'ung, or Huang Li-Chou) was the Son of a Ming dynasty official who had crossed the clique of corrupt eunuchs who dominated the court. The father was executed when his son was sixteen. When he was eighteen, he came to the capital and exacted vengeance with his own hand. Huang Tsung-Hsi was a native of Yü-yao, a town in Chekiang province, about a hundred miles south of Shanghai.

The follower of Liu Tsung-Chou, he wrote a great compilation of Neo-Confucianism, the *Sung-Yüan Hsüeh-an* (*Biographical History of Confucianist Philosophers of the Sung and Yüan Dynasties*), as well as the *Ming-I Tai-Fang Lu* (*Treatise on Political Science*, written 1662, published 1673, and *Ming-ju Hsüeh-an* (*Lives and Works of Ming Scholars*, 1676).

He held the current monarchy in low esteem. However, when China was invaded by the Manchus, he joined the army and fought for the Mings. When the Manchus won, he retired to a life of study, teaching, and writing, and declined offers of appointment to public office.

He wrote that:

In ancient times, the people were the masters, and the kings the guests, and the object of the kings' labors was the people. Now it is the kings who are the masters and the people the guests, and there is not one corner of the earth where the people can live peacefully their own lives, all because of the ruler. . . .

Kings have thus become the great enemy of the people. For if there were no kings, people would be able to work for their own benefit and their own living. Alas! is this the purpose for which kings exist?

In ancient times, the people loved their kings like their father and compared them to Heaven. That was well deserved. Now the people regard their kings as their enemy and call them "that lonely person." That is well deserved, too. . . .

Could it be that (the rulers) truly believe that the whole world exists for the particular benefit of one person and one family in the heart of the Creator? . . .

It may be difficult to understand the proper functions of king and subject, but it should not be difficult to weigh the advantages and disadvantages between temporary glory and a lasting disaster. (—Huang Tsung-hsi, in Wade Baskin, *Classics in Chinese Philosophy*, 609 ff.)

HUI HAI (750-810): Student of two eminent Zen masters, Hui Hai wrote the dialogue *The Essential Gateway to Truth by Means of Instantaneous Awakening*. At the Great Cloud Monastery in Yüeh Chou, the Venerable Tâo Chih gave him the name "Ocean of Wisdom" (Hui Hai). In Kiangsi province, he entered the monastery of Ma Tsu. Ma called him the "Great Pearl," because his

162

original surname, Chu, sounds like "Pearl." The book that Ma liked includes the following section:

Q: What are the 'three methods of training (to be performed) at the same level,' and what is meant by 'performing them on the same level?'

A: They are: discipline, concentration, and wisdom.

Q: Please explain them one by one.

A: Discipline involves stainless purity (non-attachment and refusing to judge). Concentration involves the stilling of your minds so that you remain wholly unmoved by surrounding phenomena. Wisdom means that your stillness of mind is not disturbed by your giving any thought to that stillness, that your purity is unmarred by your entertaining any thought of purity and that, in the midst of all such pairs of opposites as good and evil, you are able to distinguish between them without being stained by them and, in this way, to reach the state of being perfectly at ease and free of all dependence. Furthermore, if you realize that discipline, concentration and wisdom are all alike in that their substance is intangible and that, hence, they are undivided and therefore one—that is what is meant by three methods of training performed at the same level.
(—in Baskin, *Classics in Chinese Philosophy*, pp. 430, 431.)

HUI-NENG (638-713): The sixth and last (Chinese) partriarch of Zen Buddhism, Hui-neng (in southern dialect, Wei-lang; in Japanese, Eno) was the traditional author of *The Platform Scripture (Liu-tsu t'an-ching*, also published as *The Sutra of Wei Lang*). It has been called the basic classic of Zen. The oldest known text of *The Platform Scripture* was discovered, like the Dead Sea Scrolls, in a Tun-huang cave in 1900, and taken to the British Museum in 1907. Another version of the text dates from 1291, the "Ming Canon" text.

Hui-neng's father, a native of Fan Yang, had been dismissed from his official post and banished to the status of a commoner at Sun Chow in Kwangtung (near Hong Kong). Soon afterward, he died, leaving the family poor and miserable. They moved to Canton, and made a living, such as it was, selling firewood. One day, leaving a shop, Hui-neng heard a man reciting the *Diamond Sutra* (*Ching-kang ching*, or *Vajracchedikā*, perhaps the most popular Buddhist scripture in China). He was so impressed that, after making arrangements for the support of his mother, he went to the monastery, where he met Hung-jen, the patriarch. At the Tung Monastery, in Hupei, Hui-neng was given the job of splitting firewood and pounding rice. When time came to choose a new patriarch, the monks (a thousand of them) were invited to submit a poem about enlightenment. Only one had nerve enough to apply, by writing his poem on the wall like graffiti, without signing it:

Our body is the tree of perfect wisdom,
And our mind a mirror bright.
Carefully we wipe it every hour,
And let no dust alight.

The patriarch said it was not good enough, and invited further entries. Hui-neng thereupon wrote on the wall:

There is no tree of perfect wisdom,
Nor stand of mirror bright.
Since all is nothing,
How can dust alight?

Hui-neng was selected by the patriarch to be his successor. But as he gave him the robe and bowl, he also gave him some advice: to get out of there, because the monks would be too jealous to leave him in peace. So he went back to the area of Canton, and made the temple of Fa-hsing into a strong center of Sudden Enlightenment doctrine.

He taught that meditation (*ting*) and insight (*hui*) were the same. Merely sitting motionless, in meditation, is not enough. Calmness is the lamp, but insight is the light.

Some monks were arguing about a flag, why it flapped in the breeze. The various theories were:

1) that the wind made it flap;
2) that it did not really flap, because both the wind and the flag are inanimate;
3) that the flapping is due to a combination of all the factors; or
4) that it is only the wind that moves.

Hui-neng said they were all wrong. It was not the wind, nor the flag, but their own minds that flapped!

Southern and Northern Schools differed in their concepts of mind. The Northern School held that the mind undisturbed is calmness and the senses undisturbed are wisdom. Thus:

The pure mind will arise after erroneous thoughts have been eliminated, and then from absolute quietude. The Southern School rejected those distinctions, holding that calmness and wisdom are both the same, and not two. In fact, not only the mind, but everything is unified. The mind of the Buddha is everywhere. Anything can be taken as the occasion for enlightenment.

When Hui-neng announced that he would die within a month:

The sad news moved Fat Hoi and other disciples to tears. Shin Wui, on the other hand, remained unperturbed. Commending him, the Patriarch said, "Young Master Shin Wui is the only one here who has attained that state of mind which sees no difference in good or evil, knows neither sorrow nor happiness, and is unmoved by praise or blame."

(—Wong Mou-Lam *The Sutra of Wei Lang*, 1944, p. 114.)

Hui-neng died without appointing any specific person as the successor, saying that enlightenment is available to all, and having his Buddha-robe and bowl placed in the gate of the Sokei temple, near Canton.

Under the vigorous challenge from the Southern School, the Northern School declined and vanished, despite imperial patronage. The Southern School then developed five branches during the Tang and Sung dynasties (eighth to thirteenth centuries): the Lin Chi (Japanese Rinzai), Tsao Tung (Sōtō), Yun Men (Ummon), Kuei Yang (Ikyo), and Fa Yen (Hogen). Of these, the Rinzai and the Sōtō became the most important.

HUI-YÜAN (334-416): A great scholar with wide knowledge of the Six (Confucian) Classics, Hui-yüan (or Chia) was a Taoist monk who founded the Pure Land School of Buddhism. Somewhat bewildered by this great variety of doctrines, those who listened to his lectures at the Mount Heng monastery (in northern Shansi province, west and south from Peking) began to raise objections against his theory of reality. When he explained how Chuang Tzu's ideas were similar to his, they were satisfied. Originally called the "White Lotus" religion, his followers hurriedly changed its name to "Pure Land" to avoid arrest when a secret political society also began calling itself "White Lotus." Evidently political authorities were more afraid of a white lotus than a pure land.

Hui-yüan wrote a treatise entitled, "A Monk does not Bow Down Before a King." The authorities did not object so long as Hui-yüan was content to confine the Pure Land to the Western Quarter of Heaven. After death, the ruler did not care what happened to his subjects.

HUNEIN IBN ISHAK (809-873): A Nestorian Christian born in Syria, Hunein wrote the *Sayings of the Philosophers*, presenting a Biased Plato and confusing Socrates with Diogenes. He also wrote an *Introduction into the Science of Medicine* and a Syriac-Arabic dictionary and grammar, distinguishing properly between the two languages.

HU SHIH (1891-1962): An influential philosopher in modern China, Hu Shih was educated at Cornell (agriculture) and Columbia (Ph.D. in philosophy), where John Dewey was his teacher. Attempting to introduce Pragmatism into China, he was a leading figure in the "Chinese Renaissance," or "New Tide." From 1917-1927, he was professor of philosophy and chairman of the department of English literature at National Peking University.

From 1928-1930, he was President of the China National Institute. From 1930-1937, he was Dean of the College of Arts, National Peking University, and from 1938-1942, Chancellor. From 1942-1945, he was Ambassador to the United States. Until his death, February 24, 1962, he was President of *Academia Sinicia*.

His major publications, in English, are:

The Development of the Logical Method in Ancient China (Shanghai: The Oriental Book Co., 1928); *The Chinese Renaissance* (Chicago: The University of Chicago Press, 1934).

In Chinese:

A History of Chinese Philosophy (1919); *History of Vernacular Literature*; The Philosophy of Tai Chen; *Collected Essays*; *Recent Essays on Learned Subjects*; and *Forty Years: An Autobiography*.

Hu said that mankind must dominate nature, so that Taoism was wrong in teaching us merely to enjoy it and to leave it alone. Furthermore, since liberty and individualism are to be highly valued, Confucianism was wrong in teaching subordination to rulers and authority figures, such as fathers. The point of departure for philosophy should be the study of life, thought only being an instrument: "To examine the facts attentively, to risk a hypothesis boldly, finally to strive to find the proofs." In judging beliefs, we must use the historical method, and call a theory good only if its practical results were good. Hu wrote:

The knowledge that mankind needs is not the way or principle which has an absolute existence, but the particular truths for here and now and for particular individuals. Absolute truth is imaginary, abstract, vague, without evidence, and cannot be demonstrated.

Perhaps absolute truth could not be demonstrated, but absolute politics certainly could.

167

I

IBN-HANBAL (800-855): Founder of the Hanbalite school of Moslem law, the most conservative of the schools, Ibn-Hanbal lived in Bagdad during the loose and merry days of Harun al Rashid, and was shocked by the loose living. Blaming the situation on loose thinking, Ibn-Hanbal became an uncompromising op-
-ponent of "opinion," insisting upon adherence to the literal words of the *Koran*, with only secondary reliance upon *Tradition* (*Hadith*, which is the recollection of Mohammed's words and deeds as attested to by various authorities). He was imprisoned, scourged, and put in chains for his stubbornness in refusing to deny the eternity of the *Koran*. Hanbalite rulings are generally followed today in Saudi Arabia.

IBN MASKAWAIH (960-1030): Known for his theory of Ethics, Abu Ali ibn Maskawaih was treasurer and friend of Sultan Adudaddaula. In his view, the soul is a simple, incorporeal substance which is conscious of its own existence. It possesses an inborn rational knowledge, independent of the senses, which supervises and regulates the senses, comparing and distinguishing the objects presented by sense-perception, and judging the true from the false.

Some men, he said—a very few—are born good and never become bad, since they are good by nature, and what is so by nature cannot change. Many men are bad by nature, and never become good. Others are neither good nor bad, but are turned so either by education or by society.

Ibn Maskawaih's intellectual enterprise was aimed at combining the insights of Aristotle, Plato, Galen, and Islamic Religious Law. He wanted an ethical system based upon broad cultural traditions, which would be free from the casuistry of the Moralists on the one hand and the extreme self-denial of the contemporary Sufis on the other.

I CHING: The ancient Chinese book of fortune, *I Ching* (pronounced yee jing), the *Book of Changes*, is said both to foresee future events and to allow a person to control them. Commentators say that if one approaches the book sincerely and intelligently, it is an infallible means for choosing good and avoiding evil. Not only does the book tell us what will happen, but what should happen, what we might do to bring it about or to avoid it. It makes us into architects of our own fate. The *I Ching* is one of the oldest books in the world, predating the Bible.

Confucius and Carl Jung are among the eminent people who have seriously consulted the *I Ching*. Massachusetts Institute of Technology has published a version of the text (*The Portable Dragon*, R.G.H. Siu, 1968), and *Scientific American* has run an article on it, remarking on the fact that Fu Hsi's sequence of the hexagrams corresponds to the binary numbers 0 through 63. Leibniz, who had invented the binary system, was startled to hear of this sequence from Father Bouvet, a Jesuit missionary to China. Martin Gardner points out that the powers of 2 turn up everywhere, so that it is not difficult to apply the 64 hexagrams to everything from crystal structures to the 64 moods of the classical syllogism.

Jung, in his famous preface to the Wilhelm-Baynes translation of the *I Ching*, says that the predictions and events which happen in accordance with the book's text are not related causally, in the scientific sense, but *a-causally*, in the metaphysical (Eastern) sense. That is, they are both part of a vast cosmic design which lies beyond the reach of natural science but within the reach of the unconscious mind of the individual. Engraved on the collective unconscious of mankind, Jung contends, are the archetypes, among which are the hexagrams and their meanings.

The hexagrams are figures with six lines, either solid (Yang) or broken (Yin), formed from the bottom up, by the process of throwing 3 coins or 50 yarrow stalks or 6 wands. Concentrating on the question you want answered, the coins are thrown (counting heads as 3 (the blank side of the old Chinese bronze coins), tails as 2 (the inscribed side, which gives the value of the coin), and the lines are formed. When the hexagram is formed, its decision and commentary are then read (for example, if hexagram number 8, "Unity,"):

The Decision: Unity. Good fortune. Let him re-examine himself by means of the oracle to see if he is virtuous, persistent, and firm in his aims. If so, there will be no error. Those who are hesitant will gradually follow; late-comers will encounter misfortune.

The Commentary reads:

Unity signifies good fortune through cooperation. In the hexagram we see inferiors (the broken lines) docilely following their superior (the unbroken fifth line). Good fortune is indicated, but a careful assessment of his capabilities is first needed if error is to be avoided. This done, those who now hesitate will gather round in support. Any who delay too long will not share in the general good fortune.

Other features of this method of divining are equally interesting. A "changing" line in the hexagram indicates that the interpretation of that line needs to be taken especially seriously. Then the new hexagram (with the changed line) needs to be read, and the two compared in the mind of the reader to discover their true meaning.

The *I Ching* may thus be said to function as the poor man's psychiatrist. Those who consult it regularly think of it as another person, giving personal interpretations to the problems faced in life.

Different versions of the *I Ching* vary in their translation, and if the words are too obscure it will be difficult to decide how they relate to the question asked. For example, Wilhelm's translation includes the following sentences: "Release yourself from your big toe!" and "The way of wood creates success," and "He dissolves his blood; Thus he keeps at a distance from injury."

John Blofeld has a translation of the *I Ching* (Dutton) which avoids the problems caused by Wilhelm's renderings. James Legge (Dover) also has a good translation, as does Douglas (Berkley).

Besides the book itself, the various Appendices (called the "Ten Wings") attached to the *I Ching* are famous in their own right, as attempts to explain philosophically the nature of the universe as connected with the formation of the trigrams and hexagrams. They are sometimes referred to under the materials on various Neo-Confucianists.

INDIAN PHILOSOPHY: "Alps over Alps" is the phrase used to describe Indian philosophy by Dr. R. D. Ranade of Nimbal in his book, *A Constructive Survey of Upanishadic Philosophy* (Bombay: Bharatiya Vidya Bhavan, 1926). Just as levels of reality are mentioned in Indian thought, levels of philosophies may be found in the key works of Indian thought. Each level comments on the preceding level. Layer upon layer has accumulated through the centuries. As mountain peaks tower over the plains, so do these grand generalizations of Indian thought tower over the harsh realities of practical life on the flat level of the Indian subcontinent. No intermediate stage seems to be offered between the universal and the individual. No partial success is studied. It is all or nothing, the Absolute or the famine. No stopping-place is permitted on the climb to the summit.

The primary sources of Indian philosophical thought are the *Vedas, Brahmanas* (including the *Aranyakas*), *Upanishads*, and epic poems, the *Mahābhārata* (which includes the *Bhagavad Gītā*) and the *Rāmāyaṇa*. A sense of timelessness pervades the pages of these ancient Indian books. Their focus is on the external. Historical features, being details, are not considered significant. This lack of historical reference is striking (McNeill makes this point in *A World History*). The historical and personal give way to the eternal and impersonal.

The Sanskrit language enhances this tendency. It typically expresses the individual in terms of an instance of the abstract universal. For example, the sentence "He grows old" must be translated into Sanskrit as "He goes to oldness."

I. THE VEDAS

The Vedas are held by orthodox Hindus to be divinely inspired. In fact, they are so sacred that the *Laws of Manu* forbade any man of low caste to hear or recite them under penalty of having his tongue cut out and molten metal poured into his ears. The word *Veda* means "knowledge," "word," or "wisdom," with similarities to the Greek word, *logos*.

There are four Vedas: the *Rig-Veda*, the *Sama-Veda*, the *Yajur-Veda*, and the *Atharva-Veda*.

The *Rig-Veda* (" *Veda* of Hymns") contains the hymns, prayers, and mantras of ancient Aryans, which were used in the worship of various gods. It is composed of ten books of composite authorship.

The *Sama-Veda* (" *Veda* of Music" or "Knowledge of Chants") is based on the *Rig-Veda*, only 75 (out of 1225) stanzas different. Used by priests who sang at the Soma sacrifice, it is similar in conception to the book of Psalms.

The *Yajur-Veda* (" *Veda* of Liturgy") is also based quite heavily on the *Rig-Veda*, but in addition contains the rituals telling how to perform the sacrifices correctly.

The *Atharva-Veda* ("Wisdom of Arthaven") is the latest of the four *Vedas*. Containing many magic charms and incantations, together with hymns and prayers similar to those in the *Rig-Veda*, it is a book of popular religion. A large number of *Upanishads* are included in this *Veda*.

The *Rig-Veda* contains passages such as this:

To the Waters
Forth from the middle of the flood the waters—their chief
    the sea—flow cleansing, never sleeping.
Indra, the bull, the thunderer, dug their channels: here
    let those waters, goddesses, protect me.

Waters which come from heaven, or those that wander dug
    from the earth, or flowing free by nature,

Bright, purifying, speeding to the ocean, here let those
    waters, goddesses, protect me.

Those amid whom goes Varuna the sovran, he who
    discriminates men's truth and falsehood—
Distilling meath, the bright, the purifying, here let those
    waters, goddesses, protect me.

They from whom Varuna the king, and Soma, and all the
    deities drink strength and vigour,
They into whom the universal Agni entered, here let those
    waters, goddesses, protect me.

II. THE *BRAHMANAS*

Poetry requires interpretation, and the process of explanation
and clarification begins with the next layer of vedic literature, the
Brahmanas.

They contain such passages as Manu's Escape from the flood
(in the *Satapatha-Brahmana*):

In the morning they brought to Manu water for washing,
just as now also they are wont to bring water for washing the
hands. When he was washing himself, a fish came into his
hands.

It spoke to him the word, "Rear me, I will save thee!"
"Wherefrom wilt thou save me?" "A flood will carry away all
these creatures: from that I will save thee!" "How am I to rear
thee?"

It said, "As long as we are small, there is great destruction
for us: fish devours fish. Thou wilt first keep me in a jar.
When I outgrow that, thou wilt dig a pit and keep me in it.
When I outgrow that, thou wilt take me down to the sea, for
then I shall be beyond destruction."

It soon became a large fish. Thereupon it said, "In such
and such a year that flood will come. Thou shalt then attend
to me (to my advice) by preparing a ship; and when the flood

173

has risen thou shalt enter into the ship, and I will save thee from it."

After he had reared it in this way, he took it down to the sea. And in the same year which the fish had indicated to him, he attended to the advice of the fish by preparing a ship; and when the flood had risen, he entered into the ship. The fish then swam up to him, and to its horn he tied the rope of the ship, and by that means he passed swiftly up to yonder northern mountain.

It then said, "I have saved thee. Fasten the ship to a tree; but let not the water cut thee off, whilst thou art on the mountain. As the water subsides, thou mayest gradually descend!" Accordingly he gradually descended, and hence that slope of the northern mountain is called "Manu's descent." The flood then swept away all these creatures, and Manu alone remained here.

In their course, the *Brahmanas* not only commented on the *Vedas* with a view to explaining their meaning, but often changed that meaning in the process. The personalities of separate gods decreased, and the skill of priests increased in general importance. The priests (Brahmans) began to argue in the *Brahmanas* that by performing the rituals properly, they could actually compel the Gods to grant whatever was demanded of them.

III. THE *UPANISHADS*

These extravagant claims to supremacy were resented by lower ranks of society, and this dissatisfaction set the stage for the development of the last level of Vedic literature, the *Upanishads*. *Upa-ni-shad* means to sit at the feet of a master, from *upa* (connected with the Latin *s-ub*), under, *ni* (found in English be-*neath*), and *sad*, to sit. It was not by obedience to priests nor observance of ceremonies that a man could become holy, but by withdrawal from daily life, by meditation, asceticism, and self-discipline. Thus, the *Upanishads* constituted a direct challenge to the authority of the priests. The priests met this threat by saying that

174

after raising a family and honoring them (the priests), it would be quite appropriate, toward the end of one's life, to pursue solitary ideals in forest retreats characteristic of the *Upanishads*.

Instead of seeking riches, health, and a long life, the wise man, according to the *Upanishads*, wants to escape the endless round of rebirth. By following the right path of discipline, he can transcend all the imperfections of existence, all its pain and sufferings.

An individual will follow either of two routes after death, according to the *Upanishads*. One is the way of *devayana* (the way of the gods), in which one enters the flame of cremation, passing into the day, then into the half-month while the moon waxes, into the six months while the sun goes north, into the world of the gods—the sun, the moon, the lightning-fire, and then entering, guided by a person of mind (*manasa*), into Brahman (or the world of Brahma), never returning to this world.

The second route, on the other hand, is followed by one who sacrifices and practices austerity, the way of *pitryana* (the way of the fathers), in which one enters into the smoke of cremation and thus into the night, then into the half-month while the moon decreases, into six months while the sun goes south, and from these into the world of the ancestors' spirits. From this, one goes into the moon, where he stays to become food for the gods. He then begins to descend into space and enters successively into the sky, air, rain, earth, and into food (such as rice and barley) where he becomes a spermatozoon, if he enters into the fire of a man, and then enters into a womb of a woman to be reborn.

One hundred and eight *Upanishads* are listed in the most complete editions (Nirnayasagar Press, Bombay), but there are a number of others, besides. Radhakrishnan and Moore (*A Sourcebook in Indian Philosophy*, Princeton, 1957) say there are over two hundred. The principal *Upanishads*, according to the Muktika canon, are thirteen. Arranged by R. D. Ranade into five roughly chronological groups, they are:

(1) *Brihadāraṇyaka* and *Chandogya*;
(2) *Īśā* and *Kena*;
(3) *Aitareya, Taittirīya,* and *Kaushītaki*;

175

(4) *Kaṭha, Muṇḍaka,* and *Śvetāśvatara;* and

(5) *Praśna, Maitri,* and *Māṇḍūkya.*

Some of the *Upanishads* are named after great sages featured in them, for example, Māṇḍūkya (who taught the four stages of consciousness: waking, dreaming, deep sleep, and the fourth state, *turiya,* which is alone real), Śvetāśvatara (who taught theism rather than Absolutism), Kauṣītaki (who taught that the breathing spirit was the prime mover of the universe), and Maitri (who distinguished between the changing, empirical ("elemental") self (*bhūtātman*) and the essential, unchanging, universal Self (*Ātman*)). Other *Upanishads* are named after the first word of the work, and so on.

The *Brihadāraṇyaka* ("Great Forest Book") *Upanishad* is perhaps the most famous of the Upanishads, and contains the following passages:

1. In the beginning nothing at all existed here. This [whole world] was enveloped by Death,—by Hunger. For what is death but hunger? And [Death] bethought himself: 'Would that I had a self!' He roamed around, offering praise; and from him, as he offered praise, water was born. And he said [to himself]: 'Yes, it was a joy (*ka*) to me to offer praise (*arc-*).' And this is what makes fire (*arka*) fire. And joy is the lot of him who understands that this is what makes fire fire.

2. Water too is *arka.* And the froth of the water was churned together and became the earth. And on this [earth] he wore himself out. And the heat and sap [generated] by him, worn out and consumed by fierce penances as he was, turned into fire.

3. He divided [him] self (*ātman*) into three parts: [one third was fire,] one third the sun, one third the wind. He too is the breath of life (*prāna*) threefold divided.

The east is his head. The north-east and south-east are his two arms. The west is his tail. The north-west and south-west are his two buttocks. The south and north are his flanks. The sky is his back, the atmosphere his belly, this [earth] his chest. Firmly is he based on the waters; and firmly is that man based who thus knows, wherever he may go.

4. [Then] he longed that a second self might be born to him; [and so he who is] Hunger and Death copulated with Speech by means of mind. What was the seed became the year; for there was no year before that. For so long did he bear him [within himself],—for a whole year; and after so long a time did he bring him forth. When he was born, [Death] opened his mouth [as if to swallow him]. '*Bāhn*,' said he, and that became speech.

(—I, ii)

In another part of this most famous of *Upanishads* we find the questions answered by Yājñavalkya, the great sage:

1. Then Vidagdha Sakalya questioned him, saying: 'How many gods are there, Yājñavalkya?'

He answered by this invocation:

'As many as are mentioned in the invocation in the "Hymn to All the gods,—three hundred and three and three thousand and three (=3306).'

'Yes (*om*),' said he, 'but how many gods are there really, Yājñavalkya?'

'Thirty-three.'

'Yes,' he said, 'but how many gods are there really, Yājñavalkya?'

'Six.'

'Yes,' he said, 'but how many gods are there really, Yājñavalkya?'

'Three.'

'Yes,' he said, 'but how many gods are there really, Yājñavalkya?"

'Two.'

'Yes,' he said, 'but how many gods are there really, Yājñavalkya?"

'One and a half.'

'Yes,' he said, 'but how many gods are there really, Yājñavalkya?"

177

'One."

'Yes,' he said, 'but which are those three hundred and three and those three thousand and three?'

2. [Yājñavalkya] said: 'These are only their attributes of majesty. There are only thirty-three gods.'

'Which are those thirty-three?'

'The eight Vasus, the eleven Rudras, the twelve Ādityas. That makes thirty-one. Indra and Prajāpati make thirty-three.'

3. 'Which are the Vasus?'

'Fire, earth, wind, atmosphere, sun, sky, moon and stars. These are the Vasus. For to these all wealth (*vasu*) is entrusted. That is why they are [called] Vasus.'

4. 'Which are the Rudras?'

'The ten breaths in man (*puruṣa*), and the eleventh is the self. When they depart this mortal body, they make [men] weep; and because they make them weep (*rud-*), they are [called] Rudras.'

5. 'Which are the Ādityas?'

'The twelve months of the year are the Ādityas, for they carry off everything, though going on [themselves]; and because they carry off (*ada-*) everything, though going on (*yanti*) [themselves], they are [called] Ādityas.'

6. 'Which is Indra? Which Prajāpati?'

'Indra is thunder, Prajāpati the sacrifice.'

'Which is thunder?'

'The thunderbolt.'

'Which is the sacrifice?'

'Cattle.'

7. 'Which are the six?'

'Fire, earth, wind, atmosphere, sun and sky. These are the six. These six are everything.

8. 'Which are the three gods?'

'These three worlds, for all these gods are in them.'

'Which are the two gods?'

'Food and the breath of life.'

'Which is the one and a half?'

'The purifying [wind].'

9. 'It has been asked: "Since the purifying [wind] appears to be one, how can it be [called] one and a half?"'

'Because everything grows to maturity (*adhyārdhnot*) in it, it is [called] one and a half (*adhyardha*).'

'Which is the one God?'

'The breath of life, and that is Brahman, the beyond. So have [we] been taught.'

(—III, ix)

The *Upanishads, Brahmanas,* and *Vedas* proper are all recognized by orthodox Hindus as *shruti*, or revealed truth. By way of contrast, the epic poems, the *Mahābhārata* and *Rāmāyaṇa*, together with the *Laws* of Manu and the eighteen *Puranas*, are called *smriti*, not revealed but "remembered" truth (Günter Lanczkowski, *Heilige Schriften*, Stuttgart: W. Kohlhammer Verlag, 1956, p. 84.). The Vedic literature, according to one school of thought (the Nyaiyayikas), was composed by God (*paurusheya*). According to another school (the Mimāṁsakas), the *Vedas* and *Upanishads* were not composed by God (*apaurusheya*) nor by man, but rather existed from all eternity in the form of sounds in which they have come down to us. Therefore the sounds of the words of the *Vedas* have special importance, providing a direct connection with the source of the universe.

IV. THE EPICS

The *Rāmāyaṇa* was written by the poet Valmiki, the earliest poet known to classical Sanskrit literature and the pattern for all such poets following. It is dated (by Zimmer) between 400 B.C. and 200 A.D., in its present form, but its present form is greatly expanded from the original, including many rewrites of the poems or incidents of the epic, a sort of anthology of Indian poets added to by whoever was copying the manuscript over again.

The *Rāmāyaṇa*, the Epic of Rama, Prince of India, deals with the conflicts between Aryans and the native Indian population. The hero of the epic is Sri Ramachandra, whose conduct makes him the best example of a dutiful son, ideal husband, and king. Lakshmana is an ideal brother, who shares the fortunes of his eldest brother in city and forest, joy and distress. Ravana and Vali are two who seem to prosper despite their evil deeds. Sita is the beautiful and memorable wife, devoted to her lord in thought, word, and deed, whether in her own palace or in the enemy's camp. The *Rāmāyaṇa* is used as a text-book of morals for young people to "inspire them to higher and nobler ideals of conduct and character" (P.P.S. Sastri).

The *Mahābhārata* (including the *Bhagavad Gītā*) was written by a poet named Vyasa. It is dated (Zimmer) between 400 B.C. and 400 A.D., in its present form (Chandradhar Sharma dates it between "500 B.C. and 0;" Noss says the *Bhagavad Gītā* was added to the *Mahābhārata* around 300 A.D.). It tells the story of a great battle between the five Pandav princes and their hundred evil cousins, the Kurus. In the midst of the battle, an old warrior is wounded. His dying words are expanded into sermons to his descendants. By the time this process was completed, by the additions of generations of scribes, the epic contained large sections of history, philosophy, law, and religious codes. It is a sort of poem plus an encyclopedia of the times. It is now eight times as long as the *Iliad* and *Odyssey* combined. The effect, as Broomell remarks, of reading some parts is as if we opened the Bible and read that Moses took leave of the Israelites, going up Mount Nebo to die, reciting the complete Code of Motor Vehicles on the way. "If you do not find it in the Mahābhārata," Indians say, "you will not find it in the world."

The *Laws of Manu* (*Manu Shastra*), which also dates from this period, is the most famous of the *Dharma-Shastras*, Law Books, or treatises on justice and righteousness. Other *Shastras* include the *Artha Shastra* of Kautilya (the Prime Minister of the Magadha empire) on economics and politics, and the *Kama Shastra* (or *Kama Sūtra*) on sex and pleasure. Manu was supposed to be the son of Brahma, and to have preserved the ancient Vedas from destruction in the Flood. Some of the statutes from the *Laws of Manu* are:

118. In self should one behold the All, being and not-being, with mind intent; for beholding in self the All one does not turn his mind to wrong.

180

119. Self alone (are) all divinities; the All is founded in self, for self begets the chain of action in (all) these incorporate (creatures).

(—XII)

58. Ignobility, coarseness, savageness, laziness, reveal here among men a man of impure origin.

59. Whether he assume the father's or the mother's character, or that of both, the base-born man never disguises his true nature. . . .

63. Not to commit corporal injury, (to speak) the truth, not to steal, to be pure, to restrain the senses, this condensed rule of duty Manu declared for the four castes.

(—X)

77. Now one man (alone) may be a witness, (if) free from covetousness; but not (even) several women, although (they may be) pure, on account of the lack of reliableness of woman's mind; and also other men who are involved in sins (may not be witnesses).

78. Only what (the witnesses) declare of their own accord is to be accepted as having bearing on the case; if, however, they declare anything other (than this), that does not affect the consideration of justice.

79. When the witnesses are collected together in the court in the presence of the plaintiff and defendant, the judge should call upon them to speak, kindly addressing (them) in the following manner:

80. Whatever you know has been done in this affair by one or the other of these two parties, declare it all in accordance with the truth, as it is here your (duty) to give testimony.

81. A witness who in testifying speaks the truth reaches

(hereafter) the worlds where all is plenty, and (even) in this world obtains the highest fame. This declaration (of truth) is honoured by Brahmā.

82. One who in testifying speaks an untruth is, all unwilling, bound fast by the cords of Varuṇa till a hundred births are passed. Therefore one should declare true testimony. . . .

84. For self alone is the witness for self, and self is likewise the refuge of self. Despise not, therefore, (your) own self, the highest witness of men.

85. Verily the wicked think, "No one sees us," but the gods are looking at them, and also their man within.

(—VIII)

55. Women are to be honoured and adorned by fathers and brothers, by husbands, as also by brothers-in-law, who desire much prosperity.

56. Where women are honoured, there the gods rejoice; but where they are not honoured, there all rites are fruitless.

(—III)

148. In her childhood (a girl) should be under the will of her father; in (her) youth, of (her) husband; her husband being dead, of her sons; a woman should never enjoy her own will. . . .

150. She must always be cheerful and clever in household business, with the furniture well cleaned, and with not a free hand in expenditure.

(—V)

52. The intelligence of one who pisses against fire, against

the sun, against the moon, against water, against the twice-born, against a cow, and against wind, perishes. . . .

57. One should not sleep alone in an empty house, nor awaken a sleeper, nor talk with a woman in her courses, nor go to a sacrifice (when) not invited. . . .

114. The day of conjunction destroys the Guru, the fourteenth destroys the pupil; the eighth and full moon day (destroy) the Veda. Therefore one should avoid those (days).

115. A twice-born man should not recite during a dust shower, (or) redness of the quarters (of the horizon); so when a jackal howls, or dogs, asses, and camels bray, and in a company. . . .

118. When a village is invaded by robbers, and in a tumult caused by fire, and during all portents, one should know that recital is to be adjourned. . . .

260. A Brahman living by this conduct, who knows the Veda (and) treatises, freed from sin, is ever glorified in the Brahma world.

(—IV)

According to Manu, there are four ways of determining right and wrong: the revealed truth of the *Vedas*, the remembered truth (*smriti*) of the epics and other similar writings, good conduct (*ācāra*), and the voice of conscience. The first three provide social order, and the last social progress.

Other literature from the period, the greatest drama of India was by Kalidasa, *Śakuntalá* (or *Śakoontalá*), written a century and a half before the Christian Era.

Śakoontalá was the daughter of a nymph by a mortal father. In the *Śakoontalá*, the story is diversified and the interest well sustained by a chain of stirring incidents. The first link of the chain, however, does not commence until the Fourth Act, when the union of the heroine with King Dushyanta and her acceptance of the marriage ring as a token of recognition take place. Then follows the King's departure and temporary desertion of his bride; the curse pronounced on Śakoontalá by the choleric Sage; the monarch's consequent loss of memory; the bride's journey to the palace of her husband; the mysterious disappearance of the ring; the public repudiation of Sakoontalá; her miraculous assumption to a heavenly retreat; the unexpected discovery of the ring by a poor fisherman; the King's agony on recovering his recollection; his aërial flight in the car of Indra; his strange meeting with the child in the groves of Kaśyapa; the boy's battle with the young lion; the search for the amulet, by which the King is proved to be his father; the return of Śakoontalá, and the happy re-union of the lovers.

The play ends with these words by the King:
What other can I desire? If, however, you permit me to form another wish, I would humbly beg that the saying of the sage Bharata be fulfilled:

May kings reign only for their subjects' good!
May the divine Saraswati, the source
Of speech, and goddess of dramatic art,
Be ever honoured by the great and wise!
And may the purple self-existent god,
Whose vital Energy pervades all space,
From future transmigrations save my soul!

V. THE *SŪTRA* PERIOD

Written between 600 and 200 B.C., the *Sūtras* ("Strings") are aphorisms written by authors who prized brevity. It was said that an author rejoiced as much in the economizing of half a short vowel as in the birth of a son. The *Sūtras* were either orthodox or heretical (*nastika*, denier, nihilist). The difference was whether the author agreed with the authority of the Vedas. The Buddhist (*q.v.*), Jain (*q.v.*), and Cārvāka (*q.v.*) *Sūtras* were called *nastika* because they did not justify their theories by quoting the Vedas or by showing that they were in harmony with them.

184

Four *Upa-Vedas* were drawn from the four Vedas: one on medicine from the *Rig-Veda*; one on music from the *Sama-Veda*; one on warfare from the *Yajur-Veda*; and one on sixty-four mechanical arts from the *Atharva-Veda*. All the *Upa-Vedas* are now lost.

Six *Vedangas*, or "limbs of the Veda," were also produced, to develop the six sciences needed for the interpretation of the sacred books: first, pronunciation; second, grammar; third, prosody; fourth, explanation of difficult words or phrases; fifth, religious ceremonial; and sixth, astrology.

Four *Upangas*, or "additional limbs" were added: history (the *Purana*), logic (the *Nyāya*), ethics (the *Mīmāṁsā*), and law (the *Dharma-Shastra*).

Six schools of orthodox thought developed, each writing its own *Sutras*, preserving its own edition of the Vedas, and producing scholars who wrote commentaries on this body of literature.

VI. THE PERIOD OF THE GREAT COMMENTARIES

The six *darśanas*, or "aspects (of the truth)," the great accepted systems of Indian thought, are Nyāya, Vaiśeṣika, Sāṁkhya, Yoga, Mīmāṁsā, and Vedānta. The six systems agree on the authority of the Veda, intuition, and inference. Reason is subordinated to intuition. There is some kind of Super-consciousness above the self-consciousness of an individual. Any glimpse of it gives us an expanded understanding. The spirit is more important than "mere logic" (Radhakrishnan's phrase).

All six systems assume four things:

(1) the Vedas are inspired;

(2) reason is a less reliable way to know reality than the direct intuition of an individual who has been properly prepared by self-denial and years of obedient study;

(3) the purpose of knowledge is not to control the world but to attain release from it; and

(4) the goal of thought is to find freedom from frustration by extinguishing desire.

There is an objective standard of reality and truth as opposed to the (Buddhist) view that there is merely an unstable flux.

Nyāya (*q.v.*) is an intellectual system, providing an analytic, logical method for investigating the doctrines of the Vedas. Later Nyāya was to argue that a Supreme Soul was the seat of eternal knowledge, creating and providentially maintaining the universe:

The earth must have had a maker, because it is an effect, like a jar. . . . The world depends upon some being who wills to keep it from falling.

(—Udayanâchārya, *Kusumānjali*, 1200.)

Nyāya offers a scheme of saving knowledge, salvation through attendance at logic classes. As an individual rises higher in intellectual understanding, the soul becomes indifferent and is no longer disturbed by the fruits of past sins. The highest state, freedom from the pain of rebirth, can be reached only through death, whereupon presumably one can really become proficient at logic.

Vaisheshika (*q.v.*) is a naturalistic system, based on "distinctions" and "atoms" (*anu*, in Sanskrit, meaning the smallest possible division of reality). The importance of knowing true distinctions is illustrated by the example of the post and the thief. If we are walking in the twilight and we see a tall object in front of us, we do not know whether it is a post or a thief. Because we are uncertain, we are afraid. If we were able to distinguish one from the other, we would not feel fear from a false cause.

Sāṁkhya (*q.v.*), probably the most ancient philosophical system in the world, is notable for its dualism of spirit (*purusha*) and matter (*prakriti*). The observable world of nature (*prakriti*) is not created, but unfolds or evolves into intelligence and individual things, in various aspects. Over against this entire world of nature is a kind of "anti-nature," or spirit. The arguments advanced for the existence of spirit include the considerations that nature is an ordered sequence, with each part serving the needs of some higher organism, that there is no infinite regress, that some principle of intelligence must be directing the operation of the world, that every experience is experienced, the world as a whole

186

experienced by the infinite spirit, and that the universal desire for transcendence indicates that it cannot be a vain desire.

Besides these arguments, the testimony of those who have transcended the world of practical action and material reality is taken as evidence that there is a world of transcendental experience.

Freedom is the result of correct understanding, making the proper kinds of discrimination with one's mind, developing one's true inner being. Freedom does not depend upon external circumstances, but on inner knowledge.

No reason is given in Sāṁkhya for why free spirits were originally entangled in the bonds of ignorance.

It has been said with justification that Sāṁkhya provides the philosophical foundation for Eastern culture and the key to Oriental symbolism. It is without doubt one of the most important Asian philosophies.

Sāṁkhya is typically merged with Yoga. In India the two are regarded as twins, two aspects of a single discipline. Sāṁkhya provides the theoretical basis of human nature, whereas Yoga provides the method for release, "isolation-integration." Both believe in a hierarchy of principles.

Yoga (q.v.) is the system which uses philosophical concepts from Sāṁkhya, adding a method of meditation for the purpose of freeing individuals from pain and enabling them to attain union with the universal soul. Yoga is said to give its devotees knowledge of the future and the unseen world. The practice of Yoga enhances the powers and sensibilities of man. These are the *siddhis*, or miraculous powers. The yogin may know his previous existences, and the mental states of other persons. Patanjali says the yogin acquires the ability to make himself invisible. One can gain the power of knowing the moment one is to die. By practicing *samyama* (the last three stages of yogic technique, concentration, meditation, and trance contemplation) at the moon, one may gain knowledge of the solar system. Whatever the yogin desires to know, he should perform *samyama* in respect to that object.

Yet the yogin is not to be content with a mere mastery over nature, for that is only partial and provisional. Nor is the yogin to be satisfied with reaching a "divine condition," for divinity brings its own temptations, celestial women, medicine which will conquer old age and death, and supernatural sight and hearing. These things are "desirable only for the ignorant." The true yogin is to press on beyond heaven toward his final goal, complete freedom.

Yoga aims at emancipating an individual from his human condition, so that he can realize the unconditioned. The method of yoga is physiological, mental, or mystical. It is opposed to normal social life, prescribing absolute solitude and chastity. As against moving freely and breathing with irregularity, yoga recommends an immobile posture and dreams of holding one's breath indefinitely. Yoga recommends, in essence, that we do the opposite of what human nature would have us do.

Mīmāṁsā (q.v.) is the system of thought which aimed at a correct interpretation of the Vedas, particularly the earlier parts of the Vedas, dealing with ritual and ethical prescriptions. The Commandments in the Vedas are understood to be absolute, not limited by time or circumstance. The words of the Vedas are records of transcendental experience, metaphysical reality, above any physical reality or mental reasoning. The words, therefore, are eternal. They give access to the fundamental sounds of the universe. The Veda, in this sense, never had an author, not even God. In fact, when the proper sacrifices are performed in obedience to the commands of the Veda, they support the gods. No detail of Vedic religion, in the view of Mīmāṁsā, requires God's existence or assistance. The moral law was not established by God, but is part of the structure of the universe. Karma works automatically to exact retribution for wrong-doing. By determining the literal meaning of the Vedas and Brahmanas, and obeying them, one will certainly obtain release from suffering. The Upanishads, being philosophical in character, are unnecessary.

The doctrine of God was later smuggled into the system, and later writers merged Mīmāṁsā with Vedānta.

Vedānta (q.v.) is the last and in many ways most notable of the orthodox schools of Indian philosophy. Concentrating on the Upanishads, Vedānta attempts to justify the concepts of the Vedas in a consistent, systematic, philosophic manner. The dualism of Sāmkhya, with both Self and non-Self distinct, eternally real and separate, is rejected in favor of monism, the idea that there is only one basic reality. Similarly, the Nyāya and Vaisheshika theories that the world is real and pluralistic, composed of different atoms, also came in for criticism. Rather, according to Shankara, the great Vedānta scholar, the reality of Brahman is one. There is no other reality. At the level of Brahman, any multiplicity is non-existent. However, the world itself is neither real nor unreal. As long as we think of the world as real, it is real. But when we think of Brahman, everything else sinks into unreality. This is the theory of *Advaita*, Non-Dualism.

In contemporary times, Sri Ramakrishna (1836-1886) and Swami Vivekananda have spread Vedānta to the West. A large number of Vedānta societies have been formed, periodic lectures given, and opportunities for study provided.

VII. THE MODERN PERIOD

The two principal tasks of modern Indian philosophy have been (1) to come to terms with Western thought, and (2) to appreciate and export its own heritage.

Because the West was a political intruder in India, coming to terms with the West meant in large part coming to terms with Western politics. Gandhi (*q.v.*) succeeded in appropriating the Western political ideals of independence, freedom and equality, and combined them with ideals which were internal to Indian culture. This new synthesis was then turned against the British Colonial masters in such a way as to immobilize and at last expel them from the sub-continent.

The ideals which were internal to Indian culture were *ahimsa* and *satyagraha*, non-violence and soul-power. The press could not highlight the cruelties and barbarities committed by Gandhi's freedom fighters in India, because there were none. The resistance was completely non-violent. The colonialists were the ones who, both externally and internally, appeared brutal and unreasonable. Neither the press nor their own consciences could rest easy. The Indians supported non-injury as a tactic with all the depth of hundreds of centuries, sympathetic chords from the Vedas, from Jaina, and the other aspects of Indian thought.

Soul-power, *Satyagraha*, became a sort of description of the organizational success enjoyed by Gandhi and his followers as they applied political pressure. Soul-power was the reflection of the Indian preference for spiritual over material. As Gandhi renounced material possessions, there was nothing else the British could take away from him except his life, and he was prepared to lay that down.

The chief methods of resistance used by Gandhi and his followers were the rent-strike, business holiday, obstruction of traffic by lying down in the street, and the hunger-strike, or "fast unto death."

Empirical science was another feature of Western thought with which Indian thinkers needed to come to terms. Several Indian scientists have distinguished themselves in research, especially Dr. Yellapragada Subba Row (1896-1948), a high-caste Brahmin who studied at London University's School of Tropical Medicine and at Harvard and became research director at Lederle Laboratories until his death. Subba Row's research contributed to the development of aureomycin and other antibiotics. Whenever an experiment would fail, he would say:

Well, we know that doesn't work.

We will try something else.

Just remember, failure is not of God, but of man.

Subba Row was motivated by the desire to find cures for the diseases of India. He said:

Time is precious, and not enough of it is allowed to us.
Today people are dying, tomorrow people suffer and die.
We must find relief and help to save people from being devoured by death.

Resurgent pride in the Hindu heritage was encouraged by Mme Helena Blavatsky. Founder of the Theosophical Society, she came to India in 1877 and travelled widely telling her audiences that India possesses the pure Ancient Wisdom which had grown corrupt and vanished from the West. The Theosophical

Society may be interpreted as the first neo-Hindu organization. Its second leader, Mrs. Annie Besant, continued its important role in the Hindu revival.

Śri Aurobindo (Aravinda Ghose) (*q.v.*) was one of the most notable contemporary Indian philosophers. He taught a Vedānta which is largely the same as that of Shankara. Śri Aurobindo finds room in his system of thought for evolution, in a manner similar to the French philosopher, Bergson.

Sarvepalli Radhakrishnan is probably the greatest modern authority on Indian philosophy, and attempts to interpret ancient Hindu doctrines in terms compatible with twentieth-century thought.

The philosophy of religion, according to Radhakrishnan, is "religion come to an understanding of itself." The problems of religion, he argues, exist only for one who has first had the religious experience. Whether religious experience belongs to reality or *maya* he does not make clear.

Radhakrishnan goes on to assert that reason affirms God only as a possibility, whereas religion affirms God as a fact. All the world religions owe their inspiration to the personal insights of their prophetic founders. Hinduism, however, in its pure form, does not rely to the same degree upon authority as do the other religions. The explanation for this is that experience is the soul of religion. Reliance upon experience seems to provide a sort of instant reality. Expression of religion is the "body" through which it fulfills its destiny. Theology, in Radhakrishnan's view, is a sort of secondary mechanism through which experience may be explained. When, however, the explanations and dogmas become doubtful, we must be called back to experience. Religion begins and ends in experience.

Some recent criticisms of Indian philosophy have been raised by Arthur C. Danto (*Mysticism and Morality: Oriental Thought and Moral Philosophy*, New York: Basic Books, 1972), who contends with Max Weber that Indian philosophy has failed to establish a universally valid system of ethics. The Indian compartmentalization of mankind into castes also compartmentalized ethics. There is no possibility, therefore, of fraternizing between castes, which are really different species. The toleration which results from this ethical system is, in Danto's opinion, the same kind of toleration we allow between man and animal, tolerating differences in animal conduct because we see no possibility of changing animal behavior.

Caste behavior, Danto holds, is the most significant feature in Indian ethical theory. This prevents Indian thought, in Danto's view, from being completely adequate.

The most spectacular form in which Indian philosophy is being presented to the West is, without doubt, Transcendental Meditation, TM. Maharishi Mahesh Yogi, an ascetic Hindu monk from the Himalayas, recommends a method of physical and spiritual exercises designed for self-exploration, which can lead to relaxation and regeneration, joy, serenity and peace. He writes:

> Life need not be the painful struggle it is commonly represented to be. We are meant to be happy, and here is a way for everybody; a way which involves no austere discipline, no break with normal life and tradition, and which gives fuller and deeper meaning to all religions.
>
> (—*Transcendental Meditation*, New
> York: New American Library, 1963.)

Maharishi's Spiritual Regeneration Movement has its headquarters at Rishikesh on the Ganges River in the foot of the Himalayas. The movement trains meditation guides who are able to lead those interested in learning the methods of TM. Students are promised freedom from the anxieties and failures of life as they learn how to deal with mental tension and learn the relaxation response. The Maharishi believes that the art of living is the ability to supplement and reinforce individual life with the power of the absolute cosmic Being.

The testimonials given for TM by show-business personalities and the presence of several TM books on the best-seller list have led to its great popularity in the West.

TM promises to combine wisdom from the East with Western scientific knowledge about medicine, the percentage of carbon dioxide in the body, and its relation to freedom from stress.

192

Indian philosophy, which, a generation ago, was generally considered to be a parochial matter of interest primarily to Indologists, is now more widely available for adoption, adaptation, and criticism. In the sophisticated version of Radhakrishnan, the popular version of the Maharishi, or the devotional version of Hare Krishna, the insights of Indian thought are now available to everyone.

ĪSHVARAKṚṢNA (390-450): The author of the oldest surviving text of the Sāṁkhya (*q.v.*) school of orthodox Hindu philosophy, the *Samkhya-Karika*, Īshvara Krishna provides a commentary on Kapila and the older works of the school.

ITŌ JINSAI (1627-1705): A Japanese Confucian scholar of the Tokugawa Shogunate, Itō taught that the real world is nothing but change and action. In itself, action is good. The *Dōjimon* (*Children's Questions*) reads:

> Between heaven and earth there is only one reason: motion without stillness, good without evil. Stillness is the end of motion, while evil is the change of good; and good is a kind of life, while evil is a kind of death. It is not that these two opposites are generated together, but they are all one with life.

(—quoted in Hajime Nakamura,
Ways of Thinking of Eastern Peoples, 355.)

Criticizing the nihilism of Lao Tzŭ, Itō remarks:
Lao Tzŭ thinks that everything emerges out of nothing. But heaven and earth cover all from time immemorial. . . . Things inherit and ferment one another, and things go on living endlessly. How can one see what is called emptiness?

(—*Gomōjigi, Gloss on the Mencius*,
I, 15)

He was impressed by the phrase in the *I Ching*:
The great virtue of heaven and earth is called life.

Itō was a monist, repudiating any dualism of mind and matter, holding that matter is the first principle of all existence.

J

JAIMINI (430-370 B.C.): The founder of the Mīmāṁsā school of Indian thought, Jaimini was the author of the *Mīmāṁsā Sūtra* (*ca.* 400 B.C.), admitting the reality of the Vedic deities, to whom sacrifices are offered, but not arguing for the existence of a supreme deity.

The dates of Jaimini are very much in question. Tradition says he was a pupil of Bādarāyana, founder of the Vedānta system, but Bādarāyana's dates are not known with any certainty, either. Radhakrishnan dates the *Mīmāṁsā Sūtra* around 400 B.C. Bernard says the style of his writings places him between 600 and 200 B.C. Zimmer (and Campbell) place him between 200 and 450 A.D. Since the Mīmāṁsā school was flourishing about 300 B.C., it seemed reasonable to place its founder before that time.

Jaimini's main interest was to deny impious doctrines by various philosophers. He believed that reason is not able to solve the problems of metaphysics or theology. Reason is nothing more than a slave to desire. Emotions cloud our reason. We do not discover truth by thought, we merely rationalize our own pride and sensuality. We believe what we choose, and merely invent reasons for it afterwards. The way to wisdom and peace does not lie through logic, but rather through the acceptance of tradition and the careful observance of the rituals prescribed in the sacred scriptures.

The question could be asked of Jaimini, no doubt asked by an impious philosopher: "How do you *know* that knowledge does not

194

produce truth? Is it true that you know that knowledge does not lead to the truth?"

JAINISM: A heterodox system of Indian thought, Jainism emphasizes the absolute necessity of non-violence, and takes elaborate precautions to avoid accidental injuring of any living creature, including insects.

During the first century A.D., Jainism split into two sects, "White-clad" (*Shvetambara*) and "Sky-clad (*Digambara*), disputing what kind of clothes monks should wear. The former held white clothes were necessary and the latter held that nothing was, on the grounds that the only proper way to express complete renunciation of worldly values was to go nude. The former allowed women to enter the monastic order, evidently believing that such a liberal attitude could be justified as long as they kept their clothes on. The latter did not admit women, believing, with their founder, that women are "the greatest temptation in the world" and "the cause of all sinful acts." The only hope women have in winning salvation is to be reborn as men.

One of the vows of renunciation which a Jain ascetic (called a Nirgrantha, "naked one") takes is:

> I renounce all attachments,
> whether to little or much,
> small or great, living or
> non-living things; neither
> shall I form such attach-
> ments myself, nor cause
> others to do so, nor con-
> sent to their doing so.

There are about two million practicing Jainists in the world today, living mainly in the Bombay area, where their emphasis upon the renunciation of the world made a deep impression upon Gandhi in his early life.

At Mysore, once every twelve years, a fifty-seven-foot sacred statue which stands with its head against a cliff is annointed from the top by pouring a thousand pots of milk, curd, and sandal paste. At this sign of devotion, Jaina faithful shout their approval.

Founded by Mahavira ("Great Man") around the time of the Buddha, Jainism's chief source-books are the sacred canon (*Siddhānta* or *Agama*), the *Essence of Exposition* (*Pravacanasāra*) of Kundakunda, and the *Aphorisms Penetrating to Fundamental Principles* (*Tattvārthādhigamasūtra*) of Umāsvāti. The sacred books of the Jainas are available in an eleven-volume English edition.

Jainism takes the doctrine of karma most seriously, believing that bad deeds produce mutations of a sort. A karma chemistry is formed by a subtle form of matter beyond the reach of our senses which pervades the whole universe. The soul, as it travels through the material world, becomes entangled with this form of matter, and every change leaves its mark upon the organism.

The performance of austerities is the main means of improvement. Right belief, knowledge, and conduct are also recommended. Great care should be taken not to take life of any kind. Stepping on an insect, even accidentally, is forbidden, so the path should be swept before walking on it. However, the broom used in sweeping might itself injure an insect, so a non-believer is sometimes employed to do the sweeping, that any injuries might be on his conscience, not on the true believer's. If these tasks are performed properly, the end of *nirvana* will be reached.

One of the characteristics of Jainism was its logic, based on the skeptical belief that no knowledge was absolute, that all statements are relative. Negative judgment is also typical of Jainism, and one of the most striking such statements is:

> [One who has obtained enlightenment is] neither long nor short nor circular nor triangular nor square nor globular nor black nor blue nor red nor yellow nor white nor fragrant nor ill-smelling nor bitter nor pungent nor puckery nor sour nor sweet nor rough nor soft nor heavy nor light nor cold nor hot nor coarse nor smooth, he neither has a body nor departs from the body nor remains in the body, he is neither feminine nor masculine nor neuter; he has wisdom (*prajñā*) and intellect (*samjñā*). However, there is no simile [by which the emancipated soul can be known]. The essence of the emancipated soul has no form. One who has no word cannot

speak a word. There is neither sound nor color and shape nor smell nor taste nor tactile objects.

JAMCHEN CHOJE SHAKYA YESHE (1389-1449) (precise transliteration, Byams-chen Chos-rje Shakya Ye-shes): The disciple of Tsongkha-pa, who was the founder of "Those Who Follow Virtuous Works" (Geluk-pa order, the Yellow Hats), Jamchen founded (1419) the great Sera monastery. Sera (Se-ra) was the second largest monastery in Tibet, housing 5,500 monks. Jamchen also founded the monastery of Huang-ssu (Yellow Temple) in China, during his visit to Peking as the representative of Tsongkha-pa, who had declined the invitation of the Ming Emperor, Yung-lo (r. 1403-24) to come for a visit. Jamchen became the Emperor's personal lama, and received the modest title of:

All-knowing, Understanding and Benevolent Peacemaker of the World, Great Loving One, Worshipped by All, Great Prince and Lama from the Happy Steadfast Kingdom of the West, Jamchen Choje, the Great Lama of the Emperor.

Unable to surpass that, he went home to Tibet.

JAMYANG CHOJE TRASHI PELDEN (1379-1449) (precise transliteration, 'Jam-dbyangs Chos-rje): A disciple of Tsongkha-pa, Jamyang Choje founded the Drêpung monastery (1416), funded by Neu Namkha Zangpo, the prime minister. Drêpung became, in time, the largest monastery in Tibet, with 7,700 monks. It was patterned after the Tantric monasteries of India.

JAPANESE PHILOSOPHY: ("Japan" is the English form of "Jihpen," or "Zipangu," the Chinese pronunciation of "Nihon" or "Nippon," brought to Europe in the thirteenth century by Marco Polo; its designation in Chinese characters means "sun" and "source," because Japan, in the sea to the east of China, was the source of the sun; before the early seventh century, the Japanese had called their country "Yamato.") In the West, Japanese philosophy is not well understood. Some western philosophers, perhaps operating on the principle that "what I don't know isn't knowledge," have written as if whatever they did not know could not possibly have any significance.

For example, in the prestigous *Encyclopedia of Philosophy*, only Confucianism and Western thought are considered under Japanese philosophy. This is something like writing an article on American philosophy saying that the two most representative features in American philosophy are Hegelian Studies and British Analytic Philosophy, and appending a line reading: "P.S., also read 'Pragmatism.'"

Japanese philosophy is not western-philosophy-in-Japan alone, although that is part of it, nor is it Chinese-philosophy-in-Japan (Confucianism), although that is also a legitimate part of it.

Japanese philosophy may be characterized (as Hajime Nakamura has written in *Ways of Thinking of Eastern Peoples*, Honolulu: East-West Center Press, 1964) as typically phenomenalistic and this-worldly. Japanese philosophy typically emphasizes social relations over individual. It is practical in orientation, and religious beliefs in the sense of abstract doctrines are not strongly held. There is not much interest in formal consistency. Intuition and the emotions are held in much higher esteem. In any case, direct knowledge concerning objective reality, according to Japanese ways of thinking, is not available.

The phenomenalistic character of Japanese philosophy is indicated by Dōgen's statement that the "real aspect" of the world is "all things." The essence of the universe is its existence, "this wind," "this rain," "this stick," "this study," "this evergreen pine and unbreakable bamboo." There is no metaphysical idealism in this theory. The phenomenal world is being. True reality is not static, but dynamic. "Evil men," says Dōgen, "mostly think that speech and action are temporary things which have been set up by illusions, while silence and non-action are the truth. That is not the doctrine of the Buddha!"

Itō Jinsai, the Shintoist, remarks that:

Between heaven and earth there is only one reason: motion without stillness, good without evil. Stillness is the end of

198

motion, while evil is the change of good; and good is a kind of life, while evil is a kind of death. It is not that these two opposites are generated together, but they are all one with life.

Further:

When life thus evolves, without ceasing, into eternity, it may rightly be said that no one dies.

Japanese Confucian scholars also emphasized the phenomenalistic. Ogyū Sorai rejects the static character of Chu Hsi's version of Confucianism. Dualism is rejected by Japanese Confucianists in favor of the belief of phenomena as the fundamental mode of existence.

Ryokan's poem illustrates this love for natural phenomena. On his death bed, he wrote:

> For a memento of my existence
> What shall I leave? (I need
> not leave anything.)
> Flowers in the spring,
> Cuckoos in the summer, and
> Maple leaves in the autumn,
> What is special is what is natural.

The importance of social relations for Japanese philosophy is indicated by the fact that such social relationships as rank and closeness must be known before choosing the proper personal pronoun to use. Thus an individual is not perceived as an individual, but as a member of a certain social class. There is a lack of clear distinction between an individual and the social group to which he belongs. Ryōnin (1072-1132), founder of Yūzū Nembutsu, said:

> One person is all persons;
> All persons are one person;
> One meritorious deed is all meritorious deeds;
> All meritorious deeds are one meritorious deed.

199

Sō means either individual monks training in a Buddhist order or the order as a whole. Dōgen wrote:

> One should be more intimate with brethren in a Buddhist order than with oneself.

It should be emphasized that this social aspect to thought is not aimed at something universal, but limited to a group. It would be considered evil to give up everything in the search for truth, if it were contrary to the wishes of the ruler.

Japanese conversation is severely limited to the environment of the speaker and listener. The reply to a question (such as: "Aren't you going?") would refer to the opinion of the person who asked the question (thus: "Yes, I am not") rather than to the fact involved (which would reply: "No, I am not"). Things are thought of in terms of social relationships rather than as impersonal facts in the objective world.

The lack of interest in formal consistency is linked with the importance given to subjective and social relations. Loyalty is given to the family, clan, and nation. Thus intuitive and emotional ways of thinking are predominant over universal expressions and logical formulations. The Japanese language reflects this tendency. Vagueness of expression results from the fact that nouns have no clear singular and plural, there is no distinction between genders, and no article is used.

The non-rationalistic character of Japanese thought may be illustrated by Dōgen's statement:

> Life and death matter little because the Buddha exists therein. And one is not perplexed by life and death because the Buddha does not exist therein.

This formal contradiction in this case is striking.

Another illustration may be seen in Ogyū Sorai, who emphasized the importance of following the will of Heaven, while also saying:

> We need not wait to understand Heaven.
> We all know it.

Heaven, in his view, was not abstract but, rather, natural.

Again, when Hayashi Razan (1583-1657), the Confucianist, debated with a Catholic Father, the conclusion was nothing more than an *ad hominem* exchange of shouts: "You blighter," "You idiot!" and so on.

One of the reasons formal logic was lacking from the equipment of an educated man was that logic had been treated as an esoteric study. It was classified top secret and reserved for a small number of very advanced scholars. When Jōkei, in the Kamakura period, gave his *Short Commentary on Logic* (*Myō hon-sho*) to Ryō-san, his disciple, he said:

> I made only one copy. . . . I gave the first half (seven volumes) to the Vicar-General of the Tōhokuin, and the second half (six volumes) to the Preceptor of the Kōmyōin. By mutual agreement each can borrow the other half and make a copy of it. While either of the two is living, *the number of copies must not be increased*. When you transmit it in the future, you must choose a person who has the same religious disposition as you.

These conditions would tend to inhibit the wide spread of the knowledge of logic.

Dr. Hideki Yukawa, the Nobel-Prize-winning physicist, has remarked that:

> Japanese mentality is, in most cases, unfit for abstract thinking and takes interest only in tangible things. This is the origin of the Japanese excellence in technical art and the fine arts.

The "defect in abstraction" has not prevented Yukawa from abstracting on the highest levels of theoretical physics, but the point he makes agrees in the main with Nakamura's. Yet he also ties his hopes for the rejuvenation of fundamental physics to a revival of interest in "the sense of beauty" and intuition.

The key movements in Japanese thought coincide with the various historical periods of the country.

I. PRIOR TO THE AGE OF REFORM

The Jōmon (*ca.* 8000-300 B.C.), Yayoi (*ca.* 300 BC?-300 A.D.), and Tomb (*ca.* 300-552 A.D.) periods preceded the introduction of Buddhism under Prince Shōtoku. The legends explaining the creation of the islands and the manner of the founding of the royal family belong to this period. Myths and legends were transmitted orally until the seventh century A.D., and by 712, they were collected into the *Kojiki* (*Records of Ancient Matters*). In 720, the stories were re-written and entitled *Nihongi* (*Chronicles of Japan*). These are the two principal sources for our knowledge of early Japanese culture.

The *Kami*, gods or spirits, were central to the ancient Shinto belief. The *Kami* could be worshipped in a natural place without benefit of shrine or temple. Shinto shrines themselves are not particularly of great antiquity. The later shrines are rebuilt periodically. The famed Ise Shinto shrine, built of cypress wood, is rebuilt every twenty years on an alternating site.

Motoori Norinaga writes that *Kami* may be interpreted to mean "the deities of heaven and earth that appear in the ancient records and also the spirits of the shrines where they are worshipped." *Kami* also include human beings or living or non-living objects of nature whenever they "possessed superior power" or were "awe-inspiring." Not only were good creatures called *Kami*, but also "evil and mysterious things, if they are extraordinary and dreadful." No clear line is drawn between the human and the divine. Whatever was extraordinary is worthy of reverence.

II. THE AGE OF REFORM

Buddhism in Japan (*q.v.*) was first introduced from Korea to the accompaniment of various court intrigues and disputes over the rightful imperial succession. The Soga family vigorously supported the new religion, much to the dismay of Shinto traditionalists. Soga Buddhism consisted primarily of magical invocations for benefits such as wealth, health, and power, which may be gained by devout reverence to the Buddha. The power of Buddhism as practiced in China at the time and its universality throughout Asia were used as arguments for its acceptance in Japan.

Prince Shōtoku ("sovereign moral power") was the chief architect of change, the patron both of Buddhism and, to promote governmental administration, Confucianism. His *Seventeen Article Constitution* (604 A.D.) begins with a quotation from the *Analects* of Confucious (I,12):
Harmony is to be valued.
The Second Article recommends Buddhism:

Sincerely reverence the three treasures, . . . Buddha, the law, and the Monastic orders, . . . the supreme objects of faith in all countries.

It was hoped that these philosophies would help achieve the practical goal of stabilizing the country and promoting the virtues of central government. They did succeed in this.

(Article XV) To turn away from that which is private, and to set our faces toward that which is public, this is the path of a minister. Now if a man is influenced by private motives, he will surely feel resentment; and if he is influenced by resentful feelings, he will assuredly fail to act harmoniously with others. If he fails to act harmoniously with others, he will surely sacrifice the public interest to his own private feelings. When resentment arises, it interferes with order, and is subversive of law.

III. NARA BUDDHISM

Once established in Japan on an elementary level, the next task was to investigate the deeper intellectual aspects of Buddhism. The next seventy-four years saw the elaboration of six schools, the *Kusha* and *Jō Jitsu* ("Completion of the Truth"), both Hinayana, and the *Sanron* ("Three Treatises"), *Kegon* ("Flower Ornament"), *Hossō* ("Characteristics of the Dharmas"), and *Ritsu* ("Discipline"), all Mahayana schools. These schools debated the nature of reality. *Kusha* held that the self was unreal but the world real. *Jō Jitsu* held that both self and world were unreal. *Sanron* agreed with this latter point of view. *Kegon* held that no individual exists independently of the rest, but that each reflects the universe and is, in return, reflected by the universe. *Hossō* held

203

that things exist only when we think they exist. *Ritsu* said the most important thing about doctrine was that it should be transmitted in a strictly orthodox way.

One of the most significant works for Nara Buddhism was the *Sūtra of the Sovereign Kings of the Golden Light Ray* (*Konkō myō saishō ō gyō*). The *Sūtra of the Golden Light*, as it is called, has a chapter on medicine, showing the close connection between religion and medical practice at the time.

IV. THE HEIAN PERIOD

Saichō (767-822) was the founder of Tendai. He was disgusted with the worldliness and lack of devotion which he observed among the Nara priests. He left and built a hut on Mount Hiei (788), saying:

> O Buddhas
> Of unexcelled complete enlightenment,
> Bestow your invisible aid
> Upon this hut I open
> On the mountain top.

When Emperor Kammu, who was a Confucian by training, selected (794) the area near the mountain as the site of the new capital, Saichō's influence became important. Sent to China (804) to gain spiritual approval for his new order, Saichō, who was of Chinese ancestry, studied T'ien-t'ai teachings, and after a year, brought Tendai back to Japan.

Based on the *Lotus Sūtra*, Tendai held that everyone has within him the potential for gaining enlightenment. This differed sharply from the Doctrines of some of the Nara sects (such as Hossō), which held that some people are excluded from Buddhist perfection because of their inborn shortcomings.

Kūkai (774-835) was the founder of Shingon, the second main school of Buddhist philosophy during the Heian period. He returned to Japan in 806, the year of Emperor Kammu's death. Presenting many Chinese treasures to the new emperor, the court began exhibiting a preference for the beauty and simplicity of Shingon's theories, rather than adhering to the severe moralism of the Tendai school.

Kūkai taught an esoteric (secret) doctrine, sharply refusing to loan a certain esoteric sūtra to Saicho unless he would agree to become a regular student. Kūkai's emphasis upon the secret teachings of the cosmic Buddha (Vairochana) was based upon his belief that these teachings were absolute, independent of any relativity of space or time, uniting in themselves the truth common to all schools of thought.

Kūkai wrote the *Ten Stages of the Religious Consciousness* to present the upward progression of knowledge. The ten stages are:

1) Uncontrolled passion, an animal life;
2) Confucianism, with the mind ignorant of true religion;
3) Taoism (or Brāhmanism), with believers hoping for heaven but ignorant of its nature;
4) Hinayana, with a partial understanding of truth;
5) Another Hinayana, hoping for (selfish) personal extinction in Nirvana:
6) Pseudo-Mahayana, or Quasi-Mahayana (the Hossō School), compassionate (in contrast with the selfishness of Hinayana), aiming at discovering the ultimate entity of cosmic existence through contemplation, investigation of the specific characteristics of existence, and realization of the fundamental nature of the soul in mystic illumination;
7) The Sanron, following Nāgārjuna's "Eightfold Negations" as a means for eliminating whatever false conceptions hinder the mind's search for truth;
8) Tendai, in which one moment contains eternity (as a sesame seed may hold within it a mountain);
9) Kegon, with its teaching of interdependence and convertibility; and
10) Shingon's esoteric teachings.

The essence of Shingon teaching was not verbal, but artistic. Kūkai's master, Hui-kuo, said that only through art could the truth of the teaching be conveyed. Kūkai believed that whatever was beautiful partook of the nature of Buddha, and: "Art is what reveals to us the state of perfection."

Kūkai's school taught the arts as:
(1) painting and sculpture;
(2) music and literature;
(3) acts and gestures; and
(4) civilization and religion.

Thus, the highest truth is expressed in the highest culture. The implements of religion included the Diamond Mandala and the Womb Mandala, for meditation. The implements of civilization included the *kana*, Japanese syllabary, invented by Kūkai, according to traditional accounts, utilizing his knowledge of Sanskrit in the process.

For Shingon, the truths of its religious system are not the limited result of revelations by the historic Buddha alone, but of the cosmic Buddha, transcending all human limitations.

The founders of these two great schools of Heian Buddhism, Tendai and Shingon, were knowledgable about Confucianism and Taoism, and rejected them in favor of what they judged to be the superior intellectual and social qualities of Buddhism properly understood. Both men had a Chinese orientation and were proficient in Chinese (Kūkai more so than the professional diplomats he sailed with), and they were interested in taking the best of Chinese civilization back to Japan for the appreciation and use of the Imperial Court.

V. KAMAKURA PERIOD

In the Kamakura period, three additional forms of Buddhism were developed, Amidism, Zen, and Nichiren. These emphasized faith rather than reason in the development of life. An intellectual weariness seemed to set in, perhaps as a reaction to social troubles.

Admidism held that simple faith in the Amida Buddha was enough. If a person called on the name of Amida only once, he would be rewarded by being granted entrance into the Western Paradise, the "Pure Land."

Zen, as is better known, similarly insisted that reason was not the guide to ultimate truth. The Zen masters gave paradoxical or nonsensical answers to questions raised by their students. Riddling answers to devout questions provided the hammer to strike apart any reasonable connection between the two. Different connections could be made, not on the basis of reason, but rather, through meditation, on the basis of everyday life and extraordinary devotion.

Nichiren joined this retreat from reason. Rather than calling on the name of Amida Buddha for salvation, he said, the believer should call on the entire *Lotus Sūtra*. Not only a rejection of reason, but a fierce intolerance of any opposing point of view characterized Nichiren. In *The Establishment of the Legitimate Teaching for the Security of the Country* (*Risshō ankoku ron*), he wrote:

Woe, woe! During the last thirty or forty years, thousands of people have been enchanted and led astray, so that they wander in Buddhism as men without a guide. Is it not to be expected that the good deities should be angry when men depart from the truth? Is it not natural that evil spirits should make the most of their opportunities, when they see men forsake justice and love unrighteous deeds? It is far better to exert ourselves to stay as impending calamity than to repeat the vain *Nembutsu*.

VI. THE MUROMACHI PERIOD

Named for the street in Kyoto where the Ashikaga Shoguns lived, the Muromachi period (1336-1603) is generally considered to be a dark age in the history of Japanese culture. Social unrest was widespread and civil wars disrupted the land. Warriors drifted to the cities, where there were increasing opportunities for commerce, managed and encouraged by the large Buddhist monasteries. Zen priests controlled education. In response to the demand by the Samurai for culture, classes were held. The tea ceremony and screen painting were developed to their high points, and the Silver and Golden Pavilions were built. Nō drama was created by Kwanami (1333-1384) and his son, Seami (1364-1443). In the sixteenth century, movable type was introduced into the country, and a translation of *Aesop's Fables* was prepared.

Kitabatake Chikafusa (1293-1354) wrote *The Records of the Legitimate Succession of the Divine Sovereigns* (*Jinnō shōtō-ki*), a historical study of great importance to Japanese culture. Ichijō Kanera (1402-1481) developed a system of idealistic monism. Yoshida Kanetomo (1435-1511) developed a system of monism called Yui-itsu ("one and only") Shintō.

In 1542, the first Europeans to visit Japan, Portugese merchants, landed on Kyushu. Seven years later, St. Francis Xavier reached the land, and ferment over new ideas and foreign influences became more intense than before. The violent political struggles precipitated issued in the control of the capital in 1568 by Nobunaga, the destruction of the monastery on Mount Hiei, and (in 1582) Nobunaga's murder.

VII. THE TOKUGAWA PERIOD

During the Tokugawa regime, no new Buddhist philosophies were introduced except for Ōbaku Zen, Chinese in style, favored by the political leaders. The Christian influence, which had become conspicuous, was opposed as subversive. Other western influences, from the Spanish, Portugese, and other Europeans, were excluded with the expulsions of 1624, 1639, and 1640.

The famous shrine at Nikkō ("Sunshine") was dedicated to Ieyasu, the first Shogun from the Tokugawa family. One of the five great shrines of Shintō, it is the subject of a common saying:

Speak not of beauty
Until you have seen Nikkō.

Ieyasu's abbot, Tenkai, interpreted Shintō's particularism in the light of Buddhist universalism, that is, saying that particular native Shinto gods are manifestations of the cosmic Buddha. The posthumous title chosen for Ieyasu was "Buddha incarnate as the Sun God of the East," and had the effect of making him both Sun God and Sun Buddha of the East.

Confucianism dominated intellectual life in the Tokugawa period. The stability promised by Chu Hsi's variety of Neo-Confucianism seemed attractive to the rulers. The political pessimism of Buddhism, recommending that the true believers leave the world and retire to monasteries, must have seemed like a contributing cause to the chaos preceding the Tokugawa unification of the land. Confucianism promised peace and order in this world, here and now, through law and ethical behavior. The foundation of social prosperity was individual morality, it taught, and the Tokugawa could not have agreed more. However, Ieyasu did not attempt to copy the imperial institutions of China, but rather sought to follow the personal virtues of the Chinese emperor, T'ang T'ai-tsung. Rather than founding a civil bureaucracy, he founded a military government based upon a feudal system of loyalties, and solving the problem of succession by establishing a heriditary aristocracy. The government was conservative and opposed to any sort of innovation. Travel was restricted. Class restrictions were upheld as a bar to social mobility. Marriage had to be approved by the authorities. Five-man groups were held collectively responsible for the crimes of any individual member. Laws were promulgated governing military households (1615):

Offenders against the law should not be harbored or hidden in any domain. Law is the basis of social order. Reason may be violated in the name of the law, but law may not be violated in the name of reason.

Ieyasu declared:

If we cannot clarify the principles of human relations, society and government will become unstable and disorders will never cease. The only means whereby these principles can be set forth and understood are books. Thus the printing of books and their distribution to the public is the first concern of a benevolent government.

The Neo-Confucian scholar who most influenced Ieyasu was Fujiwara Seika. A graduate of instruction at the Five Zen Monasteries of Kyoto, he concluded that Zen was too negative in its attitude toward secular affairs. Further, in his view, Zen failed to offer an ethical code adequate to regulate international trade. Seika's criterion of a good philosophy was one that was acceptable to all countries and which offered a rational standard of conduct which could govern the peaceful transaction of business. Seika wrote:

209

Good faith is inherent in our nature, . . . it moves heaven and earth, penetrates metals and rocks, and pervades everything without exception; its influence is not just limited to contact and communication between neighboring countries . . . Good faith is the very nature of things.

Hayashi Razan was the strict champion of orthodox Chu Hsi Neo-Confucianism. He drafted the major regulations of the first Tokugawa Shoguns. He was interested in "the investigation of things," to quote from the *Great Learning*, a favorite text of the time, especially with regard to the constant laws of nature and human society. This provided a striking contrast to Buddhist ideas of the impermanence of the world.

In later years, beginning with Hōkō, all the Hayashi family leaders were granted the hereditary title, Head of the State University (*Daigaku-no-kami*).

The purpose of education, according to Yamazaki Ansai, is "to clarify human relationships:"

In the elementary program of education the various human relationships are made clear, the essence of this education in human relationships being devotion to [or respect for] persons.

Yamazaki taught the Neo-Confucianism of Chu Hsi's philosophy, summarizing its complexities by the slogan "Devotion within, righteousness without." Yamazaki also formulated a new system of Shintō doctrine.

Kaibara Ekken presented Confucian ethics in everyday terms which ordinary Japanese could understand, "household talk." The slogan, "Investigate things and make your knowledge perfect" (from the *Great Learning*), had been interpreted by most Chinese and Japanese Confucianists as meaning study the classics. Kaibara broadened the investigation to include the whole field of nature. Man and nature are allied and inseparable. The books he wrote include one entitled *Catalogue of Vegetables*, as well as *How to Live Well*.

Just as Chu Hsi's School of Reason (or Principle) was opposed in China by Wang Yang-ming's School of Intuition (or Mind), so

210

in Japan it was opposed by Nakae Tōju. Wang Yang-ming was called Oyōmei, in Japan, and Nakai stressed the distinction made possible by the controversy. Everyone does not have to be a scholar (as Chu Hsi was interpreted as teaching), but everyone ought to be a good man. It is not enough to talk about good deeds; one does not truly understand them until one has put them into action. The only sure guide in life is the inner light, the conscience, the moral sense, the "Divine Light of Heaven."

Kumazawa Banzan extended Oyōmei's teachings from the limited sphere of personal conduct to the more general field of political action. He recommended that the Samurai spend more time keeping in shape, and that the Shogunate take a stronger hand in managing the country's economy by discouraging cotton, tobacco, and tea production and encouraging rice. Rice instead of money should be made the medium of exchange.

Yamaga Sokō, instrumental in the development of *bushidō*, the way of the warrior, taught that he should set a high example of devotion to duty. The Samurai should serve his lord with the utmost loyalty, and put devotion to moral principle ahead of personal gain. Yamaga wrote the *Essence of Confucianism* in 1665, stating that Confucius' pure teaching had been corrupted by Chu Hsi and the Neo-Confucianists of the Sung School. Yamaga was arrested for expressing these views. However, Yamaga's theory that intelligence was one of the martial virtues had important implications for changing the Samurai from an idle and effete class into the intellectual leaders in the Restoration movement.

Itō Jinsai criticized Neo-Confucian dualism, objecting to Chu Hsi's teaching that principle (in Japanese, *ri*) and material force (*ki*) were two ultimate realities. Instead, Itō argued, material force is the first principle, understood as the vital force which underlies all three realms of existence—heaven, earth, and humanity. The universe is dynamic, not, as Chu Hsi seemed to think, static. Since the life force is real, death is unreal. Death is nothing but the absence of life, and is purely negative. Itō applies these concepts to human behavior by saying that man should conserve and develop the life force within him. Thus man will develop the virtue of humanity (*jin*) fully, which is love expressed in loyalty, good faith, reverence, and forgiveness.

Ogyū Sorai also criticized the Neo-Confucianists for wasting time on metaphysical questions. He felt that Itō was on the right track, but was too interested in personal ethics and not enough in social issues:

> They are quite wrong who say today that the way of Confucius is not the same as the way of the early kings. The basis for bringing peace and contentment to all under Heaven was personal cultivation, but always with a mind to achieving peace in the world.

Ogyū, arousing the antagonism of the Hayashi family school, which was devoted to Chu Hsi orthodoxy, taught that Hsün Tzu was a better guide to the interpretation of Confucius. Man was evil by nature, and could be improved only through social institutions.

Muro Kyūso, the son of a physician, defended Chu Hsi's philosophy more effectively than the teachers of the Hayashi school, who had an official monopoly on state education. The ethical attitudes emphasized by Muro include the sense of duty in personal relationships (*gi*), the highest duty of loyalty to one's ruler, and indebtedness or obligation (*on*) to one's parents for the gift of life and to one's ruler for protecting it.

Muro criticized Wang Yang-ming for having attacked Chu Hsi and proclaimed the doctrine of innate knowledge:

> Thus the temper of thought in the Ming underwent a change, and after Yang-ming's death such followers of his as Wang Lung-ch'i turned in the direction of Zen Buddhism. Thereafter scholars became intoxicated with intuitive knowledge and grew tired of pursuing first principles. . . . As Han Yü said, 'They sit in a well and, looking up at the sky, pronounce it small.' Nevertheless, there are countless numbers of men, shallow and deficient in knowledge, who eagerly take to new and strange teachings and love to echo the opinions of others. . . . All the dogs join in when one starts barking, and that is the reason why vile teachings and outrageous doctrines abound in the world today.

In *Conversations at Suruga-Dai*, Muro praises the virtues of the Samurai, honor and duty. The considerations of price and profits are, in Muro's opinion, perversions. Continuing in this analysis of value, he said:

> Some years ago, when Arai Hakuseki was attendant lecturer in the Confucian temple, I heard him say: 'Never say, in reporting of another man, that he is greedy. For if he is greedy of money, then you can be sure that he will ultimately be greedy of life. In that case, you should use the blunter word, and say that he is cowardly.'

Arai Hakuseki sensed the role that Japan was to play in the world at large. While he was advisor to the sixth Shogun, Ienobu, he settled some of the diplomatic questions of protocol which arose. He set up a system of budgeting and accounting for the first time to bring order to the Tokugawa finances. He also attempted to stabilize the currency by advising stricter controls on the foreign trade allowed at Nagasaki, so that the imbalance of payments would require less gold and silver to be drained from the country. Arai believed that social order depended upon clearly defined heirarchy, and encouraged those ceremonies and customs which made the status of citizens clear.

Tominaga Nakamoto's trenchant attack upon Confucianism (*Failings of the Classical Philosophers*) succeeded in motivating his expulsion both from the Confucian school which his father had established and from his father's hosue as well. "The vice of Confucianism," he wrote, "is rhetoric." Earning a living at a Zen monastery as proofreader of a new edition of the *Tripitaka*, he wrote a *Historical Survey of Buddhism (Shutsujō kogō)*, on the theme:

> The rise of the sects and denominations is due to everybody's striving for advancement.

The only reason for appealing to the authority of the founders is to get ahead of someone else. Thrown out of the monastery as well, Tominaga proceeded to attack the third religion within his

213

reach, Shinto, before he died at the age of thirty-one, persecuted and poverty-stricken. "The vice of Shinto," he wrote, "is secrecy." In his *Testament of an Old Man (Okina no fumi)*, he recommends a kind of ethical culture to replace all existing religions, called "the religion of the true fact," which seems to consist of such virtues as:

> Be normal in everything you do. Consider today's work of primary importance. Keep your mind upright. Comport yourself properly. Be careful in speech.

The religion of the true fact has no vices.

Miura Baien, a physician, philosopher, and economist (born the same year as Adam Smith and, in *The Origin of Price*, outlining similar views on currency), refused to accept authority as the sanction for knowledge. Rather, he maintained, nature and man himself is the first source of knowledge, rather than tradition or textbooks. He rejected the Buddhist view of the emptiness of things. The universe is one, infinite, real, and characterized by dynamic energy, vitality. Death is not complete extinction, but only organic change. What we must study is the "logic of things" (*jōri*). This logic "is the key for opening the gates of Heaven:"

> The essence of this logic is the dialectics of antithesis and synthesis, setting aside all bias or prejudice, and verifying everything by empirical evidence.

Miura's dialectic is similar to Hegel's in that the essential character of reality is antithesis, that one does not remain one. Yet when there is two, the essential identity of the two can be understood. In a letter to Asada Gōryū, Miura remarks that:

> Human minds are like human faces; their preferences differ. Each considers what he has arrived at to be right, a relevation from Heaven or deposit of truth from antiquity, and thinks those who do not accept his standards should be exterminated. It is my conviction, therefore, that there is no systematic truth or logic except that which enables man to

comprehend the universe without setting up standards conceived in terms of humanity or human motives.

Kaiho Seiryo writes that it is intelligence, not virtue, which makes a man a sage or a saint. Kaiho is noted for his economic theory, written in *Lessons of the Past* (*Keikodan*), which illustrates that the long process of the application of Confucian ideals to social problems issued in the secular need to solve the problems of economics. According to Kaiho, society is basically economic in character. The two principal social activities are the production and exchange of goods. The function of government is to balance the economy. Kaiho recommended few laws with much enforcement. He agreed with the Confucians that too much legal regulation is self-defeating, and he also agreed with the Legalists that it is the office, not the personal virtue of the ruler, that is the source of governing authority. He writes:

In Chinese antiquity when a death sentence was passed, the sentence was reported to the sovereign. Then the sovereign would request a reprieve three times, but the penal officer would not listen to the request and proceeded to execute the death sentence. To repay a capital crime offender with capital punishment is a matter of simple business arithmetic.

By 1790, the Shogunate was alarmed by the free-thinking manner in which philosophy was proceeding. Afraid that new ideas would imperil the stability of the regime, the Kansei Edict was issued. The effect was to prohibit the study of any but Chu Hsi's form of Neo-Confucianism. This edict discouraged students from reading books, but it did not stop the earth from turning.

Many Japanese had believed that it was important to keep foreigners out, for, once admitted, the "pure Buddhist country" would be polluted, and disaster and punishment would ensue. American Naval Commodore Perry disabused Japan of this superstitious belief, in 1853-54, by opening Japan to the outside, to merchants, tourists, and missionaries. Within the century there was war, world war, two atomic bombs, national disaster, humiliation, and punishment.

VIII. THE MODERN PERIOD

Both internal and external pressures led to the end of the Tokygawa Shogunate. The Meiji Restoration led, ironically, to an even more rapid opening to foreign influence than the one for which the Tokugawa were blamed. In 1877, one of the same leaders who had restored the emperor as the central figure in govnerment, Saigo Takamori, of the province of Satsuma, led a rebellion, angry at the "selling out" of the traditional values of Japan. After it was put down, modernization proceeded without obstacle. A large number of scholars attempted to assimilate as many Western ideas as possible. Nishi Amane began the process. Idealism was investigated by Inoue Tetsujirō of Tokyo University. Materialism was propounded by Katō Hiroyuki. Kantianism was presented by Kuwaki Gen'yoku.

Onishi Hajime and Hatano Seiichi presented the history of philosophy in a thorough-going fashion. Tanaka Odō, a graduate of The University of Chicago, argued for naturalism. Nishida Kitaro of Kyoto University attempted to create an oriental logic, *basho no ronri*, "logic of field," or "logic of place." The "Kyoto School" of Japanese philosophy included Tanabe Hajime among its members.

Watsuji Tetsuro wrote on the subject of ethics. Furukawa Tesshi cultivated the field of historical ethics, while Oshima is familiar with existential ethics.

Marxists include Miki Kiyoshi and Tosaka Jun, who both died in prison (1945), Ide Takashi, the specialist in Aristotle, and Yanagida Kenjuro, one of Nishida's students. Miyake Gōichi is an existentialist, oriented toward Heidegger. Ueda Seiji is a Pragmatist. Kawada Kumatarō and Nakamura Hajime are both interested in the comparative philosophy of East and West.

JIEN (1155-1225): A learned Tendai master prominent in Japanese Buddhism during the Heian period, Jien (or Jichin) commented on the despair and anxiety which overwhelmed the orthodox Buddhist priests and the educated upper class at the time.

216

People generally believed that they had entered the fateful Age of the Latter Law.

JŌDO-SHIN: The Pure Land sect of Japanese Buddhism, Jōdo-Shin flourished during the Heian period. Founded by Hōnen (*q.v.*), it stresses faith in Amida Buddha.

JÜAN CHI (210-263): One of the Seven Worthies of the Bamboo Grove, a group of Neo-Taoists who met in bamboo groves to drink, write poems, and argue that "following nature" meant satisfying one's desires, not denying them. Jüan Chi wrote the *Biography of Mr. Great Man (Ta-jen hsien-sheng chuan)*. He recommended that we should become one with the universe, transcend all earthly distinctions, and live beyond good and evil. Wealth and poverty are all the same to the Great Man. What does it all matter? Great job or small, rich or poor are, from an eternal point of view, all the same. Enemies of the Seven Worthies accused them of wild abandon and shameless conduct. The wild abandon indulged in by Jüan was of the following shameless kind: he would uncover his head, loosen his hair, take off his outer clothes, and sprawl upon the ground.

His followers, being rather slow learners, aped his behavior after a couple of generations had passed. For example, Juan Chan (250-312), Wang Teng, alias Wang P'ing Tzu (269-312), Hsien Kun (280-322), and Hu-mu Fu-chih, alias Hu-mu Yen-kuo got rid of their caps and also a lot more. They pulled off their clothes, behaved "like the birds" and the beasts. "Doing it" was called "comprehension." Doing it more was called "understanding."

These were the *feng-liu*, "wind and stream" men, the Neo-Taoists and their followers of the Wei and Chin dynasties. The English term "romanticism" is used as a roughly equivalent translation.

JUDAH, RABBI (135-220): Called "The Rabbi" in the Talmud, Judah Ha-Nasi committed the Mishnah (Oral Law) to writing, using the redaction of Meir as a basis. The number of people who knew the entire oral Law by heart had been drastically reduced by the political chaos in Palestine. Therefore, the achievement of Rabbi Judah was most significant, and ended the disorder which was becoming prevalent in the transmission of the Law.

	Shinto	*Buddhist*	*Confucian*	*Contemporary*
Jōmon (8000-300 B. C.)				
Yayoi (300B.C.-300 A. D.)				
Tomb (300-552)				
Age of Reform (552-710)		Prince Shōtoku Taishi (574-622) *Seventeen Articles Constitution*		
Nara (710-780)		The Six Schools (1) Kusha (2) Jō Jitsu (3) Sanron (4) Kegon (5) Hossō (6) Ritsu		
Heian (781-1185)	Ise Shintō movement. Unique Shintō myths.	Saichō (767-822): Tendai Sect. Kūkai (774-835): Shingon (True Word) sect. Eshin (942-1017): Tendai scholar. Hōnen (Genkū, 1133-1212): Jōdo-shin (Pure Land) sect, faith in Buddha Amida. Eisai (1141-1215): Rinzai School, Zen. Jien (Jichin, 1145-1225):		

Age of Unification (1568-1603):
Momoyama Period— Hideyoshi & Ieyasu
Tokugawa Shogunate

Atsutane Hirata

(EDO) (1603-1867)

(1760-1843:) Nationalist & Physician.
Study of Japanese classics:
Keichū (1640-1701)

Kada Azumamaro (1669-1736)
Kamo no Mabuchi (1697-1769)
Motoori Norinaga (1730-1801)

Suzuki Shōsan (1579-1655)

Hakuin (1685-1768): Zen master.

Hayashi Razan (Dōshun) (1583-1657): Kami (Shintō) = *li* (reason) of Chu Hsi
Nakae Tōju (1608-1648)
Kumazawa Banzan (1619-1691)
Itō Junsai (1627-1705)
Ogyū Sorai (1666-1728)
Dazai Shundai (1680-1747)
Matsumiya Kanzan (1686-1780)

Tominaga Nakamoto (1715-1746): Textual study; relativistic ethics and religion. Miura Baien (1723-1789): Objective Metaphysics.

			Learned Tendai priest, Historiography.
Kamakura (1185-1333)	Faith and experience emphasized, rather than intellectual or moral or traditional Buddhism.		Shinran (1173-1262): Jōdo Shin sect (True Pure Land). Dōgen (1200-1253): Zen Master, Sōtō School. Nichiren (1222-1282): the Hokke Sūtra.
			Ryōkan (Ninshō Bodhisattva, 1212-1303): Reviver of the Ritsu sect, faith in the Lotus Sūtra.
Kemmu Restoration (1333-1336)			
Muromachi Period (Ashikaga Shogunate) (1336-1573)	Kitabatake Chikafusa (1293-1354) Ichijō Kanera (1402-1481): Idealistic monism. Yoshida Kanetomo (1435-1511): Yui-itsu ("One and Only") Shintō, Monism.		Zen predominant
			Nisshin (1407-1488), Nichiren.
			Rennyo (1415-1499), True Pure Land.

Meiji Restoration (1868-1911)

Sakuma Shōzan: "Eastern Ethics and Western Science"
li equals the principle of Western knowledge.
Hatano Seiichi (1877-1950): *A Study of Spinoza* (1904).
Nishida Kitarō (1870-1945) *A Study of Good.*
Tanabe Hajime (1885-1962) A disciple of Nishida.
Daisetz Teitarō Suzuki: Nishida's childhood friend.
Takahashi Satomi (1886-1964)
Watsuji Tetsurō (1889-1960)

Taishō (1912-1925)

Shōwa (1926-Present)

JUDAISM: From a word coined by Greek-speaking Jews (see II Maccabees 2:21) to differentiate their way of life from their Hellenistic neighbors, Judaism (Greek *Ioudaismos*) refers to the phenomenon of Jewish spiritual life.

Some scholars distinguish between the religion of Israel, meaning before the exile, and Judaism, meaning post-exilic development. However, both are successive stages in the same religious process. Yahweh was worshipped as Israel's covenant God and savior. His will was revealed to the prophets, both former and latter. His will was embodied in the various law-codes which comprise the Torah. He jealously demanded faithful moral conduct from His worshippers. From Sinai to the present, these elements have remained the unbroken heritage of Judaism.

Shaped by Moses at Sinai and Kadesh, the religious experience of the Jewish people contains a heightened consciousness of the Sacred, embodied in the Torah, both written and Oral, Scripture and Tradition.

When settled into the agricultural economy of Canaan, the religion changed from nomadic to priestly, with an elaborate sacrificial cult with various festivals and approved sanctuaries. The kingship consolidated these developments, and the prophets advanced the concept of Yahweh from that of first-among-equals or first-in-a-region to first and only God. The prophets objected to the subordination of righteousness to ritual. Their inspired pressures led to the Deuteronomic Reformation which centralized religious worship in Jerusalem under the Zadokite priesthood.

The Exile, first under the brutal Assyrians, and then under the Babylonians, broke the geographic unity of the Jews and forced them into an ever-widening dispersion. The dynasty of King David disappeared into the hope of a coming Messiah, who would deliver the chosen people from their troubles.

After the return, spiritual life was centered in the Second Temple and, to a lesser degree, in the Synagogue. Actual political sovereignty, however, passed into the hands of Persians, Greeks, and Romans. The Reformation of Ezra and Nehemiah led to the adoption of the Torah as the supreme source of authority. Scripture was completed in its three-fold canon, the Law, the Prophets, and the Writings. In addition, the Apocrypha was produced, and the Oral Law was initiated.

In the Samaritan secession were seen instances of heroic resistance against the wave of Greek Hellenism. The party of the Pharisees arose, challenging the Zadokite priests (the nucleus of the accommodationist party called the Sadducees). The Pharisees insisted that all Jews must become a kingdom of priests, a holy nation, with the Torah as common heritage of the congregation of Jacob. As the Law gave structure to the spiritual life, the Law must be preserved in all its particulars, and in its adaptations to changing circumstances. Merging with the mystery cults of neighboring peoples, the messianic yearnings of some of the politically crushed people centered in the person of Yeshua (Jesus) and formed the world religion of Christianity.

With the destruction of the Second Temple and the fall of the Jewish state, the great divide of Judaism was reached. Now completely in foreign hands, the Jews were driven into *Galut*, exile, homeless wanderers among the nations. The Torah was all they could salvage, to serve as a spiritual fatherland.

As the synagogue necessarily replaced the Temple as the center of Jewish life, the rabbi replaced the priest. In the schools and academies of Palestine and Babylonia, the rabbinic scholars developed religious lore (Haggadah) and law (Halacha) for changing circumstances. The rich products of these labors are embodied in the Mishnah ("learning," or "second law"), the Gemaras, and the Midrashim. About the time of the rise of Islam, and with similarities to Islamic theories of the transmission of divine law (for example, from Moses to the forty "Receivers" to Rabbi Judah the Holy), the heads of the Babylonian academies, the Geonim, began a campaign to make the newly-completed Talmud ("teaching") the possession of all Jewry. Their enthusiasm prompted a reaction, the Karaite opposition. With the slogan, "Back to the Scripture," they opposed the authority both of the Rabbis and of the Talmud. To counter their influence the Rabbis turned to a closer study of the text of Scripture, Hebrew grammar, and philology.

The codification of the Halacha (rabbinic law) reached its climax in Maimonides' *Mishne Torah* (thirteenth century). How-

223

ever, the dominant force of the period was the Cabalah. A book of mysticism and magic, it teaches that mankind is a miniature universe, that numbers have mystical meaning, and that knowledge of the human spirit is as necessary as knowledge of the human body for health and peace The tetragrammaton (four-letter for Yahweh), IHVH, is divided to mean, for I (*Yod*), "Wisdom," for H (*He*), "Understanding," and for VH (*Vau He*), the two children produced from Aima, the Mother. In the cryptic *Sefer Yezira* and the *Zohar* (fourteenth century), the speculative Cabalah taught a mysticism designed to offset the rationalism characteristic of over-emphasis on Talmudic legalism.

In the sixteenth century, a practical Cabalah (of Isaac Luria) replaced the purely speculative approach. It combined the occult sciences of demonology, angelology, and astrology with neo-Platonic ideas, particularly reincarnation.

The messianism of the Cabalah led to the movements of Sabbatai Zevi and Jacob Frank. The more tragic elements of this development were overcome by the popular spiritual movement of the eighteenth century, Hasidism.

K

KALA-SUTRA: The second of the Buddhist hells, the "Black Rope Hell," reserved for those who steal. It is especially bad to steal medical supplies, or (in the Fearful Vulture Hell) to torment others to get their possessions. Residence in this hell lasts for one thousand years.

KAMO MABUCHI (1697-1769): A noted student of the Japanese classics and Shintoism during the Tokugawa Shogunate, Kamo Mabuchi was one of the founders of the School of National Learning (*kokugaku-ha*). He studied the ancient masterpiece, the *Man'yōshū*, looking for a true and original Japanese spirit, a golden age, untainted by any foreign influences. People should restore the native temper of ancient times. Kamo was the son of a functionary at a Shinto shrine. He so distinguished himself that he became lecturer to the head of one of the branch families of the Tokugawa.

K'ANG YU-WEI (1858-1927): A noted Confucian scholar, K'ang believed the reason Western powers had become so strong was because they had a state religion. He therefore attempted to establish Conficianism as the state religion of China. Confucian societies were organized, the high point of their influence being reached in 1915. K'ang's Confucian revival was known as the "New Text School."

KAPILA (550-500 B.C.): The legendary founder of the Sāmkhya (*q.v.*) philosophy, Kapila (pronounced KAW pih luh), "the Red One," was the son of Kardama and Devahūti. Kardama, his father, was an inspired sage (*Rsi*), and Kapila learned from his mother about philosophy and the nature of the soul. The last part of his life was spent on the island of Sāgara in the mouth of the Ganges River, some ninety miles from Calcutta. There he taught his philosophy to disciples. Each year on the last day of Māgha (January-February), thousands visit in his memory.

In the cave temple of Anuradhapura in northern Sri Lanka (Ceylon), a likeness of Kapila is carved. In these ways his memory is worshipped as a Great Sage and Philosopher, which is more than can be said for philosophers in most other countries.

Kapila taught the way to remove human misery. Misery, he said, is caused by the intimate association of the soul with the body. When the true nature of the soul is understood, bondage will cease and the soul will be forever freed from suffering. Bondage is an illusion caused by ignorance. Once we learn the true nature of things, we will be forever released from all unhappiness.

The effectiveness of Kapila's teaching is indicated by a celebrated episode in the *Mahābhārata* (3.107). According to the epic poem, some sixty thousand sons of "Ocean" were riding armed guard for the sacrificial horse as it wandered about. Suddenly, to their astonishment, the horse vanished. They set about digging for it, and, at last, found it deep in the underworld, with a holy man, Kapila, sitting beside it in meditation. Eager to get their horse back, they neglected to be properly respectful to a holy man. Kapila's eye flashed at them, and burnt them all to ashes.

KARMA: (Sanskrit *karman*, "deed" or "action," from *kar*, "to do" or "to create"). The concept that whatever one does in life becomes the seed which determines one's destiny in the next life. Rebirth is the endless recreation of life in obedience to moral necessity. Whenever a person dies, the karma is left. A new life must follow to work out the retribution involved. It is a matter of action and reaction. The process never ends.

The only escape possible is through the path of salvation of-

226

fered by Hindu, Buddhist, or some other system of thought.

Hindu systems recommend the suppression of karma. This suppression will bring freedom from the necessity of existence. Then the individual will be reabsorbed into the universe, universal life.

Buddhist systems regard karma as a part of cause and effect. Deliverance comes by understanding the real nature of things. When the individual is freed from the necessity of rebirth, absorption into Nirvana is possible, and the individual becomes one with the great void.

Karma may be regarded either as the work of God or the automatic result of causal law.

Action binds man to the earth. Bad action binds him to an undesirable existence, and good action binds him to a better existence. Bad karma may be used to explain such phenomena as bad luck ruining the best and most careful of plans. People may be blamed for their diseases on the basis of their actions in previous lives. Good karma may be used to explain child prodigies, gifted learners, and genius. In other words, "a man's level of being attracts his life." Life is not what you make it, it is what has been made before you were born.

Śri Aurobindo, in *The Problem of Rebirth*, writes that: the meaning of Karma is that all existence is the working of a universal Energy, a process and an action and a building of things by that action,—an unbuilding too, but as a step to further building,— that all is a continuous chain in which every one link is bound indissolubly to the past infinity of numberless links, and the whole governed by fixed relations, by a fixed association of cause and effect, present action the result of past action as future action will be the result of present action.

"Karma" does not appear in the earliest parts of the Veda, but does appear in the Brahmanas and is fully developed in the Upanishads.

KESANG GYATSO (1708-1757): The Seventh Dalai Lama, Kesang (or Kelzang or Kalsang) Gyatso (precise transliteration (*Bskal-bzang rgya-mtsho*) was established in office during the course of struggles by rival powers—competing Mongol tribes and the Chinese Manchu dynasty—for control of the country. The Qoshot Mongols who, under Lhazang Khan, had ruled Tibet for a dozen years, were attacked by the Dzungar Mongols who, after a series of bitter engagements, won control (1717). The nine-year-old Dalai Lama was receiving religious training at the Kumbum Monastery in Kokonor, under the protection of the Manchus.

The K'ang-hsi Emperor wrote:

> The Dalai Lama is like a ray of sunshine which is impossible for any one group of people to obscure. The ray of Buddhist faith will shine on everyone through him.

The Dzungar Mongols, popular at first for having deposed the false and unpopular sixth Dalai Lama, Yeshe Gyatso, aliented the Tibetan population by opposing the Nying-ma-pa sect, ruining two of its monasteries, and executing the Nying-ma-pa lamas.

Tibetan governors in the west (at Gartok) and the south (Tsang) revolted, leaving the Dzungar Mongols in control only of U and Lhasa. At this point, China intervened (1718), sending an army in, which was massacred. The second army, commanded by the emperor's fourteenth son, had better luck. Escorting the seventh Dalai Lama from Kumbum to Lhasa, they rallied the enthusiastic support of the Tibetans, and the Dzungar Mongols fled Lhasa with whatever loot they could carry.

The Chinese entered Lhasa, set up a permanent garrison, pulled down the city's defensive walls, and established a protectorate which lasted until 1912.

Kesang Gyatso's interests, despite the way he had come to power, were spiritual, not political. He left most secular matters to the Panchen Lama and the two Chinese representatives (Ambans) stationed in Lhasa. He led a simple, austere life, travelled widely, giving religious lectures, especially from the "mud throne" at a park in Lhasa. He wrote many books. He devoted his life to the "Three Precious Ones," seeking refuge not only for himself but for all his people.

KITABATAKE CHIKAFUSA (1293-1354): A Shintoist scholar of the Muromachi period, Kitabatake (pronounced Kee-ta-batak-ey) wrote *The Records of the Legitimate Succession of the Divine Sovereigns* (*Jinnō shōtō-ki*) about fifty years after the attempted Mongol invasions of Japan. In the introductory manifesto of this influential work, he wrote:

> Our Great Japan is a Divine Nation. Our Divine Ancestors founded it. The Sun Goddess let her descendants reign over it for a long time. This is the reason why Our Nation is called 'Divine Nation!'

Although he was willing to accept Buddhism in general, he argued that its political theory was inferior to Shintō's:

> The Buddhist theory [of the state] is merely an Indian theory. Indian monarchs may have been the descendants of a monarch selected for the welfare of the people, but our Imperial Family is the only continuous and unending line of family descending from its Heavenly Ancestors.

Kitabatake praised Shingon Buddhism as closest to native Shintō belief:

> Traditions from the Age of the Gods tally most closely with the teachings of [Shingon]. That is probably why, though it enjoyed only brief popularity in China, it has persisted in Japan.

KOREAN PHILOSOPHY: Since Korea has been commonly considered to have been a mere bridge between China and Japan, so far as culture was concerned, works of distinctively Korean philosophy have not been made generally available to the Western reader. Sinkyo (shamanism), Confucianism, Buddhism, Tonghak (Society of the Heavenly Way), and Sirhak (Real or Pragmatic Learning) are some topics of interest for the student of Korean philosophy.

Sinkyo was the earliest Korean belief. It is said to be practically identical with the shamanism practised by the central Asian and Siberian tribes.

229

Confucianism came to Korea in the first century B.C., probably in connection with the army from the Han Dynasty collecting tribute.

Buddhism was introduced into Korea in the fourth century A.D. The peninsula was divided into three kingdoms, Koguryo (in northern Korea), Paekje (Southwest), and Sills (Southeast). Indian monks, accompanied by Chinese guides, provided the initial contact with Buddhist sutras, images, and doctrines. Monks from Paekje later transmitted Buddhist images and ideas to Japan. Korea became so enthusiastic for Buddhism that it retained the belief long after 845, the date it was banned in China. Buddhism became a unifying influence on the peninsula, in the competition between various kingdoms for control.

Sirhak, which means Real or Pragmatic Learning, was a phenomenon primarily of the seventeenth, eighteenth, and nineteenth centuries. Founded by Yu Hyongwon (1623-1673), there were three main schools: (1) the school of "governing for maximum utility", of Yi Ik, emphasizing land reform and administrative change; (2) the school of "utility for social welfare", of Pak Chiwon, author of *Story of a Yangban* (*Yangban chon*), emphasizing the encouragement of commerce, industry, and technical renovation; (3) the school of "searching for the truth in empirical evidence" of King Chonghui, emphasizing textual analysis of classics.

Scholarship, in Korea, was the function of a specialized and powerless class called the *sa*. The "Great Purge" by King Sukjong in 1680 split the ruling class (*sadaebu*) into two parts, the *poryol*, who became a hereditary privileged class with monopolistic power, and the *yangban*, completely excluded from ruling power, and allowed to retain only the position of scholars. These scholars, the *sa*, as Pak Chiwon observed in the *Yonam chip*, "above consort with kings and below . . . mingle with the common people." Actually, their choice was either to flatter the rulers in the hope of getting a reward, or to denounce the rulers for their oppression of the masses, farmers, artisans, and merchants, in which case they would probably not get a reward. It was from the critical and conscientious activities of these latter scholars that the *Sirhak* was born.

The pioneers of *Sirhak* thought were Yi Sugwang (1563-1628) and Yu Hyongwon. It was the Neo-Confucian tradition, specifically the doctrines of self-criticism and self-renewal that led them to develop a thorough criticism of the social and administrative policies of their government.

In the southern provinces, the *sa* lived as small or middle-class landowners, studying Chu Hsi Confucianism in their spare time, with special interest in such topics as "human nature" and the correct "rites." In Seoul, the *sa* lived a more precarious existence. The life-style of the capital was characteristically extravagant, and they had great difficulty just making ends meet. They had a direct personal stake in promoting social reform, and they were less likely to settle for rhetoric and slogans, demanding instead policies that really made a difference, in demonstrable, empirical terms.

Yi Ik's "School of Governing for Maximum Utility" stressed the importance of preserving family farms, a policy also recommended by Plato in the *Laws*. In Yi Ik's words:

> Nowadays there are cunning officials and overbearing merchants. By obtaining large sums of money, in one day they buy up the fields of the poor and enjoy the pleasures of wealth.

Yi Ik also opposed the use of currency on the grounds that it made capital more important than land. He also felt that Chu Hsi's theories should be criticized for being too abstract and not practical enough.

Pak Chiwon's School of Utility for Social Welfare believed that it was not possible to turn back the hand of time. Commerce was here to stay, and the need was to develop a nation-wide system of markets to move from an agrarian to a mercantile economy. The school criticized the shortages in various parts of the country, for example, hemp but no cotton, iron but no oranges, silkworms but no salt, and recommended encouraging the exchange of goods. The future was in the cities, not in the farms.

Chong Yagyong (1762-1836) combines many features of the thought of each of the *Sirhak* Schools. He believed the future lay in technology (farm tools, weaving machines, and weapons). He was noted for the commentaries he wrote on the Confucian classics, such as *Understanding the Meaning of the Great Learning* (*Taehak hoeui*), the *Basic Meaning of Mencius* (*Maengja Youi*), and *Ancient and Modern Commentaries on the Analects* (*Nono Kogumju*).

Kim Chonghui's School of Searching for the Truth in Empirical Evidence stressed that learning was an end in itself, and that a rigorously objective approach to facts would establish their truth. Kim immersed himself in the study of Korean culture, textual exegesis and stone and metal inscriptions. He greatly admired the work of the Chinese scholar Wei Yuan (1794-1856), especially his recommendations for coastal defense, as foreign invasion seemed imminent.

The *Sirhak* scholars also recommended that those of their number who did not actually farm should make themselves useful by teaching agriculture, an idea similar to that which led in America to the establishment of land grant institutions, with their schools of agriculture.

The Society of the Heavenly Way (Chondokyo or Tonghak), "Eastern Sect", was started in 1859 by Ch'oe. Combining Shamanism, Confucianism, Buddhism, and Christianity, it declined from a high of two million followers to about eighty thousand by World War II.

KUAN CHUNG (600-645 B.C.): Famous as the advisor of Duke Huan of Ch'i, Kuan Chung (or Kuan Yi-wu) was asked for a last piece of advice while on his deathbed. The Duke wanted to know who Kuan would recommend as a replacement, now that he was going to die. Even though life does not go on, politics does. Kuan did not recommend his best friend, Pao Shu, because Pao was too moral. Such a strict personality would only create opposition. Instead, Kuan recommended Pao's rival, Hsi P'eng, known to be less moral and, hence, more flexible in his administration. Pao did not like the advice, but ceased complaining after Kuan's death, perhaps feeling that it was useless to pursue the matter any further. Pao was too good to be prime minister. He would have taken to drink had not that, too, been immoral.

The seventh chapter of the *Lieh-tzu* contains some anecdotes,

probably apocryphal, about Kuan Chung. In one of them, he is described answering questions asked by Yen Ying a hundred years after his death. He seems to have been more communicative after his death than during his lifetime. Yen Ying asked how we should nourish life. Kuan replied:
Give it freedom, neither stopping it nor frustrating it.

KUAN YI-WU: See Kuan Chung.

KUMĀRILA (690-750): One of the two great commentators (along with Prabhākara) on the *Mīmāṁsā-Sūtra* of Jaimini, Kumārila Bhatta was interested in problems of epistemology and metaphysics. Kumārila divides all categories into positive and negative. The four positive categories are:
(1) substance,
(2) quality,
(3) action, and
(4) generality.
Substance includes similarity and force under its compass, and quality includes number.

Kumārila's ethical theory is that duty (*dharma*) is action enjoined by the Veda. It enters the *ātman* (soul) as a latent force (called *apūrva*) before producing its fruit. Duty is action. Prabhākara's view, by way of contrast, is that duty is the potential merit produced by action.

Kumārila, in agreement with Vedāntist thinkers, held that we have immediate perception ourselves, and hence of the *ātman*.

KUMAZAWA BANZAN (1619-1691): A Confucian scholar during the Tokugawa Shogunate, Kumazawa called Japan "the land of benevolence," and recommended the love of others as the principal ideal of the ruling class. He wrote the *Collection of Discourses* (*Shūgi washo*). The ablest student of Nakae Tōju, he applied Wang Yang-ming's teaching about "the unity of knowledge and action" to politics, entering the service of Lord Ikeda and becoming the prime minister of Okayama.

KUNG-SUN LUNG (320-250 B.C.): One of the members of the School of Names, Kung-Sun's book, the *Kung-Sun Lung-tzu*, is partially preserved. He is famous for the "Discourse on a White Horse," in which he proves that a white horse is not a horse:

> The word 'horse' denotes a shape, 'white' denotes a color. What denotes a color does not denote shape. Therefore, I say that a white horse is not a horse. . . . When a horse is required, yellow and black ones may all be brought forward, but when one requires a white horse, a yellow or black horse cannot be brought forward. . . . Therefore, yellow and black horses are each separate kinds, and can respond to the call for a horse, but *not* to the call for a *white* horse. . . . Horses certainly have color. Therefore, there exist white horses. Suppose there is a horse without color, then there is only the horse as such. But how can we get white horses? . . . A white horse is 'horse' together with 'white.' 'Horse' with 'white' is not 'horse.' Therefore, I say that a white horse is not a horse.
>
> (—*Kung-Sun Lung-tzu,* Ch. 2)

In the fifth chapter is found the "Discourse on the Hard and White:"

> "Is it possible that hard, white, and stone are three?"
> "No."
> "Can they be two?"
> "Yes."
> ". . . . There are white things, but whiteness does not specify what is white. There are hard things, but hardness goes not specify what is hard. Being non-specifying, they are general, and so how can they be in the stone [which is particular]?"
>
> (—*Ibid.*, 5)

KUNG SUN YANG: See Shang Yang.

KUO HSIANG (250-312): The third of the Neo-Taoists, after Wang Pi and Ho Yen, Kuo Hsiang wrote a famous commentary on the *Chuang Tzŭ*. Scholars have discovered that Kuo Hsiang copied much of Hsiang Hsiu's commentary into his, without giving due credit. Kuo Hsiang's use of Hsiang Hsiu results in the hyphenated designation, Hsiang-Kuo (or, if there is no objection to mixing first names with last, Hsiang-Hsiang). However, since the thought of the two thinkers was virtually identical, and since the names nearly are, as well, the controversy doesn't seem to matter much.

Kuo disagrees with Chuang Tzǔ's idea that the major category for investigation is the Way, *Tao*. Rather, he holds, it is Nature (*Tzu-jan*). "Heaven" is not properly considered to be a supernatural reality lurking behind the processes of Nature whereby things exist and change spontaneously, but rather merely its collective name. Principle does not, as Wang Pi taught, transcend things. Principle is immanent in things.

The wise man will take no unnatural action. In an interesting departure from classical Taoism, Kuo Hsiang (and Wang Pi, as well) say that the sage is not a hermit who withdraws from the world, as Lao Tzǔ did, but rather one who, with "no deliberate mind of his own" (*wu-hsin*), responds to events spontaneously. Confucius was then taken as the model of such a sage.

Kuo (unlike Wang) taught fatalism. Everything that happens is pre-determined, and hence correct. One should learn to be content in whatever station he finds himself.

KU YEN-WU (1613-1682): An outstanding seventeenth-century scholar during a period of independent and critical thought, Ku Yen-wu was greatly influenced by the philosophy of Chu Hsi (twelfth-century), whose interpretation of Confucianism (along with Ch'eng I's) was officially held to be orthodox.

L

LAMA: "Superior," or by derivation, "spiritual teacher," equivalent to *guru*. Not every monk is a Lama, because the term is properly reserved for a Tibetan or Mongolian monk (or layman) who is deeply learned in Buddhist doctrine or Tantric practices. Incarnate Lamas are called *Tulkus*.

Lama-ism is based upon the total veneration of the Lama. "The Lama is a Buddha in person," actually present, say Marpa's disciples when Mila Rêpa is initiated. They are filled with faith. The disciple's submission to the Lama is complete.

The purpose of this resignation is to receive knowledge of the techniques of Tantric Buddhism. The goals of these techniques are two-fold. The first is the ability to make the Absolute turn into perceived objects, at will. The second is the completion process, the "Great Fulfilment," fusion with the Absolute.

LAO TZŬ (570-517 B.C.):

> All men seek the first. He alone sought the last. He said: 'Accept the world's refuse.' Men all seek the full. He alone took the empty. Without storing anything, he had abundance, and this abundance was independence gained through contentment. His actions were effortless and without waste. He made nothing and laughed at inventions. Men all seek good fortune. He alone sought preservation through adaptation. He said: 'Only be blameless.' He regarded the

236

deep as the fundamental, moderation as the rule. He said: 'The hard will be crushed, the sharp will be blunted.' He was always generous and tolerant. He was not aggressive towards men. This may be called the height of perfection. Oh, Kuan Yin and Lao Tan! They were the perfect great men of antiquity.

Such was Chuang Tzŭ's summary of the general spirit and main principle of Lao Tzŭ's philosophy (quoted from the exposition by Hsiao Kung-Chuan).

Taoism ("Way-ism") is the name for the philosophy under discussion, and it was founded by Lao Tzŭ. However, Lao Tzŭ is a title, and there is some dispute among scholars as to who should have received that title. The title, Lao Tzŭ, means, elegantly, "The Eldest," or, reverently, "Old Master," or, flippantly, "Old Boy," or, "better" (in the opinion of William James Hail of the College of Yale-in-China), "Old Philosopher." The name of the founder of Taoism was Li Erh. He was presumably a contemporary of Confucius, but older. Called a "recluse gentleman," his doctrine "aimed at self-effacement and anonymity."

Lao Tan, "the Vast Perfect One of Old," is another name which may or may not, according to your point of view, be identical with Lao Tzŭ. Fung Yu-Lan argues that the two are not the same, while Wing-tsit Chan, generally following Ssŭ-ma Ch'ien (the great historian), treats them as different names for the same individual (*A Source Book in Chinese Philosophy*, 138).

The traditions about Lao Tzŭ's life are quite diverse. They assign his birth to any time between the thirteenth and sixth centuries B.C. Some say he lived for one hundred years. Others claim he never died. Ke Hung, an eclectic Taoist writer from the fourth century A.D., says that Lao Tzŭ has appeared many times throughout history, once taking a trip west to Ceylon where he was reborn as the Buddha.

The most likely historical information is that Lao Tzŭ was born on a farm in Honan province (south of Peking and an equal distance inland from Shanghai). He became the librarian (historian) of the State Archives at the court of Chou. This was during the worst of times, politically turbulent and unstable. Confucius once visited him (517) for information about rituals. Confucius began reminiscing about the heroes of old, and Lao Tzŭ said:

All those men of whom you speak have long since mouldered away with their bones. Only their words remain. When a capable man's time comes, he rises; if it does not, then he just wanders around wearily. I have heard that good merchants keep their goods buried deeply to make it look as if they had none and that a superior man whose character is perfected will pretend to be stupid. Give up your proud airs, sir, your many wishes, mannerisms and extravagant claims. They won't do you any good, sir. That's all I have to say to you!

After living at Chou for a long time, Lao Tzŭ concluded that the state was so poorly administered that it was on its way to ruin. Disgusted, he resigned his position, loaded all his possessions onto a cart drawn by two black oxen, and set off for parts unknown. At the final frontier outpost of the empire, he was recognized by the gatekeeper, who begged him to stay long enough to write down his philosophy in a book. He did, according to the legend, in two parts, a little over five thousand words, thus producing the *Lao-tzŭ*. Then he got back in his ox-cart, vanished over the mountain pass, and was never seen again. Where he died is not known. Perhaps it was in Tibet.

Taoism generally teaches retreat from civilization and a return to nature. Then we may attain harmony with the *Tao*, the external way, which is the supreme governing force behind the universe. Other schools of thought had used the term, *Tao*, to mean a system or moral truth. Lao Tzŭ's school used it to mean the One, which is natural, eternal, spontaneous, nameless, and indescribable.

LAO TZŬ, THE: See *Tao Te Ching*.

LI: The Chinese term meaning "principle," "law," "reason," "abstract right," both "*Li*" (principle) and "*li*," meaning "ceremony," "rites," "proper conduct," or "propriety" are pronounced identically, although the Chinese characters are different, and care should be taken not to confuse the two terms. Neo-Confucian thinkers gave great prominence to *Li*, writing that principle underlies all things (Chang Heng-ch'ü), that principle is reality (the Ch'eng-Chu School), that principle is always good, the eternal, incorporeal, infinite, uniform, and self-identical essence of all things, new in every new thing or event (Chu Hsi), that the Mind is principle (Lu Chiu-yüan) that the principle of Nature is the reality of the Mind (Wang Yang-ming), that principle and matter-energy should not be distinguished (Yen Yüan), that principle should be identified with natural processes and human affairs (Li Kung), and that there is no principle outside human desire (Tai Tung-yüan).

It has been mentioned that the character for *Li* suggests the grade in Jade, having the Jade radical built into it, implying, perhaps, that good craftsmen take a natural substance, find the pattern in it, and carve around it, rather than destroying what is naturally beautiful and valuable.

li: The Chinese term for "propriety," "ceremony," "etiquette," "worship," "offerings," the Chinese character which appears in the title of the *Book of Rites*. Discussed in the context of the five human relations which rest on mutual moral duties, Confucius holds that harmony is the function of propriety (*li*).

LIEH TZŬ (450-375 B.C.): A Taoist philosopher who, according to Chuang Tzŭ, could ride on the wind for two weeks at a time. Although Chuang had been born about six years after Lieh died, he may have seen the shadow still passing by. Able to accomplish such extraordinary feats, he also wrote a book posthumously, the *Lieh Tzŭ*, which was influential during the Wei and Chin periods (220-419 A.D.), Wang Pi and Ho Yen's time. More scholars dispute his writing ability than object to his flying ability. The *Lieh Tzŭ* is fatalistic, mechanistic, evolutionary and hedonistic in its outlook. He taught that man should abandon all attempts at thought and classification and instead seek peace and "emptiness."

LI KUNG (1659-1733): A Chinese Confucian philosopher who emphasized the social utility of values. Li and Yen Yüan judged even moral behavior and music according to a utilitarian standard.

LIN YUTANG (1895-1976): Born October 10, 1895, in Fukien province on the southeast coast of China, he was tutored privately, and then attended St. John's University in Shanghai, a Christian missionary school. In 1919, he entered Harvard's graduate school, studying comparative literature and essay writing. He then travelled to France and Germany, earning a Ph.D. in philology from Leipzig University. In 1923 he returned to China, teaching English philology at Peking National University. Three years later, he was forced to leave, as a "radical" professor. He went south to Amoy University as dean of the College of Arts. In 1927, he became foreign secretary of the Wuhan government. A split developed in the government, so he left politics for a life of writing. Foreign language editor for the Academia Sinica, a research academy, he also founded the first humor magazine to appear in China, entitled "The Analects Fortnightly."

In 1935, he returned to the United States. His books include: *My Country and My People; The Importance of Living* (1937); *Wisdom of Confucius* (1938) *Moment in Peking* (1939); *With Love and Irony* (1940); *A Leaf in the Storm* (1941); *Wisdom of China and India* (1942); *Between Tears and Laughter* (1943); *The Vigil of a Nation* (1945); *Wisdom of Laotse; Chinatown Family* (1948); *Wisdom of China* (1949); *Peace is in the Heart* (1950); *On the Wisdom of America* (1950); *Widow, Nun and Courtesan* (1951); *Famous Chinese Short Stories* (1952); *The Vermillion Gate* (1953); *The Unexpected Island* (1955); *Lady Wu* (1956); *The Secret Name* (1959); *From Pagan to Christian* (1960).

He considered his dictionary of Chinese-English modern usage the "crown" of his career. Beyond that, he said, his only ambition was to improve his calligraphy (the brush writing of Chinese characters, considered an art form), "when I retire at eighty." When seventy, he returned to Asia. He died March 26, 1976, in Hong Kong, aged eighty.

LIU-AN: See Huai-nan Tzŭ.

LOKAYATA: "Directed toward the world," the theory that only this world (*loka*) is real. Materialism in India. The same philosophy as Cārvāka (*q.v.*).

LU CHIU-YUAN (1139-1193): A philosopher of the Idealistic Neo-Confucian School (called the Lu-Wang School, after Lu Chiu-yüan and Wang Yang-ming), Lu Chiu-yüan (or Lu Hsiang-shan, "the master of Hsiang-shan") was noted for his debate with Chu Hsi at the Goose Lake Temple. Agreeing with Ch'eng Yi, Chu Hsi maintained that "the nature is *Li*." Lu replied that "the mind is *Li*." "The universe is my mind," he said, and: "my mind is the universe." Again, "All affairs within the universe (literally, space and time, *yü* and *chou*) come within the scope of my duty; the scope of my duty includes all affairs within the universe."

Since he had experienced his philosophical views through Sudden Enlightenment, he is noted for his emphasis upon meditation and intuition.

The Mind is Principle, Law, or Reason (*Li*). There is only one world (Mind), not two (Mind and Matter-Energy (*Ch'i*)). Principle underlies all things. It is complete in the mind. Mankind possesses an innate moral consciousness. The Principle of Nature and human desires are not to be distinguished from each other.

Lu stressed the simplicity of method. We should cultivate ourselves, search for fundamental truth, and discover the "original mind."

Any distinction between mind and nature was, Lu held, merely verbal:

> Scholars of today devote most of their time to the explanation of words. For instance, such words as feeling, nature, mind, and ability all mean the same thing. It is only accidental that a single entity is denoted by different terms.
>
> (—*Collected Works, Lu Hsiang-shan
> Ch'üan-chi*, 35.)

Lu criticized Buddhists for wanting to withdraw from the world to escape its pain, sorrow, and vexation. Compared to

Confucianists who, he says, are righteous and unselfish, the Buddhists are "profit-seeking and selfish."

Lu wrote:

> The universe has never limited and separated itself from man, but it is man who limits and separates himself from the universe.
>
> (—*Ibid.*, 36.)

LU HSIANG-SHAN: See Lu Chiu-yüan.

LURIA, ISAAC BEN SOLOMON ASHKENAZI (1534-1572): A Jerusalem-born mystic schooled in Egypt, Isaac Luria procured one of the first printed copies of the *Zohar*, and became obsessed by it. He lived as a hermit in Safed (1569), separating from his home and family, only returning on the Sabbath. He claimed to have talked with the Prophets in his sleep, and had many other trances and visions. In 1572, he died of the plague. His disciple was Chaim Vital.

M

MADHVA (1199-1260): One of the leading Vedanta thinkers, along with Shankara and Ramanuja, Madhva (also called Pūrnaprajnā Anandatîrtha) was born in a village near Udipi, about sixty miles north of Mangalore. A highly successful debater, Madhva could walk on water, an ability which seldom failed to impress judges. He toured South India debating against Shankara's doctrine of Non-Dualism. When he toured the north, he had less success, possibly because there was less water. He had to walk on the land, and suffered persecution from his opponents. His patron deity—he was said to be his manifestation—appropriately enough, for a public speaker, was Vāyu, the god of wind.

Madhva contended, in contradiction to Shankara, that the soul is a separate principle which has an independent existence of its own. The soul is only associated with, not reducible to, the Ultimate Principle. The Ultimate Principle is not the cause of the world. This theory is a dualism (*dvaita*). After renouncing the world, he founded a temple dedicated to Krishna at Udipi and taught there until his death. His biography is found in Nārayanācārya's *Madhva vijaya* and *Manimañjari*.

Madhva's works include commentaries on the *Vedānta sūtra*, the *Bhagavad gîtā*, the Upanishads, the *Mahābhārata tātparyanirnaya* (*Epitome of the Mahābhārata*), the gloss on the *Bhāgavata purāna*, and the *Anuvyākhyāna*. In addition, he wrote an illuminating work entitled the *Light on Principles* (*Tattvoddyota*).

MAHĀMUDRĀ: The "great symbol," in Tantric Buddhism, transcending any verbal expression and containing within it the universe. When Tilopa was instructing Nāropa, he said:
I understand that to see the Ultimate in this life is to have obtained the highest realization, Mahāmudrā.
Specifically, this instruction was in three parts:

1) through mystic illumination to determine the unoriginatedness of the ground (Being-in-itself), Mahāmudrā;
3) through subsequent presentational knowledge to recognize the unceasing or the path (Being-for-itself), Mahāmudrā; and
3) through the relation of coincidence to realize the ineffable or the goal, Mahāmudrā.

Mahāmudrā thus appears as reality (Brahman), as the way (Tao), and as the goal (Nirvana).

MAHARAURAVA: The fifth of the Buddhist hells, the "Great Screaming Hell" is reserved for liars. There are eighteen subdivisions of this hell. The standard length of stay is 8000 years. Those who lie to friends, lie about magical powers that they do not have, steal farm land by lying, double-cross business partners, or impersonate monks are given different parts of this hell to inhabit. Many fires, giant scissors, enormous crows, and worms are provided for various tortures.

MAHAVIRA (599-527 B.C.): The founder of Jainism (q.v.), Mahavira (meaning "Great Conquerer"), or Nataputta Vardhamana, was an older contemporary of the Buddha. Born in Bihar, near Vaisali (which is between Delhi and Calcutta, closer to the latter) not simply of one virgin, but of two (the gods did not approve of the first one, because she was a Brahmin, so they transferred the embryo to another woman, of the Kshatriya caste), he was raised enjoying the all luxuries of wealth. When he was thirty, he renounced all pleasures, gave away all his money, tore out five handfuls of hair, and entered "the state of houselessness." After living for several months with some monks, he decided that was also too pleasant a life, so he struck out for himself. He pledged to "neglect my body and abandon the care of it," threw off his last remaining robe (which had "a flamingo pattern"), and wandered naked through central India seeking release from rebirth. Village urchins built fires under the soles of his feet or drove nails into his ears in an attempt, unsuccessful, to distract him from meditation. He was bitten by dogs while entering villages. Sometimes the natives would urge the dogs on, shouting: "Khukkhu, khukkhu," at him.

One of the distinctive teachings of Mahavira was *ahimsa*, non-injury to any living creature, a doctrine which greatly appealed to Gandhi and Schweitzer, centuries later. Mahavira's interpretation of this idea required him to carry a soft broom when walking, to sweep away any insect which might be injured by his feet. He carried a cloth to strain liquid before drinking, to avoid drinking any insects. He held the cloth in front of his mouth while speaking, to prevent any living thing from flying into it. Before eating, he would carefully inspect a bowl of food looking for worms, eggs, mildew, or cobwebs, to avoid accidentally injuring any living thing.

Finally, in his forties, he reached Nirvana, called Kevala, and became the Jina (the Conquerer), after which his followers are called Jains. He taught for thirty more years that *ahimsa* and extreme asceticism are necessary to reach enlightenment. At the age of seventy-two, he died by voluntary self-starvation (*sallakhana*), and went to his place of reward, Isatpragbhara.

His biographers promptly recorded all his deeds for posterity, beginning their writing a mere thousand years after his death.

Mahavira is pictured as the last of the "ford finders" (*Tirthankaras*), of which there have been twenty-four, represented by images in Jain temples. They are not deities, and can help no one else attain salvation, but others may feel encouraged to keep trying by the example of their success.

MAHĀYĀNA BUDDHISM: Arising as a reform movement in reaction to the council of orthodox Elders, Mahāyāna (from *mahā*, meaning "great," and *yāna*, meaning "means of salvation") taught that gods and divine Buddhas are available to help one attain true understanding. Hīnayāna (q.v.) taught that salvation was entirely up to the individual.

Mahāyāna Buddhism, the "Greater Vehicle", is found in northern Asia, Japan, and Korea. Hīnayāna Buddhism, the "Lesser Vehicle," is essentially a body of teaching designed to instruct the individual how to achieve release from the cycle of life, death, and rebirth. Release, on this view, only seems open to those with special capacity, those able to follow the noble eightfold path correctly. However, just before his death, said Mahāyāna theologians, Buddha had revealed that all living beings have the capacity for Buddhahood. Gautama Buddha is transcendent, a god rather than a mere man. There must also be others who had similarly achieved enlightenment. These, the Bodhisattvas, "Buddhas-to-be," are individuals who completed all the requirements of Enlightenment, who if they wanted could go directly into Nirvana, but who held back to help others as well. Their great compassion is the key virtue.

Mahāyāna developed the theory of the "three forms" of Buddha: (1) cosmic, (2) transcendent, and (3) earthly. The cosmic form of Buddha is all-embracing and universal. The transcendent form of Buddha is one of the many heavenly figures, such as the healing Buddha (Japanese, *Yakushi*), the Buddha of the future (*Miroku*), or the Buddha of boundless light (*Amida*). The earthly form of Buddha was identified as Siddhartha Gautama (q.v.), the historical Buddha.

Mahāyāna developed in three main stages, beginning with the Second Buddha Council (about 383 B.C.), at which time a rival meeting of ten thousand, called Mahāsanghikas, was held in opposition to the Elders (Theravādins). Next, when the Third Council (about 240 B.C.) added another collection of books to the canon of approved scripture, there were three divisions (the three "baskets," *pitaka*), the Dhamma (teachings, doctrines, or laws), the Vinaya (rules of conduct for discipline and monastic life), and, now, the Abhidhamma (primarily metaphysical and psychological themes). The total number of books in the new collection was sixty-five thousand. Of these, some seven thousand were to be translated into Chinese by the tenth century. The

246

enlargement of the canon was of particular interest to Mahāyāna thinkers.

Finally, two principal schools were formed, one by Nāgārjuna (*cc.* 100-200 A.D.) and the other by Asanga (*ca.* 410-500 A.D.). The first was called the Middle Doctrine School (Mādhyamika) and the second the Idealistic, or "Mind Only," School (Yogāchāra). The Middle Doctrine School was carried to China by Kumārajīva (401 A.D.) and developed by Chi Tsang. It emphasized the Void, stating that only the Void is really real, whereas everything else is relative. Eight denials are made, in pairs: no creation and no destruction, no annihilation and no permanence, no unity and no diversity, no coming and no going. The assertion is made that these conditions must have a middle without extremes between each of these pairs. Thus, the truth is an absolute middle, the Void, which is also Nirvana. In deeper meditation, we come to realize that this is also the nature of the All. The extremes (and all dharmas) were deductions or projections from this center, by which the real is veiled.

The Idealistic School stressed the belief that the mind is the coordinator of the senses. Its store-house consciousness is the source of all characteristics and things. Thus the mind is what gives the nature ("thus-ness," *tathata*) to all things. This Kant-like formulation has the consequence that, under it, reality is not nonexistent (a Void). Further, since the mind supplies the structure of phenomena, it is not said that phenomena have any reality of their own. This school was taken to China by Paramārtha (499-569 A.D.) and, after the books had been translated, became the She-lun School and then Fa-hsiang (Hosso), founded by Hsuan-tsang.

The name Mahāyāna was first used about 100 A.D., following Ashwaghosha, the Indian author of *The Awakening of Faith* (100 B.C.). The original Sanskrit has been lost, and it was preserved only in its Chinese translation by Paramārtha and Chih-i (557 A.D.).

MANDALA: An intricate symbolic design, usually circular, with an inscribed square, used as a memory device by those who practice yogic meditation under its various forms. Sometimes

247

painted, sometimes pictured in the mind, sometimes traced in colored sand upon the ground, it is a support for instruction and meditation.

MANTRA: A sacred sound, or formula, composed of syllables for their psychic effects, a mantra is said to be full of the influence of a particular sage or bodhisattva. A mantra is always in Sanskrit and never translated.

MAO TSE-TUNG (alternate spelling: MAO ZEDONG): Revolutionary Marxist and Chinese cultural leader, Mao was born December 26, 1893, in the village of Shaoshan, Hunan province, an inland province about three hundred miles west and a little north of Formosa. Mao's father was a poor peasant who worked his way up to being a grain merchant and rich peasant. His mother was a devout Buddhist. He was a Buddhist as well, until adolescence. Although his father had only two years of school, Mao was sent to a traditional Confucian school for five years, from eight to thirteen. His father then wanted him to drop out to work full-time in field and office. He ran away from home to continue his studies, taking law from an unemployed law student and classics from an old village scholar. At sixteen, he formally enrolled in school again, despite his father's opposition. Older than the other students because of his interrupted education, he towered above them. Poorer than the other students (they were mostly sons of landlords), he dressed in frayed and ragged clothes. In his readings, he admired Napoleon and George Washington. Next he went to Changsha, the provincial capital of Hunan, hardly daring to dream, as he said, that he could "actually become a student in this great school." Revolutionary activities were sweeping China as the old patterns of authority broke up. Secret societies successfully struck against the administration. In 1911, a revolutionary army took control of all Hunan province. Within a short time, the landlords and merchants became dissatisfied with the policies of the new leaders who favored the poor. They organized a counter-revolt, murdered two popular leaders and left their bodies lying in the street, a sight which greeted

Mao's eyes one day. The lessons of this counter-revolution were not lost on him.

Mao, who was now eighteen, joined the revolutionary army as a private, hoping to "help complete the revolution." Within six months he left the army, convinced that revolution was accomplished. After drifting for a couple of years, enrolling in the kind of courses designed to fleece veterans, reading on his own at the provincial library (the works of Darwin, J. S. Mill, Rousseau and Spencer) he decided to become a teacher and enrolled at the Fourth Provincial Normal School in Changsha. There he formed friendships and developed ideas and techniques which he used from that time on.

Mao's ethics teacher, Yang Ch'ang-chi, enthusiastically urged all his students to read the magazine, *New Youth* (*Hsin Ch'ing-nien*), almost as soon as it came out. Through it, Mao found himself in touch with the mainstream of intellectual life in modern China. Yang was a disciple of Kant and T. H. Green, having studied for ten years in Germany, England, and Japan. Yang also admired Chu Hsi, the neo-Confucian, believing that:

Each country has its own national spirit, just as each person has his own personality.... A country is an organic whole, just as the human body is an organic whole. It is not a machine, which can be taken apart and put together again. If you take it apart, it dies.

His students read neo-Kantian ethics from a translation of a book by Friedrich Paulsen. Mao wrote in the margin of the book:

Wherever there is repression of the individual, wherever there are acts contrary to the nature of the individual, there can be no greater crime. That is why our country's three bonds (between prince and subject, father and son, husband and wife) must go, and constitute, with religion, capitalists, and autocracy, the four evil demons of the empire.

Mao later married Yang's daughter. She was put to death by the Nationalists in 1930.

Mao's first published article, in *New Youth* (April, 1917), was entitled "A Study of Physical Culture," a series of exercises for the strengthening of body and the building of character. He wrote:

The principal aim of physical education is military heroism.

He organized the "Association for Student Self-Government" to resist unreasonable demands by the college administrators. The students discussed how they could have an effect on national policy. Some said they should go into politics. Mao replied that they would need money and connections to get elected. Others said they should use their positions as teachers to influence future generations. Mao replied that this would take too long. They asked him what solution he would propose, he replied:

Imitate the heroes of the Liang Shan P'o (the mountain fortress where bandit heroes had gone to fight for justice and order and the Chinese way).

Mao graduated in the spring of 1918 and went to Peking, where he accepted a job as a librarian's assistant for eight dollars a month. He tried to ask questions of the leading intellectuals who visited the University library, but found that in most cases, they had no time to listen "to an assistant librarian speaking with a southern accent." Once, after a lecture by Hu Shih, he attempted to ask him a question. Upon finding out that he was not a proper student, but merely a librarian's assistant, Hu Shih refused to talk to him.

Mao joined Li Ta-chao's Marxist Study Group, where people were more friendly. Ch'en Tu-hsiu, who had long been Mao's literary idol, also influenced him by recommending all that was young, uninhibited, full of vitality, and liberating.

Li and Ch'en debated over which was more important, the freedom of the people or the survival of the state. Li maintained that it was better to suffer even the most tyrannical state rather than to have no state at all, to become "slaves without a country."

The "May 4th Movement" was a radicalizing influence upon the entire country. Used broadly to refer to the years from 1915-1921, when new ideas swept the land, it strictly refers to the student demonstrations which broke out on that date in 1919 in Peking. They were protesting the decision of the Paris Peace Conference to end the former German concessions in Shantung, instead of returning them to China, by giving them to Japan! Ch'en Tu-hsiu, Dean of the Faculty of Letters, supported the students. He was imprisoned for six months. When Mao later asked him about his experiences, Ch'en told him that he turned toward Marxism during his detention.

Mao worked as a laundry-man in Shanghai, but soon was offered a job as director of the primary school of the First Normal School in Changsha, in the wake of struggles between contending armies.

Joining the First Congress of the Communist Party, he met in Shanghai in July, 1921, in a girl's school closed for the holidays, located in the French concession of the city, thus beyond the reach of Chinese police. When a police spy joined the group, they took the warning, and all but two escaped. The final session was held on an excursion boat on South Lake, Chekiang province, disguised as a holiday party. The next year, attempting to attend the Second Congress, Mao lost the Shanghai address and had to go back home.

Mao founded a "Self-Study University," combining Marxist, nationalist, and traditional Chinese learning. He also prepared a special set of literacy booklets, to teach a basic thousand-character vocabulary, which was distributed by the YMCA. His set explained how the riches of society were produced by workers and peasants, and told of the Russian revolution and the desirability of communism.

Collaboration with the Koumintang was counseled by emissaries from the International, such as "Maring" (Henricus Sneevliet), the Dutch Communist. It was an uneasy alliance.

Foreign influence in China grew increasingly arrogant. A sign was posted at the entrance to the municipal park in Shanghai, which read: "Chinese and dogs not allowed."

A Japanese foreman, in a dispute with a Chinese worker, killed him. In the following protest, on May 30, 1925, a column of workers and students was fired upon by police of the International Settlement on the order of a British police officer. Ten were

251

killed. Protests mounted, and on June 23, British and French police again fired on a crowd, this time killing fifty-two. National indignation and political activitiy increased. Fury was directed against Chinese officials who meekly cooperated with the foreigners. Mao wrote:

A revolution is . . . an act of violence whereby one class overthrows the authority of another. A rural revolution is one in which the peasants overthrow the authority of the feudal landlord class.

Mao wrote, more specifically, that:

What we call land confiscation consists in not paying rent. There is no need for any other method. At the present time, there is already a high tide of the peasant movement in Hunan and Hupei, and on their own initiative the peasants have refused to pay rent, and have seized political power.

Land should be confiscated from "local bullies and bad gentry, corrupt officials, militarists, and all counter-revolutionary elements in the villages." "Counter-revolutionary elements" were defined as landlords owning more than four and a half acres (thirty *mou*).

In April, 1927, when the workers of Shanghai had taken control of the city and delivered it to Chiang Kai-shek, he expressed his gratitude by massacring them. This ended collaboration. In Peking, a number of Communists, including Li Ta-chao, were arrested and strangled to death.

In spite of this, Stalin ordered cooperation with Chiang and told them to restrain the "excesses" of the peasants and to talk to the Kuomintang about land reform. The recipients of these instructions said that talking about land reform with the Kuomintang was like "playing a lute to entertain a cow." They also planned—and announced openly—a complete Communist takeover of the Kuomintang. They were promptly expelled (July 15, 1927).

Military resistance was the only refuge for the Communists,

they believed, but policy was still in doubt. Mao gathered the remnants of some regiments, a thousand men, and led them up into a mountain range called the Chingkangshan, on the border between Hunan and Kiangsi. The Central Committee bitterly denounced Mao for his failure to prosecute an attack upon the city of Changsha. Mao was relieved of his command, but the communique did not reach him until several months had passed. He joined forces with two bandit chiefs who already lived in the mountains. Mao had admired, from childhood, the bandit heroes of popular Chinese novels (such as *Water Margin*). Mao and his comrades were able to hold a meeting and elect a new Special Committee with a secretary favorable to Mao.

Chiang Kai-shek's troops attacked ferociously, with one "encirclement campaign" after another. He was more interested in attacking Mao than in fighting the Japanese. As the military situation became more precarious, the Red Army began the famous Long March, which lasted for two years, beginning in October, 1934. The longest route (the First Front Army) went from Kiangsi west to Yünnan, and then north to the Kansu-Shensi border. Altogether, one hundred thousand started out. Neither their destination nor their purpose was entirely clear. The desire to resist the Japanese and to escape the Kuomintang motivated them. A third of the way along, at Tsunyi, the secretary-general, Ch'in Pang-hsien, who insisted that they drag along all the machines, printing presses, and bullion of a fully-organized state, was ousted, and a leader sympathetic to Mao's desire for swift mobility installed. Mao was given the newly-created post of chairman of the Politburo.

The march covered six thousand miles. They had to fight all the way. In the course of one delaying action, Mao's own brother was killed.

Finally reaching Shensi province, Mao proceeded to establish a base for national operations and resistance against foreign operations and resistance against foreign invasion. He called Chiang Kai-shek a "traitor who sells out his country," and the "running dog" of the imperialists. Chiang attempted to "quarrantine" the area he was in.

After a short time, Mao's intense concern for the fate of China led him to propose collaboration with Chiang Kai-shek. The insults ceased and Mao mobilized the patriotic sentiments of the Chinese masses against the Japanese invasion. He started the "North-west Anti-Japanese Red Army University," with 2700 students, many of whom were students from Peking that the Kuomintang leadership made unwelcome because of their participation in demonstrations.

In 1937, the well-known movie star from Shanghai, Lan-p'ing, went to Yenan. Mao ended his relationship with Ho Tzu-chen, who had borne him five children since 1928, when they first had begun to live together, and married Lan-p'ing.

Mao's sister had been executed in 1930, the same time as his first wife. In 1943, his brother, Mao Tse-min, was executed by a local war-lord who shifted his allegiance from Moscow to the Kuomintang.

During this period, he wrote *Basic Tactics* (*Chi-ch'u Chan-shu*), counseling "avoiding strength and striking at weakness," and stating that the military objective is the destruction of enemy soldiers, not the capture of territory or strong points.

By 1945, "the thought of Mao Tse-tung" was enshrined as necessary to "guide the entire work" of the party. Liu Shao-ch'i said Mao was "not only the greatest revolutionary and statesman in Chinese history, but also its greatest theoretician and scientist." A few days after the capture of Nanking, Mao wrote:

The true way that governs the world of men is that of radical change.

By 1949, Mao had won the civil war, and he said:

The poor peasants conquered the country; the poor peasants should now sit on the country. (*ta chiang-shan, tso chiang-shan*).

Full-scale land reform was instituted, along with "a small-scale reign of terror" against the "local bullies and evil gentry." Some "tens of thousands" of landlords were put to death.

The Marriage Law was promulgated to establish equal rights for women and make "free choice the basic principle of every marriage." The law also had the result of weakening feudal ties and dissolving parental control over children.

On June 25, 1950, the Korean War broke out, just as the Agrarian Reform Law was about to be put into effect, and two days after Mao had declared that the "trial of war" was "basically" over. A "Resist America and Aid Korea" campaign was inaugurated.

On November 29, 1950, the Chinese intervened in Korea with an army of 850,000 men. Among the casualties suffered was Mao's son (by his first wife), Mao An-ying, killed in combat.

By the first half of 1951, between one and three million persons were executed as "counter-revolutionaries" by the regime.

The war ended in 1953. By 1955, agricultural cooperatives were established, and Mao wrote:

As this is being written, more than sixty million peasant households in various parts of the country have already joined cooperatives. It is as if a raging tidal wave has swept away all the demons and ghosts.

"Let a Hundred Flowers Bloom," proclaimed Mao in the middle of 1956, relaxing restrictions against internal criticism. As criticisms became too intense for comfort, a "rectification program" was instituted in the beginning of 1957. "Rightists," often intellectuals, were "sent down" into the country to do hard physical labor, which often ruined the health of those not used to it. Many university professors were ordered to clean lavatories in the school as a means of breaking their spirit.

In May of 1964, the first edition of *Quotations from Chairman Mao*, the "little red book," was published, on the eve of the Youth League Congress. It was published by the Political Department of the Army. This book has been made to serve as the central source of wisdom for contemporary China. Belief in Mao's thought is enthusiastically recommended as the chief virtue for a progressive society. For example, one author writes:

What I call "belief" means believing in Mao Tse-tung's thought. Moreover, this belief must be steadfast and immovable. . . . Mao Tse-tung's thought is the only correct thought. It is the incarnation of Marxism-Leninism in China. It is the symbol of truth. Therefore, if a person at any time whatever, in any place whatever, regarding any question whatever, manifests wavering in his attitude toward Mao Tse-tung's thought, then, no matter if this wavering is only momentary and slight, it means in reality that the waverer departs from Marxist-Leninist truth and will lose his bearings and commit political errors. So we must follow Chairman Mao steadfastly and eternally! Forward, following a hundred per cent and without the slightest reservation the way of Mao-Tse-tung.

(—Liu Tzu-chiu, quoted by Stuart Schram, *Mao Tse-tung*, p. 326.)

Some of the more noted passages from the little red book include the following:

Policy and tactics are the life of the Party; leading comrades at all levels must give them full attention and must never on any account be negligent.

(I. "The Communist Party")

In class society everyone lives as a member of a particular class, and every kind of thinking, without exception, is stamped with the brand of a class.

(II. "Classes and Class Struggle")

A revolution is not a dinner party, or writing an essay, or painting a picture, or doing embroidery; it cannot be so refined, so leisurely and gentle, so temperate, kind, courteous, restrained and magnanimous. A revolution is an insurrection, an act of violence by which one class overthrows another.

(—*Ibid.*)

We should support whatever the enemy opposes and oppose whatever the enemy supports.

(—*Ibid.*)

The socialist system will eventually replace the capitalist system; this is an objective law independent of man's will. However much the reactionaries try to hold back the wheel of history, sooner or later revolution will take place and will inevitably triumph.

(—III. "Socialism and Communism")

It is only the working class that is most far-sighted, most selfless and most thoroughly revolutionary.

(—*Ibid.*)

Even administrative regulations for the maintenance of public order must be accompanied by persuasion and education, for in many cases regulations alone will not work.

(—IV. "The Correct Handling of Contradictions Among the People")

War is the highest form of struggle for resolving contradictions, when they have developed to a certain stage, between classes, nations, states, or political groups, and it has existed ever since the emergence of private property and of classes.

(—V. "War and Peace")

History shows that wars are divided into two kinds, just and unjust. All wars that are progressive are just, and all wars that impede progress are unjust.

(—*Ibid.*)

Revolutionary war is an antitoxin which not only eliminates the enemy's poison but also purges us of our own filth.

(—*Ibid.*)

"Political power grows out of the barrel of a gun."

(—*Ibid.*)

The army is the chief component of state power.... Yes, we are advocates of the omnipotence of revolutionary war.

(—*Ibid.*)

War can only be abolished through war, and in order to get rid of the gun it is necessary to take up the gun.

(—*Ibid.*)

War, this monster of mutual slaughter among men, will be finally eliminated by the progress of human society, and in the not too distant future, too.

(—*Ibid.*)

The imperialists ... will never become Buddhas, till their doom.

(—*Ibid.*)

Imperialism will not last long because it always does evil things. It persists in grooming and supporting reactionaries in all countries who are against the people.

(—VI. "Imperialism and All Reactionaries Are Paper Tigers.")

Strategically we should despise all our enemies, but tactically we should take them all seriously.

(—*Ibid.*)

We should rid our ranks of all impotent thinking. All views that overestimate the strength of the enemy and underestimate the strength of the people are wrong.

(—VII. "Dare to Struggle and Dare to Win.")

Our strategy and tactics are based on a people's war; no army opposed to the people can use our strategy and tactics.

(—VIII. "People's War.")

Our principle is that the Party commands the gun, and the gun must never be allowed to command the Party.

(—IX. "The People's Army.")

Place problems on the table. This should be done not only by the "squad leader" but by the committee members, too. Do not talk behind people's backs.

(—X. "Leadership of Party Committees.")

"Have a head for figures".... Every quality manifests itself in a certain quantity.

(—*Ibid.*)

The masses are the real heroes.... The masses have boundless creative power.

(XI. "The Mass Line")

You can't solve a problem? Well, get down and investigate the present facts and its past history! When you have investigated the problem thoroughly, you will know how to solve it.

(XXIII. "Investigation and Study.")

Liberalism is extremely harmful in a revolutionary collective. It is a corrosive which eats away unity, undermines cohesion, causes apathy and creates dissension.

(XXIV. "Ideological Self-Cultivation.")

(1) The individual is subordinate to the organization;

(2) The minority is subordinate to the majority;

(3) The lower level is subordinate to the higher level.

(XXVI. "Discipline.")

Be pupils of the masses as well as their teachers.

(XXVIII. "Communists.")

Knowledge is a matter of science, and no dishonesty or conceit whatsoever is permissible. What is required is definitely the reverse—honesty and modesty.

(XXXIII. "Study.")

Mao died on the 10th of September, 1976, apparently of Parkinson's disease.

MAPPŌ: Japanese eschatological term for the latter days of Buddhist law.

MARPA (1012-1096): The disciple of Drogmi (who had secured a monopoly on Tibetan education by paying a large sum of gold to an Indian master for his wisdom), Marpa was a sort of brigand businessman saint. Born in southern Tibet, in the rich district of Lhotrak, his violent behavior convinced his parents to send him away for religious training. The tuition payment ("initiation" fee) charged by Drogmi was paper enough for sixteen volumes and two pack-animals. He gave Marpa language lessons for three years, Sanskrit and contemporary Indian. Dissatisfied, Marpa went home, demanded all of his inheritance, sold it, and went to India, saying:

> If, for the sake of religious teachings, one goes to India without having much gold, it is like drinking water from an empty bowl.

He studied in India for twelve years, then returned to Tibet for more money. He went into partnership with one of his clansmen, Marpa Golek, in Dam, raising horses, working the mines, curing the sick, and giving initiations. He became rich and successful, married several wives and had several sons, and travelled to India again for more instruction. All of his religious training did not improve his personality. Marpa remained a strong, violent man given to fits of temper. One of the chronicles comments of him:

> In the eyes of ordinary people, he reared a family, quarrelled with his countrymen, and only occupied himself with agriculture and building.

Marpa used his magic for selfish purposes, to frighten away the "cousins" who were attacking a fort which he had built in violation of the spirit of a treaty at a strategic location.

His pupils (called the "Four Pillars") included Mila Rêpa and Ngoktön. To learn the "particularly deep instructions," of the "manuscripts of the oral transmission" which bore the seal of prohibition, Ngoktön had to bring him all of his possessions, including even a lame old nanny-goat he had left at home. Even after such a payment was made, Marpa's style of education seems to have been setting nearly impossible tasks for his students to perform.

This information is from the *Biography of Mar-pa*, sPung-thang edn., by gTsang-smyon He-ru-ka, late fifteenth century.

MATSUMIYA KANZAN (1686-1780): A Japanese Confucian scholar of the Tokugawa Shogunate, Matsumiya maintained that Confucianism and Shintoism have much in common. Chinese and Japanese "customs and manners" are similar, and are to be contrasted with those of the people of India:

> In India, . . . people are old and feeble in spirit and they like the sombre teachings of Buddhism, which is always talking about the problem of death.
>
> (—*Sankyō Yōron, Essentials of the Three Schools*, in *Nihon Jurin Sōsho, Series on Japanese Confucianism*, Kaisetsubu,
> II, 7.)

He was critical of the exclusive attitude of esoteric Shintoism, concentrating on occult instructions, which he called "trifles." He characterized the cultural interests of his countrymen by saying:

> The Japanese are high-spirited and fond of arms. Valor and fearlessness make up their distinctive style.
>
> (—*Ibid.*, 2.)

MĀYĀ: The power of illusion, Māyā (pronounced MAW-yuh) is appearance as opposed to reality, phenomena being appearance,

Brahman (*q.v.*) being the only permanent and unchanging reality. Māyā is the veil of change and things.

Māyā is said to be illusion but not delusion because something real is there, but wrongly seen. A delusion is the case when nothing at all is present. However thickly veiled, reality is still behind the illusions of everyday life. Māyā is a sort of mirage created by reality.

The world as māyā is a sub-psychological inhibition capped by positive "madness," or make-believe in action. This process occurs whenever we think of anything. We first choose the subject of our thought. This is a limiting act by the mind. We select, we screen out other possibilities and concentrate on one thing. This is the veiling. Then, on the basis of these limitations, we make a plan and do something about it. This plan is called a "projection" (*vikshepa*). Through this process arises the "world of action," which is "a māyā."

Another word often used by Vedāntist scholars to describe the manifest is *mithya*, which means "false." It differs from māyā in that it is positively false. It is that which the creative or projecting power builds upon the defects brought about by the veiling power. It is a wrong notion based on careless or disordered perceptions, incorrect references, or mistaken considerations. It is a sort of second-order illusion, a false idea based upon illusion to begin with. More deeply, according to Sureshwarācharya, the very notion of falseness is false. Only the experience in samādhi (deep meditation) is truly true.

Māyā is said to be not a reality, because it is an ever-present power (*shakti*), not something in the current of events, and yet it is real because it is an ever-present law wherever there is any event or thing.

Śri Aurobindo writes (in *A Practical Guide to Integral Yoga*): Nothing can arise from Nothing. Asat, Māyā, nothingness, is a creation of our mind. Out of its own incapacity it has created the conception of a zero; but it is an incalculable Infinite. Our sense by its incapacity has invented darkness. In truth there is nothing but Light. God is everywhere and wherever God is, there is Light.

MEIR (80-150): The disciple of Rabbi Akiba, Meir continued and completed the classification of the Law begun by Akiba. In the Mishnah (i.e., oral teaching), when a statement was not attributed to any other authority, Rabbi Meir was understood to be the source.

Friend of cynic (Oinomaos of Gadara) and atheist (Elisha ben Abuyah, a noted teacher who denounced the faith), Meir spoke Friday evenings in the little synagogue at Tiberius. "Every day," he said, "a man should utter a hundred benedictions."

MENCIUS (372-289 B.C.): Mang Tzǔ, "Master Mang," the great successor of Confucius, was the contemporary of Plato, Chuang Tzǔ (the famous Tzoist), and Hsün Tzǔ (of the "realistic" wing of Confucianism).

Mencius was unable to obtain a fair hearing for his views among the rulers or professional philosophers of the time at the great center of Chinese learning, Chi-hsia (in present Shantung), so he retired and wrote seven books called the *Mencius*. Later his work was honored by being included among the famous "Four Books," one of the main foundations of the Confucian education.

Human nature, Mencius declared, is originally good. Whereas Confucius had only implied such a view, Mencius made it into the basis for his entire philosophy. This natural goodness implies:

1) that man has an innate knowledge of the good;
2) that man has the "innate ability" to do good;
3) that one can "develop his mind to the utmost" both serving Heaven and fulfilling his own destiny;
4) that evil results from external influences;
5) that we must at all costs try to recover our original nature; and
6) that the end of learning is to "seek for the lost mind."

Mencius asserted that: "All men can become Yao or Shun," referring to two legendary sage-rulers. In contemporary terms, he might have said: "Everyone can become Christ or Buddha or Muhammed."

262

That is not to say everyone is born Confucius, a sage. But everyone is born with the capacity to become a wise man.

Mencius tangled with the Mo-ists over the question of whether one should have universal love. Mencius, with the rest of the Confucianists, said no. There should be degrees in love:

> Treat the aged in your family as they should be treated, and extend this treatment to the aged of other people's families. Treat the young in your family as they should be treated, and extend this treatment to the young of other people's families. (—*Mencius*, Ia, 7.)

We should "extend our scope of activity to include others."

> The superior man, in his relation to things, loves them but has no feeling of human-heartedness. In his relation to people, he has human-heartedness, but no deep feeling of family affection.(—*Mencius*, VIIa, 45.)

There are grades, or degrees, of love, according to Mencius.

"Supreme Spiritual Force," *Hao Jan Chih Ch'i*, is one of Mencius' prominent concepts (also translated "Great Morale," Fung Yu-lan). This kind of positive attitude is the morale of a person who identifies himself with the universe and its forces. It is cultivated by (1) Understanding the way (*Tao*) of elevating the mind, and the (2) accumulation of righteousness, behaving as a citizen of the universe. Once you understand the way and perform enough righteous deeds, the Supreme Spiritual Force will appear naturally. Its presence can never be forced. We can never "help it to grow," for just that effort will harm it:

> We should not be like the man from Sung, who was disturbed because his grain was not growing fast enough. So he pulled on it. Then he went home and innocently said: "I am very tired today, because I have been helping the grain to grow." His son ran out to look at the field, and found all the grain withered.(—*Mencius*, IIa, 2.)

263

MILA RÊPA (1040-1123): One of the most famous figures in the transmission of esoteric (secret) knowledge, Mila Rêpa, or Milarepa (precisely transliterated *Mi(d)-la ras-pa*) means "cotton-clad Mila." Named Töbaga ("delightful to hear") by his father, he was a great Tibetan poet, ascetic, and master of psychic powers. His life is recounted in the *Biography of Mi-la Ras-pa* (Peking edition, xylograph, written by gTsang-smyon He-ru-ka, "the madman of Tsang," also called "the Yogin who roams in cemeteries," in an edition by de Jong, the Hague, 1959). His father died when he was only seven, leaving his son, daughter, and twenty-four-year-old wife in the care of his younger brother (Mila's uncle), as was the custom. The uncle was greedy, took all their property for himself and then made them work for him. Mila's mother was able to keep one field which her own brother worked. Later she sold it and used the money to send Mila to study sorcery, to get vengeance. Mila learned how to bring hailstorms to ruin his uncle's crops. Then a giant scorpion was conjured up, which pulled down the house where everyone was assembled for a wedding reception, killing everyone but the uncle and aunt. Finally, the wicked uncle gave them back the property which he had stolen from them.

Although his mother was delighted, Mila was horrified by what he had done. He went off in search of other teachers, a Nyingmapa and others.

Finally, Mila Rêpa went to Marpa, the fat, famous, drunken, bad-tempered Lama. Marpa had received from the Indian sage Nāropa the knowledge of the only certain way to attain Liberation, and Mila Rêpa was determined to become his disciple. Marpa, however, was not interested in taking him on. Mila was poor and unable to afford the initiation fee (*dbang-yon*). His persistence made Marpa give him work to do, which Mila interpreted as necessary penance for his past misdeeds. Marpa ordered him to build five houses with his own hands. When the first stone house was almost finished, Marpa, instead of giving the promised instruction, said he had built the wrong kind of house, ordered him to tear it down, and return each stone to its exact original location. A second and a third proceeded in the same way. Mila's back was sore and bleeding from carrying the stones. Marpa insulted him

264

and struck him, humiliated him and drove him to despair. Marpa ordered him to build a fourth house, and then a fifth. Still, he did not teach him any secret doctrine. Marpa required him to make use of the sorcery he had learned to kill some enemies.

Mila became despondent and thought of suicide. Lama Ngok dissuaded him:

> The Lama grasped me and, shedding tears, he said, "Do not so, great magician! According to the doctrine of the secret mantras (Tantrism) which is the culmination of the teachings of the Buddhas, our body with all its senses is inseparable from the gods. If we perform transference ('pho-ba, passing from one life to another or into a paradise) before the right time, we commit the sin of killing the gods. Hence there is no sin greater than suicide."

At last convinced of Mila Rêpa's sincerity, Marpa accepted his total gift of "body, speech, and mind," ended his trials, and initiated him into the secret doctrine. Together, they drank wine from a cup made of a human skull.

Mila then spent six years in solitude and self-purification, in a cave. Deciding to return home, he had a vision in which he saw his mother dead, the house in ruins, and his sister in rags. When he reached home, it was as he had forseen. Overcome by grief, he resolved to spend the rest of his life as a hermit, pursuing a life of hardship, until he found liberation.

> Mila called himself "mad," and mocked at the monks: Your belly filled with pride, you belch vanity and vomit jealousy. You fart comtempt for others and excrete sarcasm!
> (—*Songs of Mi-la Ras-pa (m Gur-'bum)*,
> Peking edition.)

He became the patron of strolling comedians and actors and is usually pictured singing, holding his right hand to his ear.

Mila Rêpa wrote poems and songs to popularize Buddhist thought, creating folk-songs as a mode of instruction. He entered song contests at plowing time. Some of the verses from his "hundred thousand songs" read:

If you understand this song, then once you've scored a point,
If you understand it not, I can simply go away. . . .
Well then, little child so handsome, who would understand,
then listen!
What man am I? Do you know me? If you know not who I am,
Kungthang's
Mila Cloth-clad am I.

. . . .

Of myself, I've nothing to say: I am the son of the oral
teaching's *guru*;
I entered the religious life directly from my mother's womb,
And from the years of adolescence spent in study of the
doctrine.
Grown at last, great mediator, mountain hermitages I haunt.
Faced by demons, I do not waver, I fear not their phantom.
Once, while going from one cave to another, his clay bowl
broke. He burst into song praising it and saying it had now
become a great teacher, for it reminded him of the transitory
nature of all things.

When a great scholar came to visit him, he sang him a song:
Accustomed long to meditating on the Whispered Chosen
Truths, I have forgot all that is said in written and in printed
books.
Accustomed, as I've been, to study of the Common Science,
knowledge of erring Ignorance I've lost.
Accustomed long to keep my mind in the Uncreated State of
Freedom, I have forgot conventional and artifical usages.
Accustomed long to know the meaning of the Wordless, I
have forgot to trace the roots of verbs and source of words
and phrases;
May thou, O Learned One, trace out these things in standard
books.

(—from Evans-Wentz, *The Tibetan
Book of the Great Liberation*,
quoted in Thubten Jigme Norbu,
Tibet, 189.)

His diet consisted of wild fruits around his cave until he decided they were too luxurious, and ate only the nettles. His sister and the woman to whom he had once been engaged begged him to give up his terrible hardships, but, when he persisted, brought him food and clothing.

He wrote:

Send waves of grace over this beggar that he may cling to solitude. Keep me free from the distractions of the Evil Ones and of the World. Grant me advancement in meditation (*samādhi*).
My growing old, unknown to my friend; my sister unaware of my last illness.
If I can die in this solitude; this devotee will be fully content.
My death unknown to any being; my rotting corpse unseen by birds.

If I can die in this solitude; this devotee will be fully content. None to ask where I have gone; no place to point to, saying "There!"
If I can die in this solitude; this devotee will be fully content. May the prayer about the death of this beggar be fulfilled for the benefit of all beings in a rocky cave in an uninhabited country! Then will my mind be fully content.

Mila died, as he wished, in lonely isolation. According to one tradition, when he died, the clouds formed mystic symbols in the sky, the gods descended to earth and walked among men, and heaven wept tears of blossoms.

MĪMĀMSĀ: One of the six classical systems or points of view (*darshanas*) of Indian philosophy, Mīmāmsā (exposition, reflection, consideration, deep thought, exegesis) aims at drawing out the truth from the Veda. There are two schools of Mīmāmsā, called "earlier" (*pūrva*) and "latter" (*uttara*), referring to the Vedas, the earlier parts mainly ethical, the latter mainly philosophical in nature. Purva Mīmāmsā is usually called

Mīmāṁsā, for short, or sometimes Karma Mīmāṁsā, referring to its emphasis on actions. Uttara Mīmāṁsā is called Vedānta (q.v.), or sometimes Brahma Mīmāṁsā, referring to its contemplation of Brahman.

With the proliferation of priestly readings from the Vedas, the demand increased for definitive explanations of the deeper meanings of passages. Mīmāṁsā offered clarification of the liturgical aspects of the Vedas. It declared that Brahman is beyond the two principles which support the world.

The founder of Mīmāṁsā was Jaimini (q.v.). His *Pūrva Mīmāṁsā Sūtra* is the original text of the school. His arguments are presented in a formalized manner:

(1) thesis,
(2) doubt about the thesis,
(3) antithesis,
(4) synthesis, or the right conclusion, and
(5) agreement, consistency.

This might remind the reader of the formalized style of St. Thomas Aquinas' works. Besides the first twelve chapters of the book, four additional chapters are included which are written in a different style. They are generally considered apocryphal and referred to as the *Samkarsakānda* or *Devatākānda*.

The outstanding commentator on Jaimini's *Sūtra* whose work still survives was Sabara (fifth century A.D.), in a commentary entitled *Commentary (Bhāsya)*.

Prabhākara, who founded Mīmāṁsā's first division, or school, wrote a commentary on the *Commentary* entitled *Brhatī*. Sālikanātha wrote a commentary on the *Brhatī* named *Rjuvimalā*.

Kumārila (eighth century A.D.), founder of the second school of Mimaṁsa, wrote the *Sloka Vārttika (Verse glosses)*, commenting on the *Sūtra* of Jaimini and the *Bhāsya*. Sucarita Miśra wrote the *Kāśikā*, commenting on the first third of Kumārila's work. Someśvara Bhatta wrote the *Nyāya sudhā* on the second third. Venkata Dīksita wrote the *Vārttikābharana* on the third third.

A third school of Mīmāṁsā, founded by Murāri, did not produce any works which survived.

In the fourteenth century, Madhava put the whole system into a poem, in the *Jaiminīya Nyāya mālāvistara*, and then wrote a prose commentary on his own work.

Appaya Dīksita (1552-1624) wrote the *Vidhirasāyana*, an attack on Kumārila.

Khandadeva's (seventeenth century) *Bhāttadīpikā* is well known for its logic.

Vedānta Deśika's *Seśvara mīmāmsā* argued that Mīmāmsā and Vedānta are both parts of one philosophy, with basically compatible views.

Mīmāmsā holds that the Vedas are infallible. Further, the language of the Vedas, Sanskrit, is in itself an emanation of being. It is the sacred language of reality, of the universe, of God. If, in this sense, God spoke Sanskrit, the least we can do, according to the Mīmāmsā writers, is to do everything we can to understand the words and meanings of the Vedas. The words in the Veda are eternal. They have no beginning and no end. When they are spoken, that does not indicate their creation, but merely indicates the manifestation of the word-form. Then, after a word has been spoken, it reverts to its original status to await another call. Non-eternal things can be destroyed, but words, being eternal, cannot be destroyed. Meanings are eternal forms. Truth is eternal. It is impersonal, having nothing to do with the discoverer. Since words are eternal, the Vedas of which they are composed are also eternal.

We should add, as Prabhākara did, that proper names are not words. They are applied to persons or things after they have come into existence, and their meaning is due to convention. Also, words used by ordinary people outside the language of the Vedas, since they talk of things that can be verified by other means of knowledge, are of questionable authority. Only the transcendent topics of the Vedas, described in the language of the Vedas, are self-authenticating.

Jaimini did not argue that every word in the Vedas was a record of the experiences of the sages. Rather, he divided the Vedas into two main divisions. The one consisted of the Sentences or Commands (*vākyas* or *vidhis*). This was the main category. This contained metaphysical knowledge. The other consisted of the Supplements (*vākya-śesas*) to the Sentences, or in other words, sentences which related to perception or reasoning. This category served only to bring out the implications of the Sentences, not as a record of metaphysical knowledge in itself.

The question would then arise as to which parts of the Vedas were to be classified as Sentences and which as Supplements. Jaimini argued that all the Upanishads and mantras are Supplements, subsidiary sentences, *arthavādas*:

> Arthavādas have to be construed as integral in sense with the Commands, being meant to eulogize them, etc. Arthavādas do not carry an import of their own.

The Upanishads, then, do not deserve our serious attention, according to this theory.

Shankara, the great Vedāntist thinker, tacitly agreed with Jaimini that the Mantras were supplemental, but disagreed with his estimate of the Upanishads. Shankara argued that the Upanishads were most emphatically essential, containing the most important doctrines in the whole of the Vedas.

Mīmāṁsā is interested in the ethical aspects of the Vedas, whereas Vedānta is interested in the philosophical. Every sentence either prohibits or commands something. Mīmāṁsā inquires into the nature of Right Action (Dharma). Action is the essence of human existence. Knowledge without action is fruitless. Happiness is impossible without action. Human destiny cannot be fulfilled without action. The opening verse of the *Mīmāṁsā Sūtra* is:

> Now is the enquiry of duty (*dharma*).

Taken as the basis for interpreting the whole Veda, Jaimini went on to say:

> Duty is an object distinguished by a command.

Mīmāṁsā then goes into an exposition of all the commandments in the Veda, rituals and ceremonies which are said to lead to enlightenment for the mind and spiritual evolution for the soul.

In the beginning, according to Jaimini, was the sound (*Sabda*), or word. Knowledge of dharma can be obtained only by the word, or verbal testimony. Since we are dealing with the invisible effects of ritual, any other means of finding knowledge, besides verbal testimony, may be mistaken.

The form or nature of a thing, which is denoted by a word is:

that which is common to all objects and the means of a collective idea of all these as forming one composite whole.

Universals are real and are the objects of perception.

The doctors of Mīmāṁsā developed interesting theories of logic, epistemology, and semantics, in the process of defending the Vedas against critics. Truth, Kumārila argued, is its own guarantee. Thoughts are valid by themselves. Invalidity can be shown only by recognizing discrepancies in their causes or by the contrary nature of their objects. When in doubt about something seen far off, or in dim light, we can resolve the doubt by a second observation made under improved conditions. This general theory of truth is called self-evidence (*svatah pramana*).

Since knowledge is self-validating, what is to be proven is not the truth of something, but its falsity. The main trend of Mīmāṁsā epistemology is its search for falsity. This often involves a form of indirect proof, assuming the opposite of what is to be proved and demonstrating that it is self-contradictory.

MIURA BAIEN (1723-1789): Physician, philosopher, and economist during the Tokugawa Shogunate, Miura was the author of three outstanding works: *Gengo*, *Zeigo*, and *Kango* (*Discourse on Metaphysics*, literally "Abstruse Talk," *Discourse on Corollaries*, literally "Talking On and On," and *Discourse on Morality*, literally "Presumptuous Talk"). In addition, he wrote *Heigo Hōji*, on politics, and *Kagen* (*The Origin of Price*). For more information on his philosophical position, see Japanese Philosophy.

MO TZǓ (479-438 B.C.): The philosopher who recommended universal love for both personal and political situations was Mo Tzǔ (pronounced MOE dzuh) (or Mo Ti (MOE dee), other varia-

271

tions of the name being Mu Ti, Micius, Motse, Mihtse, Meh Tzŭ, Moh-tse, Meh-tse, Mei-ti, and Mu Tzŭ). His thought was received with a notable lack of enthusiasm by politicians, who did not wish to encourage love, as it tends to interfere with cold-blooded imperial expansion.

Master Mo was born in Lu (western Shantung province), although some scholars believe that he was born in Ch'i (eastern Shantung) because he spent so much time there. By that reasoning, he was born where he was buried, because he has spent even more time there. However, since no one knows where he was buried, no one has shown an interest in recommending this theory. Mo Ti was an official in the state of Sung, an economist and specialist in defensive warfare. He became angry at the elaborate and expensive Confucian rituals, especially for funerals, which, he felt, were "detrimental to the living and harmful to public affairs." He therefore took the regulations from Yü, the Hsia Regulations, which were much simpler, as his pattern to follow. The historian, Ssŭ-ma Ch'ien, described his manner of living:

> (He) lived in a very small thatched hut built of rough, unworked timber. His utensils were of earthenware, his food of the coarsest kind. In the summer he wore garments of coarse, yellow cloth, and in the winter he wore a coat of deerskin. When he was buried, he was laid in a coffin of thin boards.

The politicians of the time employed brutal military tactics. A system similar to the "body count" method was used, with a bounty paid for each enemy head brought in. After each battle, the dead were decapitated, the heads counted, and the total entered in an official register. Mencius wrote that there "were no righteous wars," and that:

> The slain bodies filled the cities and the wilds.

Mo Ti, through a combination of logic, daring, and religious zeal, tried to influence events at the time. For example:

272

Kung Shu Pan (a noted mechanical inventor of the time) had completed the construction of Cloud-ladders for the state of Ch'u, and was going to attack Sung with them. Mo Tzŭ heard of it and set out from Lu, arriving at Yin (the capital of Ch'u) after a journey of ten days and nights. When he saw Kung Shu Pan, the following conversation ensued:

Kung Shu Pan: "What is your pleasure, Sir?"

Mo Tzŭ: "Some one in the North had insulted your humble servant: I wish to procure your assistance to kill him." (Kung Shu Pan was evidently offended by this request.)

Mo Tzŭ: "Allow me to offer you ten pounds of gold."

Kung Shu Pan: "My principles forbid me to commit an act of homicide."

Mo Tzŭ (who rose and bowed twice): "Permit me to explain. I heard in the North that you have constructed ladders and are going to attack Sung with them. Has Sung done any wrong at all? Moreover, the state of Ch'u possesses land in excess and is deficient in population. Now to sacrifice what is insufficient in a mortal contest for what is already superfluous can hardly be said to conform to the principle of benevolence. Failure to protest against the injustice of this action can hardly be regarded as loyalty toward your ruler. To protest without consequence can hardly be an indication of firmness of will. Your principles forbid you to kill one man, but permit you to slaughter whole armies; this can hardly be deemed conversant with the logic of analogy." (Thereupon Kung Shu Pan indicated that he was convinced of his mistake.)

Mo Tzŭ: "If so, why don't you stop the undertaking?"

Kung Shu Pan: "No. I cannot retract; for I have already reported the matter to the King."

Mo Tzŭ: "Why don't you present me to His Majesty?"

Kung Shu Pan: "Yes, I will be glad to do so."

Mo Tzŭ (after being introduced to the King): "Suppose there is a man who abandons his own richly adorned carriage and desires to steal the shabby wagon of his neighbor; who relinquishes his own elegant vestments and desires to steal the coarse jacket of his neighbor; and who forgoes his own

273

tasty fare of millet and meat and desires to steal the unpalatable food of his neighbor; what sort of fellow would he be?"

King: "Surely, he must be a man with a pathological tendency toward stealing."

Mo Tzǔ: "Well, the territory of Ch'u measures five thousand square li, whereas that of Sung a mere five hundred. These remind me of the ornamented carriage and the shabby wagon. Ch'u has the marsh land of Yunmeng full of valuable animals such as rhinoceros and deer; she is in possession of rivers Kiang and Han in which fishes, turtles and alligators abound. It is one of the wealthiest of states under the sun. Sung does not even have pheasants, hares and silver carps. Those remind me of the tasty fare and the unpalatable food. Ch'u has all kinds of useful trees, pine, catalpa, nanmu and camphora. Sung has no tall trees at all. These remind me of the elegant vestments and the coarse jacket. In short, your humble servant is of the opinion that in deciding to attack Sung, Your Majesty bears a close resemblance to the above mentioned person."

King: "Well, indeed! But Kung Shu Pan has built Cloud-ladders for me; I shall certainly be able to conquer Sung."

Thereupon the King summoned Kung Shu Pan into the court. Mo Tzǔ untied his belt and laid out a city with it, using small sticks of wood for defensive weapons. Kung Shu Pan set up nine different machines of attack, and Mo Tzǔ nine times repulsed him. Kung Shu Pan came to the end of his machines of attack, while Mo Tzǔ was far from being exhausted in the defense. Kung Shu Pan was thus defeated. But he said: "I know how to deal with you; I shall not tell you." Mo Tzǔ also said: "I know how you will deal with me; I shall not tell you, either." The King inquired the reason of them. Mo Tzǔ replied: "Kung Shu Tzǔ's intention is no other than to murder me. He seems to believe that when he has put me out of his way, nobody would be able to defend Sung, and she will fall an easy prey to his attack. But my disciples, Ch'in Ku Li and others, numbering three hundred men, are already armed with my implements of defense, waiting on the city wall of Sung for the invader from Ch'u. Though I be

274

murdered, you cannot terminate the defence of Sung." The King of Ch'u declared: 'Well, indeed! Let us not attack Sung any more."

On his returning journey, Mo Tzǔ passed by the city of Sung. It was raining, and he sought shelter under the gate. The gatekeeper refused to take him in, not knowing that this was the very man who had saved the whole country from ruin!

The gatekeeper was not the only one who refused to take Mo Ti in, but Mo persisted in his belief that universal love was the only profitable course of action. Love must be undiscriminating. It must not make distinctions. The fundamental principle of life is:

Indiscriminate love and mutual benefit (*Chien hsiang ai, chiao hsiang li*).

He asks:

What is the source of the present disorder? It is the lack of mutual love. . . . When a son loves himself and not his father, he will cheat his father to benefit himself. When a younger brother loves himself and not his elder brother, he will cheat his brother to benefit himself. . . . A thief loves his own home, but because he does not love the homes of others, he steals from them to benefit himself. A ruler loves his own state, but because he does not love the other states, he attacks them to benefit himself.

> (—*Mo-tzǔ*, quoted in Sverre Holth,
> *Micius*, 27, 28.)

The remedy for the disorder caused by selfishness, or partial love, is:

Indiscriminate love must take the place of partial love. . . . If we regard the property of others as we regard our own, who will then steal? If we regard others as we regard ourselves, who will then do any harm to another?

The contrasting terms are *Chien ai*, love without any discrimination, the Mo-ist doctrine, and *Pieh ai*, love with distinctions, the Confucian doctrine. The Confucians insisted that there are distinctions which must be observed. Differences of rank, privilege, and love must be graded to the level appropriate. Mo countered by arguing that privileges should not be reserved for a few. There should be equality for all. Mo called the princes of his time *Pieh chün*, "discriminating princes," and the officials *Pieh shih*, "officials who practice discrimination." He wrote:

To say that one loves, one must wait until love has been extended to all. To say that one does not love, it is not necessary to wait until one loves nobody at all.

Universal love is the natural state of human affairs: I think that for people to practice the principle of indiscriminate love and mutual benefit is as natural as for the flame to go upward and for water to run downward.

Mencius objects to Micius, arguing that universal love would destroy the obligation of a son to put his father's welfare first, and be destructive of all loyalty and social relationships. If we must love everybody in general we will love nobody in particular. Mencius wrote:

Mo's principle is undiscriminating love, and this is to ignore the affection due to one's father. But to fail to acknowledge the affection due to one's father is to be in the state of a beast. . . . Whoever is able to oppose Mo is a disciple of the sages.

However, what Mo actually said in this regard was:

The basic principle of filial love is that the son should place first the welfare of his parents. . . . If people regard their fathers and elder brothers and rulers as they regard themselves, how would un-filialness find expression? How would there yet be any who lacked in propriety?

276

Mo Tzŭ believed that his concept of love would have the utilitarian virtue of profitability, as the following quotations indicate:

He who loves will be loved again. . . .
To love and thereby profit all the people, . . . it is the will of Heaven that men should love and mutually benefit each other. . . . From what source does every benefit flow? From mutual love.

Mo Tzŭ's religious zeal in the propagation of his gospel of love was legendary. Three points of doctrine were important, in his view: (1) belief in the will of Heaven, (2) the existence of the Manes or Spirits, and (3) an attack on the belief in Fate. Whereas Confucius always conceived of Heaven as impersonal, Mo ascribed personal attributes to it. The "will of Heaven" enables one to "measure conduct," as a carpenter uses the square and a wheelmaker the compass. Heaven's providential care is the motivation for universal human love.

Mo did not doubt the existence of spirits, good and evil: Yes, however deep a valley may be, however gloomy a forest, however dark a cavern, the spirits see what goes on there: one cannot escape their sight as that of men!

Further:

The partiality of the officials and the disorderliness of men and women—the spirits see it all. When people are licentious, cruel, tyrannical, rebellious, thievish, and plundering . . . so that they snatch away men, carriages, horses, clothes and furs to benefit themselves, there are spirits watching them.

Widespread doubt of their existence is, in Mo's mind, irrelevant to their real existence:

The fact that people no longer believe in the existence of the spirits, in the efficacy of their blessing or cursing, is a great

277

misfortune for the rulers and for men in general. How can one doubt their existence or their power, seeing that they have manifested themselves so many times in full daylight, and before numerous spectators?

Like Plato, in the *Laws*, Mo denounced the belief that deity does not intervene providentially in human affairs, that whatever happens takes place by fate:

The theory of fatalism is a great evil in the Empire. This belief in blind destiny, which has extinguished the faith in Heaven and the manes, and which therefore has deprived men of the benedictions of Heaven and the spirits, is causing the ruin of morality, suppressing the belief in the differing sanctions of good and evil.

Mo's views on the economy were that:

An outlay that does not profit the people should cease.

We should always ask:

Does that which is gained correspond to that which has been spent?

The state should limit its expenditures to alleviating the three causes of human distress:

to be hungry without getting food, to be cold without being clothed, and to be tired without finding rest.

As for music, loved by the Confucians, he asked:

Can music relieve any of these anxieties?

Candidates for political office should be individuals who possess political ability. Birth, wealth, kinship, or military prowess should not be accepted as substitutes for ability:

278

When the rulers need clothes, they send for a skilled tailor. When they want to have a banquet, they send for skilled butchers to slaughter the cattle. But when they need one to fulfill the duties of government, they send for one of their personal friends or one who is good-looking.

All theories, he taught, are to be tested by the practical consequences they produce. Conduct is:
the completion of knowledge.
Despite his lack of lasting influence, he was, Dr. Hu Shih has noted, "perhaps the greatest mind China has produced." Such is sometimes the fate of a great mind.

MOTOORI NORINAGA (1730-1801): One of the greatest students of the Japanese Classics, he remarked on the fact that the Japanese authors accept man's natural dispositions more readily than do Chinese authors:

The fact that the Book of Poetry (*Shih Ching*) lacks love poems reveals something of the customs of the people of [China]. . . . In contrast, the abundance of love poems in our empire reveals the way to express one's geniune dispositions.
(—*Motoori Norinaga Zenshū, Collected Works of Norinaga Motoori*, IV, 236, quoted in Hajime Nakamura, *Ways of Thinking of Eastern Peoples*, 373.)

Motoori characterized *The Tale of Genji* as a novel of "the sadness of things," *mono no aware*, also translated as "sensitivity to things," such as the fall of a flower or an unwept tear.

N

NĀGĀRJUNA (100-165): The Indian Buddhist philosopher who founded the Middle Doctrine School (Mādhyamika, or Doctrine of the Middle Position), one of the chief schools of Mahayana Buddhism. A Brahmin from South India, Nāgārjuna taught at the Buddhist university in Bihar, North India, Nālanda, as well as at the Nāgārjunikonda in Andhra Pradesh.

Teaching that the phenomenal world has only a qualified reality, the illustration was used of a monk with defective eyesight who may imagine that he sees flies in his begging bowl. They have full reality for the old monk. Though the flies are not real, the illusion is. All our experience, taught the school, is like this. All beings labor under the illusion of seeing things where actually there is only emptiness. The Emptiness, the Void, is all that really exists.

His main work was the *Middle School Verses* (*Mādhyamika-kārikā*), the basic text of the School of Non-Being. He also wrote the *Four Hymns* (*Catuh-stava*), a devotional booklet.

There was another Nāgārjuna who lived in the eighth century, was an alchemist, and an exponent of the Tantra. The Tibetans identified the two.

NAKAE TŌJYŪ (1608-1648): A Japanese Confucian scholar during the Tokugawa Shogunate, Nakae Tōjyū was called "the saint of Omi." The highest virtue, he taught, was honoring one's parents (*kō*). However, a distinction is drawn between what he called the small filial duty (*shō-kō*) and the great filial duty (*dai-kō*).

The former is the ordinary duty of serving parents well, because they gave birth to us. However, if the parents are in the wrong, the correct filial duty is to encourage them to mend their ways. This is the great filial duty, because the divine parents gave birth to all human parents (— *The Collected Works of Professor Nakae, Nakae Tōjyū sensei zenshū*, Shiga: Toju-shoin, 1928).

NANAK: See BABA NANAK.

NĀROPA (1016-1100): Tilopa's student and the teacher of the famous Tibetan, Marpa, Nāropa (Nāro-pa, Nādapāda, or Nārotapa, also called the Elder bsTan-pa 'dzin-pa, and, later, 'Jigs-med grags-pa or Abhayakîrti) was born in Bengal in the year of the Fire-Male-Dragon. He was a famous transmitter of esoteric (secret) doctrine in the Kargyupa tradition. The secret doctrines of Tantric Buddhism were not written for the general public to read, but rather were passed down from master to disciple.

Nāropa was from a well-to-do family, his father even called "king" and his mother "queen," which, however, did not mean a ruling monarch but rather a member of the upper class. When eleven, he was sent to Kashmir, then a center of Buddhist learning. When fourteen, he returned home with a large number of scholars, and they studied together for three more years. At seventeen, he was forced to marry Ni-gu-ma, a strong-willed woman who became a writer in her own right (her works are preserved in the *bsTan-'gyur*). After eight years, they were divorced, with the statement: "countless are the woman's defects." He went back to Kashmir. Three years later (1040), he went to Puspahari/Pullahari, where he stayed for six years. This place was to become famous in Tibetan Buddhism when, later, Mar-pa received his last instruction from Nāropa.

In 1049, Nāropa went to the university of Nālanda (the famous Buddhist center, located between Delhi and Calcutta, near the Ganges river, south of Nepal) for the debates. Elected an abbot, he served for twelve years.

In 1057, he resigned his post and set out in search of a teacher who had been revealed to him in a vision. The guru's name was Tilopa. The vision was of an old woman:

With thirty-seven ugly features: her eyes were red and deep-hollowed; her hair was fox-coloured and dishevelled; her forehead large and protruding; her face had many wrinkles and was shrivelled up; her ears were long and lumpy; her nose was twisted and inflamed; she had a yellow beard streaked with white; her mouth was distorted and gaping; her teeth were turned in and decayed; her tongue made chewing movements and moistened her lips; she made suck-ing noises and licked her lips; she whistled when she yawned; she was weeping and tears ran down her cheeks; she was shivering and panting for breath; her complexion was darkish blue; her skin rough and thick; her body bent and askew; her neck curved; she was hump-backed; and, being lame, she supported herself on a stick.

The woman asked Nāropa what he was reading. He replied:
"Books on grammar, epistemology, spiritual precepts, and log-ic." She asked if he understood them.
"Yes."
"The words or the sense?"
"The words."
She was delighted. Thinking to make her still happier, he added:
"I also understand the sense."
She began to weep and threw down her stick. He asked why she had become unhappy. Because he had turned from telling the truth to lying, she replied, because he did not understand the sense. He asked:
"Who understands the sense?"
"My brother."
"Introduce me to him."
"Go meet him for yourself, and beg him for understanding."
With that, she disappeared "like a rainbow in the sky."
Nāropa then began his famous search for the guru Tilopa, having his course obstructed by a leper woman, a stinking bitch crawling with vermin, a man carrying a load, a man cheating his parents, an undertaker cutting the intestines out of a human corpse, a violent man who had stabbed a man in the stomach who was still living, a king who wanted to marry off his daughter, a

dark man with a pack of hounds hunting deer with bow and arrow, two old people plowing a field and killing and eating the insects they found in the furrows, a man who had impaled his father on a stake and imprisoned his mother and asked help in killing them, an old beggar frying live fish over a fire, and a freak show. Each of these repulsive people was revealed to be Tilopa, but too late for Nāropa to ask him anything. Their counsel to him was:

> Out of confidence, devotion, and certainty, become
> A worthy vessel, a disciple with the courage of conviction.
> Cling to the spirituality of a Teacher in the spiritual fold,
> Wield the razor of intuitive understanding as the viewpoint,
> Ride the horse of bliss and radiance as the method of attention,
> Free yourself from the bonds of this and that as the way of conduct.
> Then shines the sun of self-lustre which understands
> One-eyedness as the quality of many,
> Blindness as seeing without seeing a thing,
> Deafness as hearing without hearing a thing,
> Muteness as speaking without saying anything,
> Lameness as moving without being hurried,
> Death's immobility as the breeze of the un-originated.

In Western thought, Occam's razor is important, choosing only the simplest of any possible explanation. In Eastern thought, we see Tilopa's razor, "the razor of intuitive understanding," of vital significance for correct thinking.

Nāropa took the razor literally, as he had taken literally the presence of all the illusory people who had blocked his way to the Teacher. He decided, out of despair, to commit suicide:

> Since I have been hindered by this body which is the result of former deeds, I shall discard it with the resolve to meet the Guru in some later life.

As he was about to cut his veins, a voice said:

If you have not found, how will you find The Guru, if you kill the Buddha? Is it not me whom your evil thoughts desire?

Tilopa then appeared, a dark man dressed in cotton trousers, his hair knotted in a tuft, and with protruding, blood-shot eyes. The process of instructing Nāropa began. He taught him how to rely on the Gurus of the four transmissions:
(1) recognizing all Sūtras and Tantras, the Mahāmudrā teaching;
(2) the teaching of the Mother-Tantras;
(3) the teaching of the Father-Tantras; and
(4) the doctrine of the Radiant Light.

Fourteen of the works of Nāropa are extant, in the *bsTan-'gyur* (Derge edition), including the following:
(1) *Sṛhevajrasādhana (dPal dGyes-pa rdo-rje'i sgrub-thabs)*,
(2) *Ratnaprabhā (Rin-po-che'i'od)*,
(3) *Ekavīraherukasādhana (dPa'-bo gcig-pa He-ru-ka'i sgrub-thabs)*,
(4) *Sṛguhyaratnacintāmani (dPal gsan-ba rin-po-che'i yid-bzin nor-bu)*,
(5) *Vajrayoginīsādhana (rDo-rje rnal-'byor-ma'i sgrub-thabs)*.

Nāropa is famous for his "six teachings" on the "completion process," a fusion between the central channel of the body (to some extent confused with the spinal column) and its power centers with the channels to the left and the right, the white and the red, Wisdom and Means. The six are:
(1) generating great internal heat;
(2) light, maintaining a state that is conscious but free from any thought;
(3) illusory body;
(4) intermediate state between death and the next life (*Bardo*);
(5) mind-transference (*'pho-ba*), and
(6) the art of taking over someone else's newly dead body (*grong'jug*).

One of the objects of such training is to remain in a constant state of meditation, so that at the moment of death, one may succeed in catching the instant of intense light, and thus emerge from the cycle of rebirth, avoiding being dragged into *bar-do*.

At the age of eighty-five, he died in the hermitage of Pullahari, his "rainbow" radiant in a five-fold light.

NASTIKA: (Sanskrit *n'asti*, "it is not") Systems of Indian Philosophy which *deny* the authority of the *Vedas*. Opposed to *Astika* systems. The chief *Nastika* systems are Buddhism, Jainism, and Chārvākism.

NGAWANG LOZANG GYATSO (1617-1682): The Fifth Dalai Lama, also called "the Great Fifth," Ngawang Lozang (or Lopsang) Gyatso (precise transliteration, Ngagdbang blo-bzang rgya-mtsho) instituted the high office of the Panchen Lama of Trashilhünpo, declared to be an incarnation of Amitabha, on the basis of "discoveries" of "hidden texts." Ngawang Lopsang Gyatso built the Potala palace (1645-1694) in Lhasa, named for Mount Potala, which was believed to be the abode of Avalokiteśvara. His regent Sangye Gyatso, "the flatheaded Desi," kept the fact of his death secret for fifteen years so that construction on the Potala could be completed. There was a great upsurge in literary, cultural, and economic activity during his reign. He wrote an autobiography, *Du-ku-la'i gos-bzang*, in three volumes, completed by three more volumes of biography written by Sde-srid Sangs-rgyas rgya-mtsho. The Dalai Lama also wrote a book on temporal and spiritual matters, entitled *Bslab-bya mu-thi-la'i 'phreng-ba*, remarking that no pity should be wasted on a man who was sentenced to death and executed for his crimes.

When he died, his Desi carried out an elaborate scheme to conceal that fact. An announcement was made that the Dalai Lama had gone into meditation for an indefinite period of time and did not wish to be disturbed. The hand-drum and bell used in rituals could be heard from his room. Meals were taken in as usual. Foreign dignities from Mongolia were shown a look-alike monk dressed in the Dalai's ceremonial robes. The double tired of his confinement and tried to run away on several occasions. A combination of bribery and beatings kept him at his post.

The Desi carried on the administration faultlessly. He would turn up unexpectedly at courts, offices, and even at bars, to ask what people were thinking. Once the disguised Desi asked a beer-drinker for his opinion on the government. "My business is drinking beer," he replied. "All other business is the Desi's."

When the Potala was completed, the Desi announced that the fifth Dalai Lama had died in 1682, and that his reincarnation was already thirteen years old.

NIRVANA (Sanskrit for "blown out," or "extinguished," as of a lamp or fire): The Buddhist conception of Nirvana is that it is the painless peace which rewards the moral annihilation of self. It is:

(1) Happiness attainable in this life through the complete elimination of selfish desires,
(2) Liberation from rebirth.
(3) Annihilation of individual consciousness,
(4) Union of individual consciousness, and
(5) Heaven, happiness after death.

Those who achieve Nirvana in this life do so by acquiring its seven constituent parts, which are:
(1) self-possession,
(2) investigation into truth,
(3) energy,
(4) calm,
(5) joy,
(6) concentration, and
(7) magnanimity.

Used frequently in Buddhist literature, the term also occurs in Vedantic writings, as, for example, the *Bhagavad Gītā* (ii 72, v. 24-26, vi 15) and the *Viveka Chudamani* (v. 70). It refers to the extinction of all worldly desires and effects. It will be noted that these expressions are negative, in order to avoid ascribing any worldly qualities to the Beyond. Nirvana, thus, is a state of perfection so subtle that it defies adequate description.

NISHIDA KITARO (1870-1945): The first Japanese philosopher to be internationally respected as an original thinker following the transplantation of Western philosophy into Japan. Author of *A Study of Good* (*Zen no kenkyū*), he wrote:

286

Our true self is the basic substance of the universe, and, when we know the true self, we not only unite with the good of mankind, but we merge with the basic substance of the universe and spiritually unite with the divine mind.

NYĀYA: One of the six orthodox systems (*darshanas*, "demonstrations") of Indian Philosophy, together with Vaisheshika, Sankhya, Yoga, Pūrva-Mīmāṁsā, and Vedānta, Nyāya (pronounced nyah yah) means "going into a subject," an analytic investigation of a topic.

The outstanding Nyāya thinker was Gautama (not to be confused with the Buddha) who lived between the sixth century B.C. and the first century A.D. He wrote the *Nyāya Sūtra*.

He recommends the Nyāya "syllogism," in five propositions: theorem, reason, major premise, minor premise, and conclusion (Aristotle's syllogism had three). For example:

(1) Socrates is mortal,
(2) for the reason that he is a man;
(3) Whoever is a man is mortal.
(4) Socrates is a man who is invariably mortal.
(5) Therefore, Socrates is mortal.

"Logic" teaches four methods for establishing valid knowledge:

(1) Perception,
(2) Inference,
(3) Analogy or Comparison, and
(4) Credible testimony.

Perception (*pratyaksa*), or intuition, initially meaning only sense-perception, was later broadened to include any kind of immediate experience. Later theorists, such as Dharmakirti, said there were four kinds of perception: sense perception, mental perception, self-consciousness, and Yogic intuition.

Inference (*anumāna*) is defined as knowledge that follows other knowledge. Both deductive and inductive reasoning may be included. Every inference, it is argued, presupposes a universal connection. The Nyāya "syllogism" includes:

(1) the proposition to be proven, the conclusion;
(2) the premise, the reason;
(3) the example;

(4) the application; and

(5) a statement of the final conclusion.

Analogy (*upamana*) is defined as the knowledge gained when we compare an unknown thing to a known object, classifying by similarities.

Credible testimony may be relied upon as a source for truth, when that testimony has been given by a reliable person.

These four methods indicate the truth of the Vedas, the Nyāya scholars maintain.

Five kinds of fallacies are listed in the *Nyāya Sūtra*:

(1) The "erratic," a reason which leads to more than one conclusion (the example given suggests that this is similar to *non sequitur*, as usually understood);

(2) The "contradictory," a reason which opposes what is to be established;

(3) The "equal to the question," in which it provokes the same question it was supposed to have solved;

(4) The "unproved," a reason which stands as much in need of proof as did the original proposition (this seems similar to "begging the question"); and

(5) The "mis-timed," a reason which is offered when the time in which it would be true has passed.

The *Nyāya Sūtra* was commented on by Vātsyāyana (fifth century A.D.), Vācaspati (ninth century), Jayanta (tenth century) and others. By the time of Udayana the viewpoints were fully merged. About A.D. 1200 the school of *Navyanyāya* (New Logic) was formed—mainly through the work of the logician Gangesa.

O

OGYŪ SORAI (1666-1728): The eminent Japanese Confucian scholar and rival of Jinsai Itō, he rejected Chu Hsi's doctrines on the grounds that they were too static. Phenomena are the fundamental mode of existence. Modifying Confucius' tendency toward silence about supernatural beings, and contradicting the *Analects*, Ogyū wrote:

> There is evidence that Confucius himself approved the existence of spiritual beings. So whoever denies spiritual beings does not believe in Confucius.

Ogyū agreed with Hsün Tzŭ that man is basically evil, and needs to be corrected by education and political control. The laws must be strictly enforced. He took a position close to the Chinese Legalists.

Ogyū became an expert in the Chinese language, and communicated to his disciples (including Dazai Shundai) a love of all things Chinese.

He died at the age of sixty-three, which prevented him from occupying a post in Shogun Yoshimune's government, although the pension payments would have been nominal.

OM (or AUM): A sacred syllable, according to the Brahmanas. A word of invocation, benediction (like "Amen"), and affirmation, often placed at the beginning of any scripture or prayer considered of unusual sanctity. It is said that the sound of the word will re-echo inside the skull, causing vibrations that affect different nervous centers of the body beneficially, if the aspirations be pure.

An incident is related about a lecture given by Alan Watts, in which he invited his listeners to shout out loud any word they wanted to. After a few minutes of yelling and screaming, the sound settled down to one tone. Alan Watts smiled and left the platform. That tone was "Om."

ORMAZD: See AHURA MAZDA

P

PARSIS: Contemporary Zoroastrians, who live in Bombay, India.

PATANJALI (240-180 B.C.): The traditional founder of classic Yoga, Patanjali (pronounced pah tahn jolly) is currently the subject of a scholarly debate as to whether he is two or one, whether he is identical with Patanjali the grammarian (who composed the Great Commentary (*Mahābhāsya*) to Kātyāyana's Critical Gloss (*Vārttika*) on Pānini's Sanskrit Grammar) or not. Liebich, Garbe, and Dasgupta say he is, while J. H. Woods, Jacobi, and Keith say he is not. There is less controversy among the scholars as to whether, as tradition claims, he is the incarnation of the serpent-king Sesa, who surrounds and supports the universe as the Cosmic Ocean.

However these controversies are resolved, Patanjali was not the inventor but rather the codifier of the Yoga philosophy and methods of practice which had been known from very ancient times.

He wrote the *Yoga-sūtras*, in four books or chapters, dealing with:

(1) contemplation (*samādhi*),
(2) the practice of yoga,
(3) psychic powers, and
(4) liberation (*kaivalya*).

The first three of these books may belong to the second century B.C., but the fourth is apparently later (fifth century A.D.) because it contains arguments against later Buddhist thought.

PHAGMOTRU (1110-1170): The "man from Sow's Ferry," founder of an important noble family and of the monastery of Thel (or Thil) at a place of the same name, Phagmotru (or Phagmo Drupa, Phag-mo gru-pa), or Dorje Gyalpo, came from Kham in eastern Tibet. Called the "precious protector of beings," the "great man from Kham" was a very learned monk who attracted many disciples. He won the territory of the "king of Tsharong" in a game of chess, a form of territorial acquisition so civilized that it has never caught on, compared to war.

PRATAPANA: The seventh of the eight Buddhist hells, the "Hell of Great Burning Heat," for those sinners who have defiled religion sexually, such as by raping virtuous laywomen, sending call girls to monks, or having relations with daughters-in-law. The tortures of Pratapana include fire and having flesh peeled off from head to toe.

PŪRVA-MĪMĀMSĀ: See Mīmāmsā.

R

RAB (160-247): The affectionate title of Abba Arika, Rab was a market inspector in Babylonia, towering in height and friendly, who pursued his studies in the Talmud so effectively that he was offered the presidency of the Nehardea Academy. He refused, instead founding a new academy at Sura (219), which was destined to last for eight centuries and outshine all the other Babylonian schools. Classes were offered early in the morning and late at night, the only times that students were free to come. During the national holidays, twelve thousand people gathered at Sura to hear him speak. From being an Amora ("speaker," or "interpreter"), Rab advanced to the point where he was considered to be a Tanna ("first and major teacher of the Talmud"). Rab was a contemporary of Jerome and Origen.

In 226, political changes drastically altered life in Babylonia. The old Arascid dynasty, which had been relatively tolerant, was replaced by the Sassanian dynasty, which encouraged fire-worship. Believing that burial of the dead polluted the soil, Ardashir I ordered many bodies disinterred. Synagogues were burned down and the Nehardea Academy was destroyed (in 259).

RADHAKRISHNAN, SARVEPALI (1888-1975): "Poverty is good for the soul," said Dr. Radhakrishnan, "only when it is voluntary." President of India (1962-1967), knighted by King George V (1931), Radhadrishnan was born a Telugu Brahmin, September 5, 1888, into an extremely poor family. He was sent to a school run by German Christian missionaries. There, his instructors criticized Hindu beliefs, a fact which motivated him to learn more so as to be able to defend them.

He taught philosophy at Madras Presidency College (1909-1917). When Rabindranath Tagore won the Nobel Prize for Literature (1913), Radhadrishnan wrote *The Philosophy of Rabindranath Tagore*, a book which became immensely popular. From 1921-1931, he taught philosophy at Calcutta University, and published *Indian Philosophy* in two volumes. He taught at Oxford for three years (beginning in 1931). He was a member of the Indian Assembly that drafted the country's first constitution, and headed up India's delegation to UNESCO. Nehru appointed him ambassador to the Soviet Union, where he quoted the Bible to Stalin: "What does it profit a man if he gain the whole world but lose his own soul?" Stalin, as a former theology student, had probably heard the verse before.

Radhakrishnan's view of Indian politics was expressed in his saying:

> The worst sinner has a future, even as the greatest saint has had a past.

Among his other books are commentaries on Hindu texts, entitled *The Bhagavad-Gita* and *The Principal Upanishads*. His short autobiography is called *My Search for Truth*.

RĀMAKRISHNA (1834-1886): A modern Tantrist teacher, Srî Rāmakrishna was one of the most eminent religious teachers in India. His thought first reached America in 1893, when his pupil, Swami Vivekānanda, spoke at the World Parliament of Religions in Chicago.

Rāmakrishna said:

> Someone once gave me a book of the Christians. I asked him to read it to me. It talked about nothing but sin. . . . The wretch who constantly says, 'I am bound, I am bound,' only succeeds in being bound. He who says day and night, 'I am a sinner, I am a sinner,' really becomes a sinner. . . . (But) a

man is free if he constantly thinks: 'I am a free soul. How can I be bound, whether I live in the world or in the forest? I am a child of God, the King of Kings. Who can bind me?' If bitten by a snake, a man may get rid of its venom by saying emphatically, 'There is no poison in me.'

RĀMĀNUJA (1040-1137): As Shankara was the great logician of Vedanta, Rāmānuja was the great intuitionist, valuing feelings highly in the formulation of his religious views.

Born in Srperumbudūr (or Bhūtapurî) in South India, a few miles west of Madras, his father died early. At sixteen, he married. An unhappy domestic life convinced him that he should renounce the world to attain perfection. He settled in Srîrangam and converted large numbers of people to Vaisnavism. He toured South India restoring many temples, and North India, including Benares. He was persecuted by one king, converted another, and wrote many works, including the *Great Commentary (Srîbhāsya)* on the *Vedānta Sūtra*, the classic text for Vaisnavism; the *Vedānta sara (Essence of Vedanta)*; *Vedānta samgraha (Epitome of Vedānta)*; *Vedānta dîpa (Lamp of Vedānta)*; and a commentary on the *Bhagavad gîtā*.

His version of Vedānta is called Qualified Non-Dualism (Viśistādvaita). Agreeing with Shankara that the Ultimate Principle alone is what exists, he qualifies that position by arguing that souls are also real, although their reality is dependent upon the Ultimate Principle. After the individual soul is released from its worldly chains, it continues to exist. In the end, there is nothing but the Ultimate Principle. But during this period of manifestation, the world and souls, in order to serve the Ultimate Principle, are separate.

Salvation is available through devotion (*bhakti*). Rāmānuja, like Schleiermacher and Rudolph Otto in the West, finds the origin of religion in feeling rather than doctrine.

RAURAVA: The fourth of the Buddhist hells, Raurava, the "Screaming Hell" is for sins connected with intoxicating liquors. For example, liquor dealers who overcharge customers will be ambushed by demons in the Hell of Complete Darkness. Individuals who may have gotten an elephant drunk will suffer the punishment of having a giant elephant toss them in the air over and over again and stomp them into pieces. In this hell, the length of stay is 4000 years. Tortures are also available for those who talked a monk or devout layman into becoming their drinking companion.

REINCARNATION: The rebirth (Sanskrit, *punarjanma*, "again birth") of a person into another life, reincarnation is also called transmigration or metempsychosis, by some authors. It is to be distinguished from the pre-existence of the soul, which does not necessarily imply a previous bodily existence, and also from metamorphosis, a temporary change of bodily form.

Reincarnation is a widespread doctrine in India, Tibet, and Japan. In the West, the Orphics, Pythagoras, Empedocles, Plotinus and the Neo-platonists held some version of it. It is also found in Islam, in the Sūfîs, and in Judaism, in the Cabalah.

Evidence for the belief is cited as the inborn facility found in child prodigies, memories of past lives, *déjà vu* ("already seen") experiences, love at first sight, strength or deformity, purity or vice, health or disease, happiness or pain, and one's social rank. Many people have felt that an unfamiliar place is disturbingly familiar, and thus have entertained the belief in the possibility of reincarnation. Psychiatrists at the University of Virginia (e.g. Dr. Ian Stevenson) report that small children who have a genuine fear of firearms recall having been killed by guns.

Śri Aurobindo, in a passage written before the widespread publication of Einstein's theory of relativity, wrote that:

One feels certain that admirable theories could be invented to account for the facts of gravitation if our intellects were not prejudiced and prepossessed by the anterior demonstrations of Newton.

(— *The Problem of Rebirth*, 13.)

Similarly, he argues, the unprejudiced mind could appreciate the evidence collected in behalf of reincarnation. He continues:

The theory of rebirth coupled with that of Karma gives us a simple, symmetrical, beautiful explanation of things; but so too the theory of the spheres gave us once a simple, symmetrical, beautiful explanation of the heavenly movements. Yet we have now got quite another explanation, much more complex, much more Gothic and shaky in its symmetry, an inexplicable order evolved out of chaotic infinities, which we accept as the truth of the matter. And yet, if we will only think, we shall perhaps see that even this is not the whole truth; there is much more behind that we have not yet discovered. Therefore the simplicity, symmetry, beauty, satisfactoriness of the reincarnation theory is no warrant of its certitude.

When we go into details, the uncertainty increases. Rebirth accounts, for example, for the phenomenon of genius, inborn faculty and so many other psychological mysteries. But then Science comes in with its all-sufficient explanation by heredity,— though, like that of rebirth, all-sufficient only to those who already believe in it. Without doubt, the claims of heredity have been absurdly exaggerated.

(—*Ibid.*, 14.)

The existence of child prodigies, such as Mozart, who at the age of five wrote a piano concerto that was too difficult for anyone to play; Mendelssohn, who had composed thirteen symphonies by the age of fifteen; Samuel Reshevsky, a great chessmaster who had beaten three European chess champions at five; or William Rainy Harper, later president of The University of Chicago, who finished high school in Ohio at the age of ten, and earned his B.A. by thirteen, delivering the Salutatory in Hebrew, deserve a satisfactory explanation to account for their abilities.

The West accepts the Pythagorean Theorem, but rejects the Pythagorean proof, if even aware of it, that he had fought at Troy under the name of Antenorid and was slain by the younger son of Atreus, offering as evidence his identification of the Trojan shield at the temple of Apollo at Branchidae, the shield having become so rotten that only the ivory facing was left.

When the Tibetan lamas searched for the reincarnation of the Dalai Lama, they often consulted the oracle, the sacred Lake Lhamoi Latso, high up in the mountains, at Chokhorgyal, some ninety miles southeast of Lhasa. In the depths of the waters can be seen wonderful sights. Like a television set, it sometimes reveals to the regent the exact location of the infant successor. In 1875, a member of the search party, Gyutod Khensur, reported seeing a reflection of the birthplace of the future (thirteenth) Dalai Lama Thakpo Langdun in Southeast Tibet (see Thubten Jigme Norbu, *Tibet*, New York: Simon & Schuster, 1968, p. 229 ff.; and Tsepon Shakabpa, *Tibet, a Political History*, New Haven: Yale, 1967). The same procedure was followed to find the fourteenth Dalai Lama. When the search party arrived at the house, the test of the young child proceeded. Duplicate copies of possessions were offered to him, and he was asked to select the one which is genuine. Sometimes, Tibetans believe, rebirth may be divided among two or three bodies, the body of one, speech of another, and mind of a third, these three entities together making a complete person.

There are two main interpretations of reincarnation in Indian thought. The first (Vedānta, Sānkhya) is that the wheel of rebirth must be endured until the soul acquires true knowledge of its essential freedom. In Sānkhya, the soul cannot be said to be reincarnated in the technical sense, because the soul is never actually attached to a material body. The illumination of the soul produces a psyche which acquires karma and passes from one life to the next, thus encumbered. When the soul at last becomes aware of its true nature, it detaches from the body, the karma-body disintegrates at death, and the soul is eternally free.

The second (Buddhist, Jainist) is that release from the bonds of karma may be secured by discipline. In Buddhism there is, of course, no soul entity which is reborn, but merely an aggregate of qualities which is the bearer of the karma and which passes to the next existence.

The Russian mystic and mathematician, Ouspensky (1878-1947) quotes Gurdieff's theory of reincarnation, to the effect that reincarnation is the survival of the "astral body," but that not everyone has an astral body, only those who have obtained it by hard work and struggle. If formed, it can live after the death of the physical body, for a time, and be born again in another physical body.

RINCHEN SANGPO (958-1055): One of the two (the other was Lekpe Sherab) of twenty-one who survived the heat and rigors of the journey to Kashmir, sent to learn Sanskrit and study Buddhist doctrine, Rinchen Sangpo (Rinchen Zangpo) lived to become a famous translator and lecturer, and his work marked the beginning of the renaissance of Buddhism in Tibet, "a spark rekindled in the east and spread by a wind blowing from the west." His work was mentioned by His Holiness, the Dalai Lama, in a speech given at New Delhi, India, in 1956.

RINZAI (785-867): The Japanese name for the renowned Chinese Ch'an (Zen) master, Lin-Ch'i or I-hsüan, Rinzai Gigen's collected sayings, known as the *Rinzai-roku* (*Lin-ch'i Lu*), are widely considered the supreme example of Zen literature.

Rinzai's (sudden) enlightenment took place after he had spent three years at Ōbaku's school. He approached the master personally and asked him if he would kindly explain the essential truth in the Buddha's teaching. Ōbaku replied by giving him twenty blows with a stick.

He went to another master, Daigu (Ta-yu), to complain, but was told that Ōbaku had given the right "answer," and further emphasized the point by choking Rinsai and shouting at him. This time, Rinzai hit back, but, in the process, became suddenly enlightened.

When he returned to Ōbaku to tell him the good news, Ōbaku slapped him in the face and threatened him with worse treatment. Seeing his surprise, Ōbaku began roaring with laughter, and, for a mantra, shouted the meaningless word, "Katsu!"

The effect of such an unorthodox method of instruction was to prevent the student from intellectualizing, and provide him with a direct experience of the truth.

RUSSELL, BERTRAND, IN CHINA: In 1920, the Chinese Lecture Association invited Russell to the country. Pronouncing his name "Luo-Su," they anticipated his enlightening words on the scientific discoveries of Einstein, on education, and various social questions. Proud of the fact that he was less "conservative" than John Dewey, also teaching in China at the time, Russell relished his reputation as "The Second Confucius," and pontificated that the most crying need of China was education, because "without it, it is hard to see how better government can be introduced." A librarian named Mao Tse-Tung was also giving thought to the method of introducing a new form of government. Russell's attention was on Miss Black, at the moment, with whom he was touring. When Russell visited Shanghai, it reminded him of Glasgow. When he visited Hangchow on the Western Lake, it reminded him of Grasmere. Nanking, he said, was "an almost deserted city." At Cheng-Sha, "a great educational conference was taking place." When he visited Peking, he did not specify what that reminded him of. He later put his views on the country into a book entitled *The Problem of China*.

RYŌKAN (1217-1303): The reviver of the Ritsu school of Japanese Buddhism during the Kamakura period, Ryōkan (Ninshō Bodhisattva) promoted faith in the *Lotus Sūtra*. He was a welfare worker who established charity hospitals to care for invalids. While at the Saidai Temple, he took pity on a leper, carried him (on his back) into the city and begged for him. On his deathbed, the leper said to him:

I shall certainly be reborn into this world and become my master's humble servant in order to reciprocate my master's virtuous deeds. (As a mark for you to identify me) I shall have a scar left on my face.

(—quoted by Hajime Nakamura, in
Ways of Thinking of Eastern Peoples,
p. 369.)

In later years, a man with a scar on his face appeared among his disciples, and served him as an attendant.

S

SAADIA (892-942): Believing that Judaism is compatible with all truth, whatever its source, Saadia ben Joseph al-Fayyumi attempted to reconcile Judaism with Islam, Hinduism, Christianity, Zoroastrianism, Manicheanism, and Greek philosophy. Born at Dilaz, Egypt, he studied Arabic, Biblical, and Talmudic literature. He went to Palestine and Babylonia, where he became Gaon or director of the college at Sura. His field of knowledge included mathematics and philosophy. His *Book of Philosophical Doctrines and Beliefs (Kitah al-Amanat)* has been called the most significant work of medieval Jewish thought before Maimonides. Saadi accepts truth validated by revelation, tradition, and reason.

SAICHŌ (767-822): Of Chinese descent, Saichō (Dengyō Daishi) was the founder of the Tendai (T'ien-t'ai) sect of Buddhism in Japan. The little temple he built on the side of Mt. Hiei, near Kyoto, became the center of education and culture for the nation until it was burned in 1571. The goal of the good life, Saichō taught, is, as the *Hokke Sūtra* declares, to become a living Buddha in a human body, *sokushin jōbutsu*.

SAKYA PANCHEN (1182-1251): The "great scholar" known for having bested the heretics in theological debates in India, Kunga Gyaltsen (called Sakya Pandita or Panchen because of his knowledge of Sanskrit) was summoned in 1244 to Kokonor where Prince Godan, the grandson of Genghis Khan, had his camp.

They made it by 1247. Sakya Panchen instructed the Prince in the teachings of the Buddha and persuaded him to refrain from throwing large numbers of Chinese into the nearby river. The Prince had nothing personal against the Chinese, but evidently felt it was an acceptable method of population control. When Sakya Panchen convinced Godan that it was against Buddhist doctrine, the practice was stopped.

If the Tibetans helped the Mongolians on matters of religion, he believed, and paid tribute money, the Mongolians would help the Tibetans with political affairs.

Sakya's book was entitled *The Buddha's Intention* (*Thub-pai Gong-sal*).

SAMGHĀTA: The third Buddhist hell, Samghāta, the "Crowded Hell," is for those guilty of indulgence in sex. Sixteen different kinds of torture are provided for the various kinds of sinners in this category, including molten copper, steel hooks, exploding horses, iron insects, and burning lotus blossoms, a fiery revenge for heeding the fires of physical passion.

SAMJĪVA: The first of the eight Buddhist hells, Samjīva, the "Hell of Repetition," is for all those guilty of killing. Sentence (prior to being allowed re-birth) is for a period of five hundred years.

SĀMKHYA: (The word may mean "enumeration," derived from the Sanskrit *samkhyā* (so Garbe), or "examination" (so Oldenberg), or "defining a concept by enumerating its content" (so Jacobi), or "discrimination," "discernment" (so Eliade).) One of the six orthodox systems of Indian Philosophy, together with Nyāya (logic), Vaisheshika (atoms), Yoga (a yoke), Pūrva-Mīmāmsā, and Vedānta (the end of the Vedas), Sāmkhya (pronounced sahm khyah), or Sankhya, is the oldest of the systems, and may well be the oldest philosophical system in the world. Some scholars say they find its influence in Pythagoreanism. The Buddhist texts refer to it. However, the classic textbook of Sāmkhya (the *Sāmkhya-kārikā* of the commentator Ishvara Krishna) dates only from the fifth century A.D. (Zimmer), or third century A.D.

(Radhakrishnan), or first or second century (Belvalkar). It was translated into Chinese in the sixth century, which provides a convenient way to date it, from one standpoint. Other literary sources are the *Sāṁkhya-pravacana-sūtra* (fourteenth century) and *Tattvasamāsa* (1380-1450, Zimmer, Garbe), ascribed (without tangible evidence) to Kapila; also Gaudapāda's *Bhāsya* (eighth century), Vācaspati Miśra's *Sāṁkhya-tattva-kaumudī* (ninth century), Aniruddha's *Sāṁkhya-sūtra-vrtti* (fifteenth century), Vijñānabhiksu's most significant *Sāṁkhya-pravacana-bhāsya* (sixteenth century), and Mahādeva's gloss of little interest, the *Sāṁkhya-vrttisāra* (seventeenth century).

The principal thinker in Sāṁkhya was Kapila (sixth century B.C.), who wrote:

the complete cessation of pain . . . is the complete goal of mankind.

The purpose of life is to quit suffering. The similarities with Buddhist thought are striking. Kapila imparted the doctrine to Asuri, who transmitted it to Pañcasikha, who then taught it to Ishvara Krishna.

If Sāṁkhya means "enumeration" (from *sam*, together, and *khyā*, to enumerate, count, sum up, calculate), it is so called because of its list of twenty-five realities:

(1) Cosmic Spirit, Self (*Purusa*),
(2) Cosmic Substance, Not-Self (*Prakrti*),
(3) Cosmic Intelligence (*Mahat*),
(4) Individuating Principle (*Ahamkāra*),
(5) Cosmic Mind (*Manas*),
(6-15) the ten Abstract Sense Powers (*Indriyas*),
(16-20) the five Subtle Elements (*Tanmātras*), and
(21-25) the five Sense-Particulars (*Mahābhutas*).

The twenty-five categories are classified under four headings:
(1) that which is neither produced nor produces;
(2) that which is not produced but produces;
(3) those which are produced and do produce;
(4) those which are produced and do not produce.
They are named:

303

(1) *Purusa*, the unevolved which does not evolve, the uncaused which is not the cause of any new mode of being;
(2) *Prakriti*, the unevolved which evolves, the uncaused cause of phenomenal existence;
(3) "evolvents," seven categories which are both caused and serve as causes of new modes of being;
    (i) Cosmic Intelligence (*Mahat*),
    (ii) Individuating Principle (*Ahamkāra*),
    (iii) the five Subtle Elements (*Tanmātras*);
(4) "evolutes," sixteen categories which are caused but do not serve as causes of new modes of being:
    (i) Cosmic Mind (*Manas*),
    (ii) Five Abstract Knowing-Senses (*Jñānendriyas*),
    (iii) Five Abstract Working-Senses (*Karmendriyas*), and
    (iv) Five Sense Particulars (*Mahābhūtas*).
The *Sāmkhya-Kārikā* opens with the words:
From torment by three-fold misery arises the inquiry into the means of terminating it.

The causes of misery are:

(1) internal, such as sickness, from intrinsic causes, disorders of body or mind;
(2) external, such as accidents, from extrinsic causes, resulting from other men, beasts, birds, or inanimate objects;
(3) acts of god, from supernatural causes, such as the influence of the atmosphere or the planets.

Sāmkhya may also be characterized as an atheistic (or non-theistic) mode of thought, an evolutionary idealism. These realities ("that-nesses," *tattwas*) make up the world as we see it and know it. Sāmkhya is a form of philosophical idealism which derives reality from perception.

How can we end misery? If known means were sufficient, we would not have to think further, but simply apply what we already know. But all known means fail. Medicine, for instance, has its limits, and cannot cure forever, any more than eating one big banquet can banish hunger forever. So we must seek further.

Investigating the nature of the soul (cosmic spirit, *purusa*), we find that it is not identical with the body nor the senses nor the brain nor the mind (*manas*) nor the ego (*ahankāra*) nor intellect (*buddhi*) nor a substance which possesses the quality of consciousness. Rather, consciousness is its essence. It is pure and transcendental consciousness.

Since it is universally agreed that the pure soul is free from suffering, misery must somehow belong to the body, and the misery of the soul must be caused by its close association with the body.

Spirit (*purusa*) and Matter (*prakriti*) are the two ultimate realities. They are the source from which all other things evolve. The evolution of matter from its cosmic cause is an unfolding. Evolution is the projection of potentialities into realities according to fixed laws. Mankind can understand those fixed laws, and control them.

Creation (*ex nihilo*) is impossible because something can never come from nothing. Change implies that something can change. Whatever is, is. Whatever is not, is not. There is no evolution, except in the sense of modification.

> Cause and effect are the same, essentially:
> The effect is of the same essence as the cause.
> (—*Sāṁkhya-Kārikā*, IX)

This argument is used to support the claim that all objective reality is ultimately the same, that it is simply the result of various transformations of one ultimate substance.

Matter (*prakriti*) is a string of three strands or qualities (*gunas*):
(1) potential consciousness (*sattva*),
(2) activity (*rajas*), and
(3) restraint (*tamas*).

The first principle of the Sāṁkhya system is *purusha*, the universal spirit, the soul of the universe, the animating principle of nature, the source of consciousness. Sometimes writers identify it with the deities, Brahmā, Vishnu, Shiva, Durgā. *Purusha* is the Sāṁkhya version of the *Ātman* or *Brahman* of the Upanishads. *Purusha* accounts for the subjective aspect of nature:

Spirit (as distinct from matter) must exist, since (a) combinations serve a purpose of some(thing) other than themselves, since (b) this other must be the reverse of (what is composed of) the three constituents, and so on, since (c) there must be control (of the combinations), since (d) there must be someone to experience, and since (e) there is an activity for the purpose of release (from three-fold misery).

> (—Sāṁkhya-kārikā, XVII, adapted from Theos Bernard, *Hindu Philosophy*, New York: The Philosophical Library, 1947.)

Koller (in *Oriental Philosophies*) notes that arguments (a) and (b) assume two premises: (1) that all experienced objects have parts ordered so that they serve the purposes of something other than themselves, and that nature as a whole is orderly; and (2) that infinite regress must be avoided by assuming that there is something indivisible served by the divisible parts.

Argument (c) assumes that some principle of intelligence must be directing the cooperation of the various parts of the world.

Argument (d) argues from analogy: since pleasure and pain only exist when experienced, the world of objects must exist for some experiences, and the principle of that experiencer is *purusha*.

Argument (e) states that because there is a universal desire for self-transcendence, *purusha* must exist. In an orderly universe, such a universal desire for the infinite could not be self-frustrating. Since it is universally sought, it exists.

Furthermore, besides all these arguments, the existence of the transcendental world is established beyond a reasonable doubt because of the experience of those who have transcended the world of matter and action.

There were numerous schools of Sāṁkhya thought. Gunaratna (fourteenth century) mentions two: the "original" and the "late." The former holds that there is a *prakriti* (*pradhāna*) for each soul (*ātman*), while the latter holds that there is but one *pradhāna* for all individual souls.

Sāṁkhya has been said to be the philosophical foundation for all Asian culture, the standard by which to measure all Indian

306

literature, the basis for knowledge of the ancient sages, and the key to all Oriental symbolism.

SENG-CHAO (384-414): The first Chinese philosopher to succeed in systematizing Buddhist thought, Seng-chao was born in Sian (approximately equidistant from Peking and the border of Tibet). As his family was poor, he earned his living by repairing and copying books. Like Benjamin Franklin, later, he took advantage of this trade to read extensively. When he read the *Scripture Spoken by Vimalakīrti* (*Vimalakīrti-nirdeśa sūtra*), he was converted and became a Buddhist monk. At fifteen, he went west to become the student of Kumārajīva, the half-Indian half-Kuchen scholar who was teaching the Middle Doctrine school of Nāgārjuna. Although over a thousand monks sat in his daily lectures, Seng-chao made himself number one, helped his master with his translations and did several of his own. He reconciled the one-sided Buddhist schools who argued for being or for non-being, and also provided a bridge for Taoist thought. Having done all this, he died when barely thirty-one years of age.

SEVEN WORTHIES OF THE BAMBOO GROVE: A group of Neo-Taoists who met in a bamboo grove for conversation and drinking. The members of this third-century group were Hsiang Hsiu, Shan T'ao the statesman, Wang Jung, Hsi K'ang, Juan Hsien, Jüan Chi, and Liu Ling. They were influential in promoting back-to-nature sentimentalism. The "wind and stream" (*feng liu*) ideas, carefree and natural, were their expression. According to Hsiang Hsiu, one should live "according to himself but not according to others."

When Wang Jung lost his child, he wept uncontrollably. One of his friends rebuked him, saying: "It was only a baby; why do you behave like this?" Wang Jung replied: "The wise man forgets emotions, and low (callous) people do not reach emotions. It is people like us who have the most emotion." His friend agreed, and they both wept together.

Many of the stories of this group are found in the *Shih-shuo*.

SHAMMAI (90-30 B.C.): A Palestinian tanna (teacher) known for his strict views and his opposition to the generally milder judgments of Hillel. For example, the "House of Shammai" allowed the husband to divorce his wife only for adultery; the school of Hillel allowed it for "anything unseemly."

SHANKARA (788-820): The greatest Indian thinker after the Buddha, Shankara (or Śaṁkara) Acharya, "Doctor Shankara" was born at Kāladi, on the southwest coast of the Indian peninsula, below Goa, in the Malabar coast. A thoughtful child, he is said to have caused a river to come closer to his mother's door so she would be saved the trouble of going so far to fetch water. Considered a genius when he was eight, he was sent to a school presided over by Govinda, Gaudapāda's student. He did not become a recluse, but traveled through India, vigorously debating leaders of other philosophical schools. At the University of Benares (sometimes called the Harvard of India), he conducted an active campaign on behalf of orthodox Brahmanism. He founded four monasteries, Srngeri in the South (Mysore Province), Pūri in the East, Dvārakā in the West, and Badārinath in the North (Himalayas). He died at the age of thirty-two in Kedārnāth, a village in the Himalayas.

Two biographies were written of Shankara, one by Madhava, the Śaṁkara digvijaya, and the other by Anandagiri, the Śaṁkara vijaya.

Non-Dualism (Advaita) was Shankara's theory, affirming the belief that the universe was basically one (monistic) rather than two (dualistic) or twenty-five (as in Sāṁkhya) or many thousands of separate parts (as in Vaisheshika). The world comes from God and returns to God. There is no part of the world that is not God, yet God is not the world.

With this theory, Shankara could refute both the dualism of Sāṁkhya, which seemed to imply that the self and the not-self were in eternal opposition, and the Buddhists, who said that this world was merely appearance, not real at all. Shankara held that this world, māyā, was real if viewed from a certain way, but from the view of ultimate reality, was not ultimately real.

Beginning with the formula from the Vedas (Chāndogya Upanishad, 6), "That art thou," "tat tvam asi," Shankara develops the theory that the self (ātman) is the sole reality. Everything else, including the cosmos and the interior ego (*ahankāra*) which is usually mistaken for the self, is the product of a lack of knowledge, or ignorance (*avidyā*).

Shankara agreed with Jaimini (of the Pūrva-Mīmāṁsā school) that reason was not a trustworthy guide in the search for truth. What we need, instead, is insight, intuition. We need the faculty of grasping at once the essential out of the irrelevant. We need not action or invention but wisdom. Any form of action, including politics and economics, must be the servant of wisdom. The philosopher himself must live above material concerns on the higher level of peace and tranquility. He must desire liberation from ignorance most of all, *moksha*, blissful absorption into infinite unity.

The individual mind is prevented from knowing Reality because it is unable to perceive things except through a film of space and time, cause and change. Illusion, *māyā*, mocks the efforts of the mind to know reality. This limitation is seen as a birthright of ignorance common to all mankind. It is the reason we see so many objects and such a flux of change. In truth, if we could understand correctly, there is only one Reality, Brahman. It cannot be reached by reason or sensation, but only by intuition of the trained spirit. The true Self is hidden deep. When, at last, the Self is finally known, ignorance and illusion will disappear. Also, since the distinction between external and internal would no longer apply, there would no longer be a world.

In the *Crest Jewel of Wisdom*, Shankara writes:

> *Māyā* (Illusion) is neither being nor non-being, nor in essence both; it is neither divided nor undivided, nor in essence both; it is neither with members nor without members, nor in essence both; it is most marvellous in its nature, and indefinable. The power of *Māyā* is to be destroyed by awakening to the pure, undivided Eternal.

Thus, there are the seen and the unseen, visible and invisible, phenomenal and noumenal (in Kant's terms). Correspondingly, there are two selves: the ego (which appears to us as an individual and quite changeable self) and the *Ātman* (which is the essence and reality of us all, and which we share with all other selves and things). There are also two deities: Ishvara (the Creator, worshipped by the masses through patterns of space, time, cause and change) and Brahman (Pure Being, worshipped by philosophical faith through understanding the basic unity of all things).

All true being is God, and Shankara allows the ascription of attributes to God. Thus God may be said to be conscious, intelligent, even happy. God includes all such states. But all other adjectives are equally applicable to God. If it is true that God is love, God is also hate. God is beyond good and evil, above all moral distinctions and desires.

As a practical matter, Shankara says, it may be good to postulate the existence of a personal God to encourage our feeble morality, but this does not alter the basic character of Brahman as the timeless essence of the world and of all that is within it.

Vedānta, as expressed by Shankara, is not quite pantheistic, because all things are part of Brahman only in their changeless essence:

> Brahman resembles not the world, and (yet) apart from Brahman there is nothing; all that seems to exist outside of It (Brahman) cannot exist (in such a fashion) except in an illusory manner, like the semblance of water in the desert.

Shankara's most important works are the commentaries on the *Prasthānatraya*, consisting of the Upanishads, *Bhagavad gītā*, and *Vedānta sūtra*. His general philosophical position is revealed in *The Crown Jewel of Discrimination* (*Viveka cūdāmani*) and *Upadeśasahasrī*. Charles Johnston has a translation entitled *The Crest Jewel of Wisdom* (London: John M. Watkins, 1925). Other works include *Aptavajrasūcī*, *Atmabodha*, *Mohamudgara*, *Daśaślokī*, *Aparokṣānubhūti*, and commentaries on *Visnurahasranāma* and *Sanatsujātīya*.

SHAN-T'AO (613-681): The Chinese philosopher who exerted a strong influence upon Japanese thought, Shan-t'ao (or Zendō) taught that a Pure Land actually exists to the west of the world. "Loathe this polluted land," he said, "and desire to be born in the pure land." Many who took this theory seriously committed suicide so that they could be born into the Pure Land sooner.

SHAO YUNG (1011-1077): Developing numerology and "emblemology" from the cosmology of Appendix III of the *Book of Changes* (*I Ching*), Shao Yung of Fan-yang was also called Yao-fu (or, posthumously, K'ang-chieh). Yung buried his parents on the banks of the Yi (river) and pursued strange and hidden knowledge, hoping to penetrate into the divine mysteries. Living in a small cottage near Loyang, his biographer said that he "never lit a fire in winter nor used a fan in summer, never stretched himself upon a mat, nor reclined his head upon a pillow."

SHEN-HUI (670-762): When Ch'an (Zen) Buddhism split into a northern and southern branch over the question of who was the legitimate sixth patriarch (Shen-hsiu in the north or Hui-neng in the south), Shen-hui represented the south in a debate against the north. The north was destroyed as a legitimate transmitter of Ch'anism.

SHINRAN (1173-1262): Leader of the Jōdo Shin (True Pure Land) sect of Japanese Buddhism during the Heian period, Shinran (Zenshin, or Shakku) was banished from Kyoto at the same time as Hōnen (1207). Shinran was guilty of marriage, having married to prove a point, namely that monastic discipline was not necessary for salvation. The center of the religious life should not be the monastery, but the family. The authorities did not appreciate his insight as much as they might, thinking instead that he merely enjoyed the company of a woman.

He wrote (1224) the *Doctrine, Practice, Faith, and Realization* (*Kyōgyōshinshō*).

Not content with his nobility of mind, biographers after his death invented and stressed an illustrious social origin for him, in order, as Nakamura remarks, to appeal more effectively to the average Japanese, accustomed to the importance of rank.

SHINTŌ: Native Japanese religion, originally nameless until the sixth century, when Buddhist scholars applied this name to it

(*Shintō* or *Shindō* is the Chinese-Japanese reading of two ideo-grams that are read *Kami-no-Michi* in Japanese, meaning "the Way of the Kami," or "The Way of the Gods").

State (*Kokka*) Shintō, sometimes called Shrine (*Jinja*) Shintō, was the national religion until disestablished by the decree of General MacArthur on December 15, 1945. Two weeks later (January 1, 1946), the Emperor issued a statement which de-clared:

> The ties between us and our people have always stood on mutual trust and affection. They do not depend upon mere legends and myths. They are not predicated upon the false concept that the Emperor is divine and that the Japanese people are superior to other races and fated to rule the world.

Sectarian (*Shūha*) Shintō, depending on voluntary rather than tax support, exists in some thirteen officially recognized sects: Shintō Honkyoku ("Main Bureau Shintō," sometimes also called Shintō Kyō or "Shintō Teaching"), Shinri Kyō ("Divine Reason Teaching"), Taisha Kyō ("Great Shrine Teaching," after the great shrine of the sect at Izumo), Shūsei Ha ("Society for Im-provement and Consolidation"), Taisei Kyō ("Great Accomplish-ment Teaching"), Jikkō Kyō ("Practical Conduct Teaching"), Fusō Kyō (from Fusō, a poetical name for Japan), Mitake Kyō ("Great Mountain Teaching," after the sacred peak of Ontake), Shinshū Kyō ("Divine Learning Teaching":, Misogi Kyō ("Purifi-cation Teaching"), Kurozumi Kyō (after the name of the foun-der, Kurozumi Munetada), Konkō Kyō ("The Teaching of the Glory of the Unifying God"), and Tenri Kyō ("Heavenly Reason Teaching").

The sects are variously devoted to mountain-worship, the rites of spirit-possession, purification-rites, faith-healing, the classical forms of Old Shintō, and even, in some cases, a Confucian heri-tage. The function of State Shintō was to offer ritualistic prayers (*norito*) by priests before the altars of the gods, asking for good crops, peaceful homes, prosperous occupations, success in war,

312

stable government, and a long and majestic reign by the Emperor.

The deities or *kami* honored in Shintō shrines include ancestors, primitive natural forces, some emperors, and heroes who have died in the service of their country.

SHŌTOKU TAISHI (573-621): Prince Shōtoku, later believed to be a reincarnation of the Bodhisattva Avalokiteśvara, was devoutly revered as "Sovereign Moral Power," strong supporter of Buddhism during its introduction into Japan. He wrote the *Commentaries upon Three Sūtras*, on the *Shōman Sūtra*, the *Yuima Sūtra*, and the *Hokke* (Lotus) *Sūtra*. Throughout, he stressed practical good deeds, loyalty to the Emperor and one's parents. He wrote:
Why should any age or people fail to esteem this truth? There are few men who are really vicious. They will all follow it if adequately instructed.

The norm of all living creatures is "the Law." The Buddha is the Law embodied. United with reason, it becomes the Brotherhood. Thus, everything converges on the fundamental principle, the Law.

SIKHISM: A religio-philosophical system taught by ten Gurus:
(1) Guru Baba (Father) Nānak (1469-1539)
(2) Guru Angad (One Body) (1504-1552)
(3) Guru Amar Dās (1479-1574)
(4) Guru Ram Dās (1534-1581)
(5) Guru Arjun Dev (1563-1606)
(6) Guru Har Govind (1595-1644)
(7) Guru Har Rai (1630-1661)
(8) Guru Har Krishan (1656-1664)
(9) Guru Tegh Bahadur (1621-1675)
(10) Guru Gobind Singh (1666-1708)
Codified in the *Ādi Granth*, a highly-venerated book, it contains writings both by Hindu and Islamic teachers, and combines the Aryan idea of God's immanence with the Semitic idea of transcendence. God is called True Name (*Sat Nam*), One God (*Ek-*

Unkar), Endless Being (*Akal-Murat*), The Uncreated One (*Ajuni-sen-bhin*):

> Why goest thou to the forest in search of God?
> He lives in all, yet is ever distinct.
> He abides with thee, as well.
> As fragrance in a flower, or reflection in a mirror,
> So does God dwell within everything;
> Therefore seek Him in thy heart.

(Guru Tegh Bahadur)

God is not the tribal deity of a chosen people. He is above all particular manifestations. He is the dispenser of life Universal.

Man must conquer the five enemies: Lust, Anger, Greed, Attachment to the things of this world, and False Pride. The Gurus provide a guide, sinless and perfect but not divine. Thus, anyone can imitate them in the reasonable hope that he will become as they are. Salvation is reunion with the Divine Soul, rather than annihilation (as in Buddhism). Salvation, said Guru Arjun Dev, may be found in laughing and eating, drinking and playing.

The Sikhs were pacifists until they were persecuted, whereupon they developed a system of fierce self-defense. For about a hundred years, from the mid-seventeenth to the mid-eighteenth centuries, the Moghul emperors turned against the Sikhs. The ninth Guru was martyred. The "sword of leadership" passed to Guru Gobind Singh, who turned the congregations into an army. Women as well as men were trained in the use of weapons.

The Sikhs are concentrated in the Punjab. The orthodox Sikh wears a distinctive turban, long hair, beard, and a steel bracelet.

SIRACH (250-175 B.C.): Author of *Ecclesiasticus* (*Wisdom of Jesus the Son of Sirach*), one of the most highly respected and widely quoted books of the Apocrypha, Yeshua ben Sira, or Jesus, son of Sirach was a contemporary of the high priest Simon II, who died in 196 B.C. Driven from his home town by the lies of character assassins, ben Sirach had time and opportunity to meditate on his misfortunes. The lack of religion, lying rich men, and wicked women brook large in his catalogue of evils. On the whole, however, his view of life was optimistic, and many of the lines he wrote have become immortal:

Let us now praise famous men,
and our fathers in their generations.
. . . . There are some of them
who left a name,
so that men declare their praise.
And there are some who have no memorial,
who have perished as though they had not lived;

they have become as though they
had not been born,
and so have their children after them.
But these were men of mercy,
whose righteous deeds have
not been forgotten. . . .

Their bodies were buried in peace,
and their name lives to all generations.
People will declare their wisdom,
and the congregation proclaim
their praise.

(Sirach 44:1, 8-10, 14-15)

Originally written in Hebrew, the book was translated into Greek
by his grandson. The Hebrew original was lost until 1896, when
parts of it were found in the cellar of the Ezra Synagogue in Cairo.

SÖNAM GYATSO (1543-1588): The third Dalai Lama, Sönam
Gyatso (*Bsodnams rgya-mtsho*) studied at Drêpung monastery and
took his final vows from Sonam Drakpa. He was a brilliant student, mediator, and peacemaker. In the summer of 1562, when
the Kyichu river broke through its stone dikes and flooded Lhasa,
Sönam Gyatso organized relief and repair measures, putting
monks to work on the dikes. In 1577, he accepted an invitation to
visit Mongolia and, on the way, was lost in the snow and ice for one
hundred and seventy days. When he finally arrived at the tent of
Altan Khan, he began a program of religious instruction and
converted the ruler to Buddhism. The monastery of Thegchen
Chonkhor was built on the site to commemorate the event. On the
return trip, the monastery of Kumbum was founded in Kokonor,

where the founder of the Ge-lug-pa, Tsongkhapa, had been born.

SONGSTEN GAMPO (617-649): Tibetan king, Songtsen Gampo (Srong-btsan sgam-po), or Tride Songtsen, known in China as Ch'i-tsung-lung-tsan, began his rule at the age of thirteen. He sent seventeen students to India to learn Sanskrit. *The Secret* was translated into Tibetan, of great importance as the introduction of Buddhism into Tibet. He married both a Nepalese and a Chinese princess, each bringing Buddhist images with them. They both built temples facing towards their respective countries, while the king engaged in expeditions, first on one front, then on the other. He finally died of a high fever at Phanpo.

SŪFĪSM: Mystical orders in Islam. The *Koran* was interpreted by "story tellers" who wrote commentaries on the holy book which also contained material from Arabian, Christian, Gnostic, Zoroastrian, Buddhist, Jewish, Syriac and Babylonian sources. This esoteric knowledge offered steps toward direct union with God. The Way (*tarīqa*) to Reality might include such steps as repentance, abstinence, renunciation, poverty, patience, and trust. The key to such ethics is love.

The word sūfī means "woolie," referring to the wool garments worn by these wandering ascetics. Earlier groups were enthusiastic, holding common devotions, methods of spiritual discipline, and attempting to strip the soul and eliminate the self so as to attain the vision of Reality. Later groups formalized the steps necessary, were devoted to a particular founder and paid attention to their spiritual ancestry. The spirit was replaced by the form.

Persia was the chief point of origin for sūfīsm. The dervishes (Persian for "beggar") and faqirs (or fakers, Arabic for "poor") are derivative, the former in the twelfth century, often chanting religious formulae and whirling, the latter referring to Moslem monks who usually belong to a religious order but who now wander independently.

Many of the most famous Persian poets were Sūfīs, such as Saadi, Hafiz, Rumi, and, of course, Omar Khayyám (despite

Quatrain 55: "let the Sūfī flout; of my Base Metal may be filed a key, that shall unlock the Door he howls without," which Fitz-Gerald, according to Indries Shah, mistranslated, the original Persian actually reading:
"When the First Cause set my being,
I received the first lesson of love;
It was then that the fragment of my heart was made
The key to the Treasury of Pearls of mystical meaning").

Abu-'l-fat'h 'Omar, son of Ibrahim the Tentmaker of Naishápúr, better known as Omar Khayyám (which means "tent-maker") was born in the eleventh century. A philosopher who expressed himself in poetic form, Omar was interested in science and mathematics, writing a treatise on Algebra and working on the reform of the calendar. Among his schoolmates were the future Vizier and Hasan, the Old Man of the Mountains who spread terror through the world with the Assassins (from *hashish*, opiate of hemp-leaves).

Omar Khayyam's poems in praise of intoxication, which are interpreted as "epicureanism" by Western writers, may reasonably be interpreted as expressing the Sūfī belief that enlightenment may come through intoxication:

Ah, my Beloved, fill the Cup that clears
today of past regret and future fears;
   Tomorrow!—Why, Tomorrow I may be
myself with Yesterday's Sev'n thousand Years.

(XXI)

. . . . You know, my Friends, with what a brave Carouse
    I made a Second Marriage in my house;
    Divorced old barren Reason from my Bed,
    And took the Daughter of the Vine to Spouse.

(LV)

. . . . And lately, by the Tavern Door agape,
    Came shining through the Dusk an Angel Shape
    Bearing a Vessel on his Shoulder; and
    He bid me taste of it; and it was—the Grape!

(LVIII)

Hafiz (which means "Reciter of the Koran"), born Shams-ud-din Mohammed, was a fourteenth-century Sūfī poet. His wife and son died young. Various patrons sponsored and protected him from attacks by his enemies. Hafiz' poems also celebrate the ecstatic joys of enlightenment through drinking:

Comrades, the morning breaks, the sun is up;
Over her pearly shoulder the shy dawn
Winds the soft floating mists of silver lawn;
Comrades, the morning cup! the morning cup!
. . . . What! they have shut the wine-house up again!
      On such a morning closed the tavern door!
      Great Opener of Doors, Thee we implore
      Open it for us, for we knock in vain.

                          (—Ode 17)

Another notable ode from Hafiz is the following:
      Brothers, attend
      How ye shall spend
      This fleeting treasure
      Of days that pass:
      Fill your measure
      With present pleasure,
      The deep sweet glass,
      Of love and leisure,
      And sunny grass.

      Let the pious thunder
      Of heaven and hell—
      He drinks, as well;
      Let the proud man rear
      His lofty towers—
      Have no fear;
      The little flowers
      That grow thereunder
      Shall last as long—
      Or, a little song.

Our Most High Lord
The Sultan's sword
Can command no more,
When he comes to die,
Than you and I
Of simple birth
Can ask of earth—
A little land
In which to lie.

And even now,
Who more would ask
Than just to bask
The blue sky under:
A little grass,
Wine in the glass,
One's liberty
And Love and Wonder:
This, HAFIZ, is
Happiness.

(—Ode 2)

Again:

Deep in my heart there dwells a holy bird:
    O but 't is weary of its earthly cage,
        And in the dark of body sadly sings;
    Its heritage
Is the ninth heaven; its right is to be heard
    Before high God; its royal nest should be—
        For wide as the empyrean are its wings—
    The Sidra tree.
When from the dunghill of this world it flies,
    Bird of the soul, it stays not in its flight
        Til on the top of heaven it proudly stands,
    Far out of sight
Of the sad straining of our mortal eyes;
    And wheresoe'er its rainbow shadows rest,
        The folk go happy in those favored lands

319

From East to West.
This earth, the lonely footstool of the stars,
    Is not thy place, O HAFIZ; nay, such songs
        Should fill the listening palaces of heaven;
To God belongs
Thy voice, sweet bird, behind these fleshly bars;
    Thy singing pastures are those fields on high,
        Heaven's roses and the dew that falls in heaven—
Bird of the sky.

                                    (—Ode 465)

Sūfī mysticism often includes numerology. Numerical values are assigned to each latter of the alphabet, the "Abjad list." In one case, *Umm el Qissa*, "Mother of Stories," adds up to 267. Another arrangement of letters also adding up to 267 is *Alf layla wa layla*, or "Thousand and One Nights." Thus, the Arabian Nights is interpreted as a collection of encoded Sūfī teaching stories describing psychological processes and similar lore. "Omar Khayyam" decodes by numerical cipher to *Ghaqi*, which means "Squanderer of Goods," the name for one who, distracted by attention to things, neglects them in favor of a deeper perception of another dimension.

The Sūfīs believe that theirs is not *a* religion, but that it *is* religion, the secret tradition behind all religious and philosophical systems.

SUN TZŬ (335-288 B.C.): Author of the *Thirteen Chapters*, or *The Art of War*, a book of strategy and tactics which inspired many of Mao Tsê-tung's military doctrines. It has gone through a hundred editions in Japan, and was published in France in 1772.

Although some scholars contend that Sun Tzŭ was mythical, not many contend that the book is mythical as well, and even fewer argue that the book was not written by anyone. War may be too serious a matter to be left solely to the generals, but books must always be left to the authors, so far as their production is concerned.

Notable quotations from the book include:

Know the enemy and know yourself. (3:31)

No country has ever benefited from a long, protracted war. (2:7)

All warfare is based on deception. (1:17)

Attack where he is unprepared. Strike when he does not expect you. (1:26)

Victory is the main object in war. If this is long delayed, weapons are blunted and morale depressed. If troops attack cities, their strength will be exhausted. (2:3)

Where the army is, prices are high. When prices rise, the wealth of the people is exhausted. (2:12)

The wise general sees to it that his troops feed on the enemy, for one bushel of the enemy's provisions is the same as twenty of his. (2:15)

Treat captives well, and care for them. (2:19)

This is called "winning the battle and becoming stronger." (2:20)

Attack the enemy's strategy. (3:4b)

Next best is to disrupt his alliances. (3:5)

The next best is to attack his army. (3:6)

The worst policy is to attack cities. (3:7a)

Do the expected to engage; do the unexpected to win. (5:5b)

Those skilled in war bring the enemy to the field of battle and are not brought there by him. (6:2)

When I wish to give battle, my enemy, though protected by high walls and deep moats, cannot help but fight, for I attack a position he must save. (6:11)

The enemy must not know where I intend to give battle. For if he does not know where I intend to give battle, he must prepare in a great many places. And when he prepares in a great many places, those I must fight in any one place will be few. (6:14)

As water has no constant form, there are in war no constant conditions. (6:29)

Humble words from envoys, together with intensified preparations, are signs that the enemy is about to advance. (9:25)

Fierce language and pretentious advances are signs that the enemy is about to retreat. (9:26)

In war, numbers alone confer no advantage. Do not advance relying on military power alone. (9:45)

"How do I cope with a well-ordered enemy host about to attack me?" I reply: "Seize something he cherishes, and he will conform to your desires." (11:28)

Speed is the essence of war. (11:29a)

(A general) should be capable of keeping his officers and men in ignorance of his plans. (11:43)

He changes his methods and alters his plans so that people have no knowledge of what he is doing. (11:45)

The crux of military operations lies in pretending to accommodate oneself to the designs of the enemy. (11:56)

Therefore, at first be as shy as a maiden. Then, when the enemy gives you an opening, be as swift as a hare and he will be unable to withstand you. (11:61)

If not in the interests of the state, do not act. If you cannot win, do not commit troops. If you are not in any danger, do not fight. (12:17)

He who is not wise, humane and just, cannot use secret agents. (13:13a)

Secret operations are essential in war. The army relies upon them to make its every move. (13:23b)

SUN YAT-SEN (1866-1925): First provisional President of the Republic of China, Sun Yat-Sen was sworn into office in 1912, after the overthrow of the Manchu Dynasty. Born in the southern coastal province of Shantung, he shipped out of Macao at the age of twelve aboard a British freighter bound for Hawaii, where his older brother had started a general store. After four years at the Iolani School, he returned home. There, he blamed conditions on the autocratic policies of the Manchu regime. He went to Hong Kong and studied medicine.

In 1894, he founded the Revive China Society (*Hsing Chung Hui*), and spent the next two decades agitating for revolution. He visited the United States, soliciting money from the Chinese communities. He admired both America and Russia, and in mid-

October, 1911, when the key uprising took place in Hupeh Province, the city of Wuchang, he was traveling by train from Denver to Kansas City. Returning to China, he took power and was involved in the intrigues of politics. He admired the single-tax doctrines of the American social philosopher, Henry George.

On March 12, 1925, he died in Peking. His wife served the Communist government in high posts, and his son, Sun Fo, served the Nationalists similarly. Dr. Sun had written that the Chinese people needed to be prepared for democracy by benevolent one-party rule, like engineers running a railroad train. His ideological heirs disagreed on which track that train should take.

SUZUKI, DAISETZ TEITARO (1871-1966): One of the best-known contemporary Japanese philosophers, Suzuki was the childhood friend of Nishida (*q.v.*). He studied at Tokyo Imperial University (1891-1894) and taught at Gakushuin, Tokyo Imperial University, and Otani University. He was sent abroad by the Japanese Foreign Ministry in 1936 to lecture as a cultural ambassador at various British universities.

In 1950, he lectured at Yale, Harvard, Cornell, Princeton, and then taught at Columbia from 1951-1957. He also lectured in Munich and Mexico. His influence accounted for the tremendous interest in Zen Buddhism awakened in the West.

His publications include, in Japanese: *On "No-Mind," Studies in the Pure Land Thought, Studies in the History of Zen Thought, The Awakening of Japanese Spirituality, Bankei on the Unborn, The East and the West*; in English: *Essays in Zen Buddhism, Studies in the Lankāvatāra Sūtra, Manual of Zen Buddhism, An Introduction to Zen Buddhism, Living by Zen, Outlines of Mahāyāna Buddhism* and *Zen and Japanese Culture*.

According to Suzuki, to study Zen means to have Zen experience. The Zen master, who characteristically gives riddling answers to serious questions, is one skilful at using either words or actions which point directly to the Zen experience as his means of expression. If the student who asks the question is mentally ripe, he will be ready to grasp the intention in what the master said or did. If not, it could not have been explained to him anyway. It is like one bright mirror facing another bright mirror with nothing in between. If the questioner has never had a similar experience, all the eloquence of the master will be wasted, like a string of pearls cast into a hog wallow.

Zen does not ignore morality, nor the aspirations and feelings which determine the value of life. Zen is essentially interested in fundamental and primary things. Whatever relates to worldly life is left where it properly belongs. Zen leaves ethics, religion, and political science in order to analyze the "dualistic sphere of existence," according to Suzuki. Thus, Zen:

> aims at taking hold of what underlies all phenomenological activities of the mind.

The Zen way of deliverance from the doubts and worries of existence is not that of religion, the blind acceptance of dogmas, but an appeal to a certain inner experience. That experience is the recognition that "suchness" of things is beyond the ability of words or reasons to describe or define. The what and why of life in the world are deeper than any intellectual formulations. According to Zen, there is a wholeness of things which refuses to be analyzed or separated into antitheses of any kind. If we know this, we shall receive inner peace, contentment, and calm.

SUZUKI SHOSAN (1579-1655): A Zen Buddhist leader during the beginning of the Tokugawa period, Suzuki wrote:

> To pray for a happy future does not mean to pray for a world after death. It means to be delivered from afflictions here and now, and thus to attain great comfort. Where, then, do you think those afflictions come from? They spring solely from the love of your own body. Had it not been for this body of yours, from what would you suffer? To be delivered, therefore, from this body of yours is to become a Buddha.
>
> (*Roankyō, Ass-Saddle Bridge—*
> *Random Sayings by Zen Priest*
> *Shosan Suzuki*, last part.)

Repelled by the self-satisfied and exclusive attitude of the traditional Zen sect, Suzuki stressed the virtue of benevolence. Warning against a hyper-critical attitude toward other sects, he says:

In this monastery the right and wrong of the world or the relative merits of other sects ought not be talked about.

He opposed the idea that exclusive merit belonged to some sacred places or possessions:

A wooden statue is nothing but wood, and an icon is merely a few strokes of the brush. There is nothing sacred in them.

A member of the Samurai class, Suzuki spoke of practicing the Zen of the Two Kings, the fierce and the brave:

In these days, it has been overlooked that the Buddhist Law is saturated with great strength of deeds and solidity. It has come to be soft, gentle, disinterested, and good-natured; none has trained himself to bring forth the spirit of a vengeful Ghost. Everyone should be trained to be brave, and to become a vengeful Ghost of Buddhism.

This fight-the-good-fight, violent method of expression was a Japanese gift to Buddhism. Thus, in Zen, swordsmanship could come to be regarded as the spiritual basis for the religion.

A sort of reincarnation of Calvin, Suzuki taught that we should torture ourselves by working hard at our vocations, because we are working off the sins of past lives. To farmers, he says:

Farming is nothing but the doings of a Buddha.

To merchants:

Renounce desires and pursue profits wholeheartedly. But you should never enjoy merits of your own. You should instead work for the good of all others.

325

The essence of Buddhism is to rely upon "the true Buddha of one's own," which Suzuki interprets as pursuing one's own vocation, whether as Samurai, farmer, craftsman, merchant, doctor, actor, hunter, or priest. Suzuki wrote *The Significance of Everyman's Activities* (*Banmin Tokuyō*), pursuing these ideas. Buddhism, he believed, was nothing but the virtue of honesty put into practice.

Suzuki's Calvinistic work ethic never quite caught on, and the virtue of honesty has had its difficulties, as well.

T

TAI CHEN (1723-1777): A noted modern Chinese Confucian scholar, Tai Chen (or Tai Tung-yüan) was known as Great-Master-of-Investigations-Based-on-Evidence. He made contributions to the theory of astronomy, mathematics, phonetics, and textual criticism. Principle, he held, was the order in things, not, as the Sung and Ming Neo-Confucianists seemed to imply, an abstract, transcendental, metaphysical reality.

Tai Chen was born into a poor family in Anhui. He passed the examination for "recommended person" (1762), failed the metropolitan examinations several times (the last, in 1775), and went on to become the greatest thinker in the Ch'ing period (1644-1912).

He wrote the *Commentary on the Meanings of Terms in the Book of Mencius* (*Meng Tzu tzu-i shu-cheng*).

T'AN-LUAN (476-542): A famous patriarch of the Pure Land School of Chinese Buddhism, T'an-luan wrote a *Commentary to Vasubandhu's Essay on Rebirth*, basing his comments on a Chinese translation of the original Sanskrit work:

> How does one apply (one's own merit) to and not reject all suffering beings? By ever making the vow to put such application first, in order to obtain a perfect heart of great compassion.
>
> "Application" has two aspects. The first is the going aspect,

327

the second is the returning aspect. What is the "going aspect?" One takes one's own merit and diverts it to all the beings, praying that all together may go to be reborn in Amita Buddha's Happy Land.

What is the "returning aspect?" When one has already been reborn in that Land and attained to the perfection of concentration and insight, and the power of saving others through convenient means, one returns and enters the withered forest of life and death, and teaches all beings to turn together to the Path of the Buddha.

(—quoted by Wade Baskin, Classics in Chinese Philosophy, New York: Philosophical Library, 1972.)

T'AN SSU-T'UNG (1865-1898): A modern Chinese Confucian philosopher associated with the Revival of the New Text School, T'an wrote a book entitled *The Science of Human-heartedness (Jen)*, which introduced some ideas from chemistry, physics, and sociology into Neo-Confucianism. He was a friend of K'ang Yu-wei and when the political reform movement failed, died a martyr's death.

TANTRA: A term which applies to any of the scriptures connected with the worship of Shakti, Mother of the Universe. She is considered to be the principle of Primal Energy, the feminine (negative) principle. Study of these texts is said to reveal clairvoyance, clairaudience, telepathy, psychometry, the power of sound, vocal expression, and the composition of music. The purpose of the Tantras is to produce liberation from ignorance and rebirth through direct knowledge. "Knowledge" is used in the Biblical sense, including the intense concentration of sex.

The word, "tantra," means "loom," the warp, or threads in the loom. By extension, it means a rule or ritual for ceremonial rites. The Tantras contain magical formulae for the attainment of magical or quasi-magical powers.

The Sūtras are public books, available to anyone, but the Tantras are secret documents, for the use of initiates only. A *kalung* is required before one is allowed to study the Tantras, and an empowerment (*wang*) is required before the given method can be practiced.

The special yogic practices are devices and methods for attaining Enlightenment swiftly.

Most of the Tantras are written in the form of dialogues between Siva and Durgâ, his divine consort. She is worshiped as his energy, or *shakti*. She is a distinct personified female power, according to the Tantrins.

Most Tantric works contain five topics:

1) The evolution and manifestation of the Universe;
2) The destruction of the Universe;
3) The adoration of the divinities;
4) The achievement of what you want, especially the six superhuman faculties; and
5) The (four) methods of union with the high God by meditation.

TAO (pronounced dow): According to Taoism, the ultimate source of all things. It has been called "a preface to God." Existing before Heaven and Earth, it alone is unchanging, and permeates everything.

Generally translated "the Way" (Giles), the problem raised by the traditional translation is that it is impossible for a way (road or path), which always leads to something else, to stand for the highest of all, the infinite, as Lao Tzŭ meant by his use of the term. Other possible translations are "Course" (Legge), "Doctrine," "Nature" (de Groot), "universal soul of Nature," or "the all-pervading energy of nature." Another possibility is to leave *Tao* untranslated, as Tao (Borel), on the grounds that the Chinese philosopher himself found no satisfactory name for this sublying conception and so stamped it with the word *Tao*.

TAOISM:

Leave all things to take their natural course and do not interfere. . . .

What is contrary to the Tao soon perishes.

(—*Tao Te Ching*, 30, 55.)

Founded by the Chinese philosopher Lao Tzǔ (*q.v.*), Taoism teaches the virtue of the simple life, communion with nature, the denial of selfishness, and mystical union with the Ultimate. Taoism recommends a retreat from civilization back to nature, in order to attain harmony with the Tao, the eternal way, the supreme governing force behind the universe. More recently (beginning in the second century A.D.), Taoism has become a mixture of magic and religion.

The simple life is advised in such passages as:

> There is no calamity greater than lavish desires. There is no greater guilt than discontent. And there is no greater disaster than greed. He who is contented with contentment is always contented.
>
> (—*Ibid.*, 46.)

> The sage does not accumulate for himself. The more he uses for others, the more he has himself. The more he gives to others, the more he possesses of his own.
>
> (—*Ibid.*, 81)

Simplicity in government is the ideal. Complexities are undesirable, and the multiplication of laws is not beneficial:

> The more laws and regulations are publicized, the more thieves and robbers there will be.
>
> (—*Ibid.*, 57.)

> When the government is searching and discriminative, the people are disappointed and contentious.
>
> (—*Ibid.*, 58.)

> To rule people and serve Heaven, there is nothing better than to be frugal. Only by being frugal can one recover quickly.
>
> (—*Ibid.*, 59.)

> Ruling a big country is like cooking a small fish. [Too much handling will spoil it.]
>
> (—*Ibid.*, 60.)

Communion with nature is indicated by the many images which appear in the *Tao Te Ching*: "cautious, like crossing a frozen stream in the winter" (15), "merry . . . like climbing a tower in the springtime" (20), "if the valley had not thus become full, it would soon become exhausted" (39), "the great rivers and seas are kings of all mountain streams because they skillfully stay below them" (66), and "if a tree is stiff, it will break" (76).

Unselfishness is recommended as the best course of human behavior:

Embrace simplicity, reduce selfishness, have few desires.
(—*Ibid.*, 19.)
Virtuous people attend to their own obligations, while those without virtue attend to other people's mistakes. 'The Way of Heaven has no favorites. It is always with the good man.'
(—*Ibid.*, 79.)

Mystical union with the Ultimate is recommended by the following passages:

To know harmony means to be in accord with the eternal. To be in accord with the eternal means to be enlightened.
(—*Ibid.*, 55.)
He who is well established (in Tao) cannot be pulled away. He who has a firm grasp (of Tao) cannot be separated from it.
(—*Ibid.*, 54.)
There was a beginning of the universe which may be called the Mother of the Universe. He who has found the mother and thereby understands her sons, and, having understood the sons still keeps to the mother, will be free from danger throughout his lifetime.
(—*Ibid.*, 52.)
Tao produces them. Virtue fosters them. Matter gives them physical form. The circumstances and tendencies complete them. Therefore the ten thousand things esteem Tao and honor virtue.
(—*Ibid.*, 51.)
One may know the world without going out of doors. One may see the Way of Heaven without looking through the windows.
(—*Ibid.*, 47.)

331

Reversion is the action of Tao. Weakness is the function of Tao. All things in the world come from being. And being comes from non-being.

(—*Ibid.*, 40.)

Tao invariably takes no action, and yet nothing is left undone.

(—*Ibid.*, 37.)

Tao is eternal and has no name. Though its simplicity seems significant, none in the world can master it.

(—*Ibid.*, 32.)

We look at it and do not see it; its name is The Invisible. We listen to it and do not hear it; its name is The Inaudible. We touch it and do not grasp it, its name is The Intangible.

(—*Ibid.*, 14.)

Non-action (*wu-wei*) is advised by the *Tao Te Ching* as the wise method of operation. Action produces reaction. Force produces resistance. A victory produces the thirst for revenge on the part of the vanquished. Rather than raise all these demons and have to deal with the hostilities released by means of some further action, the wise thing to do is nothing:

Do nothing, and do everything.

The reason for this recommendation is the strong belief that man interferes with the natural course of events. All the evils of society have been the result of the willfulness and waywardness of man, who has frustrated the cosmic order of things. The solution to this problem is to cease attempting to force things to go a certain way, but to resign one's will to the Tao and so become an instrument of its eternal way:

Soldiers are weapons of evil. They are not the weapons of gentlemen. . . . Even in victory, there is no beauty, and who calls it beautiful is one who delights in slaughter.
Repay evil with good. . . . For love is victorious in attack, and invulnerable in defense. Heaven arms with love those it would not see destroyed.

332

The distinctive contributions which Chuang Tzu made to Taoism have been summarized (by Wing-tsit Chan, in Arnold Toynbee's volume, *Half the World*, 1973) under five headings: (1) he stresses that the Tao embraces all differences and conflicts; (2) rather than agreeing with Lao Tzŭ's view of the Tao as changeless, he says it is a process; (3) whereas Lao Tzŭ said nonaction means following Nature, he says it means following Nature by self-transformation; (4) he is much more individualistic; and (5) he is more mystical and transcendental than Lao Tzŭ.

The general character of the Tao and the paradoxical statements explaining it set the stage for a radical reinterpretation of Taoism. If one begins with contradictory premises, anything can be inferred. What was inferred, beginning in the second century A.D., was a system of magic and incantations. A subtle philosophy became an esoteric mysticism. Thus, later Taoism developed into magic, with incantations to drive away the vengeful kuei, who otherwise might harm people. A Taoist named Chang Ling supposedly discovered the pill of immortality. Like Indian Yogis, Taoists sought long life, peace of mind, and other miraculous powers, such as the ability to fly through the air. They learned breathing exercises and ate powdered dragon's bones. They could look forward to entering eighty-one different kinds of heaven, with the help and intervention of such gods as the god of robbery, the god of drunkenness, the gods of various epidemics, or the god of the kitchen. The highest of the Taoist gods is the Jade Emperor, invented or recognized around 1000 A.D.

TAPANA: The sixth of the eight Buddhist hells, the "Hell of Burning Heat," Tapana, is for those who held "false views." One section is for those who believed in human sacrifice, another (the Dangerous Cliff Hell) is for "those who practice water rituals" (which sounds something like Southern Baptists), one (the Diamond Bone Hell) for those who believe and teach that things come into being by chance, without any cause (Bertrand Russell may have visited here) and one (the Black Iron Rope and Pain of Release Hell) for those who believe in predestination (where many Presbyterians may dwell). The average length of stay in this hell is sixteen thousand years.

333

THANGTONG GYELPO (1385-1464): A bridge-building saint, Thangtong Gyelpo (Thang-stong rgyal-po) did not believe in burning his bridges behind him, because he made them of iron. The approved way of crossing rivers in eastern Tibet, before that time, was to strap oneself into a saddle and slide down a rope to the other side, hoping to brake one's fall with blankets and a sharp up-turn in the rope anchored across the river. Pack animals had their feet tied upside down, and were pushed down the rope the same way.

He got the iron by begging for it and, when he collected enough, built fifty-three chain suspension bridges across rivers.

He also founded the Derge monastery.

TILOPA (988-1069): Teacher of Nāropa, Tilo-pa was one of the Indian Tantrists, one of the famous mahāsiddhas reputed to have obtained an immortal "rainbow body." He is described as "a dark man dressed in cotton trousers, his hair knotted in a tuft, and with protruding, blood-shot eyes." He said to Nāropa:

Ever since you met me in the form of the leper woman, we have never been apart, but were like a body and its shadow.

TOMINAGA NAKAMOTO (1715-1746): A Japanese philosopher and Osaka merchant during the Tokugawa Shogunate, Tominaga Nakamoto was not attached to any of the orthodox religious schools. A unique free-thinker in those still-feudal times, he studied Japanese classics, analyzed their texts, and taught an ethics which was relativistic. His purpose in studying tradition was to attack it, especially if it was foreign. His rejection of the values of foreign culture was an affirmation of the values of his own, provided his own culture were enlightened.

He wrote of Indian culture that it was based upon the pursuit of "hallucinations."

The story was told of Li Shih-Ch'ien, who was asked whether Buddhism, Confucianism, or Taoism was the superior teaching. He answered: "Buddhism is the sun, Taoism is the moon, and Confucianism the five stars." Rather than praising this answer, Tominaga called it "meaningless."

He criticized Shintoism for its habits of secret instruction and occultism, "both being tantamount simply to hiding everything. Hiding is the beginning of lying and stealing."

His works include *Monologue After Meditation* (*Shutsujō-kōgo*).

TSHANGYANG GYATSO (1683-1706): The sixth Dalai Lama, he tired of the strict moralism of the Desi, renounced his Getsul vows, the first vows of the Buddhist monkhood, and roamed through the streets of Lhasa singing drunken love-songs. He enjoyed the company of women, and the yellow houses in Lhasa and Shol are said to have once belonged to the courtesans whom he favored.

The Desi attempted to have his drinking-companion assassinated, which made relations cool.

Arrested by the Mongols for his loose living, Drêpung monks attacked the caravan and rescued him. After three days, when it was obvious that the monastery would be destroyed by the hostile Mongols, the Dalai Lama rejoined his captors. When the escort reached lake Kunganor in Kokonor, the Dalai Lama died, cause unknown.

TSONGKHA-PA (1357-1419): Founder of the Ge-lug-pa ("those who follow virtuous works") Sect, Tsongkhapa Lozang Drakpa (Tsong-kha-pa Blo-bzang grags-pa) came to the U-Tsang region from Amdo. Based on the need for monastic discipline and the gradual path (in morality), the order is also called the Ganden-pa, from the Ganden monastery, founded in 1409. His books were the *Lam-rim* and *sNgags-rim*. The monastery of Kumbum is built on the site of his birth, in Kokonor.

TUNG CHUNG-SHU (179-104B.C.): A Confucian philosopher who lived during the Han period, Tung Chung-shu was noted for his eclecticism in philosophy. Using concepts from Taoism, and recommending magical procedures, he developed moral and political philosophy. He taught the mutual influence of man and Nature, and left a system of thought which was dominant until the rise of Neo-Taoism.

TZŬ SSŬ (483-402 B.C.): The grandson of Confucius, and teacher of the teacher of Mencius. *The Doctrine of the Mean*, which is attributed to him, discusses two subjects avoided by Confucius, religion and metaphysics. It is the most mystical of the Confucian Classics. The Way of Heaven is static and eternal. It is the way of sincerity, or reality. When a person is sincere, true to his own nature, he forms a trinity with Heaven and Earth.

U

UDAYANA (920-990): A commentator on the *Nyāya-sutra* of Gautama, Udayana Acārya ("Dr. Udayana," "Acārya" meaning "one who knows or teaches the rules," a title given to great spiritual teachers) wrote that while doubt is necessary for philosophy, it must be given up when it leads to contradiction: if two terms are contradictory, they cannot be identical, nor can there be any other alternative between them.

Udayana's major work was the *Handful of Flowers* (*Kusamañjali*) (E. B. Cowell, ed. and trans.; Calcutta: Baptist Mission Press, 1864; and Ravi Tirtha, trans.; Madras: Adyar Library, 1946), in which he advances various proofs for the existence of God.

UTTARA-MĪMĀMSĀ: See Vedānta.

V

VAIŚEṢIKA: The "Atomic" school of orthodox Indian thought. One of the six orthodox systems of Indian philosophy, together with Nyāya, Sāṁkhya, Yoga, Pūrva-Mīmāṁsā, and Vedānta, Vaisheshika (pronounced vy shesh ee kah) means "particularity," the characteristics that distinguish a particular thing from all other things. The system is also called "owl" (*Aulūka*, from *ulūka*), because of its founder's habit of meditating all day and, like an owl, eating at night. It was founded by the legendary "Atom eater," Kanada, probably about 400 A.D.

> All reverence to that Kanada who, having pleased Maheshvara by the superb character of his meditation and austerities, propounded the philosophy of the Vaisheshika system

it says in the *Padārthadharmasamgraha* of Praśastapāda.

Kanada did not mention God in his *Sūtra*, only using the word "that." Others thought he should have mentioned God, and supplied, that lack in later centuries, no doubt to divine relief.

Scholars date the beginning of the Atomic school between the fifth century A.D. and the sixth century B.C. "or before." They seem to know a little more about what happened once it began. From the fifth to the tenth centuries A.D., it joined with Nyāya, the Logical school, and developed a deistic philosophy. Buddhist writers criticized the Atomists, stimulating them to postulate the existence of a Lord who can keep the natural cosmos organized.

338

Pure Atomism taught that true individuality is found in the particulars (*vishesha*) of the world, souls and atoms. Six kinds of objects are capable of being thought and named:

(1) substance (*dravya*),
(2) quality (*guna*),
(3) motion (*karma*),
(4) generality (*samanya*),
(5) particularity (*vishesha*), and
(6) inherence (*samavaya*).

Later thinkers added:

(7) non-existence (*abhava*).

Atomism presents a theory of physics, according to which the atoms are eternal. The four kinds of atoms are: air, earth, light, and water. These are the four corporeal substances. The five incorporeal substances are: ether (*ākāśa*), time (*kāla*), space (*dik*), soul or self (*ātman*), and mind (*manas*). Atoms move according to an impersonal force or law, *Adrishta*, "the invisible." Complex forms may change, but atoms remain indestructible.

The ethical theory of Atomism is framed in terms of these concepts:

Dharma, merit (or virtue) is a quality of the self. It brings to the agent happiness, the means of happiness, and final deliverance. . . . Merit is the direct cause of happiness.

Adharma, lack of merit (demerit) is also a quality of the self. It is conducive to sin and undesirable results. It is imperceptible.

VĀJÑAVALKYA (630-570 B.C.): One of the sages in the *Brihadaranyaka Upanishad*, one of the oldest and most illuminating of the Upanishads, Vājñavalkya is quoted as saying that Brahman is not conceivable, changeable, or injurable. When Uhasta Cakrayana requested an explanation of "the Brahman that is immediately present and directly perceived, that is the Self in all things," Vājñavalkya replied: "This is your Self that is within all things." Again, the question was asked: "What is within all things," and the reply is: "You cannot see the seer of seeing; you cannot hear the hearer of hearing; you cannot think the thinker

339

of thinking; you cannot understand the understander of understanding. He is your Self which is in all things."

(—III.4.2)

VALMIKI: Indian poet, author of the *Rāmāyaṇa* in its original form. The *Uttara*, a supplement to the epic, tells about the life of Valmiki, a learned and pious hermit who gave shelter to the beautiful princess Sita when she was driven from the court by the suspicions of people. She gave birth to twin boys who were trained by Valmiki to recite the *Rāmāyaṇa* by heart. He hoped this might restore the sons to their heritage and vindicate Sita. Taking the young princes to the court as boy minstrels, they chanted the great poem, twenty-four thousand verses in twenty-four days. The plan worked. Rama recognized his sons. He sent for Sita to share the throne again. But she had suffered too much. She prayed, with tears streaming down her face:

> If unstained in thought and deed
>   I have lived from day of birth,
> Spare a daughter's shame and anguish
>   and receive her, Mother Earth!

> If in duty and devotion
>   I have labored undefiled,
> Mother Earth! who bore this woman,
>   Once again receive they child!

> If in truth unto my husband
>   I have proved a faithful wife,
> Mother Earth! relieve thy Sita
>   from the burden of this life!

The earth parted, and a golden throne arose, and Mother Earth clasped Sita to her, pure and true and undefiled:

> Gods and men proclaim her virtue!
>   But fair Sita is no more;
> Alone is Rama's loveless bosom,
>   And his days of bliss are o'er!

Rama's two sons, Lava and Kusa, ruled various portions of the kingdom, Kusa founding Kusavati at the foot of the Vindhya mountains, and Lava ruling in Sravasti, which was the capital of Oudh at the time of the Buddha, in the fifth and sixth centuries before Christ.

VEDĀNTA: The sixth and most extensive of the orthodox schools of Indian philosophy, after Nyāya (logic), Vaisheshika (atoms), Sāṁkhya (enumeration of the stages of reality), Yoga (yoke or union), and Pūrva-Mīmāṁsā (investigation), Vedānta means "end" (anta) of the Vedas, referring to the last part of the Vedas, the Upanishads. The central doctrine of Vedānta is that God (*Brahman*) and the soul (*Ātman*) are one. *Brahman*, the highest Self of the Upanishads, is held to be something different from and vastly superior to such divine beings as Vishnu or Shiva, who had been the chief objects of popular worship in India.

The main sources of Vedānta philosophy are: the classic *Vedānta Sūtra* or *Brahma Sūtra* of Badarayana (dated about 200 B.C.); the commentary of Gaudapada on these *sūtras* (written nearly a thousand years later); Govinda (Gaudapada's student); Shankara (Govinda's student), who wrote the most famous Vedānta commentary and became the greatest of the orthodox Indian philosophers (before he died at the age of thirty-two); Ramanuja; Madhva; Ramakrishna; and Nikhilananda.

Shankara's theory of Non-Dualism (*Advaita*) is that there are not two basic realities, but only one, namely, *Brahman*:

> There is a certain eternal Self, on which the consciousness of selfhood rests. . . . This is he who perceives all things in waking, dreaming, dreamlessness; this is the true 'I' which perceives the intelligence and its activities, whether they be good or evil. This is he who himself perceives all, whom none perceives; who illumines the intelligence and the other powers, whom none illumines. Who penetrates and upholds this universe, whom none penetrates nor upholds; from him this universe derives the light with which it is illumined.
>
> (—*The Crest Jewel of Wisdom*)

Since there is only one reality, the question arises why there are so many things that we see around us. Shankara answers this by citing the power of *māyā*:

World Glamour, Māyā, through which this whole world comes into being, is . . . neither being nor non-being, nor in essence both.

(—*Ibid.*)

The world is not non-existent, but neither is it ultimate reality. It is illusion.

The maker (*māyā*) of illusion is ignorance (*avidyā*). Ignorance is not merely a negative force, but it is also a positive power which projects the illusion of the world.

However, when we discern the Real, we see that what we imagined to be real is only an illusion. For example, what we thought was a snake is only a rope.

Thus, Shankara writes:

There is a way of power, which destroys the terror of this life beset by death; by it crossing the wide sea of this world, thou shalt attain to the supreme joy.

(—*Ibid.*)

As to how this enlightenment may be attained:

Sons and kindred may free a father from his debts; but other than a man's self, none can free him from bondage.

(—*Ibid.*)

Badarayana maintained that the human intellect can never completely understand the nature of the Ultimate Principle, Brahman, because it lies beyond the reach of human minds just as the stars are beyond the reach of human hands. Ultimate Reality will never be revealed by logical analysis, only by direct intuition. At best, we can use logic to reconcile apparent contradictions in scripture (the Vedas), thus removing conflicts to understanding the truth. But reasoning alone will never get rid of all doubt. Because one person can prove the opposite of what someone else has proven, we must admit that reasoning is only for secular, and not for transcendental matters. Transcendental matters include God's existence, immortality, and the doctrine of salvation (re-

342

lease). The human intellect when applied to these topics is help-less. We must accept the truth on faith. Our best guides are those who have gained spiritual insight in the past, and recorded their beliefs in what are now the sacred books. Thus, the Vedas are the supreme authority for Vedānta.

Shankara's form of Vedānta, Non-Dualism, was the most com-plete and thoughtful development of the theory, and still stands as a monument to all that is best in Indian philosophy. The only difference between man and God, he held, is a matter of degree, for they are ultimately the same, just as the space inside the cup is the same space as the space outside the cup.

Māyā, or Delusion, is the force which creates all the illusions which we perceive as the objective world. On one level of truth, the ordinary pragmatic level, the world seems to have been pro-duced from a divine personality, going through many cycles, much as the Sāmkhya school taught. But on the higher level of truth, the transcendental level, the world is not real: only the Absolute, Brahman, is real.

Analysis shows that our ordinary knowledge is full of contra-dictions. What we thought was a snake turns out only to be a rope. By analogy, what we perceive as the world may be similarly different from what actually is real.

Only the Absolute, Brahman, is real, which permeates the whole universe. Brahman is identical with Ātman, the soul of the individual. When a person fully realizes this tremendous truth, not intellectually, but in one's inmost consciousness, the soul is raised above all the illusions of this transitory world and is ab-sorbed in final Truth.

Shankara's description of the Absolute is primarily in negative terms. It has no qualities or parts. It has no bounds. It does not engage in any action. It has no consciousness of "I" or "thou." It is not limited by time. It does not change. The only characteristics it may be said to have are existence, consciousness, and bliss, *sat*, *cit*, and *ānanda*.

According to Shankara, there is a series of sheaths around the soul, and truth is discovered by stripping off these sheaths, some-thing like peeling layers off an artichoke. The outer sheath is the physical body. Each of the sheaths is conditioned by the results of good or bad deeds in this life or a previous one, *karma*. By the faithful practice of virtue, piety, and meditation, the sheaths may be removed, one by one, until all the illusions are recognized as such, and we recognize that the only thing that truly exists is the Supreme Soul (*Paramātman*), the one entity that possesses true Being, Consciousness, and Bliss (*Saccidānanda*).

There are some problems with Shankara's theories, which later Vedāntists were quick to point out. For example, why should the one Ultimate Being, if it is perfect and complete in itself, evolve the great web of illusion from its own essence? If it is complete, what else does it need? If it is perfect, why should it love anything that is imperfect?

Another problem arises from the attribution of consciousness to Ultimate Being. If it is conscious, it must either be conscious of something outside itself or of itself. Nothing outside itself, by definition, truly exists. Therefore, it must be conscious of itself. But if it is self-conscious, it must have personality, in some sense. Since Shankara says it transcends personality, this seems to be self-contradictory.

Furthermore, there seems to have been an intense psychological dissatisfaction with Shankara's system. His intellectual approach to religion allowed only a qualified validity to devotion. The devotion to a personal deity which many people found emotionally satisfying was only a low-level activity, according to Shankara. The Absolute was above any God to whom a worshipper could be devoted. Any possible God was merely the primary illusory manifestation of the Absolute.

Ramanuja's form of Vedānta, Qualified Non-Dualism, is the theory that, while Brahman is real, souls are also real. The individual soul survives after its release from the body, although ultimately it depends upon Brahman, as well. Selves are real as differences *within* rather than *from* the identity that is ultimate reality.

According to Ramanuja, the Absolute does have personality. The creation was the expression of God's personality, not, as Shankara said, a sort of a sport (*līlā*) on the part of the Absolute. God, Ramanuja believed, had a need to love and be loved by something other than He. The Ultimate Reality was not an imper-

344

sonal Absolute, but a God full of love and grace for His creation. It is this personal God with whom the soul may find final peace through devotion.

Madhva's theory was dualism, that God, souls and matter are eternally distinct. The goal of salvation is not re-union with God, but rather drawing close to Him to contemplate His glory. Salvation is by grace, not by works or by devotion. Commentators (A. L. Basham) remark on the similarities of this thirteenth-century theory with Christianity, and explain it through the presence of churches at Malabar.

Ramakrishna's viewpoint is expressed in the slogan: "All religions are one." The major religions, Hinduism, Christianity, Islam, and Zoroastrianism, according to the mystic, express the oneness of all things in the Universal Spirit. The chief malady of our age, as Nikhilananda remarks, when translating Ramakrishna, is spiritual, its attachment to "girls and gold."

Swami Vivekānanda was instrumental in spreading Vedānta to the West, beginning with the Parliament of Religions held in Chicago in the fall of 1893. He said:

> Each soul is potentially divine. The goal is to manifest this divine within by controlling nature, external and internal.

Control, he continued, could be achieved by any of the Yoga methods, and a person could be free:

> This is the whole of religion. Doctrines or dogmas, or rituals, or books, or temples, or forms are but secondary details.
> (—*Birth Centenary of Swami Vivekānanda. . .* ,
> Boston: The Ramakrishna Vedānta Society, p. 16)

Some of his friends while in Boston and Cambridge included Julia Ward Howe and William James. In England, he met Canon Wilberforce of Westminster Abbey. He made a strong impression through his various lectures, appearances, and discussions.

VENKATANATHA (1268-1369): An Indian thinker who wrote a commentary on a commentary by Ramanuja on the *Brahma-*

sūtra, Venkatanatha also produced the *Classification of Logical Method* (*Nyāyaparisuddhi*). While at Srīrangam on a pilgrimmage, marauding Muslims pillaged the place, and he escaped massacre, or martyrdom, by hiding among the corpses. He then fled to Mysore for his health, returning to Srīrangam only after the temple was fully restored.

VITAL, CHAIM (1543-1620): Cabalist and disciple of Isaac Luria, Chaim (or Haym) Vital was born in Safed and died in Damascus. His main work is called the *Etz Hayyim*. Vital related stories of marvellous miracles wrought by Luria's doctrines. Vital spread Luria into every village, helped by the invention of printing, and Cabalistic Judaism rivalled Talmudic Judaism for a while.

Cabalistic studies ridicule as "simple" any study of the Bible (the Pentateuch) which is content with the plain meaning of the words. The literal meaning of the text is nothing but the "garment." The hidden meaning, the "body that the vestment covers," is what is truly important.

Among the methods devised to uncover the "exalted meaning and sublime mystery" in the Law was placing one verse over another, reading vertically, and forming new words. These new words would then be used to reinterpret the text. Words would be joined or divided in new ways. Words would be reduced to numerical value, and then read in terms of other words with the same numerical value.

VIVEKĀNANDA (1863-1902): The Vedāntist evangelist, Vivekānanda brought the thought of Ramakrishna to America during the International Religious Conference in Chicago, giving an impassioned speech for toleration (of other religions) without surrender, on September 27, 1893.

W

WANG CH'UNG (27-97): A strongly independent Chinese thinker with a skeptical and mechanistic frame of mind, Wang Ch'ung wrote that:

> Man holds a place in the universe like that of a flea or a louse under a jacket or robe. . . . Can the flea or louse, by conducting itself either properly or improperly, affect the changes or movements in the space under the jacket? . . . They are not capable of this, and to suppose that man alone is thus capable is to misconceive the principle of things and of the ether.

Critical Essays (*Lun Heng*) was the title of his principal work. The title (following Wing-tsit Chan) may also be translated *Balanced Inquiries, or Fair Discussions.* Wang refused to follow authoritative systems of belief, and instead demanded hard evidence for any assertion said to be true. He opposed the Yin-Yang school, and denied that any interaction takes place between Heaven and earth, using the following argument:

> The Way of Heaven is that of spontaneity, which consists of non-activity. However, if Heaven were to reprimand men, that would constitute action, and would not be spontaneous.
> (—*Critical Essays*, Chapter 42)

Wang's own epistemology, called "hatred of fictions and falsehoods," was that:

In things there is nothing more manifest than having results, and in argument there is nothing more decisive than having evidence.

(—*Critical Essays*, Chapter 67.)

By his rugged skepticism of current orthodoxies, Wang prepared the way for the rationalism, naturalism, and the later revival of Taoism, and was also able to maintain his own secure position in poverty. He did serve as secretary of a district for a while. When Emperor Chang Ti was told that Wang was brighter than Mencius and Hsün Tzu, he invited him to come to the royal court to shine. He declined the invitation because of ill health, and the court was forced to do without his light.

Wang wrote about the story of the king who ate a leech. As traditionally told, King Hui of Ch'u was eating a salad when he found a leech on the lettuce. He thought to himself if he scolded the cook and butler who were responsible, but did not punish them, he would look weak and lose dignity. If he did punish them, the law required the death of all those responsible. So he pretended not to notice, and promptly swallowed the leech. Then he got sick, felt a pain in his stomach, and lost his appetite. He told his troubles to the premier, who said he had been so virtuous, Heaven would reward him. The same night he was cured of his illness.

Wang asked: "Can this be considered evidence of Heaven's partiality for virtue?" He answered his own question: "No. This is idle talk," because the king did not have to kill the cook—he could have pardoned him. Furthermore, anyone, even a king, dumb enough to swallow a leech is sure to get sick. When the king recovered his health, it was undoubtedly due to natural causes, not to heaven's reward of virtue. The real blame, says Wang, belongs to the careless cooks, for a leech is so big that it could be seen in a salad even by a one-eyed man!

WANG FU-CHIH (1619-1693): Greatly admired in the People's Republic of China, the experiences of Wang Fu-chich (or Wang Ch'uan-shan) paralleled the experiences of Mao Tse-tung. Both came to maturity at the end of the one era and the beginning of another, both fought oppression in their native province of Hunan, and both fled to the mountains for protection, when military pressure against them was too intense. Wang Fu-chih developed a materialistic interpretation of Confucius, opposing both the rationalistic Neo-Confucianism of Sung and the idealistic Neo-Confucianism of Ming.

Wang passed his civil service exam in 1642, just when the Manchus were overrunning China. The Ming Dynasty fell in 1644. By 1648, the Manchus were oppressing Hunan province. Wang raised a small army to oppose them and bring back the Ming. Defeated, he fled to the mountains near his home and devoted himself to writing, a choice which considerably lengthened his life span.

"The world," he wrote, "consists only of concrete things." He denied the existence of any such abstractions as the "Great Ultimate" or the "Principle of Nature."

With regard to political theory, he said that the past cannot be a pattern for the present, since the universe is in the continual process of being renewed. A new day is literally a new day. Everything in it is new. However, things do progress and improve, as time goes by. Later ages are more civilized than earlier. Hence, it is wise to discern this developing tendency, and follow it:

> What is meant by the Way (*Tao*) is the management of concrete things. When the Way is fulfilled, we call it virtue.... Lao Tzu was blind to this and said that the Way existed in emptiness.... Buddha was blind to this and said that the way existed in silence.... One may keep on uttering such extravagant words endlessly, but no one can ever escape from concrete things. Thus, if one plays up some name that is separated from concrete things as though he were a divine being, whom would he deceive?
>
> (—*Surviving Works of Wang Fu-chih, Ch'uan-shan i-shu*)

WANG PI (226-249): The most precocious genius in the history of Chinese thought, Wang Pi (Fu-ssu) wrote a famous *Commentary on the Yi* (*I Ching*), although his enemies, those who did not share

349

his Neo-Taoist ideas, said that Wang Pi's name was its own commentary. Wang died at twenty-three. Before his death, he was an official for the Wei government. His commentary on the *Lao Tzu* is now the oldest extant.

Wang contributed to the development of the metaphysics of Chinese philosophy by going behind cosmology (the theory of the universe, such as that of the *Huai-nan-tzu*) and the cosmogony (theory of creation) of the time to ontology (theory of being as such). Wang rejected appearance, which in the philosophy of the day was the theory of names and forms, for reality, which he identified as *pen-wu*, original non-being. Non-being, he stated, was pure being, the original substance (*pen-t'i*) which transcends all descriptions or distinctions. Substance and function are one in non-being. Underlying all particular phenomena is the fundamental unity.

Where Lao Tzŭ had spoken of destiny (or fate, *ming*), Wang Pi spoke instead of principle. The Neo-Confucianists would later follow this insight, preferring to speak of the Principle of Nature (*T'ien-li*) rather than the Destiny Decreed by Heaven (*T'ien-ming*).

WANG YANG-MING (1472-1529): The noted Ming dynasty Neo-Confucianist, Wang Yang-Ming (or Wang Shou-jen, or Po-an, or Wen-Ch'eng, "Completion of Culture") wrote that it was "from a hundred deaths and a thousand sufferings" that he achieved his doctrine of the extension of innate knowledge (*chih-liang-chih*). Others studying his work seem to have felt similar sensations.

Born in Chekiang province (the coastal province just south of Shanghai), his father was an earl and an officer in the civil service. He took his two degrees ("recommended person," 1492, and "presented scholar," 1499) and entered government service. In 1506 he made the mistake of offending a eunuch, and was banished. When allowed to work again, he was permitted to repress rebellions, establish schools, rehabilitate rebels, and reconstruct the economy. His enemies then accused him of being a rebel himself, and he was banished once again. After his death, he was accused of spreading false doctrines, which was false, and of opposing Chu Hsi, which was true. Chu Hsi had shifted the chapters of the *Great Learning* around so that the part on the "investigation of things" would come before the "sincerity of the will." Knowledge precedes honesty. Wang disputed this, on the grounds that honesty must precede knowledge. There would be no principle unless the mind were first determined to realize it. We must will to know the truth. Wang shifted the chapters back to their original order in the old text of the *Book of Rites*, sincerity preceding the investigation of things. Reality is value. Wang rejected an intellectual approach in favor of a moral one.

Knowledge and action are one. Knowledge is the beginning of action and action is the completion of knowledge.

Wang was honored in 1584 by imperial decree, one of four during the Ming period, as the proper recipient of sacrifices in the Confucian temple.

His major work was entitled *Inquiry on the Great Learning*.

WATSUJI TETSURŌ (1889-1960): A noted modern Japanese philosopher, Dr. Watsuji wrote:

> In Japanese, the expression of feeling and will comes to the foreground. And, owing to this characteristic, what man understands in his direct and practical action is extremely well preserved. One of the modes of expression conspicuous in Japanese literature surely owes its high degree of development to this characteristic of the Japanese language. This mode consists in connecting together words and phrases which exhibit no connection of cognitive meaning, simply according to identity or similarity of pronunciation, and moreover through the connection of their emotive and effective content, achieving the expression of one complete concrete emotion. It seems to me that this characteristic is nothing more or less than a characteristic of the Japanese spirit.
>
> (—Tetsurō Watsuji, *Research in Japanese Intellectual History, Continued, Zoku Nihon Seishin-shi Kenkyū*, quoted in Nakamura, *Ways of Thinking of Eastern Peoples*, pp. 551-552.)

WEI YANG: See Shang Yang.

WU: The Chinese philosophical term for the concept of non-being. According to Lao Tzŭ (ch. 40): "Being (*Yu*) comes into being from Non-being (*Wu*)." Chuang Tzŭ (ch. 12) writes: "At the great beginning there was Non-being." According to the WeiChin scholars (220-420), *Wu* is not simply the opposite of being, but the ultimate, pure being, the One, completely undifferentiated. The Chinese Buddhists said that to achieve Buddhahood means to be one with Non-being (*Wu*). Ch'an Buddhists held that the First Principle is inexpressible because what is called the *Wu* is not something about which anything can be said at all. We must not fall into the "net of words."

WU-WEI: Chinese term for "taking no unnatural action" (rather than simply "inaction"). In Buddhist usage, "not produced from causes."

WU-HSIN: Chinese term for "no deliberate mind of one's own" (rather than simply "inaction").

Y

YANG CHU (420-360 B.C.): The Chinese Taoist philosopher whose doctrine of egoism angered Mencius, Yang Chu declared: "Every man for himself." Self-preservation was the basic principle, even to the point of not plucking out a single hair though we would benefit the entire world by so doing:

> If everyone would refrain from sacrificing even one single hair, and if everyone would refrain from benefiting the world, the world would be in order.
>
> (—the "Yang Chu Chapter" of the
> *Lieh Tzŭ* (the *Ch'ung-hsü chih-te
> chen-ching, Pure Classic of the
> Perfect Virtue of Simplicity and
> Vacuity*), Chapter 7.)

Yang Chu (Yang-Tse, Yang-Sheng, or Yang Tschu) was a naturalist and a hedonist. If a city were in danger, he said, he would not enter it. If the army were about to fight, he would leave the army. Even an empire, once lost, may some day be regained, but once dead, one can never live again.

Yang Chu's Garden of Pleasure was the goal: "Let us hasten to enjoy our present life. Why bother about what comes after death?"

YEN FU (1853-1921): A revolutionary Chinese philosopher, Yen Fu was noted for translating western (English) works into Chin ese, Huxley's *Evolution and Ethics* (1898), John Stuart Mill, Spencer (whom he called "the greatest Western philosopher of all time"), Adam Smith, and Montesquieu.

YEN YUAN (1635-1704): A Chinese philosopher noted for practical Confucianism, Yen Yüan (Yen Hsi-chai) was a native of Chih-li. He studied fencing and military science, and remained a poor man, until his qualities led him to become the director of an academy. He believed sitting in meditation and reading to be a sure cause of social disintegration. He practiced medicine and farming with his students, taught them dancing, singing, mathematics, archery, and weight-lifting. The "four halls" of his school were (1) classics and history, (2) literature, (3) military science, and (4) practical arts.

The "investigation of things," he believed, was not the study of principle (Chu Hsi) nor the study of the mind (Wang Yang-ming), but learning from actual experience and practical problem-solving.

YIN-YANG: The yin yang doctrine is that all things and events are products of two forces. The yin is negative, passive, weak, and destructive. The yang is positive, active, strong, and constructive.

The yin yang idea is present in the classical books of Taoism, Mo Tzŭ, the *Book of History*, and others. It is absent from all the ancient Confucian Classics except the *Hsün Tzŭ*.

The yin yang theory, as Wing-Tsit Chan remarks, has put Chinese ethical and social teachings on a cosmological basis, developing the view that all things are related and that reality is in the process of constant transformation. Yin yang provides the idea of harmony within creative tension.

YOGA: (From the Sanskrit *yuj*, "to yoke," "to bind together," "to hold fast") One of the six orthodox systems of Indian Philosophy, with Nyāya (logic), Vaisheshika (atoms), Sankhya (enumeration), Pūrva-Mīmāṁsā (desire to think), and Vedānta (end of Vedas), Yoga aims at the union of the individual spirit with the universal spirit.

Yoga aims at freeing mankind from three sorts of pain:

354

(1) pains arising from sins and sicknesses;

(2) pains arising from relations with other living things, such as from thieves or tigers; and

(3) pains arising from relations with non-living things, such as storms, natural disasters, and abstract and subtle powers.

Freedom from these pains is accomplished by:

(1) non-attachment to the world;

(2) restraining the mind and imagination, purifying the manifest consciousness; and

(3) attaining the union of the individual soul with the universal soul.

This final stage is *samādhi*, the true purpose of Yoga and its techniques.

Yoga seeks to unite the inner and outer force, Life and Death. When the individual soul reaches its own essence, it is freed from such emotions as pain and joy, and is thus released, eternally, from all misery.

The "yoke" of Yoga is discipline and self-denial which a believer takes upon himself in order to cleanse himself of all material limitations and achieve supernatural powers.

The founder of Yoga was Pantajali, author of the *Yoga Sūtra*, the most important source for the school. Patanjali begins with fifty-one aphorisms discussing the science of Yoga, the aim and nature of *samādhi*. The second book contains fifty-five aphorisms about the art of Yoga and the means for attaining its end. The third consists of fifty-four aphorisms concerning the supernormal powers which may be obtained. This book ends with the word *iti*, which appears at the end of a work. Thus, the fourth book is assumed to be of later date. It consists of thirty-four aphorisms discussing final emancipation, man's realization that he is separated from mind-matter.

Other important sources of Yoga are Vyāsa's *Bhasya* (fourth century A.D.), a commentary on Patanjali's *Yoga-Sūtra*, which contains the standard exposition of Yoga principles; Vācaspati's

Tattvavaiśāradī (ninth century), a gloss on Vyāsa's work; Bhoja's *Rājamārtānda*; Vijñānabhiksu's *Yoga-vārttika* and *Yoga-sārasam-graha*, which criticize Vācaspati and attempt to bring Yoga in closer harmony with the Upanishads.

Not only is knowledge important, in Yoga, but also *initiation*. It is impossible to learn about Yoga completely by oneself. One must be initiated by a master teacher. This is necessary to avoid the physical harm that might be done to oneself by over-zealously practicing some of the exercises and also to avoid the moral harm that might be done by the selfish acquisition of special powers.

For example, the story is told by Paramahansa Yogananda (*Augobiography of a Yogi*, 1972) of an individual named Afzal Khan who acquired extraordinary powers from a Hindu yogi who was in eastern Bengal. Given command over one of the invisible realms, he was told by his teacher never to employ those powers selfishly. Ignoring his master's warning, Afzal began to misuse them. Whatever object he would touch and replace would disappear. He began visiting jewelry stores in Calcutta, using his powers to shoplift from long distance.

One day Afzal met an old man walking with a painful limp on the road. He begged Afzal to heal his limp, but Afzal only rubbed his hand over the ball of shining gold the old man had. Soon the gold vanished. Then the old man said: "Do you not recognize me?" To Afzal's horror, the old man straightened up, became strong and youthful. It was Afzal's teacher.

"So!" he said. "I see with my own eyes that you use your powers, not to help suffering humanity, but to prey on it like a common thief!"

He withdrew Afzal's occult powers, and Afzal was no longer the "terror of Bengal."

The seven Indian systems of Yoga are:
(1) Rāja Yoga (Patanjali),
(2) Gītā-Yoga (Shrī Krishna),
(3) Gnyāna-Yoga (Shankarāchārya),
(4) Hatha Yoga,
(5) Laya Yoga,
(6) Bhakti Yoga, and
(7) Mantra Yoga.

Rāja ("Kingly") Yoga is so named because it teaches us to be king or master of our own faculties. Gītā-Yoga and Gnyāna-Yoga may be said to be varieties of Rāja-Yoga. According to this view, the inner powers of the mind can only be developed by their own exercise, not (as the varieties of Hatha Yoga hold) by any external means.

The eight "limbs" of yoga, Patanjali's regular course, are:

1) *Yama*, the five abstentions, not to:

    (i) injure (*ahimsā*),
    (ii) lie,
    (iii) steal,
    (iv) be sensual, and
    (v) be greedy:
    in this stage, the death of desire, the individual abandons all self-seeking, so that he leaves all material interests and pursuits and wishes all things well;

2) *Niyama*, the five observances, to be:

    (i) clean,
    (ii) content,
    (iii) self-controlled,
    (iv) studious, and
    (v) devoted:

3) *Asānā*, balanced posture: "the posture must be steady and pleasant" (Aphorism ii 46);
4) *Prānāyāma*, regularity of breathing;
5) *Pratyāhāra*, abstraction, in which one withdraws the mind from all sense objects;
6) *Dhāranā*, concentration;
7) *Dhyāna*, fixed meditation, an almost hypnotic condition, one which may be produced by repetition of the sacred syllable, "*Om*;"
8) *Samādhi*, trance contemplation, in which the mind is completely merged with totality, a condition which

357

cannot be described in words; thus, "through yoga must yoga be known." In this final stage, one may obtain direct, intuitional knowledge. The mind is dissolved. Self-illumination results. This is the perfect life of the spirit.

Gītā Yoga (a term used by Ernest Wood, *Great Systems of Yoga*) expresses the fact that each of the eighteen chapters of the *Bhagavad Gītā* is called a yoga, such as "Yoga of Knowledge," "Yoga of Action," "Yoga of Renunciation," "Yoga of Meditation," and so on. This is more a yoga for the emotions than for the mind.

The Teacher's instruction is that right and wrong should not be judged from the standpoint of bodily appearances, but rather from what is of value to the immortal soul. He wants Arjuna to know something more than knowledge-yoga, namely wisdom (buddhi-)-yoga. He says:

The man who performs actions without personal attachment reaches the 'beyond;' therefore always do work which ought to be done, without personal attachment.

Sri Krishna Prem's book, *The Yoga of the Bhagavat Gita* (Penguin, 1973) offers a detailed study of this kind of yoga, and states:

The Gita adds a warning against communicating this Mystery to anyone who is undisciplined, without love, without desire to serve, or who speaks evil of the Teacher.

Guyāna or Jnāna (knowledge) Yoga is derived from Shankara, the noted Vedanta scholar. Practical occultism, he contended, is aimed at the destruction of all the imperfections we suffer from, which are the result of ignorance. Shankara distinguishes between people who want to *have* and those who want to *know*. The course Shankara recommends is called the group of four accomplishments:

1) discrimination between the fleeting and the permanent (*viveka*);
2) an emotional condition of withdrawal from immediate

reaction to impressions coming from the outer world
(*vairāgya*);
3) the "six forms of success," (*shat sampatti*):

   (i) control of the mind,
   (ii) control of the body,
   (iii) contentment and tolerance,
   (iv) patience,
   (v) fidelity and sincerity, and
   (vi) steadiness; and

4) eagerness for liberation (*mumukshatwa*).

Hatha Yoga, which may be said to include Laya Yoga, Bhakti
Yoga, and Mantra Yoga as varieties, is composed chiefly of advice
for the regulation of breathing, the practice of various postures,
and body-purifications.

Laya ("latent," or "in suspense") Yoga aims at the awakening of
"the coiled one" (*kundalinī*), a force "luminous as lightning" lying
in three and a half coils, like a sleeping serpent, in a cavity near the
base of the spine, a sort of fount of bodily electricity. Through
laya-practices, the *kundalinī* will be awakened, hissing, and then
can be carried up through the series of six "wheels" (*chakras*)
threaded upon the channel going up the spinal column. The four
upper wheels, or flowers, are the navel, the heart, the throat, and
the eyebrows. Arthur Avalon's book, *The Serpent Power*, describes
the effects of this theory.

The *Hatha-Yoga Padīpikā* says:

The mind is the lord of the senses; the breath is the lord of
the mind; and that depends on internal sounds (*nāda*).
(—iv 29.)

Again:

There is talk of suspension, suspension (*laya*), but what is its
character? Suspension is the non-arising of further "perfumes" (vāsānas, the lingering essence of past attachments or
359

desires, whose memory may now produce pleasure or pain, as the smell of onions persists long after they have been eaten), and the forgetting of external things.

(—iv 34.)

The theory is that all one has to do is to cut off contact with this world, and the other state will be there. The sounds of this other state, after the yogi has closed his ears with the thumbs, the eyes with the index fingers, the nostrils with the middle fingers and the lips with the remaining four, will be like the hum of a bee, then a flute, bells, and afterwards, thunder.

Bhakti (devotion) Yoga emphasizes concentrating on goodness, refusing to think about the bad. The *bhakta*, devotee, is satisfied with the joy of goodness:

Let him meditate in his own heart upon the proper form of his desired deity; let him meditate with the *bhakti-yoga*, full of the greatest gladness; let him shed tears of happiness.

(—Gheranda Sanhitā vii, 14-15.)

The yogi wants to have his consciousness raised into the source of the intuition of divinity.

Mantra (charms, spells, magical formulas, incantations) Yoga is the employment of words so as to produce a desired effect. All the hymns of the Veda are considered *mantras*. The saying of the *mantra* must be accompanied by the right intention and belief in the mind. The *mantra* must be repeated, often with a definite intonation, such as in a loud voice, a low voice, or a chant. One of the most powerful mantras is the one from the *Gopālatāpani* and *Krishna* Upanishads:

Klīm, Krishnāya, Govindāya, Gopī-jana, Vallabhāya, Swāhā.

Those who practice laya-yoga prefer the *mantra*:

Om, aim, klīm, strīm.

Om (or *Aum*) requires special mention, as it is the word, the true name, not merely the given name, of the "one life without a second," the natural name of God, pronunciation of which is a means to harmony with the divine.

360

An excellent study of yoga is to be found in Mircea Eliade's *Yoga: Immortality and Freedom* (Princeton University Press: 1958).

YÖNTEN GYATSO (1589-1617): The Fourth Dalai Lama, Yönten Gyatso was also the great-grandson of the Altan Khan. When his attendants misinterpreted some poetry, the Mongolian cavalry, which fancied poetry, was enraged, and vented their fury by raiding the stables of Yönten Gyatso. After tempers cooled, the Emperor of the Ming Court invited him to bless the Buddhist temple at Nanking. He declined the long trip, but did agree to bless the temple by long distance, facing in the right direction and scattering grains of barley into the wind.

Yönten Gyatso died at the age of twenty-eight, of rheumatism, while he was at the Drêpung monastery. Popular even after death, his ashes were divided three ways, to his Mongolian father, to one of his Mongolian patrons, and the remainder to the monastery.

YÜAN-WU KO-CHIN (1063-1135): An eminent Ch'an (Zen) master, Yüan-wu wrote the *Records of the Emerald Rock*. This is a commentary upon the hundred examples, the *Master Biographies with Anecdotes* which was collected and embellished by Hsüe-tou in the eleventh century.

For example, Yüan-wu wrote:

The ancients went by this rule: One question, one answer. Without much ado, they complied with the time and the hour. If you ask for words, hunt for proverbs, ultimately you do not reach any agreement. Not until you arrive at the position of advancing toward and releasing the word contained in the word, the meaning contained in the meaning, the motive contained in the motive, until you are free and composed, will you perceive the place which Chi-men's answer is pointing out.

> (—*Pi-Yen-Lu , translated by Kurt Leidecker, quoted in Wade Baskin, Classics in Chinese Philosophy*, p. 496.)

361

The twenty-sixth example is as follows:

A monk asked Pai-chang: What is there that is extraordinary?
Pai-chang replied: To sit alone here on Hero Mountain.
The monk bowed reverently. Thereupon Pai-chang struck him.

Among the explanations Yüan-wu offers on this incident, he observes:

The task of the master to answer the pupil's questions required the same attention and caution as when one spars with an opponent in front of horses' hoops.

Z

ZARATHUSTRA: See Zoroaster.

ZEN: (Japanese *zenno, zenna*, from the Chinese *ch'an, ch'an-na*, from Pali *jhana*, and Sanskrit *dhyāna*, meaning "meditation"). The noted school of Mahāyāna Buddhism dedicated to the importance of meditation for achieving enlightenment, *satori*. Brought to China by Bodhidharma (516), Zen came to Japan with Eisai (1141-1215), Dōgen (1200-1253) and others.

Enlightenment may be either sudden or gradual, a difference between the main schools of Zen, Rinzai and Sōtō. The first is named for Rinzai Gigen (d. 867), or Lin-chi, who advocated *sudden* enlightenment. The second, Sōtō (Tsao-tung in Chinese), was introduced into Japan by Dōgen. Sōtō does not use *koan* and follows less dramatic methods of enlightenment which, it teaches, should be *gradual*. It is Rinzai Zen which has caught the imagination of most western students.

"Zen," according to Daisetz T. Suzuki, its most forceful contemporary advocate, "is discipline in enlightenment." Discipline is not that of a world-renouncing ascetic who eats very little and lives in a hovel, but one who approaches the world with new insight. Rinzai, once asked the essence of Buddhist teaching, grabbed the questioner's robe and slapped him in the face. The questioner was stunned. The bystanders asked, "Why don't you bow?" As he was about to, he achieved *satori*.

As they met on a bridge, three monks asked a monk from

Rinzai's monastery: "How deep is the river of Zen?" "Find out for yourself," replied the Zen monk, who then tried to throw the pilgrims into the river.

Satori, it is believed, generally occurs when an individual is at the end of his resources. Having mastered the techniques of his craft, he still feels something lacking, wanting something that will tie it all together. He wants insight that will enable him to make further discovery.

We may appreciate that Zen technique is not limited to religious or philosophical inquiry, but may be applied equally well to any field. Artists, poets, and craftsmen of Japan have been enthusiastic practitioners of Zen method. This explains the proliferation of the "Zen and" books ("Zen and Archery," "Zen and Swordsmanship," "Zen and the Art of Tea"). The Zen method of attaining insight may be applied to almost any field of knowledge or craft. The cultural value of Zen has been tremendous.

When faced with complacency, the task of the Zen master is to jar an individual loose from his customary way of thinking or acting. To accomplish this, the *koan* is often used. For example:

> "Who is Buddha?"
> "Three measures of flax."

Or again:

> "What is Buddha?"
> "The cat is climbing up the post."

Or again:

> "What is the meaning of Buddha's
> coming from the West?"
> "The cypress tree in the courtyard."

By this riddling method, the questioner could be encouraged to see the divinity in the common world, the supernatural in the natural.

The seventeenth-century artist Basho painted "Bamboos and a *haiku*." Sengai (late eighteenth-century) painted "Banana plant and Frog." Miyamoto Musashi (Niten) (early seventeenth century) painted a shrine on a dead branch. Each of these is an instance where the divine is captured through the natural scene.

The *koan* riddles have the purpose of wakening a student to a new way of looking at reality. The direct approach is illustrated by this incident:

A man is hanging over a cliff by his teeth, when someone asks him: "Why did the Bodhidharma come to China?" If he does not answer, he fails the test. If he does answer, he falls. Which should he do?

One of the most famous Zen questions is:
What sound is made by one hand clapping?
The famous "kitten *koan*" by Nansen (Chinese, Nan-ch'üan) is relevant. Some monks were quarreling over who should have a certain little kitten. Nansen, catching it, said: "If any of you can tell me why I should not kill this cat, I will spare its life." None spoke. So Nansen threw it against the ground and killed it. Later, when the monk Joshu (Chinese Chao-chou) came to the monastery, Nansen asked him what he would have said if he had been there. Joshu silently removed his sandals from his feet, placed them on his head, and walked out. Nansen then said to him: "Oh, if only you had been here, the kitten would have been saved!"

Master Tsung Kao once said: "The Mind, Intellect, and Consciousness are hindrances on the Path more deadly than poisonous snakes or wild beasts. . . . Brilliant and intellectual persons always live in the cave of conceptualization. They can never get out of it in all their activities. . . . Therefore, I say, poisonous snakes and beasts are avoidable, but there is no way to escape from mental conceptualization." The "grasping mind," says this Master, is trying to reach for the nongraspable Dharma, which cannot be conceived or measured or comprehended by the mind. Blindness is the true nature of the Buddha.

Zen is not pantheistic, because there is no Unity, no One in Zen. One is All and All is One. Yet the One remains the One. The All remains All. They are not to be confounded or confused. For example, when a monk asked Jōsu: "Am I correct to say that the Buddha asserts that all talk, however trivial or derogatory, belongs to ultimate truth?" The Master replied: "Yes, you are correct." The monk then said: "May I then call you an ass?" The Master then struck him.

Again (to Jōsu):

> "What is the Buddha?"
> "The Buddha."
> "What is the Tao?"
> "The Tao."
> "What is Zen?"
> "Zen."

Zen, in contrast with other schools of Mahāyāna Buddhism, teaches that we all possess in our inner selves the immanent nature of Buddhahood. We do not need to expound the precepts of the Sutras or depend upon external rituals. Zen advocates *jiriki* Buddhism, the Buddhism of self-power, as opposed to Jōdo's *tariki* Buddhism, the Buddhism of other-power.

In America, Zen centers are found in California (Tassajara Zen Center) and New York (International Dai Bosatsu Zendo), with a three million dollar copy of Kyoto's Tofuku Ji, in the Catskills. Zazen is taught. Posture and breathing are essential, because to sit well and to be well are the same.

Zen recommends attention to the present, to things as they are, rather than as we think they should be. The idea is not to resist distractions, but to remain attentive to them. Hear your thoughts, but do not chase after them.

ZEND AVESTA: See Avesta.

ZOROASTER (660-583 B.C.): The famous prophet from Persia, Zoroaster (the conventional Greek spelling of the Iranian term, "Zarathustra" or "Zarthushtra") founded a universal religion not subject to any regional or ethnic considerations. There is, he proclaimed, an eternal struggle between the forces of light and the forces of darkness. Good and evil are in constant and bitter contention with each other. Zoroaster's name, according to philologists, means "Star-Worshipper," "Friend of Fire," "Star of Gold," "Descended from Venus," "Devoted to Agriculture," or, oddly enough, "Tormenting Camels."

The details of the life of Zoroaster tend to be obscure because his biography was written some two thousand years after his death. One indisputable landmark in dating is 484 B.C., the death of King Darius of Persia, who used Zoroastrian phrases in his inscriptions. The *Avesta* says that Zoroaster taught at the court of King Vishtasp, possibly the father of Darius.

What is known about Zoroaster's life makes him the product of the Media, an independent state in Northwest Iran, currently the province of Azerbayejan. "Born laughing," his religious system accents the positive. Its commandments are not prohibitions, but positive recommendations.

During his childhood, wizards were said to employ the black arts in an attempt to destroy him, but without success. When fifteen, he was invested with the sacred shirt (*Sadra*) and girdle (*Kusti*). When thirty, he concluded that the wise men who had been his teachers were not so wise after all. He retired to a mountain (not located in Iran), which might not have been quite as learned, but at least it did not claim superiority. He spent the next ten years in prayer and meditation, the universe serving as his university. For two weeks, while his spirit was taken to the presence of God, his body was left entirely motionless on the mountaintop.

The name of God, the good God, is Ahura Mazda ("Lord of Life" and "Creator of Matter"). According to the *Avesta*, Zoroaster's guide on this trip was the archangel Good Thought (Vohu-Manō), a figure "nine times as large as a man." When he reached the destination, he found that he could not see the shadow on the floor beneath him, because of the brilliance of the archangels.

The name of the evil god, opposed to Ahura Mazda, and all His works, is Angra Mainyu. The author of death, Angra Mainyu created 99,999 diseases and an evil to match every good. Angra Mainyu made the killing frost of winter, the excessive heat of summer, the snakes, locusts, ants, the wicked rich, vice, lust, evil sorcerers, witchcraft, doubt, disbelief, the burying of the dead, and the cooking of carrion. Those who follow him will dwell in "the House of the Lie," an evil-smelling region, where every sufferer will forever live alone.

When he returned and began teaching, his revelations were not received with enthusiasm. After some time, he did succeed in

367

converting his cousin to the truth of his views. He started speaking in the courts of kings, eventually reaching the court of King Vishtasp. There he was opposed by the "wise men," who perceived him as a threat to their power. Anyone, they thought, who would speak so highly of truth in the presence of practical politicians must be a practitioner of the black arts. Accusing him of sorcery, they cleverly arranged to have incriminating evidence hidden in his room, nails, hairs, and heads of dogs under his bed. Jailed as a necromancer, he escaped confinement only because of the incident of the Black Horse. It seems that King Vishtasp's favorite horse had become ill, its legs tightly drawn up against its belly. Zoroaster sent word out that he could cure the horse, but only if the King would grant one wish for each of the legs he healed. The King agreed to the terms. For the first, Zoroaster asked that the King convert to the faith. For the second, he asked that the Queen convert. For the third, the Crown Prince. For the fourth, he asked that the names of the plotters be revealed and that they be punished. The horse was completely cured, the King converted, and Zoroastrianism became the official religion, or the religion of the officials. The king did waver, but two archangels, Behman and Ardi-behesht, and the Fire Burzin Meher came down to the palace to help the conversion, and the palace was filled with radiance beyond description.

Zoroaster himself healed the sick, took special care of the sacred fire, studied the laws of Nature, and summarized his knowledge in twenty-one "Nusks."

The conversion of King Vishtasp, however, was made into a cause of war by Arjasp, who twice invaded Iran. It was during the second invasion that Zoroaster was killed while praying in an Atash-gah in front of the sacred fire, by Tur Baratur.

The religion Zoroaster founded lasted a long time in Persia, and remains today principally among the Parsis of (Bombay) India. Its influence, the image of the eternal struggle of light and darkness, good and evil, had influenced the thought of many other peoples.

Ruhi Afnan's book, *Zoroaster's Influence on Greek Thought* (New York: The Philosophical Library, 1965) examines thoroughly some of the connections between Zoroaster's concepts and the ideas of the West.

ZOROASTRIANISM: The religion founded by Zoroaster, or Zarathustra, Zoroastrianism is characterized by belief in the cosmic war between Good and Evil, light and dark, reflected in the struggle within the soul of each man. Zoroaster's disciples formed the famous Maga-Brotherhood, The Magi (the "wise men from the East").

Originally centered in Persia, Zoroastrianism was affected by the changing fortunes of the Persian Empire. One of these changes was caused by Alexander the Great, who is called "Alexander the Vile," or "the Damned," by the Zoroastrians, because he burned the palaces at Persepolis (330 B.C.) and destroyed the priceless copy of the Zoroastrian scripture. Its contents were preserved only in the memories of priests, in rituals, and in a few scattered manuscripts. The attempted reconstruction of these texts produced the sacred books now used by Zoroastrians. These include the *Gāthās*, reputed to be the actual words of Zoroaster himself, now preserved in scriptures in three languages: Avesta, Pahlavi, and Persian. The Avesta texts include: (1) the *Yasna*, in seventy-two chapters, of which seventeen are the *Gāthās*; (2) the *Visparad*, a liturgical supplement to the *Yasna*; (3) the *Vendīdād*, the Laws against the Demons; and (4) the *Khordeh-Avestā*, a collection of hymns, litanies and prayers. The Pahlavi Texts are later translations of the Avesta Texts together with a commentary and various additional theological treatises. The Persian Texts are chiefly the *Revāyats*, which are answers to questions sent from India to Persian priests for decision.

The Supreme Being, Ahura Mazda, is the Lord of Life and the Creator of Matter. His nature is expressed through the "Holy Immortals" (Ameshā-Spentā), two groups of spirits (archangels, or deities standing next in rank to the Godhead), one for the Fatherhood and one for the Motherhood of God. The masculine revelations or expressions are Righteousness, Good Thought, and Power (or Dominion), *Asha*, *Vohu-Manō*, and *Kshathra*.

Asha, the first "ray" from the Godhead, stands for the Law of

God, the Law of Truth, and knowledge of that Law. In later Zoroastrian theology, "the Highest Asha" (*Asha-Vahishta*) is identified with the Sacred Fire. "There is but one Path, the Path of *Asha*; all the others are False Paths" (*Yasna*). Again: "Through the highest Righteousness (*Asha*), through the best Righteousness, may we catch a glimpse of Thee, may we draw near unto Thee, may we be in perfect union with Thee" (*Yasna* 60:12).

Vohu-Manō, the second "ray" from the Godhead, stands for Loving Mind, or Love. Wedded life is the first step on the path toward God. The wedded state is holy, and the married person is dearer to God than an unmarried one (*Vendīdād* 4:47). Love extends beyond humanity, to the animals, who are called "our younger brothers."

Kshathra, the third "ray" or aspect of God, stands for Loving Service. Representing the creative activity of the Supreme, Loving Service is service done to humanity.

The three feminine attributes represent unshakable faith in eternal Law with its resultant rewards. The first is *Armaiti*, Piety. She "stands by to solve our doubts" (Yasna 31:12). In tribulation and sorrow, she brings us strength and comfort.

Haurvatāt, Wholeness, or Perfection, is the second. She bestows upon mankind the blessing of Strength of Soul.

Ameretāt, Immortality, is the third. She gives us the blessing of "Life renewed," which comes only to those who have realized *Vohu-Manō*.

Besides the Holy Immortals, two other dieties are worthy of worship: Fire and Obedience. Fire (*Atar*) refers to the spiritual fire within each individual. To symbolize this fire, also called the "Son of Ahurā-Mazdā" (Yasna 62), a fire has been kept burning at the Sacred Shrine of the Fire of Iran, located about a hundred miles north of Bombay, for more than ten centuries.

Obedience (*Sraosha*) does not mean blind fanaticism, but rather the willing obedience of an understanding mind.

The seven commandments of Zoroastrianism are positive in form, not negative, phrased thou shalt:

(1) keep body and soul clean;

(2) love the truth;

370

(3) do good deeds and give alms;
(4) be loyal to comrades;
(5) improve the land;
(6) plant trees and breed cattle;
(7) protect useful animals and destroy noxious animals.

Each human being is perfectly free to choose one of the two paths through life, the Path of Good or the Path of Untruth. If he chooses "Mazda's Way," he does so "through *deeds* of Truth." If he chooses to follow evil, even his mind becomes dark.

The Arch-Deluder is always nearby to mislead us. When our ears are filled with the "songs of the Earth," we cannot hear the inner voice of Piety. We endlessly "dispute in doubt." Next we are attracted to the things of this earth. When we are frustrated because we cannot have everything we want, our desires are converted into wrath and hatred, and the Demon of Wrath (*Aēsh-ma*, or *Asmodeus*, in the *Book of Tobit* of the *Apocrypha*) stalks the world. Zoroaster warned of the "Evil Teachers," and the dangers to be expected from their distortions of Mazda's Word:

> Such persons in these ways defile our lives;
> Dazzled by worldly grandeur, they regard
> The wicked as the great ones of the Earth. . . .
>
> With alluring chants, they mislead all life,
> Until we meet not Truth, but hungry Wolves,
> Deaf to all else and maddened by Untruth.
>
> Whatever hopes these Wolves have to attain
> Power in realms of Lies and Evil Minds,
> This power itself destroys their Inner Life.
>
> (—Yasna 32:11-13)

Most of the Zoroastrians today live in Bombay, India, where they are known as Parsis. They do not bury their dead in the ground, but place them in "Towers of Silence," exposed to the sky.

The Parsis gained a reputation for honesty. Their word was sufficient bond for any contract. Consequently, many of them have become bankers.

The few who live in Iran are found mainly in Yazd and Kerman, remote desert towns which were way stations on the silk route to China. They had fled from Arab conquerers. Among themselves, they speak a secret language, Dari (named after Darius), which never has been written. Preserved from life at the old Persian courts, it provides the community with a unique degree of privacy from the outside world.

The central emphasis of Zoroastrianism is on practical moral living. It does not sanction flight from the world or extreme self-denial. It looks forward to a world freed at last from evil. When, with our help, the spirit of light triumphs over the spirit of darkness, a new heaven and a new earth will be created, and the kingdom of righteousness, happiness, and peace will be established, as God intended from the beginning.